VIRGINIA WOOLF

VIRGINIA WOOLF

A Collection of Critical Essays

Edited by
Margaret Homans

Prentice Hall, Englewood Cliffs, New Jersey 07632

Library of Congress Cataloging-in-Publication Data

Virginia Woolf : a collection of critical essays / edited by Margaret
    Homans.
        p.   cm. — (New century views)
    Includes bibliographical references.
    ISBN 0-13-953209-9
    1. Woolf, Virginia, 1882–1941—Criticism and interpretation.
I. Homans, Margaret,   (date).   II. Series.
PR6045.O72Z89195
823'.912—dc20   92–32468
                                                    CIP

Acquisitions editor: Phil Miller
Editorial assistant: Heidi Moore
Copy editor: Sherry Babbitt
Editorial/production supervision and
    interior design: Joan Powers
Cover design: Karen Salzbach
Prepress buyer: Herb Klein
Manufacturing buyer: Patrice Fraccio/Robert Anderson

© 1993 by Prentice-Hall, Inc.
A Simon & Schuster Company
Englewood Cliffs, New Jersey 07632

Printed in the United States of America
10 9 8 7 6 5 4 3 2 1

0-13-953209-9

Prentice-Hall International (UK) Limited, *London*
Prentice-Hall of Australia Pty. Limited, *Sydney*
Prentice-Hall Canada Inc., *Toronto*
Prentice-Hall Hispanoamericana, S.A., *Mexico*
Prentice-Hall of India Private Limited, *New Delhi*
Prentice-Hall of Japan, Inc., *Tokyo*
Simon & Schuster Asia Pte. Ltd., *Singapore*
Editora Prentice-Hall do Brasil, Ltda., *Rio de Janeiro*

Contents

Editor's Note

No attempt has been made to standardize references to the works of Virginia Woolf. British and American editions of her novels sometimes differ through Woolf's own practice of making different sets of revisions to the different editions. Moreover, the recent release of the copyright on her work means that new editions of her works are now appearing, and as yet there is no generally accepted standard edition.

I wish to thank, for their help and suggestions at various stages of work on this book, the community of Woolf scholars and in particular Patricia Klindienst Joplin (who led me to Margaret Drabble's essay, which is included here), Elizabeth Abel, Jane Marcus, Lucio P. Ruotolo, Brenda R. Silver, and Margery Sokoloff.

Introduction

Margaret Homans

But what after all is one night? A short space, especially when the darkness dims so soon, and so soon a bird sings, a cock crows, or a faint green quickens, like a turning leaf, in the hollow of the wave. Night, however, succeeds to night. The winter holds a pack of them in store and deals them equally, evenly, with indefatigable fingers. They lengthen; they darken. Some of them hold aloft clear planets, plates of brightness. The autumn trees, ravaged as they are, take on the flash of tattered flags kindling in the gloom of cool cathedral caves where gold letters on marble pages describe death in battle and how bones bleach and burn far away in Indian sands.[1]

This typical passage from the "Time Passes" section of *To the Lighthouse* (1927) evokes the transition from the civilized summer evening scene at the Ramsays' house to the indeterminate night of absence, decay, and death that follows. In it we could identify many characteristics of Woolf's style and some of her recurring concerns as a writer. Here is the modernist experimentation with language in which words are used as much for their sounds ("darkness dims . . . clear planets, plates of brightness") as for the startling images they evoke, or for abstract composition ("a faint green quickens, like a turning leaf, in the hollow of the wave"). This abstractness, the modernist attempt to image the invisible (here, the passage of time itself), will intensify in the next paragraph, where "it seemed now as if . . . divine goodness" displayed "single, distinct, the hare erect; the wave falling; the boat rocking, which, did we deserve them, should be ours always" (pp. 192–193). Here, surely, is the sheer gorgeousness for which Woolf used to be damned with faint praise, as a writer who crafted "exquisite," inconsequential prose; and here, by the same token, is the Woolf whom Arnold Bennett famously condemned to "oblivion" because she was not interested "in the full creation of [her] individual characters."[2] Whose is the sensibility reflected in this passage? No "character's," certainly; the perspective is impersonal, eternal, as even-handed and indefatigable as the night that is almost but not quite personified in the

---

[1]Virginia Woolf, *To the Lighthouse* (New York: Harcourt, Brace, 1927), 192.
[2]Arnold Bennett, "Is the Novel Decaying?" *Cassells Weekly* 28 (March 1923): 47; reprinted in *Virginia Woolf: The Critical Heritage*, ed. Robin Majumdar and Allen McLaurin (London: Routledge and Kegan Paul, 1975), pp. 112–14.

passage. Woolf here (as Erich Auerbach points out in this volume [pages 16–34]) shifts the focus away from central events in the protagonists' lives—such as the deaths of Mrs. Ramsay and two of her children, recorded briefly between brackets—and toward the seemingly unimportant: here, the passing of ordinary nights. "Description" has been discarded as "that ugly, that clumsy, that incongruous tool";[3] here, instead, is a page from the "novel about Silence" about which Terence Hewet speculates in *The Voyage Out*.[4]

At the same time, however, here is the Woolf whose analysis of war's origins in the pathologies of patriarchal family life remains as acute today as it was in the period between the world wars. "Death in battle," glimpsed so obliquely here as adjunct to a complicated metaphor for autumn leaves, looks forward to the senseless death of Andrew Ramsay, among "twenty or thirty young men" (p. 201) blown up in France. The "gold letters on marble pages," monuments to the war dead, allude, too, to the fatal masculine ethos of heroism in which Mr. Ramsay deeply believes and which, according to Woolf, causes young men to be blown up in France. Tennyson's "The Charge of the Light Brigade," a poem celebrating the Crimean War that was memorized by generations of British school boys "When can their glory fade? / Oh, the wild charge they made!" supplies Mr. Ramsay with some of his recurrent refrains.[5] The novel also traces the origins of imperialism (whose futile ends are registered by the "bones that bleach and burn far away in Indian sands") in the same patriarchal ethos: Mr. Ramsay is a disappointed intellectual quester who finds emotional support in an explorer's pathetic refrain, "We perished each alone." These oblique references to violence remind us gently that the long night of "Time Passes" is not only an extended space of natural decay, but also the world war that intervenes between the first and last sections of the novel.

Let us now juxtapose to the mystical, delicate sounds of the passage from *To the Lighthouse* a passage from Woolf's more explicitly political work, *Three Guineas*, which addresses men's and women's differing relations to war. The difference in the writing of the two passages is almost shocking, yet this passage too is typical of Woolf:

> "Our country," . . . throughout the greater part of its history has treated me as a slave; it has denied me education or any share in its possessions. . . . Therefore if you insist upon fighting to protect me, or "our" country, let it be understood, soberly and rationally between us, that you are fighting to gratify a sex instinct which I cannot share; to procure benefits which I have not shared and probably will not share; but not to gratify my instincts, or to protect myself or my country. For

---

[3]Virginia Woolf, "Mr Bennett and Mrs Brown" (1924), reprinted in Woolf, *Collected Essays* ed. Leonard Woolf (New York: Harcourt, Brace, 1966), 1: 332.

[4]Virginia Woolf, *The Voyage Out* (New York: Harcourt, Brace, 1920), p. 216.

[5]*The Poems of Tennyson*, ed. Christopher Ricks (London: Longman, 1969), p. 1036; the poem was written in 1854.

. . . as a woman, I have no country. As a woman I want no country. As a woman my country is the whole world.[6]

In apparent contrast to the passage from *To the Lighthouse*, the prose is direct and impassioned, not elusive, impressionistic, and impartial. War is the center of attention, not a figure distantly glimpsed. Figure and ground would seem to have exchanged places. And yet this passage, while not as extravagantly metaphoric as the one from *To the Lighthouse*, is just as concerned, in its own way, with the power of symbols such as "our country." Moreover, although the stirring last three sentences have deservedly become a feminist slogan, Woolf does not say them in her own voice. Speaking here is an imaginary woman, an "outsider" who takes a view of English society every bit as distanced and defamiliarizing as that of the mysterious, impersonal speaker in "Time Passes." Whether glimpsed obliquely at the end of an elaborately extended metaphor or addressed squarely in workaday prose, war, in Woolf's various presentations, is the creation of alien and irrational beings, not the site of credible ideals.

Woolf's manifold modernist styles, then, as a number of the essays in this collection will show, are not incidental but absolutely crucial to her searching critique of patriarchal institutions. Andrew Ramsay's death in battle is bracketed not because it is unimportant (far from it), but because a style that reverses the usual relations between margin and center models an anti-authoritarian world. Woolf typically employs elusive, unlocatable speakers because, among other reasons, she deeply distrusts "I." As she (or rather her fictional speaker) says about the male protagonist of a male-authored novel in *A Room of One's Own*:

after reading a chapter or two a shadow seemed to lie across the page. It was a straight dark bar, a shadow shaped something like the letter "I." One began dodging this way and that to catch a glimpse of the landscape behind it. . . . One began to be tired of "I." Not but what this "I" was a most respectable "I"; honest and logical; as hard as a nut, and polished for centuries by good teaching and good feeding. . . . But—here I turned a page or two, looking for something or other—the worst of it is that in the shadow of the letter "I" all is shapeless as mist. Is that a tree? No, it is a woman. But . . . she has not a bone in her body, I thought, watching Phoebe, for that was her name, coming across the beach. Then Alan got up and the shadow of Alan at once obliterated Phoebe. For Alan had views and Phoebe was quenched in the flood of his views. . . . [W]hy was I bored? Partly because of the dominance of the letter "I" and the aridity, which, like the giant beech tree, it casts within its shade. Nothing will grow there.[7]

The masculine egotism Woolf mocks here leads, for her, to patriarchal misuses of power, to the denigration and exclusion of women, and to war. To write as Woolf does in a decentered style, as an " 'I' [who] is only a convenient

---

[6]Virginia Woolf, *Three Guineas* (New York: Harcourt, Brace, 1938), pp. 108–9.
[7]Virginia Woolf, *A Room of One's Own* (New York: Harcourt, Brace, 1929), pp. 103–4.

term for somebody who has no real being" (*A Room of One's Own*, p. 4), requires the reader to imagine a different mode of being, one that would not subjugate others to the self's demands. Woolf writes of her plans for *Between the Acts*, her final novel:

> Let it be random & tentative; . . . "I" rejected: "We" substituted: to whom at the end there shall be an invocation? "We" . . . composed of many different things . . . we all life, all art, all waifs & strays—a rambling capricious but somehow unified whole. (second and third ellipses Woolf's)[8]

The first chapter of her next work, never completed, was to have been titled "Anon," a reference to Woolf's idea that the finest English poetry was the work of anonymous balladeers, before "the writer" became a self-conscious "I," as indeed Woolf herself, inevitably, ambivalently, became.[9]

Alex Zwerdling calls Woolf a "Proteus" who assumed many shapes as a writer.[10] In keeping with Woolf's stated dislike for a clear, single-minded "I," there are many different Virginia Woolfs, almost as many as there are readers of her, as the range of subjects and perspectives canvassed in the criticism on her suggests. Symptomatic of this diversity is the fact that, as Alice van Buren Kelley pointed out in 1973, many books on Woolf, including her own, pose their subject in terms of balanced oppositions, such as "fact and vision" (Kelley) or "life and art" (C. Ruth Miller); Kelley cites other pairings such as "flux versus permanence, or masculine versus feminine," "life and death, the solitary mind and society" (Bernard Blackstone), and "subjective thought and objective reality" (Jean O. Love).[11] Going a step further, I have tried to suggest, in reading the pair of passages above, how the aesthetic and the political do not so much balance as necessarily constitute each other. Woolf's own title for one of her essay collections, *Granite and Rainbow*, lends authority to this way of approaching the impossibility of pinning her down, as do some of the titles of her novels: *Night and Day*, *The Waves*, *Between the Acts*. Recent critics (such as Toril Moi, Pamela Caughie, and, especially persuasively, Makiko Minow-Pinkney) have found in her work a deconstructive, postmodern decentering that goes beyond even the openness suggested by these dialectical pairings.

It is perhaps because of the multiplicity and mobility of Woolf's writing selves that such heated critical controversies have broken out about her in recent years, controversies in which "Woolf's texts provide ample support for almost any position."[12] Much as Woolf herself may be "Protean," she has also,

[8]*The Diary of Virginia Woolf*, ed. Anne Olivier Bell (New York: Harcourt Brace Jovanovich, 1984), 5:135, 26 April 1938.

[9]See Brenda Silver, ed., " 'Anon' and 'The Reader': Virginia Woolf's Last Essays," *Twentieth Century Literature* 25, nos. 3–4 (Fall–Winter 1979): 356–441 (special issue on Woolf).

[10]Alex Zwerdling, *Virginia Woolf and the Real World* (Berkeley: University of California Press, 1986), p. 3.

[11]Alice van Buren Kelley, *The Novels of Virginia Woolf: Fact and Vision* (Chicago: University of Chicago Press, 1973), p. 254.

[12]Rachel Bowlby, *Virginia Woolf: Feminist Destinations* (Oxford: Basil Blackwell Ltd, 1988), p. 14.

Rachel Bowlby demonstrates, been called upon to represent a variety of opposing critical theories and political viewpoints:

> it would seem that Woolf . . . has become an "exemplary" character—and exemplary in paradoxical ways. Woolf is the only twentieth-century British woman writer who is taken seriously by critics of all casts. Whether she is seen to fit in with or to subvert what the critic identifies as established literary standards, and depending on whether subversion or conformity is the criterion of value, Woolf is vehemently celebrated or denounced from all sides.
>
> . . . She is celebrated as a modernist breaking with formal literary conventions, and thereby also with the normative structures of patriarchal—or phallocentric—language; she is also celebrated as a realist, by appeal to her authentic description of women's lives and experiences, and her commitment to the end of patriarchal society. At the same time, Woolf is also attacked from both these standpoints: as not realist enough (too much Bloomsbury aestheticism) or as not modernist enough (always falling back into a nostalgic desire for unities rather than radical breaks).[13]

For example, Bowlby points out, Toril Moi's Woolf is the stylist of decentered writing who "undermine[s] the notion of the unitary self, the central concept of Western male humanism," presenting the individual instead as the product of a network of ideological, material, and psychological forces. As such Moi enlists Woolf as standard-bearer of postmodernist feminism, against Jane Marcus's biographical and contextual approach (one that presumes that Woolf's personal self matters in her writing), and against Elaine Showalter's criticism of Woolf for not supplying enough "images of strong women," a criticism that depends upon the humanist assumption that Woolf could, and occasionally does, take up the project of realist representation.[14]

In *To the Lighthouse*, just after the selection examined above, Woolf introduces the figure of Mrs. McNab, the old woman who comes to clean and restore the Ramsays' house after years of neglect. She is at once a heroic representative of working class women's strength, as Jane Marcus points out, one of the "lives of the obscure" that Woolf wanted to write, and a depersonalized "force" enmeshed in the network of Woolf's fanciful, oblique prose.[15]

> For now had come that moment, that hesitation when dawn trembles and night pauses, when if a feather alight in the scale it will be weighed down. One feather, and the house, sinking, falling, would have turned and pitched downwards to the depths of darkness. . . . Then the roof would have fallen; briars and hemlocks would have blotted out path, step, and window. . . . But there was a force

[13]Ibid., pp. 12–13.

[14]Toril Moi, *Sexual/Textual Politics: Feminist Literary Theory* (London: Methuen, 1985), p. 7; discussing Jane Marcus, "Thinking Back Through Our Mothers," in *New Feminist Essays on Virginia Woolf*, ed. Jane Marcus (London: Macmillan, 1981), and Elaine Showalter, *A Literature of Their Own* (Princeton: Princeton University Press, 1977). See also Pamela L. Caughie, *Virginia Woolf and Postmodernism: Literature in Quest and Question of Itself* (Urbana: University of Illinois Press, 1991); and Makiko Minow-Pinkney, *Virginia Woolf and The Problem of the Subject* (Brighton: The Harvester Press, 1987).

[15]Jane Marcus, *Virginia Woolf and the Languages of Patriarchy* (Bloomington: Indiana University Press, 1987), pp. 12–13.

working; something not highly conscious; something that leered, something that lurched; something not inspired to go about its work with dignified ritual or solemn chanting. Mrs. McNab groaned; Mrs. Bast creaked. . . . Slowly and painfully, with broom and pail, mopping, scouring, Mrs. McNab, Mrs. Bast, stayed the corruption and the rot; rescued from the pool of Time that was fast closing over them now a basin, now a cupboard. (*To the Lighthouse*, pp. 208–9)

After a long, heroic catalogue of the old women's civilizing works, the novel describes the completion of their labors, as Marcus points out, with an honorific phrase used only once again, for the completion of Lily's painting: "it was finished" (pp. 212, 310). Yet at the same time that she is a heroic character of the sort Showalter and Marcus admire, Mrs. McNab is also part of the deconstructive aspect of the novel celebrated by Moi, a "force" of nature that nonetheless works against nature, not an "I" and scarcely human, "a tropical fish oaring its way through sun-lanced waters" (p. 200). Unified human form is here, but it is also dispersed: "*Unity—Dispersity,*" gurgles the gramophone at the end of *Between the Acts*.[16] Again and again it becomes necessary to say that both sides are right.

Beyond such controversies within feminist criticism lie, at the present moment, still sharper ones between feminist scholars and more traditional readers of Woolf. During the 1970s Woolf's diaries, memoirs, letters, and uncollected essays began to appear in book form, and the coincidence of these events with the emergence of feminist literary criticism (itself initiated in large part by Woolf's *A Room of One's Own*) sparked a genuine critical revolution. Zwerdling points out that "the publication of these private and fugitive writings" has not only enlarged severalfold the Woolf canon, but has also "changed our understanding of the more familiar works on which her original reputation was based."[17] Equally important, scholars, many of them feminists, have been examining and publishing the manuscripts of Woolf's novels, studying the implications of her private writings, and researching the eclectic world of her friendships and social and political affiliations. Although the present collection focuses on Woolf's novels, some essays make use of materials only recently available, and scholars are now paying serious attention to her essays, biographies, and other writings. New kinds of reading highlight previously unknown or ignored texts: feminist psychological approaches, for example, sometimes focus on "A Sketch of the Past," published in full only in 1985,[18] and political approaches frequently read the novels through the lens of *Three Guineas*, until recently less well known than *A Room of One's Own*. Starting in the mid and late 1970s, a series of special journal issues and essay collections in book form (especially around the

[16]Virginia Woolf, *Between the Acts* (New York: Harcourt, Brace, 1941), p. 201.
[17]Zwerdling, p. 2.
[18]In Virginia Woolf, *Moments of Being*, second edition, ed. Jeanne Schulkind (New York: Harcourt Brace Jovanovich, 1985), pp. 61–159.

centenary of Woolf's birth in 1982), as well as individual books and articles, recorded these scholars' findings (see "Selected Bibliography" [pages 252–254]).

The most acute of the critical controversies that arose from the conjunction of feminism with the expansion of Woolf's canon runs roughly as follows: is Woolf's writing ultimately to be valued for its aesthetic properties; or is Woolf a political writer and cultural critic, and are her writings to be valued for their radicalism? The first of these views of Woolf is the more traditional one, predominant until the 1970s, and it tends to find its adherents in England, where her elite social and economic status makes it difficult to see her as a radical (that is, socialist) thinker, so that her artistry alone remains in view. The second is more established in the United States, where it is her feminism, rather than her class politics, that has shaped recent critical appreciations, and where her reception has generally been the more enthusiastic among scholars and ordinary readers alike.[19] Brenda R. Silver points out that the influential British critic Q. D. Leavis indicted *Three Guineas* upon its publication because, as an "upperclass amateur," Woolf lacked authority to speak for women; Silver also demonstrates how consistently Woolf's "art" has been opposed to and valued over her "anger," except by feminist critics.[20] Hostility between these two sides has taken the form, as recently as the mid-1980s, of a heated and personal debate, in the scholarly journal *Critical Inquiry*, between Quentin Bell, Woolf's nephew and biographer and the co-holder of her copyrights, and Jane Marcus, who, as the editor of three collections of feminist essays on Woolf and the author of many such essays, is a leader among those in the United States who would claim Woolf for socialist as well as feminist radicalism. Marcus's Woolf was a Marxist; Bell's Woolf (writes Marcus, quoting Bell) " 'wasn't a feminist and she wasn't political.' "[21]

Whatever the merits of these antagonists' positions, Woolf's manuscripts incontrovertibly reveal a far more angry and militant side of Woolf than has usually seen the light of print.[22] To take just one example, from materials that have been in print since 1977, we could compare Woolf's 1942 published essay, "Professions for Women," with the manuscript of the 1931 speech on which it was based. A passage early in the published version reads:

19Lucio P. Ruotolo, "Preface," *Twentieth Century Literature* nos. 3–4 (Fall–Winter 1979): i–ii.
20Brenda R. Silver, "The Authority of Anger: *Three Guineas* as a Case Study," *Signs* 16 (1991): 340–70, quotation p. 351.
21Quentin Bell, *Guardian*, 21 March 1982, quoted in Jane Marcus, "Quentin's Bogey," *Critical Inquiry* 11 (1985): 492. Marcus is responding to Bell's "A 'Radiant' Friendship," *Critical Inquiry* 10 (1984): 557–566.
22See Brenda R. Silver, "Textual Criticism as Feminist Practice: Or, Who's Afraid of Virginia Woolf Part II," in *Representing Modernist Texts: Editing as Interpretation*, ed. George Bornstein (Ann Arbor: University of Michigan Press, 1991); and Susan Stanford Friedman, "Spatialization, Narrative Theory, and Virginia Woolf's *The Voyage Out*," paper delivered at the Narrative Conference, Nice, June 1991; forthcoming in *Feminist Narratology*, ed. Kathy Mezei (Toronto: University of Toronto Press, 1994), on the ways in which Woolf repressed or otherwise altered her manuscripts' vehemence when revising them for publication.

For the road was cut many years ago—by Fanny Burney, by Aphra Behn, by Harriet Martineau, by Jane Austen, by George Eliot—many famous women, and many more unknown and forgotten, have been before me, making the path smooth, and regulating my steps.[23]

The feminist theme resembles that of *A Room of One's Own*, and the tone, as in that book, is level, calm, polite, and somewhat self-ironizing (she clearly overstates the smoothness of her path). But now consider how much more vehement Woolf permits herself to be in her speech, which was made to a sympathetic audience (the London/National Society for Women's Service), and how she sounds still angrier in the lines she cut before delivering the speech:

I have no doubt that there were women two hundred years ago who [*smashed, and broke and toiled and*] drew upon themselves hostility and ridicule in order that it might not be [wicked or] ridiculous [*or impossible*] [*disgraceful*] for women [nowadays] to write books. (italics are Woolf's cancellations; roman letters in brackets are her uncanceled insertions)[24]

The acts her predecessors have had to commit were originally not described by the bland, dead metaphor "the road was cut," but by the specific acts of violence that road-cutting really entails: smashing, breaking, and toiling. And the obstacles those women faced are presented much more vividly and, one might say, truly: they drew on themselves "hostility and ridicule," for it was then, if it is not now, "wicked," "impossible," and "disgraceful" for women to write. These passionate details Woolf cancels and replaces with the list of names of great women authors, a list that elides the obstacles and labor and tends instead to emphasize the positive end result. The speech and its manuscript, however, reveal Woolf's first thoughts on the matter, thoughts that may more accurately reflect her feelings about her own experience as a writer. The difference between these two passages can be found as well in differences among Woolf's published writings, and it is significant that, while the relatively polite and evasive *A Room of One's Own* has long been a key text in women's studies classrooms, the far more explicitly political and angry *Three Guineas* is gaining in visibility. Woolf is now being discussed not only in literary contexts but as a political theorist.[25]

Although the essays collected in this volume represent a wide variety of approaches to Woolf, from formalist to psychoanalytic to narratological to poststructuralist to historical-contextual, they do not even-handedly reflect critical controversies such as that between Bell and Marcus. Rather, the

---

[23]Virginia Woolf, *"The Pargiters": The Novel-Essay Portion of "The Years"*, ed. Mitchell A. Leaska (New York: Harcourt Brace Jovanovich, 1977), p. xxviii. (The full text of "Professions for Women" is in Virginia Woolf, *Women and Writing*, ed. Michèle Barrett [New York: Harcourt Brace Jovanovich, 1979], pp. 57–63.)

[24]Ibid.

[25]See, for example, Elizabeth Meese, *Crossing the Double-Cross: The Practice of Feminist Criticism* (Chapel Hill: University of North Carolina Press, 1986), ch. 6.

selection is slightly weighted toward approaches that take Woolf seriously as an innovative political writer, but, I hasten to add, that also find Woolf's political analysis first and foremost in her writing, in the style and structure of her prose—in the very qualities of beauty and plangency that have convinced other readers that she is above politics. As Toril Moi puts it, it is important to "locat[e] the politics of Woolf's writing *precisely in her textual practice*" (italics Moi's).[26] Where some readers find in Woolf a refusal to be pinned down that would seem apolitical, others find an openness that is itself astutely political. It would be hard to decide, for example, whether Mrs. Ramsay is idealized or villified as a Victorian "Angel in the House." But this ambivalent portrait may accurately reflect the ideological bind of her spiritual daughters: she is a terrible model for any woman who desires achievement beyond her familial roles, yet it is Woolf's sharp insight to see that the difficulty of women's situation is that such models are nearly all they have. A number of the essays collected here, whether or not they focus on questions of gender, use as key terms such words as "oscillation," "interruption," "chaotic," or "threshold." But while it would be tempting to say that Woolf can, after all, be pinned down—to an aesthetics and politics of openness and indeterminacy—she defies even that sort of conclusiveness, as Lucio P. Ruotolo and Patricia Klindienst Joplin point out in this volume (see pages 162–173 and 210–226, respectively). When La Trobe's gramophone gurgles, "*Unity—Dispersity*," it presents and privileges an open choice that is between the values of closure and openness.

It would be a mistake ever to feel that one could settle upon a definitive interpretation of any of Woolf's novels. I would like to close by looking at the very open ending of *Between the Acts*, an ending that seems to take into account the values of both closure and openness. Giles and Isa, the married couple who have been silently at war all day, are left alone as night falls and the rest of the family goes to bed. The novel ends with these words:

> Left alone together for the first time that day, they were silent. Alone, enmity was bared; also love. Before they slept, they must fight; after they had fought, they would embrace. From that embrace another life might be born. But first they must fight, as the dog fox fights with the vixen, in the heart of darkness, in the fields of night.
>
> Isa let her sewing drop. The great hooded chairs had become enormous. And Giles too. And Isa too against the window. The window was all sky without colour. The house had lost its shelter. It was night before roads were made, or houses. It was the night that dwellers in caves had watched from some high place among rocks.
>
> Then the curtain rose. They spoke. (*Between the Acts*, p. 219)

In one view, to recall the options Bowlby sketches, this is a deeply conservative ending, and surprisingly so, given how profoundly the pageant (created by the lesbian artist La Trobe) and the rest of the novel have critiqued

---

[26]Moi, p. 16. See also Bowlby, p. 15.

heterosexual relations. Isa has felt nothing for Giles other than what she artificially induces in herself by repeating the empty phrase, "the father of my children" (p. 48). And Giles, mocked as the "surly hero" (p. 93), has been flirting with Mrs. Manresa, the mock-queen for whom he performs such absurdly reduced acts of "heroism" as crushing a snake with a toad in its mouth. And yet here the narrator's all-knowing, proverbial voice insists that "love" really exists between Giles and Isa. All along the novel has compared and causally linked the coming world war with the war between the sexes, and Giles's "heroic" behavior, like Mr. Ramsay's, is identified with the values that produce war. The novel, in the reading we are pursuing for the moment, suggests that Giles and Isa's alternations of fighting and embracing, which are also the world's cycles of war and peace, are as inevitable and right as nature itself, going back to prehistory, before the days of "shelter."

Some readers are reassured by this version of the ending, in which the sense of inevitability may be seen to promote a sort of intellectual passivity. In this view, Woolf is retracting her indictment of the patriarchal family by allowing, finally, that it is not a social construct but instead the product of natural sexual attraction; in this view, Giles and Isa will cyclically avert the breakdown of their marriage, just as inevitable war will be followed by inevitable peace. One could also share this reading but, by contrast, be disheartened by it, if one has admired the critique contained in the rest of the novel: here Woolf would seem to be conceding too much to the purportedly natural rightness of the interminable cycle of love and hate that Giles and Isa embody. Other readers will turn the same reading yet another way. Possibly, the very fact that Woolf seems to accede to the view that heterosexual love, and war, are natural is her depressive critique of it. This is the nature of fox and vixen, of cave man and cave woman, over which human society ought by now to have triumphed; it is a mark of human failure that we go on performing the same punishing drama eon after eon.

For still other readers, however, a focus on other details leads to different conclusions. The novel's final line ("Then the curtain rose. They spoke.") may allude to the new play La Trobe starts drowsily to envision after the pageant is over: " 'I should group them,' she murmured, 'here.' It would be midnight; there would be two figures, half concealed by a rock. The curtain would rise. What would the first words be?" (p. 210). If it is La Trobe's curtain that rises on Giles and Isa, the drama they enact will hardly be the conciliatory and natural one suggested by the narrator, if this day's pageant is any guide, with its manifold mockeries of the economic and political bases of sentiment in marriage. Perhaps La Trobe will criticize the very notion of the naturalness of heterosexuality by setting her scene in prehistory; perhaps La Trobe will save Giles and Isa from the natural cyclicality that the comparisons to fox and vixen would seem to make inevitable. Perhaps. Who could say? Many other readings are possible, and one does not foreclose the others.

Woolf's place in the canon of English literature, it would seem, is quite secure: although for years she was considered a minor modernist, only one of several in the Bloomsbury group, the claim can now be plausibly made (although not all would subscribe to it) that she was the most important writer in English of her generation. Nonetheless, just as readers are in the process of redefining Woolf's own canon, her reputation remains poised somewhere between the canonical and the non-canonical. In 1979 J. Hillis Miller (who has himself written on Woolf) could say of his "belief" in the "established canon of English and American literature," "I think it is more important to read Spenser, Shakespeare, or Milton than to read Borges in translation, or even, to say the truth, to read Virginia Woolf."[27] Although Miller has removed that remark from recent reissues of his words, this ambiguous status—neither entirely inside the canon nor really out of it—is a fitting one for Woolf, for it recalls her own remarks about being excluded as a woman from the male-dominated institutions she both admired and despised: "I thought how unpleasant it is to be locked out; and I thought how it is worse perhaps to be locked in" (*A Room of One's Own*, p. 24). Or rather, that is what Woolf's elusive, nameless speaker says. Neither a Spenser nor an unknown, Woolf is not quite, or not yet, an institution, "gold letters on marble pages," and perhaps this is for the best: Woolf's writing will remain living and challenging, its time always about to come, as long as we cannot imprison her in a shrine of perfected reading. Her uncertainties, thankfully, can be ours.

27J. Hillis Miller, "The Function of Rhetorical Study at the Present Time," *ADE Bulletin* 62 (September–November 1979); reprinted, without the controversial remark, in *Teaching Literature: What Is Needed Now*, ed. James Engell and David Perkins, Harvard English Studies 15 (Cambridge: Harvard University Press, 1988), pp. 87–109; and in J. Hillis Miller, *Theory Now and Then* (Durham: Duke University Press, 1991), pp. 201–216. Miller's prominence as a critic, especially in the late 1970s and early 1980s, gave the remark wide circulation; interestingly, it has been silently removed, not actively retracted. For his writings on Woolf, see the "Selected Bibliography," (page 253).

Characters and Human Experience

Joan Bennett

In her first two books, she takes the basic principles of the novel as she finds them and adapts them to her own vision. Characters are described and then gradually made better known to us by their sayings and doings; they are related to one another by a series of events leading to a climax. Each book is a love story. Yet it is clear that it is not the width and variety of the human comedy, nor the idiosyncrasies of human character, that most interest her. Rather it is the deep and simple human experiences; love, happiness, beauty, loneliness, death. Again and again in these two books what the reader feels is not so much "this man or woman would have felt like that in those circumstances," but rather "Yes, that is how it feels to be in love; to be happy; to be desolate."

> "We don't care for people because of their qualities," he tried to explain. "It's just them we care for,"—he struck a match—"just that," he said, pointing to the flames. (*The Voyage Out*)

Hewet says that to Evelyn Murgatroyd at a certain moment and in a certain scene; it is perfectly appropriate to the circumstances and to the characters; but it transcends them:

> She realized with a great sense of comfort how easily she could talk to Hewet, those thorns or ragged corners which tear the surface of some relationships being smoothed away. (*The Voyage Out*)

It is Rachel who has this experience; but what it reveals is not her character, it is an aspect of love:

> Very gently and quietly, almost as if it were the blood singing in her veins, or the water of the stream running over stones, Rachel became conscious of a new feeling within her. She wondered for a moment what it was, and then said to herself, with a little surprise at recognizing in her own person so famous a thing:
> "This is happiness, I suppose." And aloud to Terence she spoke, "This is happiness."
> On the heels of her words he answered, "This is happiness," upon which they

Excerpted from Joan Bennett, *Virginia Woolf: Her Art as a Novelist* (New York: Harcourt Brace, 1945). Reprinted with permission of Cambridge University Press.

guessed that the feeling had sprung in both of them at the same time. (*The Voyage Out*)

Night and Day, with its more complex story and its wider social scene, has at the heart of it this same preoccupation with the universal nature of love and happiness. Mary Datchet and Ralph Denham are walking together fiercely arguing about government, law, the social structure:

> At length they drew breath, let the argument fly into the limbo of other good arguments, and, leaning over a gate, opened their eyes for the first time and looked about them. Their feet tingled with warm blood and their breath rose in steam about them. The bodily exercise made them both feel more direct and less self-conscious than usual, and Mary, indeed, was overcome by a sort of light-headedness which made it seem to her that it mattered very little what happened next. It mattered so little, indeed, that she felt herself on the point of saying to Ralph: "I love you; I shall never love anybody else. Marry me or leave me—I don't care a straw." At the moment, however, speech or silence seemed immaterial, and she merely clapped her hands together, and looked at the distant woods with the rust-like bloom on their brown, and the green and blue landscape through the steam of her own breath. It seemed a mere toss up whether she said, "I love you," or whether she said, "I love the beech trees," or only "I love—I love." (*Night and Day*)

The reader knows Mary Datchet well, and at many points in the book it is her individual character that emerges from her action or her words; but here it is youth and love itself, the fundamental and simple experience of which poets write. Katharine Hilbery and Ralph Denham, on the other hand, are not wholly clear to the reader as individuals even at the end of the book. The idiosyncrasies that differentiate them from other people are unimportant— when we think of them from this point of view they appear a little misty; what we remember about them are those vivid experiences through which they become conscious of the bonds that unite them. Ralph meets Katharine in the street by chance:

> Thus it came about that he saw Katharine Hilbery coming towards him and looked straight at her, as if she was only an illustration of the argument that was going forward in his mind. In this spirit he noticed the rather set expression in her eyes, and the slight, half-conscious movement of her lips, which, together with her height and the distinction of her dress, made her look as if the scurrying crowd impeded her, and her direction were different from theirs. He noticed this calmly; but suddenly, as he passed her, his hands and knees began to tremble, and his heart beat painfully. She did not see him, and went on repeating to herself some lines which had stuck in her memory: "It's life that matters, nothing but life—the process of discovering—the everlasting and perpetual process, not the discovery itself at all." Thus occupied, she did not see Denham, and he had not the courage to stop her. But immediately the whole scene in the Strand wore that curious look of order and purpose which is imparted to the most heterogeneous things when music sounds, and so pleasant was this impression that he was very glad that he

had not stopped her, after all. It grew slowly fainter, but lasted until he stood outside the barrister's chambers. (*Night and Day*)

It is not Ralph and Katharine as individuals that matters here but the experience unveiled in their encounter. Similarly, in the way of the poets and of certain novelists who were also poets, Emily Brontë or Meredith or Hardy, Virginia Woolf evokes in each of these first two books scenes that communicate what it felt like to be young. At certain moments in *Night and Day* Cassandra is not so much Cassandra as youth itself:

> To Cassandra's ears the buzz of voices inside the drawing-room was like the tuning up of the instruments of the orchestra. It seemed to her that there were numbers of people in the room, and that they were strangers, and that they were beautiful and dressed with the greatest distinction, although they proved to be mostly her relations, and the distinction of their clothing was confined, in the eyes of an impartial observer, to the white waistcoat which Rodney wore. But they all rose simultaneously, which was by itself impressive, and they all exclaimed, and shook hands, and she was introduced to Mr. Peyton, and the door sprang open, and dinner was announced, and they filed off, William Rodney offering her his slightly bent black arm, as she secretly hoped he would. In short, had the scene been looked at only through her eyes, it must have been described as one of magical brilliancy. The pattern of the soup plates, the stiff folds of the napkins, which rose by the side of each plate in the shape of arum lilies, the long sticks of bread tied with pink ribbon, the silver dishes and the sea-coloured champagne glasses, with the flakes of gold congealed in their stems—all these details, together with a curiously pervasive smell of kid gloves, contributed to her exhilaration, which must be repressed however, because she was grown-up, and the world held no more for her to marvel at.
>
> The world held no more for her to marvel at, it is true; but it held other people, and each other person possessed in Cassandra's mind some fragment of what privately she called "reality." It was a gift that they would impart if you asked them for it, and thus no dinner-party could possibly be dull, and little Mr. Peyton on her right and William Rodney on her left were in equal measure endowed with the quality which seemed to her so unmistakable and so precious that the way people neglected to demand it was a constant source of surprise to her. She scarcely knew, indeed, whether she was talking to Mr. Peyton or to William Rodney. But to one who, by degrees, assumed the shape of an elderly man with a moustache, she described how she had arrived in London that very afternoon, and how she had taken a cab and driven through the streets. Mr. Peyton, an editor of fifty years, bowed his bald head repeatedly, with apparent understanding. At least, he understood that she was very young and pretty, and saw that she was excited, though he could not gather at once from her words or remember from his own experience what there was to be excited about. "Were there any buds on the trees?" he asked. "Which line did she travel by?" (*Night and Day*)

Rachel, in *The Voyage Out*, has the same unimpaired expectancy; she is, indeed, less of a "character" than Cassandra, less a peculiar, differentiated specimen of humanity, and her experience more constantly represents the quality of youth itself. Sitting next to Richard Dalloway at a meal on the ship:

> Rachel had other questions on the tip of her tongue; or rather one enormous question, which she did not in the least know how to put into words. The talk appeared too airy to admit of it.
> "Please tell me—everything." That was what she wanted to say. He had drawn apart one little chink and showed astonishing treasures. It seemed to her incredible that a man like that should be willing to talk to her. He had sisters and pets and once lived in the country. She stirred her tea round and round; the bubbles which swam and clustered in the cup seemed to her like the union of their minds. (*The Voyage Out*)

And, like Cassandra, Rachel experiences the irrational excitement or intoxication of self-discovery:

> The vision of her own personality, of herself as a real everlasting thing, different from anything else, unmergeable, like the sea or the wind, flashed into Rachel's mind, and she became profoundly excited at the thought of living. (*The Voyage Out*)

In these first two books the moments which remain most memorable are those in which we become aware of those deeper levels of experience where human beings are alike, rather than of the inexhaustible variety of human character. In the profoundly moving scenes at the end of *The Voyage Out*, what we know about Terence or Rachel or Helen or Hirst as individuals matters little compared with our sense of the capacity for suffering they have in common with ourselves. Because, in *The Voyage Out*, the characters are removed from the common-place world of everyday duties and pleasures, on the ship and then on the island, this lyrical content is less interrupted. The book, though in some ways narrower than *Night and Day* and less rich in promise, is more successfully integrated. . . .

The Brown Stocking

Erich Auerbach

"And even if it isn't fine to-morrow," said Mrs. Ramsay, raising her eyes to glance at William Bankes and Lily Briscoe as they passed, "it will be another day. And now," she said, thinking that Lily's charm was her Chinese eyes, aslant in her white, puckered little face, but it would take a clever man to see it, "and now stand up, and let me measure your leg," for they might go to the Lighthouse after all, and she must see if the stocking did not need to be an inch or two longer in the leg.

Smiling, for an admirable idea had flashed upon her this very second—William and Lily should marry—she took the heather mixture stocking, with its criss-cross of steel needles at the mouth of it, and measured it against James's leg.

"My dear, stand still," she said, for in his jealousy, not liking to serve as measuring-block for the Lighthouse keeper's little boy, James fidgeted purposely; and if he did that, how could she see, was it too long, was it too short? she asked.

She looked up—what demon possessed him, her youngest, her cherished?— and saw the room, saw the chairs, thought them fearfully shabby. Their entrails, as Andrew said the other day, were all over the floor; but then what was the point, she asked herself, of buying good chairs to let them spoil up here all through the winter when the house, with only one old woman to see to it, positively dripped with wet? Never mind: the rent was precisely twopence halfpenny; the children loved it; it did her husband good to be three thousand, or if she must be accurate, three hundred miles from his library and his lectures and his disciples; and there was room for visitors. Mats, camp beds, crazy ghosts of chairs and tables whose London life of service was done—they did well enough here; and a photograph or two, and books. Books, she thought, grew of themselves. She never had time to read them. Alas! even the books that had been given her, and inscribed by the hand of the poet himself: "For her whose wishes must be obeyed . . ." "The happier Helen of our days . . ." disgraceful to say, she had never read them. And Croom on the Mind and Bates on the Savage Customs of Polynesia ("My dear, stand still," she said)—neither of those could one send to the Lighthouse. At a certain moment, she supposed, the house would become so shabby that something must be done. If they could be taught to wipe their feet and not bring the beach in with them—that would be something. Crabs, she had to allow, if Andrew really wished to dissect them, or if Jasper believed that one could make soup from seaweed, one could not prevent it; or Rose's objects—shells, reeds, stones; for they were gifted, her children, but all in quite different ways. And the result of it was, she sighed, taking in the whole room from floor to ceiling, as she held the stocking against James's leg, that things got shabbier and got shabbier summer after summer. The mat was fading; the wall-paper was flapping. You couldn't tell any more that those were roses on it. Still, if every door in a house is left perpetually open, and no lockmaker in the whole of Scotland can mend a bolt, things must spoil. What was the use of flinging a green Cashmere shawl over the edge of a picture frame? In two weeks it would be the colour of pea soup. But it was the doors that annoyed her; every door was left open. She listened. The drawing-room-door was open; the hall door was open; it sounded as if the bedroom doors were open; and certainly the window on the landing was open, for that she had opened herself. That windows should be open, and doors shut—simple as it was, could none of them remember it? She would go into the maids' bedrooms at night and find them sealed like ovens, except for Marie's, the Swiss girl, who would rather go without a bath than without fresh air, but then at home, she had said, "the mountains are so beautiful." She had said that last night looking out of the window with tears in her eyes. "The mountains are so beautiful." Her father was dying there, Mrs. Ramsay knew. He was leaving them fatherless. Scolding and demonstrating (how to make a bed, how to open a window, with hands that shut and spread like a Frenchwoman's) all had folded itself quietly about her, when the girl spoke, as, after a flight through the sunshine the wings of a bird fold themselves quietly and the blue of its plumage changes from bright steel to soft purple. She had stood there silent for there was nothing to be said. He had cancer of the throat. At the recollection—how she had stood there, how the girl had said "At home the mountains are so beautiful," and there was no hope, no hope whatever, she had a spasm of irritation, and speaking sharply, said to James:

"Stand still. Don't be tiresome," so that he knew instantly that her severity was real, and straightened his leg and she measured it.

The stocking was too short by half an inch at least, making allowance for the fact that Sorley's little boy would be less well grown than James.

"It's too short," she said, "ever so much too short."

Never did anybody look so sad. Bitter and black, half-way down, in the darkness, in the shaft which ran from the sunlight to the depths, perhaps a tear formed; a tear fell; the waters swayed this way and that, received it, and were at rest. Never did anybody look so sad.

But was it nothing but looks? people said. What was there behind it—her beauty, her splendour? Had he blown his brains out, they asked, had he died the week before they were married—some other, earlier lover, of whom rumours reached one? Or was there nothing? nothing but an incomparable beauty which she lived behind, and could do nothing to disturb? For easily though she might have said at some moment of intimacy when stories of great passion, of love foiled, of ambition thwarted came her way how she too had known or felt or been through it herself, she never spoke. She was silent always. She knew then—she knew without having learnt. Her simplicity fathomed what clever people falsified. Her singleness of mind made her drop plumb like a stone, alight exact as a bird, gave her, naturally, this swoop and fall of the spirit upon truth which delighted, eased, sustained—falsely perhaps.

("Nature has but little clay," said Mr. Bankes once, hearing her voice on the telephone, and much moved by it though she was only telling him a fact about a train, "like that of which she moulded you." He saw her at the end of the line,

Greek, blue-eyed, straight-nosed. How incongruous it seemed to be telephoning to a woman like that. The Graces assembling seemed to have joined hands in meadows of asphodel to compose that face. Yes, he would catch the 10:30 at Euston.

"But she's no more aware of her beauty than a child," said Mr. Bankes, replacing the receiver and crossing the room to see what progress the workmen were making with an hotel which they were building at the back of his house. And he thought of Mrs. Ramsay as he looked at that stir among the unfinished walls. For always, he thought, there was something incongruous to be worked into the harmony of her face. She clapped a deerstalker's hat on her head; she ran across the lawn in goloshes to snatch a child from mischief. So that if it was her beauty merely that one thought of, one must remember the quivering thing, the living thing (they were carrying bricks up a little plank as he watched them), and work it into the picture; or if one thought of her simply as a woman, one must endow her with some freak of idiosyncrasy; or suppose some latent desire to doff her royalty of form as if her beauty bored her and all that men say of beauty, and she wanted only to be like other people, insignificant. He did not know. He did not know. He must go to his work.)

Knitting her reddish-brown hairy stocking, with her head outlined absurdly by the gilt frame, the green shawl which she had tossed over the edge of the frame, and the authenticated masterpiece by Michael Angelo, Mrs. Ramsay smoothed out what had been harsh in her manner a moment before, raised his head, and kissed her little boy on the forehead. "Let's find another picture to cut out," she said.

This piece of narrative prose is the fifth section of part 1 in Virginia Woolf's novel, *To the Lighthouse*, which was first published in 1927. The situation in which the characters find themselves can be almost completely deduced from the text itself. Nowhere in the novel is it set forth systematically, by way of introduction or exposition, or in any other way than as it is here. I shall, however, briefly summarize what the situation is at the beginning of our passage. This will make it easier for the reader to understand the following analysis; it will also serve to bring out more clearly a number of important motifs from earlier sections which are here only alluded to.

Mrs. Ramsay is the wife of an eminent London professor of philosophy; she is very beautiful but definitely no longer young. With her youngest son James—he is six years old—she is sitting by the window in a good-sized summer house on one of the Hebrides islands. The professor has rented it for many years. In addition to the Ramsays, their eight children, and the servants, there are a number of guests in the house, friends on longer or shorter visits. Among them is a well-known botanist, William Bankes, an elderly widower, and Lily Briscoe, who is a painter. These two are just passing by the window. James is sitting on the floor busily cutting pictures from an illustrated catalogue. Shortly before, his mother had told him that, if the weather should be fine, they would sail to the lighthouse the next day. This is an expedition James has been looking forward to for a long time. The people at the lighthouse are to receive various presents; among these are stockings for the lighthouse-keeper's boy. The violent joy which James had felt when the trip was announced had been as violently cut short by his father's acid observation that the weather would not be fine the next day. One of the guests, with malicious emphasis, has added some corroborative meteorological details. After all the others have left the room, Mrs. Ramsay, to console James, speaks the words with which our passage opens.

The continuity of the section is established through an exterior occurrence involving Mrs. Ramsay and James: the measuring of the stocking. Immediately after her consoling words (if it isn't fine tomorrow, we'll go some other day), Mrs. Ramsay makes James stand up so that she can measure the stocking for the lighthouse-keeper's son against his leg. A little further on she rather absent-mindedly tells him to stand still—the boy is fidgeting because his jealousy makes him a little stubborn and perhaps also because he is still under the impression of the disappointment of a few moments ago. Many lines later, the warning to stand still is repeated more sharply. James obeys, the measuring takes place, and it is found that the stocking is still considerably too short. After another long interval the scene concludes with Mrs. Ramsay kissing the boy on the forehead (she thus makes up for the sharp tone of her second order to him to stand still) and her proposing to help him look for another picture to cut out. Here the section ends.

This entirely insignificant occurrence is constantly interspersed with other elements which, although they do not interrupt its progress, take up far more time in the narration than the whole scene can possibly have lasted. Most of these elements are inner processes, that is, movements within the consciousness of individual personages, and not necessarily of personages involved in the exterior occurrence but also of others who are not even present at the time: "people," or "Mr. Bankes." In addition other exterior occurrences which might be called secondary and which pertain to quite different times and places (the telephone conversation, the construction of the building, for example) are worked in and made to serve as the frame for what goes on in the consciousness of third persons. Let us examine this in detail.

Mrs. Ramsay's very first remark is twice interrupted: first by the visual impression she receives of William Bankes and Lily Briscoe passing by together, and then, after a few intervening words serving the progress of the exterior occurrence, by the impression which the two persons passing by have left in her: the charm of Lily's Chinese eyes, which it is not for every man to see—whereupon she finishes her sentence and also allows her consciousness to dwell for a moment on the measuring of the stocking: we may yet go to the lighthouse, and so I must make sure the stocking is long enough. At this point there flashes into her mind the idea which has been prepared by her reflection on Lily's Chinese eyes (William and Lily ought to marry)—an admirable idea, she loves making matches. Smiling, she begins measuring the stocking. But the boy, in his stubborn and jealous love of her, refuses to stand still. How can she see whether the stocking is the right length if the boy keeps fidgeting about? What is the matter with James, her youngest, her darling? She looks up. Her eye falls on the room—and a long parenthesis begins.

From the shabby chairs of which Andrew, her eldest son, said the other day
that their entrails were all over the floor, her thoughts wander on, probing the
objects and the people of her environment. The shabby furniture . . . but still
good enough for up here; the advantages of the summer place; so cheap, so
good for the children, for her husband; easily fitted up with a few old pieces
of furniture, some pictures and books. Books—it is ages since she has had
time to read books, even the books which have been dedicated to her (here
the lighthouse flashes in for a second, as a place where one can't send such
erudite volumes as some of those lying about the room). Then the house
again: if the family would only be a little more careful. But of course, Andrew
brings in crabs he wants to dissect; the other children gather seaweed, shells,
stones; and she has to let them. All the children are gifted, each in a different
way. But naturally, the house gets shabbier as a result (here the parenthesis is
interrupted for a moment; she holds the stocking against James's leg); everything goes to ruin. If only the doors weren't always left open. See, everything
is getting spoiled, even that Cashmere shawl on the picture frame. The doors
are always left open; they are open again now. She listens: Yes, they are all
open. The window on the landing is open too; she opened it herself. Windows
must be open, doors closed. Why is it that no one can get that into his head?
If you go to the maids' rooms at night, you will find all the windows closed.
Only the Swiss maid always keeps her window open. She needs fresh air.
Yesterday she looked out of the window with tears in her eyes and said: At
home the mountains are so beautiful. Mrs. Ramsay knew that "at home" the
girl's father was dying. Mrs. Ramsay had just been trying to teach her how to
make beds, how to open windows. She had been talking away and had scolded
the girl too. But then she had stopped talking (comparison with a bird folding
its wings after flying in sunlight). She had stopped talking, for there was
nothing one could say; he has cancer of the throat. At this point, remembering how she had stood there, how the girl had said at home the mountains
were so beautiful—and there was no hope left—a sudden tense exasperation
arises in her (exasperation with the cruel meaninglessness of a life whose
continuance she is nevertheless striving with all her powers to abet, support
and secure). Her exasperation flows out into the exterior action. The parenthesis suddenly closes (it cannot have taken up more than a few seconds; just
now she was still smiling over the thought of a marriage between Mr. Bankes
and Lily Briscoe), and she says sharply to James: Stand still. Don't be so
tiresome.

This is the first major parenthesis. The second starts a little later, after the
stocking has been measured and found to be still much too short. It starts
with the paragraph which begins and ends with the motif, "never did anybody
look so sad."

Who is speaking in this paragraph? Who is looking at Mrs. Ramsay here,
who concludes that never did anybody look so sad? Who is expressing these
doubtful, obscure suppositions?—about the tear which—perhaps—forms and

falls in the dark, about the water swaying this way and that, receiving it, and then returning to rest? There is no one near the window in the room but Mrs. Ramsay and James. It cannot be either of them, nor the "people" who begin to speak in the next paragraph. Perhaps it is the author. However, if that be so, the author certainly does not speak like one who has a knowledge of his characters—in this case, of Mrs. Ramsay—and who, out of his knowledge, can describe their personality and momentary state of mind objectively and with certainty. Virginia Woolf wrote this paragraph. She did not identify it through grammatical and typographical devices as the speech or thought of a third person. One is obliged to assume that it contains direct statements of her own. But she does not seem to bear in mind that she is the author and hence ought to know how matters stand with her characters. The person speaking here, whoever it is, acts the part of one who has only an impression of Mrs. Ramsay, who looks at her face and renders the impression received, but is doubtful of its proper interpretation. "Never did anybody look so sad" is not an objective statement. In rendering the shock received by one looking at Mrs. Ramsay's face, it verges upon a realm beyond reality. And in the ensuing passage the speakers no longer seem to be human beings at all but spirits between heaven and earth, nameless spirits capable of penetrating the depths of the human soul, capable too of knowing something about it, but not of attaining clarity as to what is in process there, with the result that what they report has a doubtful ring, comparable in a way to those "certain airs, detached from the body of the wind," which in a later passage (2, 2) move about the house at night, "questioning and wondering." However that may be, here too we are not dealing with objective utterances on the part of the author in respect to one of the characters. No one is certain of anything here: it is all mere supposition, glances cast by one person upon another whose enigma he cannot solve.

This continues in the following paragraph. Suppositions as to the meaning of Mrs. Ramsay's expression are made and discussed. But the level of tone descends slightly, from the poetic and non-real to the practical and earthly; and now a speaker is introduced: "People said." People wonder whether some recollection of an unhappy occurrence in her earlier life is hidden behind her radiant beauty. There have been rumors to that effect. But perhaps the rumors are wrong: nothing of this is to be learned directly from her; she is silent when such things come up in conversation. But supposing she has never experienced anything of the sort herself, she yet knows everything even without experience. The simplicity and genuineness of her being unfailingly light upon the truth of things, and, falsely perhaps, delight, ease, sustain.

Is it still "people" who are speaking here? We might almost be tempted to doubt it, for the last words sound almost too personal and thoughtful for the gossip of "people." And immediately afterward, suddenly and unexpectedly, an entirely new speaker, a new scene, and a new time are introduced. We find Mr. Bankes at the telephone talking to Mrs. Ramsay, who has called him to tell him about a train connection, evidently with reference to a journey they are planning to make together. The paragraph about the tear had already taken us out of the room where Mrs. Ramsay and James are sitting by the window; it had transported us to an undefinable scene beyond the realm of reality. The paragraph in which the rumors are discussed has a concretely earthly but not clearly identified scene. Now we find ourselves in a precisely determined place, but far away from the summer house—in London, in Mr. Bankes's house. The time is not stated ("once"), but apparently the telephone conversation took place long (perhaps as much as several years) before this particular sojourn in the house on the island. But what Mr. Bankes says over the telephone is in perfect continuity with the preceding paragraph. Again not objectively but in the form of the impression received by a specific person at a specific moment, it as it were sums up all that precedes—the scene with the Swiss maid, the hidden sadness in Mrs. Ramsay's beautiful face, what people think about her, and the impression she makes: Nature has but little clay like that of which she molded her. Did Mr. Bankes really say that to her over the telephone? Or did he only want to say it when he heard her voice, which moved him deeply, and it came into his mind how strange it was to be talking over the telephone with this wonderful woman, so like a Greek goddess? The sentence is enclosed in quotation marks, so one would suppose that he really spoke it. But this is not certain, for the first words of his soliloquy, which follows, are likewise enclosed in quotation marks. In any case, he quickly gets hold of himself, for he answers in a matter-of-fact way that he will catch the 10:30 at Euston.

But his emotion does not die away so quickly. As he puts down the receiver and walks across the room to the window in order to watch the work on a new building across the way—apparently his usual and characteristic procedure when he wants to relax and let his thoughts wander freely—he continues to be preoccupied with Mrs. Ramsay. There is always something strange about her, something that does not quite go with her beauty (as for instance telephoning); she has no awareness of her beauty, or at most only a childish awareness; her dress and her actions show that at times. She is constantly getting involved in everyday realities which are hard to reconcile with the harmony of her face. In his methodical way he tries to explain her incongruities to himself. He puts forward some conjectures but cannot make up his mind. Meanwhile his momentary impressions of the work on the new building keep crowding in. Finally he gives it up. With the somewhat impatient, determined matter-of-factness of a methodical and scientific worker (which he is) he shakes off the insoluble problem "Mrs. Ramsay." He knows no solution (the repetition of "he did not know" symbolizes his impatient shaking it off). He has to get back to his work.

Here the second long interruption comes to an end and we are taken back to the room where Mrs. Ramsay and James are. The exterior occurrence is brought to a close with the kiss on James's forehead and the resumption of the cutting out of pictures. But here too we have only an exterior change. A scene previously abandoned reappears, suddenly and with as little transition as if it had never been left, as though the long interruption were only a glance which someone (who?) has cast from it into the depths of time. But the theme (Mrs. Ramsay, her beauty, the enigma of her character, her absoluteness, which nevertheless always exercises itself in the relativity and ambiguity of life, in what does not become her beauty) carries over directly from the last phase of the interruption (that is, Mr. Bankes's fruitless reflections) into the situation in which we now find Mrs. Ramsay: "with her head outlined absurdly by the gilt frame" etc.—for once again what is around her is not suited to her, is "something incongruous." And the kiss she gives her little boy, the words she speaks to him, although they are a genuine gift of life, which James accepts as the most natural and simple truth, are yet heavy with unsolved mystery.

Our analysis of the passage yields a number of distinguishing stylistic characteristics, which we shall now attempt to formulate.

The writer as narrator of objective facts has almost completely vanished; almost everything stated appears by way of reflection in the consciousness of the dramatis personae. When it is a question of the house, for example, or of the Swiss maid, we are not given the objective information which Virginia Woolf possesses regarding these objects of her creative imagination but what Mrs. Ramsay thinks or feels about them at a particular moment. Similarly we are not taken into Virginia Woolf's confidence and allowed to share her knowledge of Mrs. Ramsay's character; we are given her character as it is reflected in and as it affects various figures in the novel: the nameless spirits which assume certain things about a tear, the people who wonder about her, and Mr. Bankes. In our passage this goes so far that there actually seems to be no viewpoint at all outside the novel from which the people and events within it are observed, any more than there seems to be an objective reality apart from what is in the consciousness of the characters. Remnants of such a reality survive at best in brief references to the exterior frame of the action, such as "said Mrs. Ramsay, raising her eyes . . ." or "said Mr. Bankes once, hearing her voice." The last paragraph ("Knitting her reddish-brown hairy stocking . . .") might perhaps also be mentioned in this connection. But this is already somewhat doubtful. The occurrence is described objectively, but as for its interpretation, the tone indicates that the author looks at Mrs. Ramsay not with knowing but with doubting and questioning eyes—even as some character in the novel would see her in the situation in which she is described, would hear her speak the words given.

The devices employed in this instance (and by a number of contemporary writers as well) to express the contents of the consciousness of the dramatis personae have been analyzed and described syntactically. Some of them have been named (*erlebte Rede*, stream of consciousness, *monologue intérieur* are examples). Yet these stylistic forms, especially the *erlebte Rede*, were used in literature much earlier too, but not for the same aesthetic purpose. And in addition to them there are other possibilities—hardly definable in terms of syntax—of obscuring and even obliterating the impression of an objective reality completely known to the author; possibilities, that is, dependent not on form but on intonation and context. A case in point is the passage under discussion, where the author at times achieves the intended effect by representing herself to be someone who doubts, wonders, hesitates, as though the truth about her characters were not better known to her than it is to them or to the reader. It is all, then, a matter of the author's attitude toward the reality of the world he represents. And this attitude differs entirely from that of authors who interpret the actions, situations, and characters of their personages with objective assurance, as was the general practice in earlier times. Goethe or Keller, Dickens or Meredith, Balzac or Zola told us out of their certain knowledge what their characters did, what they felt and thought while doing it, and how their actions and thoughts were to be interpreted. They knew everything about their characters. To be sure, in past periods too we were frequently told about the subjective reactions of the characters in a novel or story; at times even in the form of *erlebte Rede*, although more frequently as a monologue, and of course in most instances with an introductory phrase something like "it seemed to him that . . ." or "at this moment he felt that . . ." or the like. Yet in such cases there was hardly ever any attempt to render the flow and the play of consciousness adrift in the current of changing impressions (as is done in our text both for Mrs. Ramsay and for Mr. Bankes); instead, the content of the individual's consciousness was rationally limited to things connected with the particular incident being related or the particular situation being described. . . . And what is still more important: the author, with his knowledge of an objective truth, never abdicated his position as the final and governing authority. Again, earlier writers, especially from the end of the nineteenth century on, had produced narrative works which on the whole undertook to give us an extremely subjective, individualistic, and often eccentrically aberrant impression of reality, and which neither sought nor were able to ascertain anything objective or generally valid in regard to it. Sometimes such works took the form of first-person novels; sometimes they did not. As an example of the latter case I mention Huysmans's novel *A rebours*. But all that too is basically different from the modern procedure here described on the basis of Virginia Woolf's text, although the latter, it is true, evolved from the former. The essential characteristic of the technique represented by Virginia Woolf is that we are given not merely one person whose consciousness (that is, the impressions it receives) is rendered, but many persons, with frequent shifts from one to the other—in our text, Mrs. Ramsay, "people," Mr. Bankes, in brief interludes James, the Swiss maid in a flash-back, and the nameless ones who speculate over a tear. The multiplicity of persons suggests that we are here after all confronted with an endeavor to investigate an objective reality, that is, specifically, the "real" Mrs. Ramsay. She is, to be sure, an enigma and such she basically remains, but she is as it were encircled by the content of all the various consciousnesses directed upon her (including her own); there is an attempt to approach her from many sides as closely as human possibilities of perception and expression can succeed in doing. The design of a close approach to objective reality by means of numerous subjective impressions received by various individuals (and at various times) is important in the modern technique which we are here examining. It basically differentiates it from the unipersonal subjectivism which allows only a single and generally a very unusual person to make himself heard and admits only that one person's way of looking at reality. In terms of literary history, to be sure, there are close connections between the two methods of representing consciousness— the unipersonal subjective method and the multipersonal method with synthesis as its aim. The latter developed from the former, and there are works in which the two overlap, so that we can watch the development. . . .

Another stylistic peculiarity to be observed in our text—though one that is closely and necessarily connected with the "multipersonal representation of consciousness" just discussed—has to do with the treatment of time. That there is something peculiar about the treatment of time in modern narrative literature is nothing new; several studies have been published on the subject. These were primarily attempts to establish a connection between the pertinent phenomena and contemporary philosophical doctrines or trends— undoubtedly a justifiable undertaking and useful for an appreciation of the community of interests and inner purposes shown in the activity of many of our contemporaries. We shall begin by describing the procedure with reference to our present example. We remarked earlier that the act of measuring the length of the stocking and the speaking of the words related to it must have taken much less time than an attentive reader who tries not to miss anything will require to read the passage—even if we assume that a brief pause intervened between the measuring and the kiss of reconciliation on James's forehead. However, the time the narration takes is not devoted to the occurrence itself (which is rendered rather tersely) but to interludes. Two long excursuses are inserted, whose relations in time to the occurrence which frames them seem to be entirely different. The first excursus, a representation of what goes on in Mrs. Ramsay's mind while she measures the stocking (more precisely, between the first absent-minded and the second sharp order to James to hold his leg still) belongs in time to the framing occurrence, and it is only the representation of it which takes a greater number of seconds and even minutes than the measuring—the reason being that the road taken by consciousness is sometimes traversed far more quickly than language is able to render it, if we want to make ourselves intelligible to a third person, and that is the intention here. What goes on in Mrs. Ramsay's mind in itself contains nothing enigmatic; these are ideas which arise from her daily life and may well be called normal—her secret lies deeper, and it is only when the switch from the open windows to the Swiss maid's words comes, that something happens which lifts the veil a little. On the whole, however, the mirroring of Mrs. Ramsay's consciousness is much more easily comprehensible than the sort of thing we get in such cases from other authors (James Joyce, for example). But simple and trivial as are the ideas which arise one after the other in Mrs. Ramsay's consciousness, they are at the same time essential and significant. They amount to a synthesis of the intricacies of life in which her incomparable beauty has been caught, in which it at once manifests and conceals itself. Of course, writers of earlier periods too occasionally devoted some time and a few sentences to telling the reader what at a specific moment passed through their characters' minds—but for such a purpose they would hardly have chosen so accidental an occasion as Mrs. Ramsay's looking up, so that, quite involuntarily, her eyes fall on the furniture. Nor would it have occurred to them to render the continuous rumination of consciousness in its natural and purposeless freedom. And finally they would not have inserted the entire process between two exterior occurrences so close together in time as the two warnings to James to keep still (both of which, after all, take place while she is on the point of holding the unfinished stocking to his leg); so that, in a surprising fashion unknown to earlier periods, a sharp contrast results between the brief span of time occupied by the exterior event and the dreamlike wealth of a process of consciousness which traverses a whole subjective universe. These are the characteristic and distinctively new features of the technique: a chance occasion releasing processes of consciousness; a natural and even, if you will, a naturalistic rendering of those processes in their peculiar freedom, which is neither restrained by a purpose nor directed by a specific subject of thought; elaboration of the contrast between "exterior" and "interior" time. The three have in common what they reveal of the author's attitude: he submits, much more than was done in earlier realistic works, to the random contingency of real phenomena; and even though he winnows and stylizes the material of the real world—as of course he cannot help doing—he does not proceed rationalistically, nor with a view to bringing a continuity of exterior events to a planned conclusion. In Virginia Woolf's case the exterior events have actually lost their hegemony, they serve to release and interpret inner events, whereas before her time (and still today in many instances) inner movements preponderantly function to prepare and motivate significant exterior happenings. This too is apparent in the randomness and contingency of the exterior occasion (looking up because James does not keep his foot still), which releases the much more significant inner process.

The temporal relation between the second excursus and the framing occurrence is of a different sort: its content (the passage on the tear, the things people think about Mrs. Ramsay, the telephone conversation with Mr. Bankes and his reflections while watching the building of the new hotel) is not a part of the framing occurrence either in terms of time or of place. Other times and places are in question; it is an excursus of the same type as the story of the origin of Odysseus' scar, which was discussed in the first chapter of [*Mimesis*, the book from which this reading was taken]. Even from that, however, it is different in structure. In the Homer passage the excursus was linked to the scar which Euryclea touches with her hands, and although the moment at which the touching of the scar occurs is one of high and dramatic tension, the scene nevertheless immediately shifts to another clear and luminous present, and this present seems actually designed to cut off the dramatic tension and cause the entire footwashing scene to be temporarily forgotten. In Virginia Woolf's passage, there is no question of any tension. Nothing of importance in a dramatic sense takes place; the problem is the length of the stocking. The point of departure for the excursus is Mrs. Ramsay's facial expression: "never did anybody look so sad." In fact several excursuses start from here; three, to be exact. And all three differ in time and place, differ too in definiteness of time and place, the first being situated quite vaguely, the second somewhat more definitely, and the third with comparative precision. Yet none of them is so exactly situated in time as the successive episodes of the story of Odysseus' youth, for even in the case of the telephone scene we have only an inexact indication of when it occurred. As a result it becomes possible to accomplish the shifting of the scene away from the windownook much more unnoticeably and smoothly than the changing of scene and time in the episode of the scar. In the passage on the tear the reader may still be in doubt as to whether there has been any shift at all. The nameless speakers may have entered the room and be looking at Mrs. Ramsay. In the second paragraph this interpretation is no longer possible, but the "people" whose gossip is reproduced are still looking at Mrs. Ramsay's face—not here and now, at the summer-house window, but it is still the same face and has the same expression. And even in the third part, where the face is no longer physically seen (for Mr. Bankes is talking to Mrs. Ramsay over the telephone), it is nonetheless present to his inner vision; so that not for an instant does the theme (the solution of the enigma Mrs. Ramsay), and even the moment when the problem is formulated (the expression of her face while she measures the length of the stocking), vanish from the reader's memory. In terms of the exterior event the three parts of the excursus have nothing to do with one another. They have no common and externally coherent development, as have the episodes of Odysseus' youth which are related with reference to the origin of the scar; they are connected only by the one thing they have in common—looking at Mrs. Ramsay, and more specifically at the Mrs. Ramsay who, with an unfathomable expression of sadness behind her radiant beauty, concludes that the stocking is still much too short. It is only this common focus which connects the otherwise totally different parts of the excursus; but the connection is strong enough to deprive them of the independent "present" which the episode of the scar possesses. They are nothing but attempts to interpret "never did anybody look so sad"; they carry on this theme, which itself carries on after they conclude: there has been no change of theme at all. In contrast, the scene in which Euryclea recognizes Odysseus is interrupted and divided into two parts by the excursus on the origin of the scar. In our passage, there is no such clear distinction between two exterior occurrences and between two presents. However insignificant as an exterior event the framing occurrence (the measuring of the stocking) may be, the picture of Mrs. Ramsay's face which arises from it remains present throughout the excursus; the excursus itself is nothing but a background for that picture, which seems as it were to open into the depths of time—just as the first excursus, released by Mrs. Ramsay's unintentional glance at the furniture, was an opening of the picture into the depths of consciousness.

The two excursuses, then, are not as different as they at first appeared. It is not so very important that the first, so far as time is concerned (and place too), runs its course within the framing occurrence, while the second conjures up other times and places. The times and places of the second are not independent; they serve only the polyphonic treatment of the image which releases it; as a matter of fact they impress us (as does the interior time of the first excursus) like an occurrence in the consciousness of some observer (to be sure, he is not identified) who might see Mrs. Ramsay at the described moment and whose meditation upon the unsolved enigma of her personality might contain memories of what others (people, Mr. Bankes) say and think about her. In both excursuses we are dealing with attempts to fathom a more genuine, a deeper, and indeed a more real reality; in both cases the incident which releases the excursus appears accidental and is poor in content; in both cases it makes little difference whether the excursuses employ only the consciousness-content, and hence only interior time, or whether they also employ exterior shifts of time. After all, the process of consciousness in the first excursus likewise includes shifts of time and scene, especially the episode with the Swiss maid. The important point is that an insignificant exterior occurrence releases ideas and chains of ideas which cut loose from the present of the exterior occurrence and range freely through the depths of time. It is as though an apparently simple text revealed its proper content only in the commentary on it, a simple musical theme only in the development-section. This enables us also to understand the close relation between the treatment of time and the "multipersonal representation of consciousness" discussed earlier. The ideas arising in consciousness are not tied to the present of the exterior occurrence which releases them. Virginia Woolf's peculiar technique, as exemplified in our text, consists in the fact that the exterior objective reality of the momentary present which the author directly reports and which appears as established fact—in our instance the measuring of the stocking—is nothing but an occasion (although perhaps not an entirely accidental one). The stress is placed entirely on what the occasion releases, things which are not seen directly but by reflection, which are not tied to the present of the framing occurrence which releases them. . . .

The distinctive characteristics of the realistic novel of the era between the two great wars, as they have appeared in the present chapter—multipersonal representation of consciousness, time strata, disintegration of the continuity of exterior events, shifting of the narrative viewpoint (all of which are interrelated and difficult to separate)—seem to us indicative of a striving for certain objectives, of certain tendencies and needs on the part of both authors and public. These objectives, tendencies, and needs are numerous; they seem in part to be mutually contradictory; yet they form so much one whole that when we undertake to describe them analytically, we are in constant danger of unwittingly passing from one to another.

Let us begin with a tendency which is particularly striking in our text from Virginia Woolf. She holds to minor, unimpressive, random events: measuring the stocking, a fragment of a conversation with the maid, a telephone call. Great changes, exterior turning points, let alone catastrophes, do not occur; and though elsewhere in *To the Lighthouse* such things are mentioned, it is hastily, without preparation or context, incidentally, and as it were only for the sake of information. The same tendency is to be observed in other and very different writers, such as Proust or Hamsun. In Thomas Mann's *Buddenbrooks* we still have a novel structure consisting of the chronological sequence of important exterior events which affect the Buddenbrook family; and if Flaubert—in many respects a precursor—lingers as a matter of principle over insignificant events and everyday circumstances which hardly advance the action, there is nevertheless to be sensed throughout *Madame Bovary* (though we may wonder how this would have worked out in *Bouvard et Pécuchet*) a constant slow-moving chronological approach first to partial crises and finally to the concluding catastrophe, and it is this approach which dominates the plan of the work as a whole. But a shift in emphasis followed; and now many writers present minor happenings, which are insignificant as exterior factors in a person's destiny, for their own sake or rather as points of departure for the development of motifs, for a penetration which opens up new perspectives into a milieu or a consciousness or the given historical setting. They have discarded presenting the story of their characters with any claim to exterior completeness, in chronological order, and with the emphasis on important exterior turning points of destiny. James Joyce's tremendous novel—an encyclopedic work, a mirror of Dublin, of Ireland, a mirror too of Europe and its millennia—has for its frame the externally insignificant course of a day in the lives of a schoolteacher and an advertising broker. It takes up less than twenty-four hours in their lives—just as *To the Lighthouse* describes portions of two days widely separated in time. . . . This shift of emphasis expresses something that we might call a transfer of confidence: the great exterior turning points and blows of fate are granted less importance; they are credited with less power of yielding decisive information concerning the subject; on the other hand there is confidence that in any random fragment plucked from the course of a life at any time the totality of its fate is contained and can be portrayed. There is greater confidence in syntheses gained through full exploitation of an everyday occurrence than in a chronologically well-ordered total treatment which accompanies the subject from beginning to end, attempts not to omit anything externally important, and emphasizes the great turning points of destiny. It is possible to compare this technique of modern writers with that of certain modern philologists who hold that the interpretation of a few passages from *Hamlet, Phèdre,* or *Faust* can be made to yield more, and more decisive, information about Shakespeare, Racine, or Goethe and their times than would a systematic and chronological treatment of their lives and works. Indeed, the . . . book [*Mimesis,* from which this reading was taken] may be cited as an illustration. I could never have written anything in the nature of a history of European realism; the material would have swamped me; I should have had to enter into hopeless discussions concerning the delimitation of the various periods and the allocation of the various writers to them, and above all concerning the definition of the concept realism. Furthermore, for the sake of completeness, I should have had to deal with some things of which I am but casually informed, and hence to become acquainted with them *ad hoc* by reading up on them (which, in my opinion, is a poor way of acquiring and using knowledge); and the motifs which direct my investigation, and for the sake of which it is written, would have been completely buried under a mass of factual information which has long been known and can easily be looked up in reference books. As opposed to this I see the possibility of success and profit in a method which consists in letting myself be guided by a few motifs which I have worked out gradually and without a specific purpose, and in trying them out on a series of texts which have become familiar and vital to me in the course of my philological activity; for I am convinced that these basic motifs in the history of the representation of reality—provided I have seen them correctly—must be demonstrable in any random realistic text. But to return to those modern writers who prefer the exploitation of random everyday events, contained within a few hours and days, to the complete and chronological representation of a total exterior continuum—they too (more or less consciously) are guided by the consideration that it is a hopeless venture to try to be really complete within the total exterior continuum and yet to make what is essential stand out. Then too they hesitate to impose upon life, which is their subject, an order which it does not possess in itself. He who represents the course of a human life, or a sequence of events extending over a prolonged period of time, and represents it from beginning to end, must prune and isolate arbitrarily. Life has always long since begun, and it is always still going on. And the people whose story the author is telling experience much more than he can ever hope to tell. But the things that happen to a few individuals in the course of a few minutes, hours, or possibly even days—these one can hope to report with reasonable completeness. And here, furthermore, one comes upon the order and the interpretation of life which arise from life itself: that is, those which grow up in the individuals themselves, which are to be discerned in their thoughts, their consciousness, and in a more concealed form in their words and actions. For there is always going on within us a process of formulation and interpretation whose subject matter is our own self. We are constantly endeavoring to give meaning and order to our lives in the past, the present and the future, to our surroundings, the world in which we live; with the result that our lives appear in our own conception as total entities—which to be sure are always changing, more or less radically, more or less rapidly, depending on the extent to which we are obliged, inclined, and able to assimilate the onrush of new experience. These are the forms of order and interpretation which the modern writers here under discussion attempt to grasp in the random moment—not one order and one interpretation, but many, which may either be those of different persons or of the same person at different times; so that overlapping, complementing, and contradiction yield something that we might call a synthesized cosmic view or at least a challenge to the reader's will to interpretive synthesis.

Here we have returned once again to the reflection of multiple consciousnesses. It is easy to understand that such a technique had to develop gradually and that it did so precisely during the decades of the first World War period and after. The widening of man's horizon, and the increase of his experiences, knowledge, ideas, and possible forms of existence, which began in the sixteenth century, continued through the nineteenth at an ever faster tempo—with such a tremendous acceleration since the beginning of the twentieth that synthetic and objective attempts at interpretation are produced and demolished every instant. The tremendous tempo of the changes proved the more confusing because they could not be surveyed as a whole. They occurred simultaneously in many separate departments of science, technology, and economics, with the result that no one—not even those who were leaders in the separate departments—could foresee or evaluate the resulting overall situations. Furthermore, the changes did not produce the same effects in all places, so that the differences of attainment between the various social strata of one and the same people and between different peoples came to be—if not greater—at least more noticeable. The spread of publicity and the crowding of mankind on a shrinking globe sharpened awareness of the differences in ways of life and attitudes, and mobilized the interests and forms of existence which the new changes either furthered or threatened. In all parts of the world crises of adjustment arose; they increased in number and coalesced. They led to the upheavals which we have not weathered yet. In Europe this violent clash of the most heterogeneous ways of life and kinds of endeavor undermined not only those religious, philosophical, ethical, and economic principles which were part of the traditional heritage and which, despite many earlier shocks, had maintained their position of authority through slow adaptation and transformation; nor yet only the ideas of the

Enlightenment, the ideas of democracy and liberalism which had been revolutionary in the eighteenth century and were still so during the first half of the nineteenth; it undermined even the new revolutionary forces of socialism, whose origins did not go back beyond the heyday of the capitalist system. These forces threatened to split up and disintegrate. They lost their unity and clear definition through the formation of numerous mutually hostile groups, through strange alliances which some of these groups effected with non-socialist ideologies, through the capitulation of most of them during the first World War, and finally through the propensity on the part of many of their most radical advocates for changing over into the camp of their most extreme enemies. Otherwise too there was an increasingly strong factionalism—at times crystallizing around important poets, philosophers, and scholars, but in the majority of cases pseudo-scientific, syncretistic, and primitive. The temptation to entrust oneself to a sect which solved all problems with a single formula, whose power of suggestion imposed solidarity, and which ostracized everything which would not fit in and submit—this temptation was so great that with many people, fascism hardly had to employ force when the time came for it to spread through the countries of old European culture, absorbing the smaller sects.

As recently as the nineteenth century, and even at the beginning of the twentieth, so much clearly formulable and recognized community of thought and feeling remained in those countries that a writer engaged in representing reality had reliable criteria at hand by which to organize it. At least, within the range of contemporary movements, he could discern certain specific trends; he could delimit opposing attitudes and ways of life with a certain degree of clarity. To be sure, this had long since begun to grow increasingly difficult. Flaubert (to confine ourselves to realistic writers) already suffered from the lack of valid foundations for his work; and the subsequent increasing predilection for ruthlessly subjectivistic perspectives is another symptom. At the time of the first World War and after—in a Europe unsure of itself, overflowing with unsettled ideologies and ways of life, and pregnant with disaster—certain writers distinguished by instinct and insight find a method which dissolves reality into multiple and multivalent reflections of consciousness. That this method should have been developed at this time is not hard to understand.

But the method is not only a symptom of the confusion and helplessness, not only a mirror of the decline of our world. There is, to be sure, a good deal to be said for such a view. There is in all these works a certain atmosphere of universal doom: especially in *Ulysses*, with its mocking *odi-et-amo* hodgepodge of the European tradition, with its blatant and painful cynicism, and its uninterpretable symbolism—for even the most painstaking analysis can hardly emerge with anything more than an appreciation of the multiple enmeshment of the motifs but with nothing of the purpose and meaning of the work itself. And most of the other novels which employ multiple reflection of consciousness also leave the reader with an impression of hopelessness. There is often something confusing, something hazy about them, something hostile to the reality which they represent. We not infrequently find a turning away from the practical will to live, or delight in portraying it under its most brutal forms. There is hatred of culture and civilization, brought out by means of the subtlest stylistic devices which culture and civilization have developed, and often a radical and fanatical urge to destroy. Common to almost all of these novels is haziness, vague indefinability of meaning: precisely the kind of uninterpretable symbolism which is also to be encountered in other forms of art of the same period.

But something entirely different takes place here too. Let us turn again to the text which was our starting-point. It breathes an air of vague and hopeless sadness. We never come to learn what Mrs. Ramsay's situation really is. Only the sadness, the vanity of her beauty and vital force emerge from the depths of secrecy. Even when we have read the whole novel, the meaning of the relationship between the planned trip to the lighthouse and the actual trip many years later remains unexpressed, enigmatic, only dimly to be conjectured, as does the content of Lily Briscoe's concluding vision which enables her to finish her painting with one stroke of the brush. It is one of the few books of this type which are filled with good and genuine love but also, in its feminine way, with irony, amorphous sadness, and doubt of life. Yet what realistic depth is achieved in every individual occurrence, for example the measuring of the stocking! Aspects of the occurrence come to the fore, and links to other occurrences, which, before this time, had hardly been sensed, which had never been clearly seen and attended to, and yet they are determining factors in our real lives. What takes place here in Virginia Woolf's novel is precisely what was attempted everywhere in works of this kind (although not everywhere with the same insight and mastery)—that is, to put the emphasis on the random occurrence, to exploit it not in the service of a planned continuity of action but in itself. And in the process something new and elemental appeared: nothing less than the wealth of reality and depth of life in every moment to which we surrender ourselves without prejudice. To be sure, what happens in that moment—be it outer or inner processes— concerns in a very personal way the individuals who live in it but it also (and for that very reason) concerns the elementary things which men in general have in common. It is precisely the random moment which is comparatively independent of the controversial and unstable orders over which men fight and despair; it passes unaffected by them, as daily life. The more it is exploited, the more the elementary things which our lives have in common come to light. The more numerous, varied, and simple the people are who appear as subjects of such random moments, the more effectively must what they have in common shine forth. In this unprejudiced and exploratory type of representation we cannot but see to what an extent—below the surface conflicts—the differences between men's ways of life and forms of thought have already lessened. The strata of societies and their different ways of life have become inextricably mingled. There are no longer even exotic peoples. A century ago (in Mérimée for example), Corsicans or Spaniards were still exotic; today the term would be quite unsuitable for Pearl Buck's Chinese peasants. Beneath the conflicts, and also through them, an economic and cultural leveling process is taking place. It is still a long way to a common life of mankind on earth, but the goal begins to be visible. And it is most concretely visible now in the unprejudiced, precise, interior and exterior representation of the random moment in the lives of different people. So the complicated process of dissolution which led to fragmentation of the exterior action, to reflection of consciousness, and to stratification of time seems to be tending toward a very simple solution. Perhaps it will be too simple to please those who, despite all its dangers and catastrophes, admire and love our epoch for the sake of its abundance of life and the incomparable historical vantage point which it affords. But they are few in number, and probably they will not live to see much more than the first forewarnings of the approaching unification and simplification.

Virginia's Web

Geoffrey Hartman

This goddess of the continuum is incapable of continuity.

—Valéry, on the Pythoness

Transitions may well be the hardest part of a writer's craft: Virginia Woolf shows that they are also the most imaginative. One remembers, from *Mrs. Dalloway*, the inscrutable motor car proceeding toward Piccadilly, and the way it serves to move the plot with it. Or, in the next episode, how the skywriting plane moves different minds, each guessing at the slogan being dispensed and then dispersed. The wind stealing the smoky letters before any guess is confirmed is the same that, fifteen years later, miscarries the players' words in *Between the Acts*. Suppose now that these letters or words or glimpses are divided by years, by some indefinite or immeasurable gap. We know that years pass, that words are spoken or spelled, and that cars reach their destination; yet the mystery lies in space itself, which the imaginative mind must fill, perhaps too quickly. The dominant issues in the study of Virginia Woolf have been her solipsism and her treatment of time and character; I propose to suspend these and to see her novels as mirrors held up primarily to the imagination.

Let us consider a fairly simple passage from *To the Lighthouse*. To look at it closely requires a concern, a prior interest: in our case, how the novelist goes from one thing to another. The context of the passage is as follows. Mr. Ramsay and his two children, Cam and James, are being ferried to the Lighthouse. The weather is calm, and it seems the boat will never get there; Cam and James, moreover, do not want it to get there, resenting the tyrannous will of their father. In the first section of the novel, with Mrs. Ramsay still alive, it is he who dampens the childish eagerness of James to go to the Lighthouse; and now (many years later) he insists on this outing as a commemorative act.

> The sails flapped over their heads. The water chuckled and slapped the sides of the boat, which drowsed motionless in the sun. Now and then the sails rippled with a little breeze in them, but the ripple ran over them and ceased. The boat made no

From *Chicago Review* 14 (Spring 1961): 20–32. Copyright © 1970 by Geoffrey Hartman. Reprinted by permission.

motion at all. Mr. Ramsay sat in the middle of the boat. He would be impatient in a moment, James thought, and Cam thought, looking at her father who sat in the middle of the boat between them (James steered; Cam sat alone in the bow) with his legs tightly curled. He hated hanging about.

The continuity is kept on the verbal as well as visual plane by echo and repetition (flapped, slapped, drowsed, them, them, boat, boat). This is an intensifying device any writer might use, but one is hardly aware with what skill the sentences lead inward, to that parenthesis and fine slowing-up that encompasses boat, man, and children. Mrs. Woolf's style is here at its best, and the continuities going from the freest to the stillest part of the scene (from the sail to the middle of the boat) do so with an almost humorous resistance. It is interesting to think that the rhythm should be generated by an avoidance; there is, in any case, a stop and go pattern to it, magnified perhaps by the subject of the passage. In terms of plot or subject we have a pause; in terms of the prose that describes it, a sustained if not augmented interest in continuity. As the description reaches the inside of the boat, and then the inside of the mind, the rhythm slows, and as the rhythm slows the continuity is made more obvious as if to counterpoint the pausing. This pattern, however, may be found elsewhere too and cannot be purely an intensifying or descriptive device. It may originate in the writer prior to the particular subject.

I am suggesting that continuity is a deeper matter here than craft or style. In his first important essay Valéry remarked that the extension of continuity by means of metaphor, language, or other means was the common gift of genius. His thesis implied two things: that there is "space" or apparent discontinuity, and that the genial inventor can project his mind into it. If we identify this ability to project (or better, interpolate) with imagination, then the crucial question is what this space may be. There can be only one answer which is not a gross generalization, and this is—anything. We are dealing, it must be remembered, with appearances, and there is nothing that may not succumb to blankness.[1] Art respects appearances so much that everything may become questionably blank, even the continuities firmly established by science. For though science has shown them to exist, it has not shown why they should exist so unapparently, and the formula that proves them also proves the coyness of nature.

To the Lighthouse begins with a sense of fullness and continuous life as we are led in and out of Mrs. Ramsay's mind. There are few apparent pauses to threaten the continuity of thought or existence. The dark space between the beams of the Lighthouse does, however, penetrate consciousness. "A shutter, like the leathern eyelid of a lizard, flickered over the intensity of his gaze and obscured the letter R. In that flash of darkness he heard people saying—he

---

[1]For a strictly philosophical account, see Hegel's *Phenomenology of Mind* (1807), introduction and opening section on "Sense-Certainty"; Heidegger's *What Is Metaphysics* (1929); and Sartre's *L'Imaginaire* (1940).

was a failure—that R was beyond him. He would never reach R. On to R, once more. R—" Mr. Ramsay's intellectual ambitions are described, and there are other fine sequences of the same kind.

These darker intervals, rare in the first part, consolidate as the encroaching and live darkness of the second part, which traces the gradual abandonment of the Ramsay house and its last minute rescue from oblivion. Then, in the last section of the novel, a horrid calm moves directly into the heart of the characters. The becalming of the boat is part of a larger sequence, in which all are involved with death, present as distance or the sea's calm or the absence of Mrs. Ramsay. Each person is compelled by a stilling glance, like the wedding guest by the Mariner. They must suffer the suspense, endure the calm, and ultimately resist it—its intimations of peace and of a happy death of the will.

Resistance is the major theme of this novel. The lighthouse itself is a monitory object, warning off, centered in hostile elements. Mr. Ramsay, an enemy of the sea that becalms his boat, is a stronger resister than Mrs. Ramsay, who lives toward the sea. Resistance is a matter of imagination which can either actively fill space or passively blend with it and die. Imagination could also die to itself and become pure will, as in the case of Mr. Ramsay, who wishes to cross the sea, or from Q to R, by force. He denies space and violates the privacy of others. Yet to keep imagination alive involves staying alive to space, to the horrid calms of Virginia Woolf's ocean.

The imagination itself neither acknowledges nor denies space: it lives in it and says to every question "Life, life, life," like Orlando's little bird or Blake's cricket.[2] Affirmation, not meaning, is basic to it, and the problem of meaning cannot even be faced without considering the necessity or fatality of some primary affirmation. Religious belief is such a primary act, but a special form of it. The founding of a fictional world is such a primary act. Fiction reveals something without which the mind could not be, or could not think. The mind needs a world, a substantialized Yes.

Yet every great artist rebels against this, and today his rebellion is conventional. By beginning to question the necessity of fiction, i.e., the inherently affirmative structure of imagination, he joins the philosopher who seeks a truth greater than that arbitrary Yes. The more Henry James seeks the definitive word, the more his mind shrinks from affirmation. It is, similarly, Mrs. Woolf's resistance, her continuous doubting of the continuity she is forced to posit, that we are interested in. At the end of *To the Lighthouse*, Lily Briscoe's "It is finished," referring in turn to the reaching of the Lighthouse and to her picture, is deeply ironic. It recalls a suffrance greater than the object attained by this last term, by any term. Each artist resists his own vision.

2*Orlando*, chap. 6; *Auguries of Innocence:* "A Riddle or the Cricket's Cry/Is to Doubt a fit Reply."

This resistance, however, cannot take place except in the space of fiction and requires the creation of a work of art which is its own implicit critique. The reason that an artist's critique cannot be discursive, or purely so, is that it still involves an affirmation— the new work of art. It is therefore quite proper to put our question in strictly literary terms: What kind of novel does Mrs. Woolf write? And how does it criticize its origin in the affirmative impulse?

I shall try to define Virginia Woolf's novel as the product of a certain kind of prose and a certain kind of plot. This dyad should justify itself as we proceed, but what I say is experimental and may lead to some undue generalizing. The reason for omitting character should also appear: there is only one fully developed character in Mrs. Woolf's novels, and that is the completely expressive or androgynous mind.

Her concern for the novel is linked everywhere with that for prose style. She often remarks that prose, unlike poetry, is still in its infancy, and her first experimental novel, *Mrs. Dalloway*, matures it via the peregrinations of a woman's mind. It may be said with some truth that the novel is, for Virginia Woolf, simply the best form of presenting a completely expressive prose.

A Room of One's Own (1928) illustrates in slow motion how this mature prose came to be. Mrs. Woolf's "sociological essay" is about the future of fiction and woman's part in it. But we are not given a straight essay. She refuses to separate her thought from certain imaginary accidents of time and place and writes something akin to the French *récit*. Her mind, porous to the world even during thought, devises a prose similar to that of *To the Lighthouse*, which makes continuities out of distractions. It is as if a woman's mind were linked at its origin, like the novel itself, to romance; and one is quite happy with this natural picaresque, the author walking us and the world along on the back of her prose.

Still, prose in a novel is different from prose in some other form. Its function can be determined only within a particular structure, and a novel or story requires some finite series of events necessary to produce suspense and move the reader toward the resolving point. This raises the question of the relation of plot and prose.

In the modern novel there are at least two significant ways of making prose subsume the suspense previously offered by plot. One is to structure it as highly as the verse of the seventeenth-century classical drama in France, so that even the simplest conversation becomes dramatic. Henry James's prose has affinities to this. The other is to have the plot coincide with the special perspective of a character. Faulkner and many others (including James) may use this method, which creates a kind of mystery story, the mystery being the mind itself. Mrs Woolf's prose has some affinities here, but it is not made to issue from a mind limited or peculiar enough to make us suspect the darkness it circles.

The curious fact is that neither the prose nor the plot of Mrs. Woolf's novels can explain the suspense we feel. Perhaps suspense is the wrong word, since we are not avid for what happens next but fascinated by how the something next will happen. To understand this let us take *Mrs. Dalloway.* Its plot is simple and realistic, as is always the case with Virginia Woolf (*Orlando* is only an apparent exception). The suspense or fascination cannot come from that source. Nor does it come, in isolation, from the rich prose woven by Clarissa's mind, since the plot often parts from her to present other people or views, yet our attention does not flag at those points. But if Mrs. Woolf goes at will beyond Clarissa's consciousness, it is on condition that some line of continuity be preserved. There are no jumps, no chapters; every transition is tied to what precedes or has been introduced. The first line of the novel, "Mrs. Dalloway said she would buy the flowers herself," presupposes some immediate prior fact already taken up in consciousness and is emblematic of the artist's mood throughout the novel. Our fascination is involved with this will to continuity, this free prose working under such strict conditions.

The plot, however, does play an important role. Clarissa waiting to cross the street, then crossing, is part of the plot; her thoughts while doing so effect many finer transitions. A tension is thus produced between the realistic plot and the expressive prose; the latter tends to veil or absorb the former, and the former suggests a more natural continuity, one less dependent on mind. We know that certain things happen in sequence, that a play will go on, that people fall in love or cross streets, that a day moves from dawn to dusk. The simpler continuity of the plot tempts the mind forward, as a relief from the essential prose, or as a resting place in something solid.

This tension between two types of continuity also makes the mind realize the artificial or arbitrary character of both. It is moved to conceive the void they bridge. A void is there, like the pauses or thoughts of death in Mrs. Dalloway. But the mind conceives it joyfully, rather than in terror, because of the constant opening up of new perspectives, and the realization through this of its connective power. The continuities we have labeled "plot" and "prose" are, moreover, not unrelated or without special value. I would now like to show that they stand to each other dialectically as major types of affirmation, the plot line coinciding mostly with what we call nature, and the prose line intimating something precarious but also perhaps greater—the "Nature that exists in works of mighty Poets." To do so I return to *A Room of One's Own*, in which Mrs. Woolf (or her persona) is thinking about women writers, and the last of her thought sequences suggests the structure of her novels in microcosm.

Mrs. Woolf looks from her window at London waking for the day's business in the fall of '28. She looks out, not in, allowing herself to be distracted. The city seems to be indifferent to her concerns, and she records the fact strongly:

> Nobody, it seemed, was reading *Antony and Cleopatra* . . . Nobody cared a straw—and I do not blame them—for the future of fiction, the death of poetry or

the development by the average woman of a prose style completely expressive of her mind. If opinions upon any of these matters had been chalked on the pavement, nobody would have stooped to read them . . . Here came an errand-boy; here a woman with a dog on a lead.[3]

Something is wrong. Can a writer be so calm about indifference, especially when it threatens art? But Mrs. Woolf is hastening the end. Not her own, but the end of a civilization which had exalted one part of the soul at the expense of the rest. The twenties are reaching their close; the first world war is not forgotten; Proust, Bergson, and Freud have advertised human possessiveness and male arbitrariness, the subtlest workings-out of the patriarchal will. The bustle she welcomes has, at least, the arbitrariness of life rather than of the will: an errand boy here, a funeral there, business men, idlers, shoppers, each going his way.

But her thought does not stop at this point; she lets it found its dialectic. The mind, to begin with, accepts a life indifferent to itself. The affirmative movement is not overcome, though what Virginia Woolf affirms is life rather than her will. Yet she is less interested in life as such than in the life of the mind, which can only appear if thought is left as apparently free as the goings and comings beneath her window.

That this freedom may be an illusion does not matter. It is still a window to the truth and, in any case, lasts a short time. As Mrs. Woolf continues to look, the life disappears, and only the indifference remains: "There was a complete lull and suspension of traffic. Nothing came down the street; nobody passed. A single leaf detached itself from the plane tree at the end of the street, and in that pause and suspension fell." Her mind, however, will not accept this pause, this emptiness. The affirmative movement attaches itself the more strongly to the slightest sign. "Somehow it was like a signal falling, a signal pointing to a force in things which one had overlooked."

What the mind has overlooked seems at first to be nature, an impersonally and constantly active principle of life. This certainly has a presence in Mrs. Woolf's novels. It is much more important to her than the spice of illusionistic realism. In her wish for a purer affirmation, one which does not merely go toward the male will, she often has her characters go toward nature. Their direct relationships are diverted by a second one: "human beings not always in their relations to each other but in their relation to reality; and the sky too, and the trees or whatever it may be in themselves." No human being, she adds, should shut out the view.

Yet it becomes clear, as Mrs. Woolf continues, that the mind had also overlooked something in itself. The falling leaf reminds her, it is true, of a natural force—but in the artist. It is the artist, the person at the window, who affirms a world where there is none. She imagines that the signal points to "a

---

[3]The thought-sequence from which I quote in this section is found in the last chapter (6) of *A Room of One's Own*.

river, which flowed past, invisibly round the corner, down the street, and took people and eddied them along." In *Mrs. Dalloway* the author's consciousness is precisely this: a stream of prose that moves people together and apart, entering at will this mind and that. Nature, as she now conceives it, is one in which the artist participates, so that Shakespeare, poetry, and the finding of a new prose style become once again vital issues.

The artist, at this point, is clearly a Prospero figure. She stages an illusion whose object is a marriage: the mind coming together outside of itself by means of the world or the stage. Nature and art conspire for this illusion or prothalamion; the river, we notice, is a natural and artificial image of rhythm and leads directly to the closing event. As if the river had eddied them together, a girl in patent leather boots and a young man in a maroon raincoat meet a taxi beneath Virginia Woolf's window and get in. "The sight was ordinary enough," she remarks; "what was strange was the rhythmical order with which my imagination had invested it."

Only now does she withdraw from the window, reflecting on the mind. Because of her topic—the woman as writer—she had been thinking intensely of one sex as distinct from the other. But, seeing the couple, the mind felt as if after being divided it had come together again in a natural fusion. Perhaps, she goes on, a state of mind exists in which one could continue without effort, because nothing is required to be repressed and no resistance develops. Interpreting the event literally as well as analogically, she concludes that the fully functioning mind is androgynous.

There is much fantasy in this. What remains is a sustained act of thought, a dialectic that comprises certain distinct types of affirmation. *Dialectic* is not, at first glance, the right word, since all we see is an affirmative movement increasing in scope. There comes, however, a critical pause, a moment of discontinuity, in which the *negative* almost appears. "Nothing came down the street; nobody passed." Such "power failures" are not rare in Virginia Woolf and not always so lightly overcome. They assume a cosmic proportion in her last novel [*Between the Acts*]. Miss La Trobe, the illusionist, cannot sustain her country pageant. The wind is against her, life is against her, the rhythm breaks. She learns the depth of space between her and her creation; the vacuum, also, between it and the audience. "Miss La Trobe leant against the tree, paralyzed. Her power had left her. Beads of perspiration broke on her forehead. Illusion had failed. 'This is death,' she murmured, 'death.'" At this very moment, as in the scene beneath Virginia Woolf's window, nature seems to take over and reestablish the rhythm in an expressionistic passage revealing the complicity of art and nature: "Then, suddenly, as the illusion petered out, the cows took up the burden. One had lost her calf. In the very nick of time she lifted her great moon-eyed head and bellowed. All the great moon-eyed heads laid themselves back. From cow after cow came the same yearning bellow. . . . The cows annihilated the gap; bridged the distance; filled the emptiness and continued the emotion."

Between the Acts reveals the same voracious desire for continuity as *Mrs. Dalloway* and *To the Lighthouse*, yet in this last work the novelist has dropped all pretense as to the realism of her transitions. She is outrageously, sadly humorous. "Suddenly the cows stopped; lowered their heads, and began browsing. Simultaneously the audience lowered their heads and read their programmes." This is how she gets from the cows to the audience, with the result, of course, that one feels the space she bridges more intensely. Yet does not the whole novel turn on what is between the acts, on the interpolations of the novelist who continually saves the play for Miss La Trobe? As in the example from *A Room of One's Own*, it is finally irrelevant whether the continuities discovered by Mrs. Woolf are in nature or in the artist.

Our question as to the kind of novel Virginia Woolf writes can now be answered. There is a line of development which goes from the realism of *The Voyage Out* (1915) to the expressionism of *Between the Acts* (1941), and passes through the experimental period of 1925–31 containing *Mrs. Dalloway, To the Lighthouse, Orlando,* and *The Waves*.[4] Mrs. Woolf sought to catch the power of affirmation in its full extent, and her effort to do so includes this shuttling between realistic and expressionistic forms of style. She never abandoned realism entirely because it corresponds to an early phase of affirmation. It is realism of the simple and illusionistic kind which guides our powers of belief toward the world we see, when we see it most freely. We can call this world nature, understanding by that a continuous yet relatively impersonal principle of life, even when (as in the bustle beneath Virginia Woolf's window) it assumes a more human shape. The next phase, more complex, raises the problem of "interpolation." The falling leaf is a signal from Nature, but it points to the artist who sees or affirms a nature persisting through the negative moment. Art, therefore, becomes interpolation rather than mimesis. Though Mrs. Woolf retains a realistic plot, everything of importance tends to happen between the acts, between each finite or external sign. *Mrs. Dalloway* and *To the Lighthouse* are distinguished by this indefinite expansion of the interval, of the mind-space, for example, between the beams of the lighthouse. The realistic plot is sustained by an expressionistic continuity.

Let us provisionally omit *The Waves* and go to Virginia Woolf's last novel. Though its plot is as realistic as ever, we cannot any longer tell with complete certainty what really happens between the acts that make up the action. The novel has a movement like that of Zeno's arrow: we know it flies continuously, and will reach some end, yet are still amazed it does not break in mid-flight. The author, another La Trobe, might fail the continuity, and history, the

4I am probably unfair in omitting *Jacob's Room* (1922) from the experimental novels. The link between imagination and interpolation is gropingly acknowledged: "But something is always impelling one to hum vibrating, like the hawk moth, at the mouth of the cavern of mystery, endowing Jacob Flanders with all sorts of qualities he had not at all—for though, certainly, he sat talking to Bonamy, half of what he said was too dull to repeat; much unintelligible (about unknown people and Parliament); what remains is mostly a matter of guesswork. Yet over him we hang vibrating."

subject of the play, might fail likewise and not reach the present moment. But life and the novel continue in the same country manner because the artist's interpolations are imaginative enough.

In the case of *The Waves* we cannot even tell what happens. It is not that the plot line is unclear, but now everything is interpolation, even the characters who are simply their speeches, and these speeches interpret acts that might and might not have been. What happens is what the speeches make happen. The purple prefaces alone, describing a day from dark to dark, seem to be founded in reality, or rather nature: the human parts are pushed between as a supreme interpolation standing against the impersonal roll of time.

Considered as notes toward a supreme fiction the novels of Virginia Woolf say "It must be affirmative." They suppose a mind with an immense, even unlimited, power to see or build continuities. It is almost as if the special attribute of the unconscious, that it does not know the negative, belonged also to mind in its freest state. The artist is either not conscious of the negative (i.e., his unconscious speaks through him), or fiction is generically the embodiment of the negative—and whatever dialectic characterizes mind—in purely affirmative terms. The reader, of course, may reconstitute the negative; this task is one of the principal aims of interpretation. We have done a similar thing by pointing to the precarious and interpolative character of Virginia Woolf's continuities. In parts of *To the Lighthouse*, in the last chapter of *Orlando*, and in *The Waves*, the novel is brought to the limit of its capacity to show death, decay, repression, and discontinuity in terms of thought, speech, and prose rhythm. Irony is no longer a device; art becomes irony, and the reader sees that the extreme eloquence of *The Waves* hides silence and incommunicability, or that Mrs. Ramsay thinking to affirm life really affirms death.

I wish to make this irony more cogent by a last glance at Mrs. Ramsay. The first section of *To the Lighthouse* is called "The Window." Mrs. Ramsay (like her creator in *A Room of One's Own*) sits near a window and knits. Her hands knit—so does her mind. Every strain that comes from without is absorbed by the regularity of her hands and the continuity of her mind. The strains are endless; she is besieged by eight children, by memory, by nature, and above all by a husband who constantly if surreptitiously demands her attention. Yet, as if another Penelope, apart from the clamoring suitors, she sits and weaves an interminable garment.

Is it a dress or a shroud? A reddish brown stocking, of course, in expectation of visiting the Lighthouse Keeper and his son, though we will not see her arrive. She dies suddenly one night, and her death reveals what she has woven. Darkness and decay creep over the house, which even now is none too tidy. Mrs. Ramsay alive keeps the disorder vital and prevents it from overrunning. She is the natural center, the sun, and however confused relationships get, all come back to her and are resolved into simplicity by her word or presence. But when she dies, impersonality, waste, and vagueness flood the house like a delayed judgment.

The second part of the novel, "Time Passes," describes the near-ruin of the House of Ramsay. It reverts to the sea, to nature; and the human events breaking that slope are reported parenthetically, as interpolations. The structure of *The Waves* comes directly out of this second part. What can the author be saying but that there existed a strange (perhaps unavoidable) correspondence between the mind of Mrs. Ramsay and the will of nature? Although most open to life, sitting by the window, knitting every impulse into a fabric of thought and feeling, what she worked proved finally to be a shroud. But the male will survives in the form of Mr. Ramsay, a sparse, old, domineering man still feeding on the sympathy of others.

It is, therefore, a tragic choice which confronts us. Mrs. Ramsay is the feminine part of the soul, with its will to bypass the will, its desire to let things be and grow in their own time, and above all with its frightening power for mystical marriage, that refusal to sustain the separateness of things in an overly great anticipation of final unity. This last is her most profound trait (she is also literally a matchmaker), and it reveals her identification with death:

> Not as oneself did one find rest ever, in her experience (she accomplished here something dexterous with her needles) but as a wedge of darkness. Losing personality, one lost the fret, the hurry, the stir; and there rose to her lips always some exclamation of triumph over life when things came together in this peace, this rest, this eternity; and pausing there she looked out to meet that stroke of the Lighthouse, the long steady stroke, the last of the three, which was her stroke, for watching them in this mood always at this hour one could not help attaching oneself to one thing, especially of the things one saw; and this thing, the long steady stroke, was her stroke. Often she found herself sitting and looking, sitting and looking, with her work in her hands until she became the thing she looked at— that light for example. And it would lift up on it some little phrase or other which had been lying in her mind like that—"Children don't forget, children don't forget"—which she would repeat and begin adding to it. It will end, it will end, she said. It will come, it will come, when suddenly she added, We are in the hands of the Lord.

This is Mrs. Ramsay's mind knitting, and she knows she has gone too far, hypnotized by her own rhythm. It was not she who said, "We are in the hands of the Lord." "She had been trapped into saying something she did not mean." It is curious how at this moment Mrs. Ramsay echoes a mood which breaks into Shakespeare's tragedies imminently before the end. Do we not hear Desdemona's "All's one" and Hamlet's "If it be now, 'tis not to come; if it be not to come, it will be now; if it be not now, yet it will come"?[5] Despite her great longing for privacy, she cannot but help the reconciliation of all things—

---

[5]Similar echoes and rhythms weave through the thoughts of Mrs. Dalloway ("Fear no more the heat o' the sun") and play an interesting part in *Between the Acts*.

she plots to marry off Paul and Minta, William Bankes and Lily Briscoe, subdues her judgment, and always finally gives in to her husband, betraying her soul and others for the sake of peace.

Virginia Woolf's use of a realistic plot and an expressionistic continuity seems to me as deep a solution to the structural problems of prose fiction as that found in *Ulysses*. Though the form cannot be said to originate with her, she gave it a conscious and personal perfection, and it remains a vital compromise with the demands of realism. She learned, of course, a great deal from (and against) Joyce, and to mention her in that company is itself a judgment. Her weakness, bound up with her virtues, lies less in any formal conception than in her subject, which is almost too specialized for the novel. I suspect that it is her subject, not her form, which is poetic, for she deals always with a part of the mind closest to the affirmative impulse. We do not find in her great scenes, passionate and fatal interviews with the characters restricted to and revolving about each other. For however complex her characters may be, they are caught up essentially in one problem and are variations of the "separatist" or "unifier" type. The one lives by doubting, and the other by affirming, the illusion of a divine or childhood nature. Poetry gives us this nature more vividly than Virginia Woolf, but it is she who makes us aware of its daily necessity and deception.

Virginia Woolf: A Personal Debt

Margaret Drabble

When I write about Virginia Woolf, I must be personal. I cannot write about her coolly and politely, as a literary critic should, for my relationship with her has not been cool. It has been personal; indeed, passionate. She herself was not an objective critic, though she was an excellent one; she disliked the thought of teaching English literature in a university, an idea new in her day. So she would not, I think, object to my response. A highly emotional woman, she demanded emotion in return. Had one met her, one would have loved her. And yet, for years, as perhaps with one's greatest loves, I avoided her, through fear and misunderstanding. This is the story of my discovery.

Her reputation was what put me off, initially. I thought of her as a "difficult" writer, overfond of technique, self-important about her use of the stream of consciousness, a somewhat disdainful creator of a literary avant-garde. Along with this went the fact that she was an elitist, that she belonged to a small inbred artistic group, that she wrote for a minority about a minority. She was one of those idle rich, childless, late Victorian women who suffered from endless migraines because they had too many servants. She was rude and dismissive about older writers who disagreed with her, and those who were not of her own social class. She was, in fact, not at all the kind of character to appeal to a writer like myself, provincial in background, brought up in and inclined to admire traditional realism and social concern in literature. A dull dilettante, she was, I said to myself; out of date, out of touch, and so I did not bother to read her.

I might never have met her, as one feels with some alarm of a friend whom one met by accident, and came to love by chance. I was set against the novels; not even duty could bring me to them. But one day, casually, I stumbled upon *A Room of One's Own*. I read it with mounting excitement and enthusiasm. Could it be true that she herself had assembled these ideas that were my daily life? In the book, which is based on two lectures she delivered in Cambridge, she outlines the social position of women in literature. She quotes from their history; she protests, with good humor but entirely without compromise, against their lot. A more militant, firm, concerned attack on women's subjection would be hard to find. I could hardly believe that a woman from her

Essay originally published in 1973. Reprinted with the permission of the Peters Fraser & Dunlop Group Ltd.

background, thinking still, wrongly, that she had an easy moneyed life, could speak so relevantly to my own condition. She, too, had noted the points in other people's work that had most struck me—Jane Eyre's cry for freedom, Lady Winchilsea's dislike of embroidery, the fact that a woman turned to the novel rather than to poetry because "all the older forms of literature were hardened and set by the time she became a writer. The novel alone was young enough to be soft in her hands." Here, after all, was a woman who knew what the problems were—economic problems, problems of prejudice and lack of education and lack of privacy. Jane Austen wrote in a corner of the drawing room, furtively, covering her novels with the blotting paper if anyone came in, as though she were committing an offense. We need privacy, said Virginia Woolf; each woman needs a room of her own. And here I sit, in my own room in Bloomsbury, feeling myself uncannily a product of her imagination.

Her essays and polemic works are nearly all of this high class. She was a good fighter, a brave speaker, and a loyal addresser of envelopes. For so shy and sensitive a nature, her braving of the scorn of the majority must have been an ordeal, but she never flinched. When one thinks of her as a member of a clique, one must also consider that without a group of loyal friends— sister, husband, sister's husband and lovers, brother's friends—she could hardly have survived, her position was so unorthodox. She felt deeply about the problem of women's rights, and far from considering herself an intellectu- ally superior person, she continued to feel herself ill-educated—because her brothers had been sent to university as a matter of course, and she and her sister had not. She knew her privileges well enough, as one can see from her novels, but unlike some of her contemporaries, such as Beatrice Webb, she didn't let her own advantages or disadvantages blind her to the plight of others. Her social sympathies were wide, as was her range of friends. Long before Germaine Greer and Kate Millett, she could write, "Women haters depress me and both Tolstoi and Mrs. Asquith hate women." How lovely of her to imagine a novel in which occurs the sentence "Chloe liked Olivia," for until that point in time it was taboo to believe that women could like other women, that they could be anything other than rivals for a man's love. How shrewd of her to point out in *Three Guineas* that women write rather than paint or compose because writing paper is cheaper than oils or orchestras.

An excellent fighter, then—but what of her novels? Hopefully, I turned to them. At first, I must admit, I was disappointed. Who were these women who peopled her pages—Mrs. Dalloway giving dinner parties, Mrs. Ramsay knitting socks and humoring her husband, the lovely widow Mrs. Flanders? What had they to do with the brave new world of liberation? They did, indeed, seem to come from a gracious past, where servants waited at table, where one dressed for dinner, where one idly cut flowers of an afternoon, and sneered at jumped-up working-class intellectuals, in witty conversations, of an evening. They were luminous, they were beautiful, but they were irrelevant. Her true self lay in her thoughts, not in her fictions, and yet, despite oneself, one is drawn back again and again. The novels are haunting. They work in the mind long after they are back on the shelf. And after a while, as I reread, and read new ones, I began to feel shame for the meanness and gracelessness of my judgment. For the novels are wonderful, various, and they contain everything. There is the girl addressing envelopes for the suffrage movement, done honorably and with deep affection; there is the society hostess; there is the madman; there is the brilliant undergraduate; there is the girl who wants nothing but marriage and tennis; there are the poets; and above all, there are the old ladies. There are, it is true, no dustmen, and as another critic remarks, a slight chill always enters the prose with the charwoman—but she has explained the reasons for this so cogently and truly in her own essay, "The Niece of an Earl," that one can hardly quarrel with her omissions. It is in vain, she says there, to look for dukes or dustmen in her fiction: such extremes are not to be found. And, when one looks at what she has included, it would be vain to ask for more. Nor was she indifferent to the few servants she and her husband, Leonard, employed. All her daily relationships were personal and intense.

Her response to the living detail and variety of life is so intense that to enter each novel is to enter a world of color, light, landscape. Her descriptive writings, which Quentin Bell tells us she used to practice as a child, are superb. Her sister was a painter, but she has herself a painter's eye. Her seascapes, her weather, her gardens, her evocation of St. James's Park on a June morning—bits that one usually skips in other people's novels—are wonderfully done. But she's not a nature writer, with great chunks of description, purple passages, that can be lifted straight out of the text. The whole thing is so woven together, so human, so full of the odd and the unexpected. London she evokes by the mud in the streets, the milkjugs (not milk bottles) left out for the milkman on the doorsteps and windowsills, the colors of the horse that pulls the colonel in the cab. Where, in any Victorian novel, does any character speculate about the color and health of the horse that is pulling his cab? It is a dying age that she records in such details, but with what fidelity, what vision, the very detail, the very moment, which will make a scene live forever: the hunt for the lost brooch on the seashore, for instance. How trivial an incident and yet how eternal.

Perhaps it is partly the fact that she describes holidays so lyrically that gives the impression that her life was one long idle stroll along the seashore. But the truth is more likely that every holiday, particularly in her childhood, was so intensely remembered, that it became for her, as for us, so intensely significant. The profound significance of childhood experience was only just, in her lifetime, acknowledged, and she was one of the first writers to catch the links between the child and the man; the unspoken loves, rivalries, and hostilities between parent and child. She had no children, but she remembered what childhood was like. In *Jacob's Room*, there is an enchanting description of little Jacob on the beach in Cornwall, climbing a rock, getting lost, sobbing, and then "he was about to roar when, lying among the black sticks and straw under the cliff, he saw a whole skull—perhaps a cow's skull, a skull, perhaps, with teeth in it. Sobbing, but absentmindedly, he ran farther and farther away until he held the skull in his arms." Granted that the image of the skull, first introduced here, is part of the pattern of imagery with which she structures her novel, but it remains a skull—concrete and irreducible— always seen *first* as Jacob, the child, experiences it.

Seascapes, holidays, dinner parties. A trivial domestic world, maybe, unworthy of the pen of a militant. It was for these preoccupations that she was rejected by succeeding generations. But there is hardly a writer who has not been affected by her. Her fluid sentence structure, her poetic prose, her perceptions of the slightest connections, her lack of interest in a heavy conventional narrative, her passion for the inconsequential psychological detail—all these things have gone into the novel and remained there. She said herself that women found the novel soft in their hands—she made it even more flexible by doing away with the heavy monstrosities of the Victorian plot. She found daily life of such absorbing interest, so rich in terror and joy, that she needed no other stimulants. As Lily Briscoe, the painter, thinks in *To the Lighthouse*, "The great revelation perhaps never did come. Instead there were little miracles, daily illuminations, matches struck unexpectedly in the dark . . . in the midst of chaos there was shape; this eternal passing and flowing (she looked at the clouds going and the leaves shaking) was struck into stability." Woolf allows, never forces, the "chaos" to take shape in her novels— but never at the expense of recording the "thousands of tiny atoms as they fall."

It is in vain to look in her work for a modern woman, leading the kind of life that we lead. All we can look for is prophecies of ourselves, and she was our prophetess. There were, in her day, no professional women running homes and jobs with the aid of deep freezers and washing machines; there were no businesswomen; there were no women novelists with many children, rushing from typewriter to school to butcher. There were no middleclass housewives giving dinner parties of extreme sophistication and Elizabeth David cuisine, with no servants in the kitchen and no nanny behind the green baize door, but they were about to be born and she welcomed them. She did her best to create them. In her novels, what she does is to record the age that is going out. She loved people, she loved society, she could not say to the world she lived in that she wouldn't mix in it because she didn't approve of it and thought it was on the way out.

Her love of parties and dinners and events, and her continual efforts to describe them in fiction, might seem surprising in one of her depressive temperament, but one of her qualities that, finally, one most admires, is her determination not to allow her own illnesses to color her view of others, her heroic success in remaining loving and cheerful and hopeful till the end. Touchy she was, ill she was, but she never spread round her waves of despair, as do some of the ill and the mad. She contained herself and continued to offer hope. Her books are the least depressing of novels though they record, faithfully, the tragedies that crossed her life—the early death of her mother, brother, half-sister; her father's savage melancholia. But always, they offer more than tragedy. One cannot help comparing her with Sylvia Plath, whose death has also been interpreted as a symbol of the impossibility of the survival of the creative woman; woman is torn in two, by her creative urges, by her conflicting roles, by her desire to be an artist and to have children, say the critics. But what they overlook is the amount of joy and love that can be found in Sylvia Plath's poetry, as, luminously, in Virginia Woolf's novels. Her genius is not as dark as it is said to be.

Perhaps the most tender and lovely manifestation of her faith lies in her portraits of old age. They are particularly moving, coming from the pen of one who probably knew that she would never achieve the states she describes. For example, in her last novel, *Between the Acts*, which she wrote very near her death, there is the enchanting old Mrs. Swithin, sitting down to her morning tea, "like any other old lady with a high nose, thin cheeks, a ring on her finger and the usual trappings of rather shabby but gallant old age, which included in her case a cross gleaming gold on her breast." Wonderful Mrs. Swithin spends a great deal of time reading an Outline of History and thinking about the days when rhododendrons grew along Piccadilly and iguanodons, mammoths, and mastodons surged, writhed, and barked about. Her last line in the novel—after the tiring village fete—is addressed to her niece: she says, "in the evening, I looked in and saw the babies, sound asleep, under the paper roses." What a sentence! Then she goes back to read her book on prehistoric birds.

Best of all Mrs. Swithin's many predecessors is Eleanour in *The Years*—a late novel, a long novel, with a large cast, spanning more than half a century. It is one of her most traditional, the story of three generations of a family— almost like the Forsytes, whom she despised. She began it with joy, but finished with some difficulty, for it needed much sustaining. Also, she must have felt uneasy, reverting to the form she had openly condemned. Her fear of criticism from the young, which comes through again and again in her diary, is one of her more curious and inexplicable characteristics. Why should she have cared? But she did care and she often comments on whether her novels are likely to be seen as "technical" or "human." This is a human novel. A large family grows up, watches its mother die; some marry, some remain single, some have children, grand-children, great-nieces; they survive air raids; grow old. There are dinner parties—Oxford ones, aristocratic ones, high teas in working-class intellectuals' houses, dingy suppers in the lodgings of modern intellectuals, with raw mutton, a "slabbed-down mass of cabbage in oozing green water," a dish of fly-blown fruit.

And there, living through all this history, is Eleanour Pargiter. When the novel opens, she is a young woman, running her dying mother's household. When it ends, she is single still, and in her seventies, just returned from a trip to India, at a party with all her family, unable to understand why people expect her to be interested in the past, for "here she was, alive, now, listening to the fox trot." Being old, she dozes off, snores, dreams, and wakes, feeling "extraordinarily happy." She tries to explain her happiness to her nephew. "It's been a perpetual discovery, my life," she says. "A miracle." The party swirls on around her. It ends. It is dawn. They go out into the square, where "the sun had risen and the sky above the houses wore an air of extraordinary beauty, simplicity and peace."

That is what I call heroism. To imagine an old age fulfilled and beautiful, doubting if one may ever reach it. To seize the moments of calm in the very midst of smoke and music and noise and flux—Mrs. Dalloway poised on her staircase to greet her guests; Mrs. Ramsay ladling out soup, endlessly concerned about her family, feeling suddenly the "still space that lies at the heart of things," alone in the midst of company—this is triumph indeed.

Virginia Woolf had an unhappy, doomed nature, but she achieves every now and then a pure happiness, a pure conciliation. She embodies it in the simplest images—a man and a woman together getting into a taxi, together opening the door of their house. It was not for her, but she gives it to us. Like Mrs. Dalloway, she stands poised in welcome, loving the past without regret. I feel that could she see us now, as we struggle through the noise and smoke and exhaustion of our social upheavals, our new freedoms, she would wish us well and wave with cheerful encouragement. We have not yet reached the future she envisaged and which her moment in history denied her, but she helped to create it. She imagined us and we owe it to her to survive.

The Loudspeaker and the Human Voice: Politics and the Form of *The Years*

Margaret (Comstock) Connolly

Among Virginia Woolf's novels, *The Years* is the work that most strikingly asks its readers not only to feel, or to see, but also to think—to think, in effect, about the issues Woolf addresses in her essay "Thoughts on Peace in an Air Raid" (1940).[1] There we are asked to think about peace as "the only efficient air-raid shelter"; to think peace "into existence," if we can. Though the sound of German war-planes overhead, "the zoom of a hornet, which may at any moment sting you to death," is "a sound that interrupts cool and consecutive thinking," nevertheless Woolf invokes Blake's words, " 'I will not cease from mental fight,' " which she defines as "thinking against the current, not with it." Mainstream thought, however, "flows fast and furious . . . from the loudspeakers and the politicians. Every day they tell us that we are a free people, fighting to defend freedom"; but when Woolf consults her own experience, she finds "it is not true that we are free"; neither the English airman who is "boxed up in his machine with a gun handy," nor "we lying in the dark with a gas-mask handy." What is it that denies us our liberty? " 'Hitler!' the loudspeakers cry with one voice." But Woolf proposes a more difficult answer, and asks us to look at our own "subconscious Hitlerism," our

From *The Bulletin of the New York Public Library* 80 (2, Winter 1977): 252–75. Copyright © 1976 New York Public Library, Astor, Lenox, and Tilden Foundations. Reprinted by permission.

[1]*Collected Essays* (NY: Harcourt 1967) IV 173ff. References to the collected essays are cited hereafter in the text as *CE*, with the appropriate volume number.

The first part of this essay is an expanded version of "Politics and the Form of *The Years*," a paper read at the MLA [Modern Language Association] convention in December 1974. I would like to express my appreciation to Ellen Hawkes, who organized the 1974 seminar on the relation between Woolf's writing and her politics, and with whom I have often discussed Virginia Woolf. Her work on Woolf opened up new ways of seeing, without which the present essay would not have been written. Since then, I have benefited from the 1975 MLA papers on *The Years*, published [with this one in *The Bulletin of the New York Public Library* 80 (Winter 1977), 2.] Among these, Joanna Lipking's reading of *The Years* is closest to my own; I am pleased that we have arrived independently, within different frameworks, at similar understanding of the novel's structure. I have also found valuable Donna Rae Mandelblatt's M.A. thesis, "Virginia Woolf's *The Years*: Read with the Guidance of *Three Guineas*" (San Francisco State College, 1969), cited hereafter as Mandelblatt; and the view of Woolf's politics put forward by Margaret Blanchard in "Socialization in *Mrs. Dalloway*" *College English* 34:ii (Nov 1972) 287–307; and by Jane Marcus in "No More Horses" *Women's Studies* 4 (1977), 265–29.

own desires to dominate, to enslave, or even to be enslaved, which, she believes, lead to war or support war. Thus if women "could free ourselves from slavery we should free men from tyranny," she writes; for "Hitlers are bred by slaves."

This "mental fight" reflects the kind of thinking that shapes *The Years* (1937). The novel is based on the premise, as Woolf puts it in *Three Guineas* (1938), "that the public and the private worlds are inseparably connected; that the tyrannies and servilities of the one are the tyrannies and servilities of the other."[2] Hitlers are bred by slaves, Woolf wrote during the war; "good Germans," it was said after the war, made Hitlerism possible. *The Years* examines what it is in the way we live that props up customs or institutions of domination and slavery, and lets us see what it would mean to "live differently."

Hitler came to power in 1933; while *The Years* was being written (1932–36), his broadcasts could be heard on the radio. During the war, in "The Leaning Tower" (1940), Woolf noted how his amplified voice invaded civilian life, so that the English people could "hear Hitler's voice as we sit at home of an evening"; and in the same essay she criticized the political poets of the 1930s for adopting, even while they opposed Hitler, a voice that perhaps too much resembled his in its magnification: "the pedagogic, the didactic, the loudspeaker strain that dominates their poetry" (*CE* II 164, 175). Woolf's repeated references to the loudspeaker, in her essays written after *The Years* and in *The Years* itself, show how much concerned she was to avoid that "strain" in her own work, and how much she cared to preserve "the human voice at its natural speaking level"—a phrase that appears, or variants of which appear, again and again in her novel.

In *The Years* Woolf lays bare the forces in daily life that, like the loudspeaker or the war-planes overhead, invade our consciousness and usurp the power of mental fight. But she also examines the desire that we ourselves have to abdicate that power, the fusion of thought and feeling whereby we make or find the meaning of our lives. We surrender it both by looking for leaders who will relieve us of the responsibility of thinking and by worshipping the lives of people we idealize, or idolize—even in the creation, for example, of what used to be called matinee "idols," seen at picture "palaces." So in *The Years* we find Peggy Pargiter critical of "faces mobbed at the door of a picture palace; apathetic, passive faces; the faces of people drugged with cheap pleasures; who had not even the courage to be themselves, but must dress up, imitate, pretend."[3] These people are the same sort who in *Mrs. Dalloway* wait stolidly and "listlessly" to see the royal motor-car go by: who by mistake "bestowed emotion, vainly, upon commoners out for a drive . . . and all the time let rumour accumulate in their veins and thrill the nerves in their

---

2(1938; rpt NY: Harcourt 1963) 142 (cited hereafter in the text as *TG*).
3(1937; rpt NY: Harcourt 1964) 388 (this edition cited hereafter in the text).

thighs at the thought of Royalty looking at them . . . at the thought of the heavenly life divinely bestowed upon Kings. . . ."[4] But this desire must be faced up to in ourselves, for "we too want to see the Dukes and Kings," Woolf wrote in 1939 ("Royalty" *CE* IV 212–15). "There is no denying it," our desire to "live in them, vicariously," because they are "always smiling, perfectly dressed, immune, we like to imagine, if not from death and sorrow, still from the humdrum and the pettifogging"; finally, "from the drudgery, about which there is no sort of glamour, of being ourselves."

Woolf finds a connection, then, between the apparently private desire to gaze at glamorous people and a political fact: the creation in various forms of "royalty" and so of mobs, the lookers-on who are "apathetic" about their own lives and therefore eager to follow leaders. This configuration Susan Sontag finds characteristic of "fascist aesthetics" broadly considered, the mutual dependence of "submissive behavior" on the one hand and "extravagant effort" on the other, of "egomania and servitude," or the "grouping of people/ things around an all-powerful, hypnotic leader figure or force."[5]

From this point of view, *The Years* may be said to be written on aesthetic principles that are the opposite of fascist. It has no center or central figure around which subordinate elements can be arranged. The reader cannot possibly surrender to the glamour of a life that seems more elevated than one's own. The way the novel is written discourages a reader's inclination to "march in step after a leader"—a phrase central to *The Years*. There is no character whose life is captivating; the author's voice is unusually unobtrusive; there is not even any "beautiful prose." The novel is made up largely of people talking to one another, and not very articulately at that. Out of these materials Woolf creates for her readers the opportunity available to some of her characters: the chance to achieve meaning in a fragmentary world and join the attempt to fill "the present moment . . . fuller and fuller, with the past, the present, and the future, until it shone, whole, bright, deep with understanding" (428). People who experience their own lives in this way are not the sort who will stand waiting to see the king.

But what prevents ordinary people from reaching this sense of themselves, so that they locate their place in history, find their past, and embrace their future? What keeps ordinary people from arriving at the use of the ordinary voice? Even further back in consciousness, what keeps them from knowing what they think or having anything to say? Conversely, when does the right to "free speech" take on important reality? These are questions at the heart of *The Years*, which Woolf thinks it worth her while to examine with great care.

In *The Years* real talk is impossible, for example, across class lines. Martin Pargiter finds that when talking with servants, with Crosby, "either one simpers, or one's hearty. . . . In either case it's a lie" (222). In the Pargiter

---

4(NY: Harcourt 1925) 27.
5"Fascinating Fascism" *New York Review of Books* 22:i (Feb 6 1975) 26.

family Crosby herself "never answered but only grinned" (152). Even when she is pensioned off, she restricts her mumblings in the public park to "a conciliatory tone"; " 'I'm quite ready to oblige you,' " she says aloud, addressing her new employers in her imagination, still servile "even out here, in the mist, where she was free to say what she liked . . ." (303).

Prohibitions against speech surround female lives. The most frightening is the one that descends on Rose when she is little; a man exposes himself in front of her, and she knows she "could not tell Eleanor what she had seen. She had a profound feeling of guilt; for some reason she must lie . . . 'I had a bad dream,' she said. 'I was frightened.' " Eleanor knows that something important is being hidden, but she does not really help Rose to say it. " 'I saw . . .' Rose began. She made a great effort to tell the truth; to tell her about the man at the pillarbox. 'I saw . . .'." The blank is never filled (40–42).

Conventions governing womanly behavior curtail speech in ways that are less appalling but still important. The talk Martin intends to offer his virginal dinner partner is too condescending to be fruitful: "what little piece of his vast experience could he break off and give to her, he wondered." Though their talk might develop, it is cut short because "Lady Lasswade had risen" and the ladies must retire. Among the ladies after dinner, conversation seems to Kitty "battledore and shuttlecock talk," something "to be kept going until the door opened and the gentlemen came in." Even here, the selection Lady Warburton offers her niece from her memoirs, the "edition with asterisks," deletes "stories unfit for girls in white satin" (251, 255, 258, 260). The demands of respectability keep talk safely within the bounds of meaninglessness. So too in the City chophouse Martin shushes Sara as she tries to discuss religion "in her ordinary voice"; she might be overheard. When Martin cuts her off, she assumes, "in deference to him . . . the manner of a lady lunching with a gentleman in a city restaurant," obviously not a manner in which anything real is going to get said (229). With City men watching, Martin thinks he "must damp" Sara's "excitement"; Sara feels "as if the engine of the brain were suddenly cut off" (231–32).

One final example: in 1917, a German air-raid stops talk "as if some dull bore had interrupted an interesting conversation" (288). Because the comparison cuts the air raid down a notch or more, it allows the private talk about "Napoleon and the psychology of great men" to grow correspondingly: the political nature of brute force heightens the political importance of talk about creating not Napoleonic codes but laws "that fit." Also, to say that German bombers interrupt conversation suggests the brutality and finally the political repressiveness of the forces that in daily life do interrupt talk: the blocks enforced by class and sex divisions and by the false propriety they give rise to.

In contrast to the talk that is forever being cut off or made servile, the talk that moves *The Years* forward is free from deference or condescension. It resists the oppressive currents that degrade talk, but not in any spectacular or posturing way. It is often described as taking place in an ordinary tone of voice, and the words can be entirely ordinary too. Edward Pargiter, for example, discussing the admission of "Runcorn's boy" to the university, says " 'of course, of course' " in what North recognizes as "the human voice at its natural speaking level" (411). Maggie restores ordinary life after the air raid of 1917 by saying, " 'Let's finish our pudding' . . . in her natural voice" (291). A third example of "human, civilised" speech is the conversation of the aged couple who talk as they have talked for the last fifty years (260).

Each of these exchanges is perfectly everyday in itself, even "humdrum," but each has a political dimension as well. There is, for example, an implied equality in the way the old couple seek each other out. In contrast to the man who "talk[s] away at a great rate" to a "young married woman," producing "a slight look of strain on her face" (253), or the young man talking to Peggy at the party in "Present Day" who had to be "I," who could not be "you" (361), the elderly man begins conversation with a " 'Well . . . ?' " that leaves an opening for Lady Warburton. Though it is only a single boy from the working class who is to be let into the university, still Edward is doing what Woolf calls for in *Three Guineas*, seeing to it that his profession is not closed off by reason of class (*TG* 80). Maggie's invitation to "finish our pudding" connects in the reader's mind with the fear entertained by North, by no means a foolish one, that in attempting to "down barriers and simplify" one might create "a rice pudding world," a bland world of conformity, without distinction (410).[6] In their 1917 dinner party, however, the Pargiters and Nicholas and Renny have downed barriers and simplified, and yet the important things have survived. They eat in the basement because they have no servants to serve their meals; with the presence of Renny the Frenchman and Nicholas the Pole and homosexual, the party crosses national and sexual "barriers."[7] This is not to say that everything about the 1917 evening represents a social ideal. Renny helps make shells to carry on the war; Nicholas lectures; Maggie breaks into the private talk between Eleanor and Nicholas. But still the evening described in "1917" is so filled with communion that Eleanor, going home, discovers she has forgotten the air raid. The German planes have not ended conversation after all.

What lets Eleanor transcend the air raid is the fact that for the first time in her life her talk takes on real meaning for her. That evening she at first finds herself in her usual dissociated state, unable to follow what's being said, walled off in the woman's condition of internal exile that used to prevent her from understanding what Morris' law-cases were about well enough to discuss them with him (33–34). But in an exchange with Nicholas in 1917 (280–82)

---

[6]Woolf used the same words to voice her own fears for the novel when it had received hostile criticism: "Dead and disappointing . . . that odious rice pudding of a book . . . a dank failure" (Apr 2 1937; *A Writer's Diary* [1953; rpt NY: Harcourt 1973] 270; cited hereafter as *AWD*). Woolf's diary also includes a good deal of high praise for *The Years*, but it is time for criticism of *The Years* to stop relying on Woolf's diary.

[7]Mandelblatt (98) also makes this observation.

Eleanor moves from a state of feeling cold and mentally numb, a reaction similar to Sara's feeling when Martin shushes her in the chophouse, to a state of warmth in which a meaningful whole is created. When Nicholas tells Eleanor that " 'we are talking about Napoleon' " she answers, " 'I see.' . . . But she had no notion what he was saying. . . . I've interrupted them, she felt, and I've nothing whatever to say. She felt dazed and cold. . . . She wished the argument had been more within her reach. . . . She felt numb all over—not only her hands, but her brain." Slowly she leaves her numbness behind and begins to join this conversation about the relation between great leaders and the way ordinary people live. She and Nicholas create meaning cooperatively, in a way in which no one dominates or speaks for anyone else. In fact, Nicholas' switch from "we were saying" to "I was saying" may signify his unwillingness to sum up on behalf of Renny, who has left the room:

> "We were saying–" He paused. She guessed that she found it difficult to sum up their argument . . .
> "I was saying," he went on, "I was saying we do not know ourselves, ordinary people; and if we do not know ourselves, how then can we make religions, laws that—" he used his hands as people do who find language obdurate, "that—"
> "That fit—that fit," she said, supplying him with a word that was shorter, she felt sure, than the dictionary word that foreigners always used.
> "—that fit, that fit," he said, taking the word and repeating it as if he were grateful for her help.
> ". . . that fit," she repeated. She had no idea what they were talking about. Then suddenly, as she bent to warm her hands over the fire, words floated together in her mind and made one intelligible sentence.

Clearly this moment of warming up and making an intelligible sentence is important for Eleanor; but is the intelligible sentence so wonderful? The speech that leads up to it is so broken it sounds almost silly ("that fit—that fit—that fit"). We are accustomed to highly articulate characters in Woolf's novels, especially in *The Waves*. And it has been claimed that Nicholas' fondness for this sentence shows him to be no more than a broken record[8]— he repeats throughout *The Years* his thought about laws "that fit." In my view the broken speech and repetition address themselves to some important realities in the lives of "ordinary people." Most people are not highly articulate, and most people do repeat themselves throughout their lives. Character takes on distinctive lines early, most people do not live under conditions that allow radical change, and lives are shaped by a small number of themes or concerns. Even when a leader articulates a vision, it cannot be widely effective unless it is carried forward by "ordinary people"—one of the working titles for *The Years*[9] and a phrase that occurs throughout the novel. There are

[8]See Josephine O'Brien Schaefer, "The Vision Falters: *The Years*, 1937" 1966; rpt in *Virginia Woolf: A Collection of Critical Essays* ed Claire Sprague (Englewood Cliffs, NJ: Prentice-Hall 1971) 138.

[9]*AWD* 228 (Jan 1 1935).

important senses in which, as Nicholas says (426), the human race "is now in its infancy"—etymologically, "inability to speak"—especially if the achievement of freedom is taken as the measure of maturity. It was only during the lifetime of Woolf's parents that slavery was outlawed in the British Empire and married women won the legal right to keep the money they earned; it was only during Woolf's own lifetime that women won the right to vote or enter the professions. If the human race is going to "grow to maturity," as Nicholas hopes, it will have to depend on ordinary people making what changes they can to free themselves and one another from what oppresses them.

Of course Nicholas' toast—"to the human race . . . which is now in its infancy, may it grow to maturity!"—is undercut when he thumps his glass down on the table and "it broke," just as Eleanor's intelligible sentence is followed by the return of self-doubt and alienation: " 'I was thinking about this war—I don't feel this, but other people do . . .' She stopped. . . . probably she had misunderstood what he had said . . ." (282). *The Years* constantly makes room for doubt and disappointment in a way analogous to an aesthetic principle Woolf stated in "The Narrow Bridge of Art" (1926):

> There trips along by the side of our modern beauty some mocking spirit which sneers at beauty for being beautiful; which turns the looking-glass and shows us that the other side of her cheek is pitted and deformed. It is as if the modern mind, wishing always to verify its emotions, had lost the power of accepting anything simply for what it is. Undoubtedly this sceptical and testing spirit has led to a great freshening and quickening of soul. (*CE* II 223)

In *The Years* it is almost as if the novel's push toward truth and beauty gains validity by giving ugliness and viciousness so fully their due. Of course the novel is full of ugly things. It is an economic fact of Crosby's life that she will have to wash the bathtub with the count's spittle on it (303). Likewise, Sara eats badly cooked mutton and cabbage because a boardinghouse is the only place she can afford to live. (Her dinner is bad and the chophouse lunch Martin treats her to is good, just as, in *A Room of One's Own*, dinner at the women's college is dreary and lunch at the men's is sumptuous; and for the same reason.) Characters continually fall back from the degrees of freedom they have achieved into old habits. Though Edward Pargiter would admit Runcorn's boy to the university, he remains a priest, a guardian of beauty (409). Even Maggie seems to lapse into the ferocity of " 'my' children . . . 'my' possessions" (380). The party in "Present Day" is not without sinister and submissive aspects: the partygoers sound like "a flock of sheep" (364) and they play "God save the King" to close off their festivities (433). Probably the bleakest "sneer" in the novel is the despair Maggie and Sara feel about human character in "1910," a despair directed at others and themselves alike:

> "In time to come," [Sara] said, looking at her sister, "people, looking into this room—this cave, this little antre, scooped out of mud and dung, will hold their fingers to their noses . . . and say, 'Pah! They stink' " . . . .

Maggie looked at her. Curled round, with her hair falling over her face and her hands screwed together she looked like some great ape, crouching there in a little cave of mud and dung. "Pah!" Maggie repeated to herself, "They stink."

She agrees with Sara: "It was true, she thought; they were nasty little creatures driven by uncontrollable lusts. The night was full of roaring and cursing; of violence and unrest"—and, the text continues, "also of beauty and joy" (189). But to say that the novel's dark underside validates its sense of beauty and joy, freedom and hope, is to say that these affirmative emotions are meant to be felt, finally, as the more persuasive. I think that this is the case, and I will try to say how, in the political terms in which I am discussing *The Years*, the novel builds honestly toward its final sentence: "The sun had risen, and the sky above the houses wore an air of extraordinary beauty, simplicity, and peace."[10]

The liberating quality of Eleanor's conversation with Nicholas in "1917," for example, stands out clearly by comparison with an earlier and closely parallel conversation that takes place in "1911." Here again Eleanor visits relatives, this time Morris and his wife Celia, and again finds an unexpected guest, this time William Whatney. Sir William has just completed his imperial career, ruling a district in India. Since Eleanor is just back from Greece, Sir William opens the dinner conversation by asking her about her trip, but the conversation immediately veers away from Eleanor's interest in Greece to Sir William's own official concerns: " 'Did you meet anyone at the Embassy?' Sir William asked her. Then he corrected himself. 'Not an Embassy though, is it?' 'No. Athens is not an Embassy,' said Morris." Note that it is not Eleanor who replies; the humor in the rendering of this fatuous conversation is quiet but precise.

Here there was a diversion; what was the difference between an Embassy and a Legation? Then they began to discuss the situation in the Balkans.

"There's going to be trouble there in the near future," Sir William was saying. He turned to Morris; they discussed the situation in the Balkans.

Eleanor's attention wandered. (200–01)

Of course Eleanor's attention wanders. She gets from Sir William nothing of the mutuality and respect Nicholas is prepared to offer her. The parallels between the dinner conversation of 1911 and that of 1917 allow the reader to see how much freer, how much better, the relation between Eleanor and Nicholas is. And that progress over the course of time allows the reader to see that *The Years* is a hopeful novel. Without denying how bad the state of the

---

10In his work "*The Years*" James Hafley makes a similar point about the coexistence of beauty and ugliness in this novel (1954; rpt in *Virginia Woolf: A Collection of Criticism* ed Thomas S. W. Lewis [NY: McGraw-Hill 1975] 113–24). He also says that *The Years* moves toward affirmation, but in ahistorical and nonpolitical terms that do not correspond to my sense of the novel's outlook: "This is another major idea . . . that human nature is in the process of becoming less imperfect, becoming in a creative evolution during which evil will be overcome and good triumph" (118).

world was in the "Present Day" of the 1930s, *The Years* affirms the possibility—not the inevitability—that a freer society can be achieved if people renounce the situations and manners that numb their brains and mute or distort their voices. The fact that various Pargiters do leave behind the silences and the lies of the Victorian and Edwardian eras creates a steady opening toward the future, a hopeful movement that gathers strength as the novel advances.

Another important instance of progress toward freer thought and speech illustrates this point. Sara arrives late for the basement dinner party because she has just said good-by to North as he goes off to war. She is furious with the thoughtlessness that has literally "regimented" him. In their parting conversation he has been totally acquiescent; since he has no mind of his own, he can only agree with everything Sara says, and that makes her angry: " 'whatever I said, "Good, Good," he said, "Good, Good," until I took up the poker and tongs . . . and played "God save the King, Happy and Glorious, Long to reign over us—" ' " (285). The national anthem taunts his subjction. But when North returns to England, after the war and after his experience as a colonial farmer in Africa, he has changed. In Africa (here one might think of *The Golden Bough*) North has killed the king who ruled his mind and told him war was good, colonies were good. He comes back to England ready for the liberation of comedy and inclined to agree with Sara's severe judgment that war is poppycock and so, by extension, are the colonial careers England sends its sons out to. " 'He's killed the king,' " Sara says in "Present Day," reading from a book." 'So what'll he do next?' " " 'Comedy,' " North answers. " 'Contrast,' he said, remembering something he had read. 'The only form of continuity,' he added at a venture" (346).[11]

Of the three generations of Pargiter men, North comes back from the colonies the least damaged by the colonial experience and the most detached from what it represents. Colonel Pargiter comes back from India literally injured, three fingers lost in the Mutiny, but with no criticism to make of the Empire. His son Martin has enough sense to leave the military career in India he never wanted, but not enough courage to become an architect, as he would really have liked to do. North sells his farm, leaves Africa, and comes back to England not knowing what he wants to do next.

In contrast to what the other men of his family have done, however, his uncertainty can easily be seen positively; it comes, at least, out of his knowing what it is he does not want to do, and moreover *The Years* puts his lack of closure in a positive context. In the party of the Present Day, North's saying " 'I don't know what I want' " confirms Eleanor's happy feeling about the openness of her own future, despite her old age:

[11]Mandelblatt (140) also reads this scene as I do.

Her feeling of happiness returned to her, with unreasonable exaltation. It seemed to her that they were all young, with the future open before them. Nothing was fixed; nothing was known; life was open and free before them.

. . . "I mean," she tried to explain . . . "old age they say is like this; but it isn't. It's different; quite different. . . . it's been a perpetual discovery, my life. A miracle." (382–83)

True to its own forward motion and open-endedness, *The Years* offers no summing up, but only "perpetual discovery." True to its own conception of democratic society, it presents no central character who will tie things together for the reader in a way that would put the reader in the position of marching in step after a leader. Not that that isn't what we as readers often want, just as North "wished there were someone, infinitely wise and good, to think for him, to answer for him" (423). Eleanor wants this too; her relationship with Nicholas "relieved her of the need of thinking; and [but also] gave her mind a little jog" (369). When "her mind slipped" and "she could not finish her thought," she "wanted him to finish it; to take her thought and carry it out into the open unbroken; to make it whole, beautiful, entire" (369). Though it is one thing for Eleanor to help Nicholas complete his thought as Nicholas is still trying to realize it, looking for words, it is something else for Eleanor to want to give up and have someone else speak for her.

Nicholas' professional willingness to speak for others is the thing about him that Sara scorns—those talks about the soul that cost ten and six, or less for a seat from which one catches only " 'half the lesson of the Teacher, the Master' " (323). "Why lecture? Why be lectured?" Woolf asked in an essay of 1934 ("Why?" *CE* II 278–83). Why

continue an obsolete custom which not merely wastes time and temper, but incites the most debased of human passions—vanity, ostentation, self-assertion, and the desire to convert? Why encourage your elders to turn themselves into prigs and prophets, when they are ordinary men and women? Why force them to stand on a platform . . . ? Why not let them talk to you and listen to you, naturally and happily, on the floor? Why not create a new form of society founded on poverty and equality? . . . Why not abolish prigs and prophets? Why not invent human intercourse? Why not try?

All these are questions that relate to the form of *The Years*. Oratory, Edward Pargiter observes (418), is " 'now practised as an art' " only in " 'the church,' " hardly a model of the society Woolf admired. Therefore it is no tragedy at all but a triumph that Nicholas cannot make his speech at the party in the Present Day (415ff). His speech would have been an act of domination; the interruptions that prevent it show not the party's dissolution but its vitality.

No one will sum up the party of *The Years*; not Nicholas, not Peggy, who is asked to speak "for the younger generation" but who refuses; not even the caretaker's children, who sing their song for sixpence. Any feeling of finality one might want to repose in their singing, as representing the voice either of future generations or of the working class, is bound to be of the most qualified nature (" 'Beautiful?' " Eleanor asks. " 'Extraordinarily' " Maggie answers. "But Eleanor was not sure that they were thinking of the same thing" [431]). To take the children's singing as a final word would be to submit to the temptation Woolf described in "Royalty" (1939; *CE* IV 215), that of "making workers into kings."

The king-making propensity, however, the process in which "Hitlers are bred by slaves," is obdurate. So strong is the desire to surrender the responsibility of thinking and speaking that North would choose a perfect stranger, an "intelligent-looking young man" at the party in "Present Day," to "think for him" (423). The impulse shows that North's king is not thoroughly killed, and may be resurrected at any moment. In the Present Day, however, North has a layer of self-consciousness about the king-making process he did not have in 1917; he realizes that the very man he would choose to think for him is

> afraid too, he thought, looking at the young man with a fine forehead and a weak chin who was gesticulating, too emphatically. We're all afraid of each other, he thought; afraid of what? Of criticism; of laughter; of people who think differently. . . . He's afraid of me because I'm a farmer. . . . And I'm afraid of him because he's clever. (414)

It is comfortable to think of other people as being so clever or so wise that they can think and judge for us. North finds this out, for example, when he wants Maggie to confirm his judgment that the Gibbses are dreadful people (380): "Why should she not take the weight off his shoulders and give him what he longed for—assurance, certainty?" Because of Maggie's seeming refusal to relieve him of perplexity, North loosens the configurations of dominance and submission in his own psyche: "disagreeable as it was to him to remove her from the eminence upon which he had placed her, perhaps she was right, he thought, and we who make idols of other people, who endow this man, that woman, with power to lead us, only add to the deformity, and stoop ourselves" (380).

But once the Pargiters have found their own voices and have stopped marching in step after leaders, what will they say and which way will they go? They face essentially the same question Woolf put to her audience in an address that sparked, for her, both *The Years* and *Three Guineas* (*AWD* 161 & n, 162): "Professions for Women." To "discuss and define" the obstacles to freedom, she says there, is "of great value and importance; for thus only can the labour be shared, the difficulties be solved." Even more emphatically, however, she says it is "of the utmost importance and interest" to discuss "the aims for which we are fighting." She tells her audience of women in the professions that

You have won rooms of your own in the house hitherto exclusively owned by men. You are able, though not without great labour and effort, to pay the rent. You are earning your five hundred pounds a year. But this freedom is only a beginning; the room is your own, but it is still bare . . . How are you going to furnish it, how are you going to decorate it? With whom are you going to share it, and on what terms? These, I think are questions of the utmost importance and interest. For the first time in history you are able to ask them; for the first time you are able to decide for yourselves what the answers should be. (*CE* II 288–89)

In *Three Guineas*, less metaphorically, Woolf states that for the first time women have the chance to "change our position from being the victims of the patriarchal system . . . to being the champions of the capitalist system, with a yearly income in our own possession of many thousands . . . It is a thought not without its glamour" (*TG* 67). She hopes, however, that women beginning to earn professional incomes will not follow the professional men who "kept in step, walked according to rule," circling the mulberry tree of property and keeping the family house in the West End (*TG* 61, 66). She hopes that women will locate their rooms in "the new house, the poor house, the house that stands in a narrow street where omnibuses pass and the street hawkers cry their wares," a house around which women can dance and sing " 'We have done with war! We have done with tyranny!' " (*TG* 83), not the greedy old song that goes " 'Give it all to me, give it all to me' " (*TG* 59).

So in *The Years*, the Pargiter women move out of the patriarchal home into cheap rooms on a "shabby street on the south side of the river" that "was very noisy," where "a man trundling a barrow opened his mouth and bawled up at the windows as he passed" (162); or to cheap lodgings, where "children were screaming in the street below" (314). Eleanor, who used to try to build housing for the poor, goes to live " 'in a sort of workman's flat at the top of six flights of stairs' " (331). The "furnishings and decorations" of these various rooms seem to be very spare; and as for the question with whom are they shared, and on what terms, the answer seems to be that the lodgings, if not the rooms themselves, are shared with all kinds of people. Sara, for example, lives in a boardinghouse, and shares a bath with a Jew in the tallow trade—a circumstance to be examined in some detail below. Pargiter women, then, take *The Years* furthest away from the paths trod out by men toward other visions and other realities—as a reading of some of the novel's more important metaphors will show.

In 1911, as Morris and Sir William discuss embassies, legations, and the situation in the Balkans, Celia leads Eleanor and Peggy out to the terrace with the traditional words, " 'Shall we leave the gentlemen to their politics' "; and so "they shut the door," the narrator tells us, "upon the gentlemen and their politics" (202). The repetition asks the reader to think what gentlemen's politics are: what exactly is being left behind? One could choose many examples of gentlemanly politics from *The Years*, but clearly for Woolf the most important is war: "For though many instincts are held more or less in common by both sexes, to fight has always been the man's habit, not the woman's," she says in *Three Guineas*. "Law and practice have developed that difference, whether innate or accidental" (*TG* 6).

War, then, she would like to have us leave behind, and in *The Years* she accomplishes that psychologically by deflating its importance. The Great War becomes "poppycock," as Sara writes in a letter to North. She seems to have got the word from Nicholas in 1917: " 'Poppycock, poppycock . . . don't talk such damned poppycock—that's what you really said,' " Nicholas tells her, commenting on the conversation Sara had with North before he went to war (286). " 'But what was the word—the word I used?' " Sara asks North in Present Day; she is trying to recall what she said in the "cruel letter" she wrote North during the war when the sight of a war procession and of a wealthy couple in a Rolls Royce had fired her anger (322). " 'Poppycock!' [North] reminded her. She nodded" (321–22). The rightness of the word seems to be confirmed by having so many people use it, and the interlocking time scheme gives it the same durability as the phenomena it is used to describe. It is still all too useful for the politics of the 1930s: "halls and reverberating megaphones . . . marching in step after leaders, in herds, groups, societies caparisoned. . . . black shirts, green shirts, red shirts— always posing in the public eye; that's all poppy-cock," North thinks (410). The repetition of "poppy-cock" asks us to dwell on the word; if we listen, we hear that it conveys not only "silliness" but "maleness" too.[12]

When Eleanor and Peggy leave gentlemanly politics behind in 1911, they turn their backs on another kind of "cocky politics," the peacock umbrella that enforces Sir William Whatney's imperial authority in India:

> "and I found myself in an old pair of riding-breeches standing under a peacock umbrella; and all the good people were crouching with their heads to the ground. 'Good Lord,' I said to myself, 'If they only knew what a bally ass I feel! . . . That's how we were taught our job in those days". . . .
>
> He was boasting, of course; that was natural. (210)

---

[12]Woolf spells "poppycock" both with and without the hyphen. The OED identifies the word as "U.S. slang" and cites usages in England in the late nineteenth century; in "American Fiction" Woolf cites "poppycock" among her examples of the "expressive ugly vigorous slang which creeps into use among us first in talk, later in writing"; she remarks that "in England, save for the impetus given by war, the word-coining power has lapsed"; and so "to freshen our speech" England turns to America and to such words as "poppycock" (1925; *CE* II 120–21). Eric Partridge, in *A Dictionary of Slang and Unconventional English* 7th ed (NY: Macmillan 1970), says that "poppycock" was anglicized by about 1905 and colloquial by about 1930. There is no reason to suppose that Woolf was unaware of the possibilities for sexual innuendo in the term. Compare her usages in *A Room of One's Own* (1929; rpt NY: Harcourt 1957). Reflecting on the relentlessness with which "the stockbroker and the great barrister" go "indoors to make money and more money and more money," the speaker says that "they are bred . . . of the lack of civilisation, I thought, looking at the statue of the Duke of Cambridge, and in particular at the feathers in his cocked hat . . ."; or, referring to the abusive ways men tell women they can't paint and can't write, "opinions that one now pastes in a book labelled cock-a-doodle-dum . . . once drew tears, I can assure you" (39, 57).

Very literally, Peggy and Eleanor turn their attention away from this peacock in order to see a white owl that swoops across the landscape every night. Though the owl is an archetypal bird not without many ties to European culture, this particular owl seems to represent qualities that Woolf would like to see substituted for those of the peacock; its presence breaks the set of gentlemanly politics and opens up larger, more impersonal vistas. Some free flights of interpretation, however, will be necessary in order to see what those vistas are.

The reader can easily sense how important the owl is simply for its beauty; it is also a relief from Sir William's stories and the drip of Celia's dreary questions. But there is something more too. In *The Waves* the birds in the lyrical interludes resemble human beings: "Each sang stridently, with passion, with vehemence," for example, "as if to let the song burst out of it, no matter if it shattered the song of another bird with harsh discord"; or, as Woolf noted in her diary in January 1931, "the first spring birds: sharp egotistical, like man."[13]

The owl in the *The Years* seems to be not sharp and egotistical but something very different. One is reminded of the wild goose pursued by Orlando, the spirit of genius and beauty and Shakespeare that always eludes her, but from which a grey feather falls to earth as her reward. It may be that both the wild goose and the white owl have their immediate source in Olive Schreiner's white bird of Truth, which likewise lets fall a single feather to reward a faithful follower. *The Story of an African Farm*, a novel Woolf knew and admired,[14] includes the parable of a hunter who pursues the beautiful white bird of Truth. He learns from an old man, Wisdom, that she may be caught only if enough people seek Truth over ages by climbing the "mountains of stern reality" and gathering single feathers dropped from her body. With these feathers a rope and a net can be made from the materials of truth itself. The hunter sets off to scale the "mountains of Dry-facts and Realities" and spends a lifetime cutting out stairs in their rock. As his death approaches the hunter says that "I have sought . . . for long years . . . but I have not found her . . . Where I lie down worn out other men will stand, young and fresh. By the steps that I have cut they will climb; by the stairs that I have built they will mount." Something Peggy Pargiter thinks in Present Day suggests that Woolf (though not necessarily Peggy) may well have had this parable in mind: "The steps from brain to brain must be cut very shallow, if thought is to mount them, she noted" (352).

The hunter continues:

"They will never know the name of the man who made [the stairs]. At the clumsy work they will laugh; when the stones roll they will curse me. But they will mount,

13*The Waves* (1931; rpt NY: Harcourt 1959) 108; *AWD* 162.
14See Virginia Woolf "Olive Schreiner" *New Republic* (March 18 1925) 103.

and on *my* work; they will climb, and by *my* stair! They will find her, and through me! And no man liveth to himself, and no man dieth to himself" . . .

Then slowly from the white sky above, through the still air, came something falling, falling, falling. Softly it fluttered down, and dropped on to the breast of the dying man. He felt it with his hands. It was a feather.[15]

The Story of an African Farm is a story of bigotry and oppression, including the particular forms of oppression suffered by women. A central character, Waldo, is a sheepherder who confronts solitude in ways that resemble the story of North's experience on his own African farm, contained by indirection in *The Years*. Waldo's excitement on discovering a copy of John Stuart Mill's *Political Economy* is a link to important themes in *The Years*; he is entranced by the "chapter on property," on "Communism, Fourierism, St. Simonism"; furthermore, "All he read he did not fully understand; the thoughts were new to him; but this was the fellow's startled joy in the book— the thoughts were his, they belonged to him. He had never thought them before, but they were his."[16] In *The Years*, the idea that thoughts are shared, not always knowingly, is an important thematic and structural principle: " 'We all think the same things; only we do not say them' " (282). Then too, the parable of the white bird of Truth is told to Waldo by an articulate stranger, in response to Waldo's interpretation of his own wood-carving; like conversations and other forms of statement in *The Years*, the parable is a collaborative product. Very possibly, then, the white owl in *The Years* derives from Schreiner's white bird, and brings with it echoes of a halting, broken, collective search for Truth, like that carried on, for example, by Eleanor and Nicholas.

Woolf's essay "The Moment: Summer's Night" offers complementary ways of thinking about the owl of *The Years* (*CE* II 293–97). The language describing an owl in this essay parallels that of *The Years*: "An owl, blunt, obsolete looking, heavy weighted, crossed the fading sky with a black spot between its claws," and later it "flutes off its watery bubble," or makes its lovely sound. As in "1911," people sit in "The Moment" watching the evening fall. They are "spectators and also passive participants in a pageant," the pageant of nature and human nature. "And as nothing can interfere with the order, we have nothing to do but accept, and watch." But not forever. It is also true that the members of this human "knot of consciousness . . . are not subject to the law of the sun and the owl and the lamp. They assist it." They change "the moment" radically "when they speak." What is said sounds bland enough: " 'He'll do well with his hay.' " Fallen on the consciousness of a hearer, however, the words seem to "let fall . . . the self-confidence of youth" (so the speaker is young, we learn); they express youth's "urgent desire, for praise, and assurance." "That he should be" (so the speaker in "the moment" is

---

[15]Olive Schreiner, *The Story of an African Farm* (London: Hutchinson 1883; rpt Harmondsworth, Middlesex: Penguin 1971) 168–69.

[16]Schreiner 109.

male, we learn) "at once so cock-a-hoop and so ungainly makes the moment rock with laughter, and with the malice that comes from overlooking other people's motives . . . so that one takes sides; he will succeed; or no he won't. . . ." All this feeling of judgment and mockery "shoots through the moment, makes it quiver with malice and amusement; and the sense of watching and comparing."

But with the reappearance of the owl, the moment changes again, and the hearer is released from preoccupation with the young man who is so "cock-a-hoop."[17] The moment's

> quiver meets the shore, when the owl flies out, and puts a stop to this judging . . . and with our wings spread, we too fly, take wing, with the owl. . . . Could we not fly too, with broad wings and with softness; and be all one wing; all embracing, all gathering, and these boundaries, these pryings over hedge into hidden compart-ments . . . be all swept . . . by the brush of the wing . . . and so visit in splendour, augustly, peaks.

Schreiner's white bird of Truth leads one to mountains of reality; with the white owl of "The Moment" we fly, augustly, to peaks.

Though a great deal more goes on in "The Moment," this much will gloss the owl in *The Years* as representing a state of mind beyond that of "judging, and overseeing"; the owl, Minerva's bird, may take us to mountains, perhaps of understanding and wisdom. This same cluster of images occurs in *The Years*. The mountain and the owl are linked, as against the peacock, and this potent context, closing the 1911 section, gives heightened importance to the lines from Dante that are introduced there. At the end of 1911, Eleanor hears William Whatney in his room next door and wonders whether he's thinking "about India?—how he stood under a peacock umbrella"; she hears, "to her delight, the liquid call of an owl going from tree to tree, looping them with silver"; a mark on the ceiling reminds her "of one of the great desolate mountains in Greece or in Spain, which looked as if nobody had ever set foot there since the beginning of time"; by chance she picks up a volume of Dante and sleepily reads first the Italian and then the English translation:

> For by so many more there are who say "ours"
> So much the more of good doth each possess.

Since, like the owl's wing itself, Eleanor merely "brushes" the words lightly with her mind while "listening to the call of the owl," the words do "not give out their full meaning"; but "there was a meaning however." The lines from Dante (*Purgatorio* XV 56–57) sum up a discussion of the light of heavenly love: the more people who possess it, the more it is reflected, as with light given back by shining surfaces, and so the more good each single person has. Following the lament of a purgatorial soul whose earthly life was ruled by

---

[17]The *OED* defines "cock-a-hoop" as "crowing with exultation."

envy and "exclusion of partnership,"[18] the lines contrast material wealth, of which one person increases his share at the expense of another, and spiritual wealth, which can be shared without diminishing. In "1911," then, Eleanor leaves behind "the gentlemen and their politics," their exclusionary talk, and their peacock umbrellas, in favor of a white owl and a scrap of Dante: an embracing, gathering ascent toward truth that ends in a vision of shared possession.

Though it is difficult to translate this idea of shared possession from a dream-world to the world we live in, nevertheless one can imagine a condition in which one could feel the richer by reason of having less and sharing more. In fact *The Years*, in its treatment of class, race, Empire, and economics, involves the reader in imagining just that. In showing how, I shall be reading a long sequence of events in Present Day, with attention both to its content—the kind of world its projects—and to its form—the way it calls upon the reader to create meaning, as Eleanor, Nicholas, and others do, by allowing elements to "float together" into a suggestive whole. In Present Day especially, the cooperative, anti-Fascist form of *The Years* opens out to include its readers among the "ordinary people" needed to carry on the search for truth and beauty. Unlike fiction in which the "philosophy" of the author blares as if by loudspeaker from every page, any meaning the Present Day sequence may convey is very much left to be discovered. It does not form a unity in the mind of any of the novel's characters or in authorial commentary; it can do so only in the writer's mind, and in the reader's. This fact gives some prominence to the role of the reader, and perhaps answers Eleanor's question about the pattern of her experience: "The thought gave her extreme pleasure: that there was a pattern. But who makes it? Who thinks it?" (369). Virginia Woolf makes it; but the reader is needed to think it out.

The sequence (380–91) begins when the visionary lines from Dante seem to take on reality in social life: at the party in Present Day, Eleanor falls asleep and dreams of a golden light, not unlike the light Dante describes, that fills her with happiness. The sequence ends with Peggy's exhortation to North that he not " 'write little books to make money' " but instead try to " 'live differently.' "

Eleanor wants to hoard the feeling of happiness she gets from her dream of golden light: "Covered up from observation it might survive, she felt." Trying to hide it, she asks North if he has accumulated enough wealth from his African farm to be able to live in England: " 'You've saved enough, haven't you?' " When she gives Maggie a pencil and paper to figure out whether North has enough to live on, Maggie draws a caricature of her brother, "the

18I quote here from *La Divina Commedia* ed H. Oelsner, trans J. A. Carlyle, Thomas Okey, and P. H. Wicksteed (London: Dent 1933). This seems to have been the edition Woolf used, since its translation of *Purgatorio* XV 56–57 corresponds exactly to the quotation in *The Years*.

man in the white waistcoat" who used to take her for rides "on an elephant." What is caricatured here, I think, is the imperial rule that has given England a ride on the elephants of India and Africa and kept England supplied in white waistcoats. (A second caricature drawn later in Present Day, and discussed below, supports this view.) When Eleanor again discusses North's future and what he will need to do if he wants to live in England, he interrupts: " 'I don't know what I want,' " he says. His lack of closure, noted above, restores Eleanor's feeling of happiness, and she shares her sense of life, even in her old age, as perpetual discovery. Here the reader's thoughts, along with Eleanor's and North's, are cast into the future, and colored by a context in which a young man abandons his colonial career, Empire is mocked, and Eleanor tests the possibility of sharing the happiness that comes from "golden light."

This is, however, a glowing vision of the future, and one might rightly feel a good deal of skepticism about it. It makes perfect sense that *The Years* next examines it from a deeply distrustful point of view, which comes to us logically from Peggy—isolated, misanthropic, "marooned when the dance started" (383). She has considered the Dantean question with regard to emotion, whether or not "pleasure is increased by sharing it"; but the frequency with which sharing fails leads her to feel that "this 'sharing,' then, is a bit of a farce" (382–83).

Peggy enters the sequence under discussion in a condition like Eleanor's, wanting to hide an emotion: "In order to cover her loneliness she took down a book." Opened at random, it says exactly what she thinks, which is very much the opposite of the flowing solidarity implied in Eleanor's vision: *La médiocrité de l'univers m'étonne et me révolte . . . la petitesse de toutes choses m'emplit de dégoût . . . la pauvreté des êtres humains m'anéantit.*[19] Then Eleanor, with Peggy beside her, says that " 'things have changed for the better . . . We're happier—we're freer' "; and she shares more explicitly the feeling she wanted to cover before: " 'I feel . . . as if I'd been in another world! So happy!' " When Renny "toshes" her for " 'always talking of the other world . . . Why not this one,' " she insists that her vision of glowing light was not otherworldly: " 'But I meant this world! . . . I meant, happy in this world— happy with living people.' " Peggy continues to react skeptically, and very thoughtfully, but she is soon pulled out of her isolation by hearing laughter around her, which she joins involuntarily. She finds that what is being laughed at is the second of the evening's caricatures—which is, like other important statements in *The Years*, a collective creation: "Each of them had drawn a different part of a picture. On top there was a woman's head like Queen Alexandra . . . then a bird's neck; the body of a tiger; and stout elephant's legs

[19]"I am astonished and revolted by the mediocrity of the universe . . . and filled with loathing at the pettiness of everything . . . the sheer poverty of human beings reduces me to nothingness."

dressed in child's drawers . . . ". Here again we have the animals of India and
Africa, now surmounted by the Queen, " 'the face that launched a thousand
ships!' "—not those of Greece, but those of Britain.

The Empire, it would seem, has become a joke. In any case Peggy's
laughter has "relaxed her, enlarged her," so that she felt or saw "a state of
being, in which there was real laughter, real happiness, and this fractured
world was whole; whole, vast, and free." She is impelled to speak to the
question of how North is to live: What's the use, she asks, of going on living as
young men of his class have always lived,[20] making money by writing " 'one
little book and then another little book . . . instead of living . . . differently,
differently.' " Having "tried to say it," but made the mistake of being personal
when she had meant to be impersonal, she slumps back against the wall and
"think[s] herself away . . . into the country [where] it seemed . . . an owl
went up and down, up and down; its white wing showed on the dark of the
hedge . . . ." Just as the owl is connected earlier with Dante's lines about
shared light, it reappears here as if to confirm Peggy's desire for a world in
which hedges might be transcended. Her effort is rewarded some time later
when, for a moment, North sees the truth of what she meant (422). Once
again in this sequence we have moved from emotional hoarding through the
ridicule of imperial barriers to a kind of communion. The possibility of
transcending economic hoarding is raised as well. As Lévi-Strauss says about
the repetition common in myths, "the function of repetition is to render the
structure of the myth apparent."[21]

North would like to do something other than write books to make money.
To be sure, he already has the money from his African farm. He has returned
from his farm to a wealthy England: "Everywhere profusion, plenty" (308); or,
" 'What a rich country England is!' " as Delia says (399). Both Eleanor's return
from Spain and North's from Africa bring into *The Years* the sense of
England's lushness, compared with the poorer countries of the world; but
even in England the well may run dry, though there's " 'quite enough for
everyone at present,' " to quote a phrase emphasized by repetition in "1911"
(207). Yet Delia's husband, the reactionary Irishman, complains that "the old
days were over" and "they had to cut things down." " 'Yes, we're all finding
that,' " Peggy says "perfunctorily" (354). She won't waste time crying over it.
The next words of the text say that "the room was filling with people she did
not know. There was an Indian in a pink turban." Here, in the context of talk
about cutting down, not only an awareness of the Empire but England's
colonial subjects themselves press into the novel. Its space begins to get
crowded.

Earlier in Present Day there is an acid test of what it might mean to "cut
down" and share resources with the people English society has excluded.

[20]See "The Leaning Tower" *CE* II 162–81, especially 167.
[21]"The Structural Study of Myth" in *Structural Anthropology*, trans Claire Jacobson and
Brooke Grundfest Schoepf (NY: Basic Books 1963; rpt Garden City, NY: Anchor 1967) 226.

After we learn of Sara's anger at the war and at the man and woman in the Rolls-Royce, we find North reciting "The Garden"; and as he comes to the lines "Society is all but rude/To this delicious solitude," the privacy of North and Sara is violated by the sound, in the room opposite, of " 'the Jew having a bath.' " Sara shares the bath across the hall with a Jew who leaves grease and hair in the tub. As she tells this to North—she has had some time to come to terms with the situation—she is relatively matter-of-fact; it is North who feels "physically sick . . . . He made a noise like 'Pah.' "

But this "Pah!" had been Sara's initial reaction, too. When she had first faced the dirty bathtub, she had come back into her own rooms and seen the slovenly serving-girl "with her blouse torn" and heard "the unemployed singing hymns under the window." Her reaction had been disgust and the desire to escape; in expressing it Woolf gives Sara the voice of T. S. Eliot: " 'Polluted city, unbelieving city, city of dead fish and worn-out frying pans . . .' " (340ff). Sara rushes out " 'in a rage' " and " 'stood on the bridge, and said, "Am I a weed, carried this way, that way, on a tide that comes twice a day without a meaning?" ' " (341). Am I, in other words, helpless; am I at the mercy of a meaningless life? Like Eliot, she sees a crowd flowing over London bridge: " 'people passing; the strutting; the tiptoeing; the pasty; the ferret-eyed; the bowler-hatted, servile innumerable army of workers. And I said, "Must I join your conspiracy? Stain the hand, the unstained hand . . . and sign on, and serve a master; all because of a Jew in my bath, all because of a Jew?" ' " She does start to "sign on"; she approaches an employer, a "man in a newspaper office," with " 'a talisman, a glowing gem, a lucent emerald' "—her class privilege, apparently, the connection that might get her a job because, as the employer says, " 'I knew your father at Oxford' " (341). As Sara tells North the tale of this interview, she suddenly falls silent. North begins to figure out what she has said: "the actual words floated together and formed a sentence in his mind." They "meant that she was poor; that she must earn her living," he supposes, and thinks "but then there's something true—in the silence perhaps" (342).

Sara's silence is the only instance in *The Years*, to my recollection, of a character's voluntarily falling silent in mid-sentence without having been interrupted by someone else. But there are one or two other instances of silence, on the part of female characters, that imply integrity: when Maggie is at first "silent," for example, as she receives the necklace from Colonel Pargiter that is not at all pretty and "her mother at once supplied the words she should have spoken" (121); or when Peggy, in 1911, "was silent" and "there was a pause" in response to her mother's saying that William Whatney is "such a delightful man" (203). Woolf calls attention to this silence and pause by giving them a whole line of their own, just as she calls attention to Sara's silence by saying North thinks "there's something true—in the silence perhaps." I think the silence points, as with Maggie and Peggy, to Sara's integrity; what we see here, I think, is the moment Sara confirms her membership in the Society of Outsiders, as Woolf calls it in *Three Guineas*. She adopts the secrecy that Woolf says is at times "essential," especially so as to avoid the "glare of advertisement and publicity" that "inhibits the human power to change and create new wholes"; for "ease and freedom, the power to change and the power to grow, can only be preserved by obscurity" (*TG* 113–14).

Rather than work for the rich man's press—whose power "to burke discussion of any undesirable subject was, and still is, very formidable," Woolf says in *Three Guineas* (162 n)—Sara will not sign on and serve a master, but will continue to live in something approaching poverty. Her decision affirms that she is not "a weed" carried on a tide "without a meaning"; or, as Woolf says in *Three Guineas*, that "we are not passive spectators doomed to unresisting obedience" (142). Standing on that bridge, like the women in *Three Guineas* who stand "on a bridge over the Thames" with Westminster and the Houses of Parliament in view (*TG* 60), a bridge between the patriarchal system of the private house and the capitalist system of the professions (*TG* 67), Sara can choose "never to side with the servile, the signers-on" (*TG* 16). She can choose to live in the poverty that has always been the condition of ghettoized Jews, the poverty and ghettoization that are and have been the condition of women. "You are feeling in your own persons," Woolf says in *Three Guineas*, addressing men, "what your mothers felt when they were shut out, when they were shut up, because they were women. Now you are being shut out, you are being shut up, because you are Jews, because you are democrats, because of race, because of religion. . . . The whole iniquity of dictatorship, whether in Oxford or Cambridge, in Whitehall or Downing Street, against Jews or against women, in England or in Germany, in Italy or in Spain is now apparent to you" (102–03). Sara begins by thinking of Jews in a voice like Eliot's, perhaps expressing and confronting her own anti-Semitism. That she should choose to go on sharing a bath with a Jew seems a direct reply to Eliot's Jews, the Jew of "Gerontion" who "squats on the window sill, the owner"; or the Jew who, apparently, undermines European civilization (" . . . Who clipped the lion's wings/And flea'd his rump and pared his claws?"): "The jew [who] is underneath the lot" as "The rats are underneath the piles."[22]

"And here I am plagued by the sudden wish to write an anti-Fascist pamphlet," Woolf wrote as she was getting *Three Guineas* under way; later, in retrospect, it made sense to her to consider "the *Years* and *Three Guineas* together as one book—as indeed they are" (*AWD* 231, 284). So what do we make of *The Years* as an anti-fascist novel?

The Years itself raises significant questions about the nature of a work of art, its relation to its audience, and the concepts we apply when we judge the success of a work of art. Most notably, if *The Years* is anti-fascist in that it shuns the loudspeaker in favor of the human voice and the leader in favor of ordinary people, if its metaphors and its structure imply the need for

[22]"Burbank with a Baedeker: Bleistein with a Cigar," in *The Complete Poems and Plays 1909– 1950* (NY: Harcourt 1952) 24. These words and those from "Gerontion" are quoted with the permission of Harcourt Brace Jovanovich.

collaborative effort, if its white owls and golden light ask for cooperative pursuit of truth and communion in vision, as do its conversations, caricatures, and the gathering of the Present Day; if its poor houses are to be shared, and if its patterns need to be both "made" and then "thought," then *The Years* treats the cooperative task of its readers with great respect, and practically makes room for its readers within its own pages.

Repeatedly in *The Years* Woolf shows a work of art not so much as a timeless entity the beauty of whose formal properties has inherent power to affect the observer, but as a work whose beauty becomes real only when, or as, it is grasped by particular people. For example, the words of "The Garden" when recited "seemed like actual presences, hard and independent; yet as [Sara] was listening they were changed by their contact with her" (339). When Martin looks at St Paul's, "all the weights in his body seemed to shift. He had a curious sense of something moving in his body in harmony with the building . . . It was exciting—this change of proportion" (227). But after lunch, the affluent City lunch interrupted briefly by the beckoning finger of his stockbroker, Martin catches the waiter trying to cheat him. He flares up, walks out, sees St Paul's again and finds that "the queer thrill of some correspondence between his own body and the stone no longer came to him. He felt nothing except anger" (233). Is anger, Woolf "wondered" in *A Room of One's Own*, "the familiar, the attendant sprite on power? Rich people, for example, are often angry because they suspect that the poor want to seize their wealth."[23] When Martin feels angry because a social inferior has tried to take his money, his ability to respond to beauty is interfered with.

Something similar may hold true for the creator of art: as the writer confronts a difficult question about her own "prosperity," the flow of creative revery may be disturbed. Or so Woolf indicates in "Street Haunting" (1930), an essay in which she portrays metaphorically the wanderings of the writer's consciousness. The artist-persona, rambling through London streets at night, enjoys release from the self and its paraphernalia; dallies with beauty; becomes conscious of surfeit on this "simple, sugary fare"; and finds relief in the observation of a dwarf, whose presence allows her to explore the psychology of beauty and its opposite. Then, placidly observing a "maimed company of the halt and the blind," who live "in the top rooms of these narrow old houses between Holborn and Soho," the artist is just "musing" that these have-nots

> do not grudge us . . . our prosperity; when, suddenly, turning the corner, we come upon a bearded Jew, wild, hunger-bitten, glaring out of his misery; or pass the humped body of an old woman flung abandoned on the step of a public building with a cloak over her like a hasty covering thrown over a dead horse or donkey. At such sights the nerves of the spine seem to stand erect; a sudden flare is brandished in our eyes; a question is asked which is never answered. (*CE* IV 159)

---

[23]Jane Marcus discussed this in "Art and Anger," a paper read at the NEMLA [North East Modern Language Association] Conference in April 1976, published in Marcus's book of that title (Columbus: Ohio State University Press, 1988).

In *The Years*, however, Sara seems to have faced a similar question and answered it in a way that leaves her, unlike Martin, still open to the experience of beauty. When North's recitation of "The Garden" is interrupted by the sound of " 'the Jew having a bath,' " it is Sara who first finds herself ready to continue the poem, North who refuses to do so, though Sara invites him to " 'go on' " (340). Again, openness to aesthetic experiences seems to require the absence of resentment or fear toward outsiders who may encroach on one's way of life. The reader, to use that convenient term, needs to be emotionally without impediment, from whatever source, so that the words actually can be "changed by their contact with her." How the words may change is shown in Woolf's rendering of Sara reading *Antigone*; a scene which also shows the reader willing to enter into the work and be changed by *Antigone* in turn: "She was buried alive . . . There was just room for her to lie straight out. Straight out in a brick tomb, she said. And that's the end, she yawned, shutting the book. She laid herself out. . . . " The vultures that eat the body of Antigone's brother touch Sara as she falls asleep and "a dark wing brushed her mind . . . " (135–36). In "1911" we see the same motif repeated, affirmatively: Eleanor falls asleep and her own mind, linked with the wing of the white owl, "brushes . . . the words" of the *Divine Comedy*. Dante's golden light enters Eleanor's life and her unconscious remakes it for her as a dream. Reader and work are interfused.

The pattern is made and thought. The words and the readers change. *The Years* is not so much self-reflexive, in good modernist form, as it is other-reflexive: it considers the process of its own reading. And this is interesting, formally or philosophically. But even more interesting are the reasons behind Woolf's concern for the human voice of the reader. The issues *The Years* raises are so important that it deserves readers who will engage with its words, the lives of its characters, and its view of history, money, and politics. All but outright, *The Years* asks how it will enter its readers' lives, and what we will make of it. Thus the novel's final spoken words: " 'And now?' "

Jacob's Room: Woolf's Satiric Elegy

Alex Zwerdling

Jacob's Room appeared in 1922, the *annus mirabilis* of modern literature that also produced *Ulysses* and *The Waste Land*. Perhaps because it was associated with these works, and because the novel was the first of Woolf's longer fictions to break with conventional narrative technique, it is often interpreted as a quintessential modernist text rather than as a unique work. Its peculiarities are treated as illustrative of the revolution in twentieth-century literature, though in fact some of them are idiosyncratic. The book was certainly Woolf's first consciously experimental novel, and it has remained her most baffling one. Its narrative techniques are so innovative that they call attention to themselves; its central character, Jacob Flanders, seems to be a classic instance of psychological inscrutability in fiction; and its rapidly shifting tone, now somber, now mocking, deprives Woolf's audience of a stable sense of her own attitude toward the world she describes. These problems of narrative method, characterization, and tone are interrelated, but they can be illuminated only by attempting to understand Woolf's fundamental aims in writing the particular novel *Jacob's Room*, rather than by assuming she was interested in fictional innovation for its own sake.

Jacob's Room is often taken to be simply a technical exercise. David Daiches, for example, suggests that it was written, "one might say, for the sake of style."[1] And indeed Woolf's first thoughts about the book in her diary are concerned with method rather than matter: "Suppose one thing should open out of another—as in An Unwritten Novel—only not for 10 pages but 200 or so—doesn't that give the looseness & lightness I want: doesnt that get closer & yet keep form & speed, & enclose everything, everything?"[2] Her diary entries as she works on the book continue to deal more with narrative strategy than with defining the "everything, everything" the novel is designed to present. Essentially, Woolf was trying to work free of the conventions of

Excerpted from *Virginia Woolf and The Real World* (Berkeley: University of California Press, 1986); first published in *ELH* 48 (1981); 894–913. Copyright © 1986 The Regents of the University of California Press.

[1]David Daiches, *Virginia Woolf* (New York: New Directions, 1963), 61.
[2]*The Diary of Virginia Woolf*, ed. Anne Olivier Bell with Andrew McNeillie, 5 vols. (London: Hogarth, 1977–1984), II, p. 13. Subsequent quotations cited as *D* with volume and page numbers.

realism she attacked with such devastating wit in "Mr. Bennett and Mrs. Brown," that style of fiction in which the character is kept waiting in the wings until his entire environment and life history have been exhaustively described.

The style of *Jacob's Room* is that of the sketchbook artist rather than the academic painter. Scenes are swiftly and allusively outlined, not filled in, the essential relationships between characters intimated in brief but typical vignettes chosen seemingly at random from their daily lives: a don's luncheon party at Cambridge, a day spent reading in the British Museum, a walk with a friend. No incident is decisive or fully developed. Nothing is explained or given special significance. The narrative unit is generally two or three pages long and not obviously connected to the one before or after. The effect is extremely economical and suggestive but at the same time frustrating for an audience trained to read in larger units and to look for meaning and coherence. All of this was clearly innovative, as Woolf's first readers saw. Lytton Strachey writes her: "The technique of the narrative is astonishing—how you manage to leave out everything that's dreary, and yet retain enough string for your pearls I can hardly understand."[3] And E. M. Forster is similarly baffled; he wonders how Woolf keeps the reader interested in Jacob when almost everything that would have defined his character has been eliminated. "I don't yet understand how, with your method, you managed it," he writes, but he is certain that this is the book's greatest achievement.[4]

Not all of Woolf's readers have been convinced that the narrative technique, interesting as it is, *was* successful, however. The book is often attacked on the grounds that it has no unity and that Jacob himself remains unknowable. Joan Bennett, for example, insists that the novel's vividly realized episodes "build up no whole that can be held in the mind" and that "Jacob remains a nebulous young man, indeed almost any young man."[5] J. K. Johnstone complains that the very vividness of the incidents "detracts from the unity of the novel," while the character who might unite all its various scenes, is—not there; his effects upon others are there; but he himself is absent."[6] Such dismissive judgments seem to me based on an unwillingness to think about Woolf's technique in relation to purpose. Both the obvious fragmentation of the novel and the inscrutability of its central character are, I think, deliberate. But in order to understand why Woolf chose to write a novel that can be characterized in these ways, one has to move beyond speculation about narrative technique as such to an understanding of why she

---

[3]Virginia Woolf and Lytton Strachey, *Letters*, ed. Leonard Woolf and James Strachey (London: Hogarth, 1969), 103.

[4]*Selected Letters of E. M. Forster*, ed. Mary Lago and P. N. Furbank (Cambridge: Harvard Univ. Press, 1985), II, 21.

[5]Joan Bennett, *Virginia Woolf: Her Art as a Novelist*, 2nd ed. (Cambridge: Cambridge Univ. Press, 1964), 95, 96.

[6]J. K. Johnstone, *The Bloomsbury Group: A Study of E. M. Forster, Lytton Strachey, Virginia Woolf, and Their Circle* (London: Secker and Warburg, 1954), 332, 334.

needed these particular techniques in the particular book she was writing. For despite her obvious interest in technical experiment, she always thought of narrative style as purposive—a means to an end. Since the ends of her individual novels were never the same, her technical choices ought to be looked at not as attempts to "revolutionize modern fiction" but as individual solutions to the problem at hand. And the problem at hand cannot be intelligently discussed without considering the book's subject matter.[7]

Jacob's Room is about a young man who is killed in the First World War. By naming her hero Jacob Flanders, Woolf immediately predicts his fate. As her first readers in 1922 would certainly have known, Flanders was a synonym for death in battle. The words of John McCrae's "In Flanders Fields"—"the most popular poem of the war"[8]—were common property:

> In Flanders fields, the poppies blow
> Between the crosses, row on row. . . .
> We are the Dead. Short days ago
> We lived, felt dawn, saw sunset glow,
>   Loved and were loved, and now we lie
>   In Flanders fields.[9]

According to official sources, nearly a third of the million British soldiers killed in World War I lost their lives in the Flanders mud. And the heaviest losses were among the young officers of Jacob's class. In the words of A. J. P. Taylor, "The roll of honour in every school and college bore witness to the talents which had perished—the men of promise born during the eighteen-nineties whose promise was not fulfilled."[10]

Although *Jacob's Room* is not in any direct sense a war novel, references to the coming conflict are carefully embedded in the narrative and would have constantly reminded Woolf's first readers of the imminent catastrophe. Jacob goes up to Cambridge in 1906. His growth from adolescence to young

---

[7]Woolf's most interesting comment on her own experimental methods in fiction was a direct response to critics who treated her next novel, *Mrs. Dalloway*, as a conscious methodological experiment. Her insistence on the inaccuracy of this view is equally pertinent to an understanding of *Jacob's Room* and is worth quoting at some length: "The book, it was said, was the deliberate offspring of a method. The author, it was said, dissatisfied with the form of fiction then in vogue, was determined to beg, borrow, steal or even create another of her own. But, as far as it is possible to be honest about the mysterious process of the mind, the facts are otherwise. Dissatisfied the writer may have been; but her dissatisfaction was primarily with nature for giving an idea, without providing a house for it to live in. . . . The novel was the obvious lodging, but the novel it seemed was built on the wrong plan. Thus rebuked the idea started as the oyster starts or the snail to secrete a house for itself. And this it did without any conscious direction. . . . It was necessary to write the book first and to invent a theory afterwards" (Virginia Woolf, "Introduction" to *Mrs. Dalloway* [New York: Modern Library, 1928], vii–viii). It is evident from this description that Woolf begins with a subject rather than with a method and that the subject seems to have a will of its own rather than allowing the novelist to shape it according to a preconceived theory of narration or a preexisting form.

[8]Paul Fussell, *The Great War and Modern Memory* (New York: Oxford Univ. Press, 1975), 248.

[9]John McCrae, *In Flanders Fields and Other Poems* (New York: Putnam's, 1919), 3.

[10]A. J. P. Taylor, *English History, 1914–1945* (Harmondsworth: Penguin, 1970), 126n, 165–66.

manhood takes place against the relentless ticking of a time bomb. We may be reading about his intellectual and amorous adventures, but we are also witnessing the preparation of cannon fodder. Woolf keeps us aware of Jacob's impending fate by moving back and forth in time: for example, when she rounds off the story of a young couple in Jacob's social set with the words "And now Jimmy feeds crows in Flanders and Helen visits hospitals."[11] Her novel alludes to certain well-known public events of the years just before the war—the Irish Home Rule Bill (97), the transformation of the House of Lords (129)—in a way that indirectly would have reminded her original audience of dates—1911, 1912, 1913.[12] Toward the end of the book the preparations for war become direct. The ministers in Whitehall lift their pens and alter the course of history (172); and the young men die. Woolf's only description of the fighting is remarkable for its contained rage, its parody of reportorial detachment: "Like blocks of tin soldiers the army covers the cornfield, moves up the hillside, stops, reels slightly this way and that, and falls flat, save that, through field-glasses, it can be seen that one or two pieces still agitate up and down like fragments of broken match-stick" (155).

Many readers have seen that such references to the war are significant and that *Jacob's Room* is a response to that event even though it records the years before it begins. Winifred Holtby, in the first book-length study of Virginia Woolf, suggested that Woolf was less interested in trench warfare (about which she knew nothing) than in the group identity of its victims: "When such a young man was killed, she seems to ask, what was lost then? What lost by him? What was lost by his friends? What exactly was it that had disappeared?"[13] These still seem to me the essential questions to ask in reading *Jacob's Room*. I hope to show that they also illuminate the book's technical innovations and its experiments in portraiture, as well as Woolf's puzzling shifts in tone.

The question of what might have become of the Jacobs is asked by Woolf herself in a review of a book on Rupert Brooke, that classic example of the gifted young man killed before his time: "One turns from the thought of him not with a sense of completeness and finality, but rather to wonder and to question still: what would he have been, what would he have done?"[14] As her

[11]Virginia Woolf, *Jacob's Room* (1922; London: Hogarth, 1971), pp. 95–96. Subsequent quotations cited by page number in the text.

[12]For a detailed chronology, see Avrom Fleishman, *Virginia Woolf: A Critical Reading* (Baltimore: Johns Hopkins Univ. Press, 1975), 49–50.

[13]Winifred Holtby, *Virginia Woolf* (London: Wishart, 1932), 116. More recent critics who have commented on the significance of the war in the book include Josephine O'Brien Schaefer, *The Three-Fold Nature of Reality in the Novels of Virginia Woolf* (The Hague: Mouton, 1965), 70–71; Carolyn G. Heilbrun, *Towards Androgyny: Aspects of Male and Female in Literature* (London: Victor Gollancz, 1973), 164; Nancy Topping Bazin, *Virginia Woolf and the Androgynous Vision* (New Brunswick, N.J.: Rutgers Univ. Press, 1973), 92–93; and Fleishman, 54. See also the excellent essay on Woolf's critical depiction of prewar British culture by Carol Ohmann, "Culture and Anarchy in *Jacob's Room*," *Contemporary Literature* 18 (1977); 160–72.

[14]*Books and Portraits: Some Further Selections from the Literary and Biographical Writings of Virginia Woolf*, ed. Mary Lyon (London: Hogarth, 1977), p. 89. Subsequent quotations cited as *BP* with page numbers.

questions suggest, the truncated lives of such men provoke doubt rather than certainty. "Promising" they surely were. But their early deaths only magnified the absence of achieved identity and accomplishment. As she says of a different young casualty in another review, "What the finished work, the final aim, would have been we can only guess" (*BP,* 96). Such questions are unanswerable, and Woolf does not really deal with them in *Jacob's Room.* Rather, she writes the book largely to give us a sense of what this particular stage in a young man's life—the promising stage—is like.

The major obstacle in her way was the almost universal impulse to sentimentalize the subject. Obituaries for the war dead are not noted for their realism; Woolf, however, was determined to write an honest account rather than a heroic one. She does not avoid the likelihood that such young men, for all their native gifts and youthful promise, were confused and immature. Her novel emphasizes the image of Jacob *adrift,* moving rapidly but lightly from one social set to another, from one romantic attachment to another, without either the intention or the ability to "settle." In his own rather despairing words, "One must apply oneself to something or other—God knows what" (71).

Woolf's fragmented narrative creates a kaleidoscopic picture of the range of Jacob's opportunities. Particularly in the London chapters, she gives us the sense that the world is all before him. His family connections, his education, and his good looks provide him with an entry into many different social circles—bohemian, professional, aristocratic. And his romantic experiments suggest a similar smorgasbord: the amiable, promiscuous Florinda, the emotionally unstable Fanny Elmer, the steady but frozen young heiress Clara Durrant, the "sophisticated" older married woman Sandra Wentworth Williams. These opportunities and experiences are deliberately presented in an incoherent way because for Jacob they do not add up; they cannot be thought of as sequential steps leading to his definition as an adult human being. Unlike the classic *Bildungsroman, Jacob's Room* lacks a teleology. Woolf's hero remains an essentially molten personality interrupted by death at the stage of experimenting upon himself, a young man by turns brashly self-confident and utterly confused. The novel treats this situation as an inevitable but early stage of growing up. Woolf's perspective is that of an older person who can describe "the obstinate irrepressible conviction which makes youth so intolerably disagreeable—'I am what I am, and intend to be it,' for which there will be no form in the world unless Jacob makes one for himself" (34). But as the last part of her sentence suggests, it is by no means certain that such attempts to define oneself will be successful, no matter how long we are given. There is always the possibility, perhaps even the likelihood, that our rebellious adolescence will give way not to strong adult individuality but to a stale, despairing conformity.

No one has written about this stage of life better than Erik Erikson, and though Woolf could not, of course, have read him, certain passages in his work illuminate Jacob's situation because both writers focus on the same phenomenon. In *Childhood and Society* (1950) and more fully in *Identity: Youth and Crisis* (1968), Erikson defines a stage of deliberately prolonged adolescence which he calls a *"psychosocial moratorium,"* a period in which "the young adult through free role experimentation may find a niche in some section of his society, a niche which is firmly defined and yet seems to be uniquely made for him." Before he is expected to take on any of his life commitments—in love, in work—the young man is offered a legitimate period of delay "often characterized by a combination of prolonged immaturity and provoked precocity."[15] His reluctance to bind himself vocationally or to choose a mate is honored or at least tolerated for a period of years because his society accepts his need for self-exploration and social mobility before demanding that the ultimate choices be made.

By its very nature, such a stage cannot be a record of triumphs, and those who are going through it often seem simply confused and self-indulgent to their elders, particularly those with short memories. Furthermore, a person in this position remains in some sense a blank—undefinable, unknowabl —and therefore not an easy subject for fiction. We expect a novel to give us characters who have an identity or whose progressive change we can follow sequentially, as in the *Bildungsroman*. In *Jacob's Room*, however, Woolf was faced with the problem that this fictional convention does not hold good for all human beings at all stages of life. She had tried to deal with a similarly inchoate personality in her first novel, *The Voyage Out*, and would do so again in *The Waves*. All three of these characters (Rachel, Jacob, Percival) die young, before they have been fully defined. But it is notable that in trying to depict such people, Woolf's technique becomes more and more stylized, until in Percival she creates a mythical rather than a realistically conceived character.

Why did she move in this direction? Why did she deliberately avoid the technique of interior monologue that might have given her readers a vivid sense of the inner turmoil in which such people find themselves? In certain obvious ways, the record of a fictional character's thoughts is ideally suited to depicting identity confusion, yet in *Jacob's Room* (and even more in *The Waves*) the characters who might have been illuminated by it are never presented in this way. The inner lives of Jacob and Percival remain a mystery. In *The Waves* this is clearly a deliberate choice, since the six major characters surrounding Percival all soliloquize at length, whereas Percival himself has no voice. It is sometimes assumed that Woolf depicts Jacob without recording his inner life in detail because when she was writing *Jacob's Room* she had not yet perfected the techniques of rendering consciousness she learned to use so brilliantly in her later fiction. But the explanation is unconvincing, since in the first place the thoughts of many minor characters in the novel *are* consistently recorded, even if not in the elaborate form found in *Mrs.*

[15]Erik Erikson, *Identity: Youth and Crisis* (New York: Norton, 1968), 156.

Dalloway or *To the Lighthouse.* Woolf deliberately minimized the reader's access to Jacob's thoughts. This is evident if one reads the holograph draft of the novel alongside the revised, final version. Again and again Woolf eliminates the vestiges of Jacob's inner life. For example, in the potentially romantic scene in which he helps Clara pick grapes while the younger children scamper about, Woolf excises the hints of Jacob's attachment from the first version:

> "Little demons!" she cried.
> ~~"I haven't said it"~~ Jacob thought to himself.
> ~~I want to say it. I cant say it. Clara! Clara! Clara!"~~
> They're throwing the onions," said Jacob.
> (holograph version, with Woolf's deletions)[16]

> "Little demons!" she cried. "What have they got?" she asked Jacob.
> "Onions, I think," said Jacob. He looked at them without moving.
> (published version, 61)

As a result of such excisions, we never know exactly what Jacob feels about Clara, nor about most of the other people whose lives touch his.

There is something obviously artificial and deliberate in such narrative reticence. Any attempt to account for it must be speculative, but two reasons suggest themselves for Woolf's peculiar strategy. It is possible that she wants to give us the sense of a character still so unformed that even the relatively chaotic record of interior monologue seems too defining. The flux of feelings must be recorded in words, and words give shape. Even Jacob's conflicted "I want to say it. I cant say it. Clara! Clara! Clara!" clearly suggests romantic attachment, when it is possible that what he feels about her is less easily describable. By their very nature, words articulate confusion too neatly to be true to the extremes of the state. This is why Jacob's letters home communicate so little: "Jacob had nothing to hide from his mother. It was only that he could make no sense himself of his extraordinary excitement, and as for writing it down—" (130). It is possible that Woolf refused to record Jacob's deepest feelings because such a transcript comes too close to presenting a finished product rather than a consciousness in process. She wanted to give the sense of someone who remains a permanently unknown quantity. And so she concentrates on the conflicting impressions of Jacob among all the people he meets, and our point of view shifts abruptly every few pages as we move from one unreliable observer to another, none of them managing to fathom this young man because, as Woolf concludes, "nobody sees any one as he is. . . . They see a whole—they see all sorts of things—they see themselves" (28–29).

---

[16]Virginia Woolf, *Jacob's Room*, holograph dated April 15, 1920–March 12, 1922, pt. I, 123, Berg Collection, New York Public Library.

But to pose the problem in this epistemological way does not fully explain the absence of anything resembling stream of consciousness. Mrs. Ramsay is similarly unknowable, Lily Briscoe tells us in *To the Lighthouse* ("One wanted fifty pairs of eyes to see with, she reflected. Fifty pairs of eyes were not enough to get round that one woman with, she thought"),[17] and yet this fact does not prevent Woolf from recording her character's inner life in detail. For a better explanation, we must go back to the problematic tone of *Jacob's Room*. Uninterrupted stream of consciousness tends to create sympathy and to work against satiric intent in fiction. And there are many indications in *Jacob's Room* that Woolf wanted to maintain an ironic distance between her reader and her main character. Her tone in describing him and his friends is often patronizing. For example, when Jacob first becomes involved with the brainless Florinda, Woolf describes his feelings with obvious mockery:

> Jacob took her word for it that she was chaste. She prattled, sitting by the fireside, of famous painters. The tomb of her father was mentioned. Wild and frail and beautiful she looked, and thus the women of the Greeks were, Jacob thought; and this was life; and himself a man and Florinda chaste.
> She left with one of Shelley's poems beneath her arm. Mrs. Stuart, she said, often talked of him.
> Marvellous are the innocent. (77)

Such ironic detachment is evident not only in the narrator's attitude toward Jacob but in her treatment of most of the young characters in the book. The narrative voice is that of an older, more experienced, highly skeptical consciousness, determined to puncture youthful illusion and under-cut intense feeling of any kind. This satiric narrator often steps in to correct romantic excess—for example, when describing Richard Bonamy's passion for Jacob:

> "Urbane" on the lips of Jacob had mysteriously all the shapeliness of a character which Bonamy thought daily more sublime, devastating, terrific than ever, though he was still, and perhaps would be for ever, barbaric, obscure.
> What superlatives! What adjectives! How acquit Bonamy of sentimentality of the grossest sort; of being tossed like a cork on the waves; of having no steady insight into character; of being unsupported by reason, and of drawing no comfort whatever from the works of the classics? (164)

The cumulative effect of such passages is to make it impossible for the reader to sympathize fully with the character. We are, in effect, told to keep our distance. And in one way or another, the narrative techniques of the novel reinforce this sense of a wide gap. Woolf frequently pretends ignorance: she imagines herself so far from the action that she can't hear the words of the characters. In one of the Cambridge scenes, for instance, the perspective suddenly lengthens, like an aerial shot in film:

17Virginia Woolf, *To the Lighthouse* (1927; London: Hogarth, 1967). p. 303.

The laughter died in the air. The sound of it could scarcely have reached any one standing by the Chapel, which stretched along the opposite side of the court. The laughter died out, and only gestures of arms, movements of bodies, could be seen shaping something in the room. Was it an argument? A bet on the boat races? Was it nothing of the sort? What was shaped by the arms and bodies moving in the twilight room? (42–43)

In such passages the omniscient narrator suddenly and rather disturbingly pleads ignorance, becomes at best "semiscient." There are also many instances in the book in which our involvement with and understanding of the characters is [are] made more difficult because our view is filtered through an alien consciousness—for example, that of Richard Bonamy's charwoman, who gives us an obviously garbled version of what she overhears the young friends saying in the next room as she washes up in the scullery: "'Objective something,' said Bonamy; and 'common ground' and something else—all very long words, she noted. 'Book learning does it,' she thought to herself" (101). The effect is to deflate the intellectual pretensions of these budding philosophers and bring them down to earth.

Is this any way to treat a young man whose life is about to be snuffed out? Why does Woolf challenge the ancient wisdom that dictates "de mortuis nil nisi bonum"? Is there some meanness of spirit evident in the games she plays with her characters? Such irreverence might well have seemed offensive to a generation of readers trained to think about the dead soldiers by the literature World War I produced. These works, written during and immediately after the conflict, convey a sense of high idealism or heroic indignation or romantic intensity. One has only to recall some of the classic passages:[18]

If I should die, think only this of me:
　That there's some corner of a foreign field
That is for ever England.
　　　　　(Rupert Brooke, "The Soldier")

What passing-bells for these who die as cattle?
　Only the monstrous anger of the guns.
　Only the stuttering rifles' rapid rattle
Can patter out their hasty orisons.
(Wilfred Owen, "Anthem for Doomed Youth")

Have you forgotten yet?. . .
Look down, and swear by the slain of the War that
you'll never forget.
　　　　　(Siegfried Sassoon, "Aftermath")

---

[18]*The Poetical Works of Rupert Brooke*, ed. Geoffrey Keynes (London: Faber and Faber, 1946), 23; *The Collected Poems of Wilfred Owen*, ed. C. Day Lewis (Norfolk, Conn.: New Directions, 1964), 44; Siegfried Sassoon, *Collected Poems, 1908–1956* (London: Faber and Faber, 1961), 119; H. G. Wells, *Mr. Britling Sees It Through* (New York: Macmillan, 1916), 431–32.

Massacres of boys! That indeed is the essence of modern war. The killing off of the young. It is the destruction of the human inheritance, it is the spending of all the life and material of the future upon present-day hate and greed.

(H. G. Wells, *Mr. Britling Sees It Through*)

Whether the sentiment is patriotic or bitterly disillusioned, such passages treat the war dead with absolute seriousness, in a style that is characteristically intense and even reverent and that works at a high level of generalization.

By contrast, Woolf's elegiac novel is persistently small-scaled, mischievous, and ironic.[19] As we have seen, she had an instinctive distrust for reverence of any kind, treating it as a fundamentally dishonest mental habit that made symbols out of flesh-and-blood human beings. She was no more interested in a cult of war heroes than she had been in a religion of eminent Victorians. For one thing, such attitudes indirectly glorified war, even if the writer was, like Wilfred Owen, consciously working against the martial myth. Woolf's elegy for the young men who died in the war is revisionist: there is nothing grand about Jacob; the sacrifice of his life seems perfectly pointless, not even a cautionary tale. *Jacob's Room* is a covert critique of the romantic posturing so common in the anthems for doomed youth. Its author's attitude anticipates Dylan Thomas's World War II Poem, "A Refusal to Mourn the Death, by Fire, of a Child in London":

I shall not murder
The mankind of her going with a grave truth
Nor blaspheme down the stations of the breath
With any further
Elegy of innocence and youth. [20]

Woolf's bedrock pacifism, then, helps to account for her ironic distance from Jacob and his contemporaries. But she would probably have felt much the same about the milieu that produced him if he had never fought in the war at all, since there was something about his whole life pattern that she disliked intensely. Jacob Flanders is a paradigmatic young man of his class. Handsome, clever, and well-connected if not rich, his credentials are impeccable and his future course apparently secure. Rugby; Trinity College, Cambridge; a London flat; a couple of mistresses; the Grand Tour: everything in his life is a traditional step on the road to establishment success. The class was Woolf's own, but the sex was not, and between the training and expectations of its young men and of its young women there was a great gulf. Woolf's satiric

---

[19]Carol Ohmann's finely judged description of Woolf's tone in *Jacob's Room* is worth quoting: "Neither is the novel an angry one. It is elegiac, rather, in its treatment of Jacob, and serenely so, mourning in tranquility its hero's death and the end of what appeared to be his promise" (Ohmann, 171).

[20]*The Collected Poems of Dylan Thomas* (New York: New Directions, 1953), 112.

detachment is in part attributable to her feeling that Jacob's world was created by men for men and essentially excluded her. She reacted with a characteristic mixture of condescension and apprehension. As she says in describing her own attitude toward him, "Granted ten years' seniority and a difference of sex, fear of him comes first" (93).

The fear is not so much of Jacob himself as of the "patriarchal machinery" that guaranteed him a powerful position in his society. Woolf describes the rites of passage for such young men in an illuminating autobiographical essay written shortly before her death. She considers the career of her illustrious cousin, H. A. L. Fisher: "What, I asked myself the other day, would Herbert Fisher have been without Winchester, New College, and the Cabinet? What would have been his shape had he not been stamped and moulded by the patriarchal machinery? Every one of our male relations was shot into that machine and came out at the other end, at the age of sixty or so, a Headmaster, an Admiral, a Cabinet Minister, a Judge."[21] Jacob too appears to be on such a trajectory. Woolf's feelings about her exclusion from this world are quite complex. She envies the men their guaranteed success (assuming they follow the rules) while pitying them their lack of freedom. The whole exploratory stage of life through which Jacob is passing is subtly undermined by the preordained, mechanical program he is acting out; and the machinery that would have assured him a place in *Who's Who* sends him off to war instead. In *Jacob's Room* Woolf describes a "dozen young men in the prime of life" whose battleship has been hit; they "descend with composed faces into the depths of the sea; and there impassively (though with perfect mastery of machinery) suffocate uncomplainingly together" (155).

The public schools and ancient universities were the training grounds for such complaisant attitudes, and Woolf's feelings about these institutions differed sharply from those of the Bloomsbury males. When people like Lytton Strachey and Leonard Woolf looked back on their undergraduate years, they saw paradise lost. Strachey writes Leonard an ecstatic letter about a visit to Cambridge: "Good God! The Great Court is the most thrilling place in the world, it's no good trying to get over it; whenever I come in through the great gate my heart thumps, and I fall into a million visions."[22] Virginia Woolf's picture of the university in *Jacob's Room* is much more ambiguous. On the one hand, she understands its magical spell, as in the passage that describes Cambridge as a city of light, "the light of all these languages, Chinese and Russian, Persian and Arabic, of symbols and figures, of history, of things that are known and things that are about to be known" (40). On the other, she constantly emphasizes the disparity between the university's high ideals and the pettiness and complacency of its distinguished scholars. Jacob's

21Virginia Woolf, *Moments of Being: Unpublished Auobiographical Writings*, ed. Jeanne Schulkind (Sussex: The University Press, 1976), p. 132.

22Lytton Strachey to Leonard Woolf, 17 September 1908, Berg Collection, New York Public Library.

Cambridge bears the stamp of pretension and provinciality: "It is not simple, or pure, or wholly splendid, the lamp of learning. . . . How like a suburb where you go to see a view and eat a special cake! 'We are the sole purveyors of this cake' " (38).

Her critical distance was a response to feeling shut out, a reaction she would examine at length in the first of her feminist books, *A Room of One's Own*. The Cambridge suburb admitted women only on sufferance, and it taught its male products to patronize them. So Jacob fails to understand why women are allowed to attend service at King's College Chapel: "No one would think of bringing a dog into church," he reflects, "a dog destroys the service completely. So do these women" (31). It is interesting that Woolf's first draft version of the novel included a chapter about a young woman student at Cambridge which in some ways parallels the Jacob portions of the narrative; the chapter was excised from the final version, however, probably to under-line the fact that the university was still a young man's world, despite the presence of a few female interlopers.[23]

From Woolf's point of view Jacob fits all too easily into this world. His rebellious gestures are relatively superficial, and the picture of him at Cambridge stresses his confident appropriation of his position: "He looked satisfied; indeed masterly; which expression changed slightly as he stood there, the sound of the clock conveying to him (it may be) a sense of old buildings and time; and himself the inheritor; and then to-morrow; and friends; at the thought of whom, in sheer confidence and pleasure, it seemed, he yawned and stretched himself" (43). His Cambridge training reinforces the sense of membership in an elite, and there is more than a hint of arrogance in his makeup. The attitude provokes Woolf's sarcasm, though the tone remains good-humored: "The flesh and blood of the future depends entirely upon six young men. And as Jacob was one of them, no doubt he looked a little regal and pompous as he turned his page" (106).

There are many indications that Jacob is far from extraordinary, despite his membership in this exclusive fraternity. The novel records the classic events in the life of a presentable young man. Jacob's thoughts and experiences are treated as typical rather than unique, and his individual identity is made to merge with that of a group. Woolf's descriptions of him at Cambridge, in London, and on the continent often seem to efface his defining characteristics and turn him into a representative figure, as in this passage:

> But Jacob moved. He murmured good-night. He went out into the court. He buttoned his jacket across his chest. He went back to his rooms, and being the only

[23]See chapter 10 of the *Jacob's Room* holograph (pt. I, 85–91), Berg Collection, New York Public Library. The chapter was later revised for publication as a short story, "A Woman's College from Outside," in *Atlanta's Garland: Being the Book of the Edinburgh University Women's Union 1926* (Edinburgh: Edinburgh Univ. Press, 1926, 11–16, and is reprinted in *BP*, 6–9. On Woolf's irreverent attitude toward Cambridge, see Irma Rantavaara, *Virginia Woolf and Bloomsbury* (Helsinki: Annales Academiae Fennicae, 1953), 102.

man who walked at that moment back to his rooms, his footsteps rang out, his
figure loomed large. Back from the Chapel, back from the Hall, back from the
Library, came the sound of his footsteps, as if the old stone echoed with magis-
terial authority: "The young man—the young man—the young man—back to his
rooms." (45)

They move in packs, these young men, and their most antisocial ideas are
quickly ratified by their fellows. For Jacob's friend Richard Bonamy, life is
"damnably difficult" because he feels the world neglects its gifted youth;
"but"—the narrator comments—"not so difficult if on the next staircase, in
the large room, there are two, three, five young men all convinced of this—of
brutality, that is, and the clear division between right and wrong" (42).

In such ways the unexamined idea of the promising young man is challenged by Woolf's vision of incipient conventionality. It is instructive to
contrast Jacob's rather banal and predictable effusions on Greece with Woolf's
own first vision of that country. His thoughts are not individualized but reflect
the familiar romantic Hellenism of his society and set: "He could live on bread
and wine—the wine in straw bottles—for after doing Greece he was going to
knock off Rome. The Roman civilization was a very inferior affair, no doubt.
But Bonamy talked a lot of rot, all the same. 'You ought to have been in
Athens,' he would say to Bonamy when he got back" (134). Contrast this with
a passage from a diary Woolf kept on her first trip to Greece in 1906, when
she was, like Jacob, in her mid-twenties. Her description of the Acropolis is
clearly the product of a keen observer who does not rely on potted history or
Baedeker's sense of the sublime:

> No place seems more lusty and alive than this platform of ancient dead stone. The
> fat Maidens who bear the weight of the Erectheum on their heads, stand smiling
> tranquil ease, for their border is just meet for their strength. They glory in it; one
> foot just advanced, their hands, one conceives, loosely curled at their sides. And
> the warm blue sky flows into all the crevices of the marble; yet they detach
> themselves, and spring into the air, with edges unblunted, and still virile and
> young. (Berg Diary, 14 Sept. [1906]–25 April 1909, 9)

A description like this, though it has a self-conscious air and is clearly an
attempt at fine writing, stands out as genuinely "promising" because it
suggests freshness of observation and expression. It shows us how far Jacob
still was from finding his own voice.

What would have happened to such young men had they been permitted
to live out their term? It is a question the novel constantly raises but can
never, of course, answer. Woolf's attempts at prediction are cut short by her
sense of their group fate, which makes her hastily withdraw the question:
"Behind the grey walls sat so many young men, some undoubtedly reading,
magazines, shilling shockers, no doubt; legs, perhaps, over the arms of chairs;
smoking; sprawling over tables, and writing while their heads went round in a
circle as the pen moved—simple young men, these, who would—but there is
no need to think of them grown old" (41). There are, however, a few passages

in the novel in which Woolf allows herself to imagine a future life for Jacob and some of his companions, and the picture is seldom radiant with hope. Respectability, responsibility, establishment success: that is the image in the crystal ball. As Jacob rails against women in youthful fervor, the narrator comments dryly in a parenthesis: "This violent disillusionment is generally to be expected in young men in the prime of life, sound of wind and limb, who will soon become fathers of families and directors of banks" (150). And after giving us a sense of his "desperate" infatuation with Sandra Wentworth Williams, Woolf notes that Jacob "had in him the seeds of extreme disillusionment, which would come to him from women in middle life" (158).

Such passages make it clear that *Jacob's Room* is a novel much more about a stage of life than about a particular person. The fate that lies ahead for her young man is extinction in the war. But the fate from which he is saved is not presented as much more attractive: middle age, in the novel, is a kind of slow death or betrayal of youthful promise. The book is filled with poignant images of the brevity of youth: "And for ever the beauty of young men seems to be set in smoke, however lustily they chase footballs, or drive cricket balls, dance, run, or stride along roads. possibly they are soon to lose it" (116). The very intensity of the experimental stage is too violent to be sustained, as Woolf suggests in a vivid metaphor: "Why, from the very windows, even in the dusk, you see a swelling run through the street, an aspiration, as with arms outstretched, eyes desiring, mouth agape. And then we peaceably subside. For if the exaltation lasted we should be blown like foam into the air" (119). And even those who do not agree to fit themselves into the comfortable niches society has prepared for them when the season of youth is over are not presented as heroic rebels. In one of her predictive passages, Woolf draws a bleak picture of what lies ahead for a young bohemian painter whose work so excites Jacob in Paris:

> And as for Cruttendon and Jinny, he thought them the most remarkable people he had ever met—being of course unable to foresee how it fell out in the course of time that Cruttendon took to painting orchards; had therefore to live in Kent; and must, one would think, see through apple blossom by this time, since his wife, for whose sake he did it, eloped with a novelist; but no; Cruttendon still paints orchards, savagely, in solitude. (130)

An elegy is a work of consolation as well as desolation. If anything in Jacob's early death can be thought of as consoling, it is the fact that he is spared the disillusionment that awaits him. Never to be defined means never to be bounded. Middle age in Woolf's work is regularly seen as a diminution. In *The Waves*, the novel in which she follows her characters through all their life stages from childhood to old age, one of them sums up the difference between youth and "maturity" in this bleak way: "Change is no longer possible. We are committed. Before, when we met in a restaurant in London with Percival, all simmered and shook; we could have been anything. We have chosen now, or sometimes it seems the choice was made for us—a pair of tongs pinched us between the shoulders."[24] Jacob's life does not reach the treadmill stage, and he seems fixed forever at the moment of infinite possibility, before the seeds of conventionality Woolf notices in him have sprouted. In her preliminary notes for the novel, there is this cryptic notation: "Intensity of life compared with immobility." [25] It is possible that her terms define the two life stages her book consistently contrasts: the experimental intensity of youth and the fixity of what follows. Jacob dies young, but he never dwindles into the banal life he sees ahead of him, that of "settling down in a lawyer's office, and wearing spats" (49).

Woolf's sharp sense of the brevity of life, of the inevitability of death, puts Jacob's "tragic" fate in longer perspective. To die young, to die later: the book seems to say that the distinction borders on the trivial. From the first page of her novel, we hear the note of mortality. Mrs. Flanders weeps for her husband, long since dead. Though Seabrook Flanders was no war victim, he too died young, before the world knew what to call him. And Woolf comments: "Had he, then, been nothing? An unanswerable question, since even if it weren't the habit of the undertaker to close the eyes, the light so soon goes out of them" (14). The book's focus on the present moment constantly blurs to give us a sense of time past and time future. For Julia Eliot, walking down Piccadilly, "the tumult of the present seems like an elegy for past youth and past summers, and there rose in her mind a curious sadness, as if time and eternity showed through skirts and waistcoats, and she saw people passing tragically to destruction" (168). This elegiac note is not connected exclusively to the carnage of the war but seems rather a response to the inescapable fact of mortality. It is, Woolf says, a sorrow "brewed by the earth itself. . . . We start transparent, and then the cloud thickens. All history backs our pane of glass. To escape is vain" (47). The sense of death broods over the novel, and Woolf's images constantly reinforce it: Jacob finding the sheep's skull on the beach; the momentary illumination of faces on Guy Fawkes night, before the fire is extinguished "and all the faces went out" (73); a mason's van passing "with newly lettered tombstones recording how some one loved some one who is buried at Putney" (111); Mrs. Jarvis walking through the cemetery or telling her friend, "I never pity the dead" (130).

This atemporal awareness of mortality Woolf carried with her always. She asks herself in her diary as she works on *Jacob's Room*, "Why is life so tragic; so like a little strip of pavement over an abyss. I look down; I feel giddy; I wonder how I am ever to walk to the end" (*D*, II, 72). Though she says later in the same entry that this tragic sense is pervasive "for us in our generation," her novel's repeated stretching of time and space suggests a fundamentally religious perception of the issue, though without a religious consolation. Her vision recalls the "Ithaca" chapter in *Ulysses*, in which Joyce's sense of cosmic

[24]Virginia Woolf, *The Waves* (1931; London: Hogarth, 1972), p. 151.

[25]Virginis Woolf, "Reflections upon beginning a work of fiction to be called, perhaps, Jacobs Room," *Jacob's Room* holograph, pt. I, 1, Berg Collection, New York Public Library.

time nearly obliterates his characters. He sees the "so-called fixed stars, in reality evermoving from immeasurably remote eons to infinitely remote futures in comparison with which the years, threescore and ten, of allotted human life formed a parenthesis of infinitesimal brevity."[26] Similarly, in *Jacob's Room*, one of the guests at the Durrants' evening party examines the constellations through the telescope only to find herself suddenly deserted by all her companions: " 'Where are you all?' she asked, taking her eye away from the telescope. 'How dark it is!' " (59).

This sense of the universal darkness surrounding us both elevates and trivializes Jacob's death. From the aspect of eternity individual death is meaningless, and even the annihilation of a million young men in battle is a fact that history will swallow without special effort. But, at the same time, the extinction of any life inevitably recalls the fate that awaits us all and is invested with that resonance. This is why the lament for Jacob becomes, for all the novel's irony, so moving: "Ja-cob! Ja-cob!" his brother calls in the novel's first scene, and the narrator comments: "The voice had an extraordinary sadness. pure from all body, pure from all passion, going out into the world, solitary, unanswered, breaking against rocks—so it sounded" (7). "Jacob! Jacob!" It is a refrain that will be heard again and again in the book, from Mrs. Flanders, from Clara Durrant, from Richard Bonamy, from all those fellow mortals who make the mistake of attaching their deepest feelings to someone who precedes them into the earth. For all Woolf's ironic distance and critical awareness of Jacob's limitations, she knows that such composure dissolves when our emotions are engaged. Her complex attitude is conveyed in an important reflective passage in the book:

> In any case life is but a procession of shadows, and God knows why it is that we embrace them so eagerly, and see them depart with such anguish, being shadows. And why, if this and much more than this is true, why are we yet surprised in the window corner by a sudden vision that the young man in the chair is of all things in the world the most real, the most solid, the best known to us—why indeed? For the moment after we know nothing about him.
>
> Such is the manner of our seeing. Such the conditions of our love. (70–71)

This double awareness of the sharpness of grief and its absurdity gives Woolf's satiric elegy its special edge and accounts for the novel's rapid shifts in tone. She worked hard to avoid sentimentalizing her subject and casting her book in the romantic mold. As Strachey writes her after reading *Jacob's Room*, romanticism is "*the* danger for your genre," and she agrees that he has put his "infallible finger upon the spot."[27] But Strachey was hardly the standard of feeling in such matters, as some of his own letters attest. When Thoby Stephen, Virginia's brother and Strachey's intimate friend, died of typhoid fever at the age of twenty-six, Strachey's letter to Leonard Woolf

---

[26]James Joyce, *Ulysses* (New York: Random House, 1946), 683.
[27]Virginia Woolf and Lytton Strachey, 103, 104.

exemplifies the uninhibited and unreflecting expression of grief Virginia Woolf came to distrust: "I don't understand what crowning pleasure there can be for us without him, and our lives seem deadly blank. There is nothing left remarkable beneath the visiting moon. It is idle to talk; but it is only to you that I can say anything, that he was the best, the noblest, the best—oh god! I am tired out with too much anguish. Oh god!"[28]

Such threnodies, Woolf came to feel, were finally self-serving and insincere, a rhetorical exercise in pulling out all the stops. The literary allusions, the exaggerated sense of Thoby's qualities, the indulgence of intense emotion would have struck her as more like a public performance than a private expression of loss. Her own very different style of lament deliberately understates or withholds such sentiment. In the book's last scene Bonamy can say no more than "Jacob! Jacob!" and Mrs. Flanders unpredictably focuses on a pair of her son's old shoes, as though their emptiness conveyed everything: "What am I to do with these, Mr. Bonamy?" (176). The significance of the scene is clarified by an anecdote about Woolf told by one of her friends: "The only other remark 1 remember from that afternoon was when she was talking about the mystery of 'missing' someone. When Leonard went away, she said, she didn't miss him *at all*. Then suddenly she caught sight of a pair of his empty shoes, which had kept the position and shape of his feet—and was ready to dissolve into tears instantly."[29]

"Such is the manner of our seeing. Such the conditions of our love." Jacob's death, like his life, has no intrinsic significance. He is not clearly "the best, the noblest, the best." Rather, he is an engaging young man, in many ways typical of his class and training, who has unintentionally managed to secure the love of a few human beings. His absence, like his presence, is not likely to alter the world significantly. His youthful promise might well have been betrayed, his eager ambition have turned into the ordinary life choices. Only on the small canvas appropriate to such a view, rather than on the grand frescoes of the heroic imagination, could Woolf allow herself to sketch—in a deliberately halting and fragmented style and a conspicuously impure tone— her vision of a permanently inscrutable young man.

The hesitation of her style and the impurity of her tone are manifestations of the impacted satiric impulse expressed in *Jacob's Room* and in many of Woolf's other works. It should be clear that this experimental novel is not merely a technical exercise but a book that raises issues to which she would return again and again: class identity, the conflict between the sexes, the cost of war. . . . Woolf brooded about these and related problems in all of her works. Her concern with them helped to direct her reading and is clearly expressed in her discursive prose. . . . [W]hat she writes is often a response

---

[28]Lytton Strachey to Leonard Woolf, 21 November 1906, Berg Collection, New York Public Library.

[29]Frances Marshall, in *Recollections of Virginia Woolf*, ed. Joan Russell Noble (London: Peter Owen, 1972), 76.

to the treatment of such issues in the culture of her time. But it is a mistake to think of that response as direct and straightforward: she was neither a social theorist nor a polemicist. Rather, her imagination absorbed and processed the discussion of "issues" until what emerged in her imaginative writing became a very different, often elusive product. . . .[T]he public discourse on social issues is indispensable to an understanding of some of Woolf's greatest works; but its terms and assumptions are only the raw material she used to shape structures that were finally very much her own.

Narrative Structure(s) and Female Development: The Case of *Mrs. Dalloway*

Elizabeth Abel

I wish you were a Kangaroo and had a pouch for small Kangaroos to creep to.

—Virginia Stephen to Violet Dickinson, June 4(?), 1903

Our insight into this early, pre-Oedipus, phase comes to us as a surprise, like the discovery, in another field, of the Minoan-Mycenean civilization behind the civilization of Greece.

—Sigmund Freud, "Female Sexuality" (1931)

We all know Virginia Woolf disliked the fixity of plot: "This appalling narrative business of the realist," she called it.[1] Yet like all writers of fiction, she inevitably invoked narrative patterns in her work, if only to disrupt them or reveal their insignificance. In *Mrs. Dalloway*, a transitional work between the straightforward narrative of an early novel like *The Voyage Out* and the experimental structure of a late work like *The Waves*, Woolf superimposes the outlines of multiple, familiar yet altered plots that dispel the constraints of a unitary plan, diffuse the chronological framework of the single day in June, and enable an iconoclastic plot to weave its course covertly through the narrative grid. In this palimpsestic layering of plots, *Mrs. Dalloway* conforms to Gilbert and Gubar's characterization of the typically female text as one which both inscribes and hides its subversive impulses.[2]

The story of female development in *Mrs. Dalloway*, a novel planned such

[1] *A Writer's Diary* (London: The Hogarth Press, 1953), November 28, 1928, p. 139.

[2] In *The Madwoman in the Attic: The Woman Writer and the Nineteenth-Century Literary Imagination* (New Haven: Yale University Press, 1979), Sandra M. Gilbert and Susan Gubar claim that "women from Jane Austen and Mary Shelley to Emily Brontë and Emily Dickinson produced literary works that are in some sense palimpsestic, works whose surface designs conceal or obscure deeper, less accessible (and less socially acceptable) levels of meaning. Thus these authors managed the difficult task of achieving true female literary authority by simultaneously conforming to and subverting patriarchal literary standards" (p. 73).

that "every scene would build up the idea of C[larissa]'s character,"³ is a clandestine story that remains almost untold, that resists direct narration and coherent narrative shape. Both intrinsically disjointed and textually dispersed and disguised, it is the novel's buried story. The fractured developmental plot reflects the encounter of gender with narrative form and adumbrates the psychoanalytic story of female development, a story Freud and Woolf devised concurrently and separately, and published simultaneously in 1925. The structure of Woolf's developmental story and its status in the novel illustrate distinctive features of female experience and female plots.

Woolf repeatedly acknowledged differences between male and female writing, detecting the influence of gender in fictional voice and plot. While insisting that the creative mind must be androgynous, incandescent, and unimpeded by personal grievance, she nevertheless affirmed that differences between male and female experience would naturally emerge in distinctive fictional shapes. She claims,

> No one will admit that he can possibly mistake a novel written by a man for a novel written by a woman. There is the obvious and enormous difference of experience in the first place. . . . And finally . . . there rises for consideration the very difficult question of the difference between the man's and the woman's view of what constitutes the importance of any subject. From this spring not only marked differences of plot and incident, but infinite differences in selection, method and style.⁴

The experience that shapes the female plot skews the woman novelist's relationship to narrative tradition; this oblique relationship may further mold the female text. In a remarkable passage in *A Room of One's Own*, Woolf describes one way in which the difference in experience can affect the logic of the female text:

> And since a novel has this correspondence to real life, its values are to some extent those of real life. But it is obvious that the values of women differ very often from the values which have been made by the other sex; naturally, this is so. Yet it is the masculine values that prevail. . . . And these values are inevitably transferred from life to fiction. This is an important book, the critic assumes, because it deals with war. This is an insignificant book because it deals with the feelings of women in a drawingroom. A scene in a battlefield is more important than a scene in a shop—everywhere and much more subtly the difference of value persists. The whole structure, therefore, of the early nineteenth-century novel was raised, if one was a woman, by a mind which was slightly pulled from the straight, and made to alter its clear vision in deference to external authority. . . . the writer was meeting

³June 18, 1923, entry in Woolf's holograph notebook dated variously from November 9, 1922, to August 2, 1923; cited by Charles G. Hoffmann, "From Short Story to Novel: The Manuscript Revisions of Virginia Woolf's *Mrs. Dalloway*," *Modern Fiction Studies*, 14, 2 (Summer 1968), 183.
⁴"Women Novelists," in *Women and Writing*, ed. Michèle Barrett (New York: Harcourt Brace Jovanovich, 1979), p. 71.

criticism. . . . She met that criticism as her temperament dictated, with docility and diffidence, or with anger and emphasis. It does not matter which it was; she was thinking of something other than the thing itself. . . . She had altered her values in deference to the opinions of others.[5]

Woolf explicitly parallels the dominance of male over female values in literature and life, while implying a different hierarchy that further complicates the woman novelist's task. By contrasting the "values of women" with those which "have been made by the other sex," Woolf suggests the primacy of female values as products of nature rather than culture, and of the named sex rather than the "other" one. No longer the conventionally "second" sex, women here appear the source of intrinsic and primary values. In the realm of culture, however, masculine values prevail and deflect the vision of the woman novelist, inserting a duality into the female narrative, turned Janus-like toward the responses of both self and other. This schizoid perspective can fracture the female text. The space between emphasis and undertone, a space that is apparent in Woolf's own text, may also be manifested in the gap between a plot that is shaped to confirm expectations and a subplot at odds with this accommodation. If the early nineteenth-century woman novelist betrayed her discomfort with male evaluation by overt protestation or compliance, the early twentieth-century woman novelist, more aware of this dilemma, may encode as a subtext the stories she wishes yet fears to tell.

Feminist literary criticism, Elaine Showalter states, presents us with "a radical alteration of our vision, a demand that we see meaning in what has previously been empty space. The orthodox plot recedes, and another plot, hitherto submerged in the anonymity of the background, stands out in bold relief like a thumbprint."[6] The excavation of buried plots in women's texts has revealed an enduring, if recessive, narrative concern with the story of mothers and daughters—with the "lost tradition," as the title of one anthology names it, or, in psychoanalytic terminology, with the "pre-Oedipal" relationship, the early symbiotic female bond that both predates and coexists with the heterosexual orientation toward the father and his substitutes. Frequently, the subtleties of mother-daughter alignments, for which few narrative conventions have been formulated, are relegated to the background of a dominant romantic or courtship plot. As women novelists increasingly exhaust or dismiss the possibilities of the romantic plot, however, they have tended to inscribe the maternal subplot more emphatically. In contemporary women's fiction, this subplot is often dominant; but in the fiction of the 1920s, a particularly fruitful decade for women and women's writing, the plot of female bonding began to vie repeatedly with the plot of heterosexual love. Woolf, Colette, and Cather highlighted aspects of the mother-daughter narrative in works such as *My Mother's House* (1922), *To the Lighthouse* (1927), *Break of Day* (1928), *Sido*

---

[5]*A Room of One's Own* (New York: Harcourt Brace Jovanovich, 1957), pp. 76–77.
[6]"Literary Criticism," *Signs*, I, 2 (Winter 1975), 435.

(1929), and "Old Mrs. Harris" (1932).[7] In *Mrs. Dalloway*, written two years before *To the Lighthouse*, Woolf structures her heroine's development, the recessive narrative of her novel, as a story of pre-Oedipal attachment and loss.

In his essay "Female Sexuality," Freud parallels the pre-Oedipal phase of female development to the allegedly matriarchal civilization lying behind that of classical Greece, presumably associated here with its most famous drama; his analogy offers a trope for the psychological and textual strata of *Mrs. Dalloway*.[8] For Freud conflates, through the spatial and temporal meanings of the word "behind" (*hinter*), notions of evolution with those of static position. Clarissa Dalloway's recollected development proceeds from an emotionally pre-Oedipal female-centered natural world to the heterosexual male-dominated social world, a movement, Woolf implies, that recapitulates the broader sweep of history from matriarchal to patriarchal orientation. But the textual locus of this development, to revert to the archaeological implications of Freud's image, is a buried *subtext* that endures throughout the domestic and romantic plots in the foreground: the metaphors of palimpsest and cultural strata coincide here. The interconnections of female development, historical progress, and narrative structure are captured in Freud's image of a pre-Oedipal world underlying the individual and cultural origins we conventionally assign the names Oedipus and Athens.

Woolf embeds her radical developmental plot in a narrative matrix pervaded by gentler acts of revision; defining the place of this recessive plot requires some awareness of the larger structure. The narrative present, patterned as the sequence of a day, both recalls the structure of *Ulysses*, which Woolf completed reading as she began *Mrs. Dalloway*, and offers a female counterpart to Joyce's adaptation of an epic form.[9] *Mrs. Dalloway*

7On women novelists' dissatisfaction with the plot of romantic love, see Nancy K. Miller, "Emphasis Added: Plots and Plausibilities in Women's Fiction," *PMLA*, 96, 1 (January 1981), 36–48, and Marianne Hirsch, "A Mother's Discourse: Incorporation and Repetition in *La Princesse de Clèves*," *Yale French Studies*, 62 (1981), 67–87. On the particular shift that took place in the early twentieth century, see Ellen Moers, *Literature Women* (Garden City: Doubleday, 1977), especially pp. 352–68; Jane Lilienfeld, "Reentering Paradise: Cather, Colette, Woolf and Their Mothers," in *The Lost Tradition: Mothers and Daughters in Literature*, ed. Cathy N. Davidson and E. M. Broner (New York: Frederick Ungar, 1980), pp. 160–75; and Louise Bernikow, *Among Women* (New York: Crown Publishers, 1980), pp. 155–93. In " 'Women Alone Stir My Imagination': Lesbianism and the Cultural Tradition," *Signs*, 4, 4 (Summer 1979), Blanche Wiesen Cook points out that "were all things equal, 1928 might be remembered as a banner year for lesbian publishing" (p. 718).

8In his essay "Femininity," published the following year, Freud explicitly uses the metaphor of strata: "A woman's identification with her mother allows us to distinguish two strata: the pre-Oedipus one which rests on her affectionate attachment to her mother and takes her as a model, and the later one from the Oedipus complex which seeks to get rid of her mother and take her place with her father." The essay is reprinted in *Women and Analysis*, ed. Jean Strouse (New York: Grossman Publishers, 1974), p. 92.

9Woolf's reaction to *Ulysses*, recorded in her journal entries in September and October 1922, suggests her interest in counteracting the perspective of this "callow school boy, full of wits and powers, but so self-conscious and egotistical that he loses his head" (*The Diary of Virginia Woolf*, vol. 2: 1920–1924, ed. Anne Olivier Bell [New York: Harcourt Brace Jovanovich, 1978]), inverts the hierarchy Woolf laments in *A Room of One's Own*. Her foregrounded domestic plot unfolds precisely in shops and drawing rooms rather than on battlefields, and substitutes for epic quest and conquest the traditionally feminine project of giving a party, of constructing social harmony through affiliation rather than conflict; the potentially epic plot of the soldier returned from war is demoted to the tragic subplot centering on Septimus Warren Smith. By echoing the structure of *Ulysses* in the narrative foreground of her text, Woolf revises a revision of the epic to accommodate the values and experience of women while cloaking the more subversive priorities explored in the covert developmental tale.

A romantic plot, which provides the dominant structure for the past in *Mrs. Dalloway*, also obscures the story of Clarissa's development. Here again, Woolf revises a traditional narrative pattern, the courtship plot perfected by Woolf's elected "foremother," Jane Austen. Woolf simultaneously invokes and dismisses Austen's narrative model through Clarissa's mistaken impression that her future husband is named Wickham. This slight, if self-conscious, clue to a precursor assumes greater import in the light of Woolf's lifelong admiration for Austen and Woolf's efforts to reconstruct this "most perfect artist among women" in her literary daughter's image; these efforts structure Woolf's essay on Austen, written shortly after *Mrs. Dalloway*.[10] Woolf's treatment of the romantic plot in *Mrs. Dalloway* reveals the temporal boundaries of Austen's narratives, which cover primarily the courtship period and inevitably culminate in happy marriages. Woolf condenses the expanded moment that constitutes an Austen novel and locates it in a remembered scene thirty years prior to the present of her narrative, decentering and unraveling Austen's plot. Marriage in *Mrs. Dalloway* provides impetus rather than closure to the courtship plot, dissolved into a retrospective oscillation between two alluring possibilities as Clarissa continues to replay the choice she made thirty years before. The courtship plot in this novel is both evoked through memories of the past and indefinitely suspended in the present, completed when the narrative begins and incomplete when the narrative ends, sustained as a narrative thread by Clarissa's enduring uncertainty. The novel provides no resolution to this internalized version of the plot; the final scene presents Clarissa through Peter Walsh's amorous eyes and allies Richard Dalloway with his daughter. The elongated courtship plot, the imperfectly resolved emotional triangle, becomes a screen for the developmental story

---

September 6, 1922, p. 199. For structural echoes of *Ulysses* in *Mrs. Dalloway*, see Margaret Church, "Joycean Structure in *Jacob's Room* and *Mrs. Dalloway*," *International Fiction Review*, 4, 2 (July 1977), 101–9.

[10]The essay on Jane Austen in *The Common Reader* (1925) incorporates a review Woolf wrote just after completing *Mrs. Dalloway*. Woolf had also reviewed works by and about Austen in 1920 and 1922. In *The Common Reader* essay, Woolf tacitly assigns herself the role of Austen's heir by speculating that the novels Austen would have written in middle age would have manifested Woolf's and Austen's concern with silence.

that unfolds in fragments of memory, unexplained interstices between events, and narrative asides and interludes.

When Woolf discovered how to enrich her characterization by digging "beautiful caves" into her characters' pasts,[11] her own geological image for the temporal strata of *Mrs. Dalloway,* she chose with precision the consciousness through which to reveal specific segments of the past. Although Clarissa vacillates emotionally between the allure of Peter and that of Richard, she remembers Peter's courtship only glancingly; the burden of that plot is carried by Peter, through whose memories Woolf relates the slow and tortured end of the relation with Clarissa. Clarissa's memories, by contrast, focus more exclusively on the general ambience of Bourton, her childhood home, and her love for Sally Seton. Significantly absent from these memories is Richard Dalloway, whose courtship of Clarissa is presented exclusively through Peter's painful recollections. Clarissa thinks of Richard only in the present, not at the peak of a romantic relationship. Through this narrative distribution, Woolf constructs two diversified poles structuring the flux of Clarissa's consciousness. Bourton is to Clarissa a pastoral female world spatially and temporally disjunct from marriage and the sociopolitical world of (Richard's) London. The fluid passage of consciousness between these poles conceals a radical schism.

Though the Bourton scenes Clarissa remembers span a period of several years, they are absorbed by a single emotional climate that creates a constant backdrop to the foregrounded day in June. Woolf excises all narrative connections between these contrasting extended moments. She provides no account of intervening events: Clarissa's marriage, childbirth, the move and adjustment to London. And she indicates the disjunction in Clarissa's experience by noting that the London hostess never returns to Bourton, which now significantly belongs to a male relative, and almost never sees Sally Seton, now the unfamiliar Lady Rosseter. Clarissa's life in London is devoid of intimate female bonds: she is excluded from lunch at Lady Bruton's and she vies with Miss Kilman for her own daughter's allegiance. Woolf structures Clarissa's development as a stark binary opposition between past and present, nature and culture, feminine and masculine dispensations—the split implicit in Woolf's later claim that "the values of women differ very often from the values which have been made by the other sex." Versions of this opposition reverberate throughout the novel in rhetorical and narrative juxtapositions. The developmental plot, which slides beneath the more familiar romantic plot through the gap between Peter's and Clarissa's memories, exists as two contrasting moments and the silence adjoining and dividing them.

Woolf endows these moments with symbolic resonance by a meticulous strategy of narrative exclusions that juxtaposes eras split by thirty years and omits Clarissa's childhood from the novel's temporal frame. There is no past in

---

[11]*The Diary of Virginia Woolf,* vol. 2: 1920–1924, ed. Anne Olivier Bell (New York: Harcourt Brace Jovanovich, 1978), August 30, 1923, p. 263.

Mrs. Dalloway anterior to Clarissa's adolescence at Bourton. Within this selective scheme, the earliest remembered scenes become homologous to a conventional narrative point of departure: the description of formative childhood years. The emotional tenor of these scenes, moreover, suggests their representation of deferred childhood desire. Clarissa's earliest narrated memories focus on Sally's arrival at Bourton, an arrival that infuses the formal, repressive atmosphere with a vibrant female energy. The only picture of Clarissa's early childhood sketched in the novel suggests a tableau of female loss: a dead mother, a dead sister, a distant father, and a stern maiden aunt, the father's sister, whose hobby of pressing flowers beneath Littré's dictionary suggests to Peter Walsh the social oppression of women, an emblem of nature ossified by language/culture. In this barren atmosphere, Sally's uninhibited warmth and sensuality immediately spark love in the eighteen-year-old Clarissa.[12] Sally replaces Clarissa's dead mother and sister, her name even echoing the sister's name, Sylvia. She nurtures Clarissa's passions and intellect, inspiring a love equal to Othello's in intensity and equivalent in absoluteness to a daughter's earliest bond with her mother, a bond too early ruptured for Clarissa as for Woolf, a bond which Woolf herself perpetually sought to recreate through intimate attachments to mother surrogates, such as Violet Dickinson: "I wish you were a Kangaroo and had a pouch for small Kangaroos to creep to."[13] For Clarissa, kissing Sally creates the most exquisite moment of her life, a moment of unparalleled radiance and intensity: "The whole world might have turned upside down! The others disappeared; there she was alone with Sally. And she felt she had been given a present, wrapped up, and told just to keep it, not to look at it—a diamond, something infinitely precious, wrapped up, which, as they walked (up and down, up and down), she uncovered, or the radiance burnt through, the revelation, the religious

---

[12]In "*Mrs. Dalloway*: The Communion of Saints," *New Feminist Essays on Virginia Woolf*, ed. Jane Marcus (London: Macmillan; Lincoln: University of Nebraska Press, 1981), p. 136, Suzette A. Henke points out that in the manuscript version of the novel Sally Seton clearly reciprocates Clarissa's love. Until recently, Sally has been remarkably absent from critical commentary on *Mrs. Dalloway*. Recent discussions include Judith McDaniel, "Lesbians and Literature," *Sinister Wisdom*, 1, 2 (Fall 1976), 20–23; Emily Jensen, "Clarissa Dalloway's Respectable Suicide," in *New Feminist Essays on Virginia Woolf*, ed. Jane Marcus. I am indebted to Tina Petrig, whose illuminating essay on female relationships in Woolf entitled "—all sorts of flowers that had never been seen together before—," first alerted me to the crucial role of Clarissa's relationship with Sally.

[13]For the power and endurance of Woolf's relationships with women, see her letters, especially those to Violet Dickinson in *The Letters of Virginia Woolf*, ed. Nigel Nicolson and Joanne Trautmann, vol. 1 (New York: Harcourt Brace Jovanovich, 1975); Jane Marcus "Thinking Back Through Our Mothers," and Ellen Hawkes, "Woolf's Magical Garden of Women," in *New Feminist Essays on Virginia Woolf*; Phyllis Rose, *Women of Letters: A Life of Virginia Woolf* (New York: Oxford University Press, 1978), pp. 109–24; and Jane Marcus, "Virginia Woolf and Her Violin: Mothering, Madness and Music" (unpublished). Although the relationship of Woolf's life to her fiction is much more pronounced in *To the Lighthouse*, there are quiet parallels between Woolf's biography and Clarissa's; the death of Clarissa's mother and sister cast Sally in the emotional role assumed by Vanessa Stephen, the primary nurturing figure throughout Woolf's life.

feeling!—when old Joseph and Peter faced them."[14] This kind of passionate attachment between women, orthodox psychoanalysts and feminists uncharacteristically agree, recaptures some aspect of the fractured mother-daughter bond.[15] Within the sequence established by the novel, this adolescent love assumes the power of the early female bond excluded from the narrative.

The moment Woolf selects to represent Clarissa's past carries the full weight of the pre-Oedipal experience that Freud discovered with such a shock substantially predates and shapes the female version of the Oedipus complex, the traumatic turn from mother to father. As French psychoanalytic theory has clarified, the Oedipus complex is less a biologically ordained event than a symbolic moment of acculturation, the moment, in Freud's words, that "may be regarded as a victory of the race over the individual," that "initiates all the processes that are designed to make the individual find a place in the cultural community."[16] For both women and men, this socialization exacts renunciation, but for women this is a process of poorly compensated loss, for the boy's rewards for renouncing his mother will include a woman like the mother and full paternal privileges, while the girl's renunciation of her mother will at best be requited with a future child, but no renewed access to the lost maternal body, the first love object for girls as well as boys, and no acquisition of paternal power. In *Mrs. Dalloway*, Woolf encapsulates an image of the brusque and painful turn that, whenever it occurs, abruptly terminates the earliest stage of female development and defines the moment of acculturation as a moment of obstruction.

Woolf organizes the developmental plot such that Clarissa's love for Sally precedes her allegiances to men; the two women "spoke of marriage always as a catastrophe" (p. 50). Clarissa perceives Peter in this period primarily as an irritating intruder. The scene that Clarissa most vividly remembers, the scene of Sally Seton's kiss, is rudely interrupted by Peter's appearance.[17] Both the action and the language of this scene hint at psychological allegory. The moment of exclusive female connection is shattered by masculine intervention, a rupture signaled typographically by Woolf's characteristic dash. Claris-

---

[14]*Mrs. Dalloway* (New York: Harcourt, Brace & World, 1927), pp. 52–53. This passage suggests an analogy between the wrapped-up present of Sally's love and the buried subplot of female bonds. All future references to *Mrs. Dalloway* will be placed in parentheses in the text.

[15]See, for example, Sigmund Freud, "Femininity," in *Women and Analysis*, ed. Jean Strouse, p. 89; Helene Deutsch, "Female Homosexuality," in *The Psycho-Analytic Reader: An Anthology of Essential Papers with Critical Introductions*, ed. Robert Fliess (New York: International Universities Press, 1948), pp. 208–30; Adrienne Rich, *Of Woman Born: Motherhood as Experience and Institution* (New York: W. W. Norton, 1976); Catharine Stimpson "Zero Degree Deviancy: The Lesbian Novel in English," *Critical Inquiry* 8 (1981), 363–379.

[16]"Some Psychical Consequences of the Anatomical Distinction Between the Sexes," in Strouse, *Women and Analysis*, p. 24; "Female Sexuality," in Strouse, p. 42.

[17]For an analysis of this scene as part of a pattern of interruption in *Mrs. Dalloway*, see Emily Jensen, "Clarissa Dalloway's Respectable Suicide," in *New Feminist Essays on Virginia Woolf*, ed. Jane Marcus. Jensen's point of view is similar to mine, though she does not adopt a psychoanalytic approach, and sees Clarissa's development in more purely negative terms than I.

sa's response to this intrusion images an absolute and arbitrary termination: "It was like running one's face against a granite wall in the darkness! It was shocking; it was horrible!" (p. 53). Clarissa's perception of Peter's motives— "she felt his hostility; his jealousy; his determination to break into their comradeship"—suggests an Oedipal configuration: the jealous male attempting to rupture the exclusive female bond, insisting on the transference of attachment to the man, demanding heterosexuality. For women this configuration institutes a break as decisive and unyielding as a granite wall. Clarissa's revenge is to refuse to marry Peter and to select instead the less demanding Richard Dalloway in order to guard a portion of her psyche for the memory of Sally. Woolf herself exacts poetic justice by subjecting Peter Walsh to a transposed, inverted replay of this crucial scene when Elizabeth, thirty years later, interrupts his emotional reunion with her mother by unexpectedly opening a door (in the granite wall?), asserting by her presence the primacy of female bonds. "Here is my Elizabeth" (p. 71), Clarissa announces to the disconcerted Peter, the possessive pronoun he finds so extraneous accentuating the intimacy of the mother-daughter tie.

Clarissa resists the wrenching, requisite shift from pre-Oedipal to Oedipal orientation, yet she submits in practice if not totally in feeling. The extent of the disjunction she undergoes is only apparent in the bifurcated settings of her history, the images reiterating radical divides, the gaps slyly inserted in the narrative. The most striking of these images and gaps concern Clarissa's sister Sylvia, a shadowy and seemingly gratuitous character, apparently created just to be destroyed. Her death, her only action in the novel, is recalled by Peter rather than by Clarissa and is related in two sentences. This offhand presentation both implants and conceals an exaggerated echo of Clarissa's split experience. A young woman "on the verge of life" (p. 118), Sylvia is abruptly killed by a falling tree that dramatically imposes a barrier to life in a gesture of destruction mysteriously associated with her father: "(all Justin Parry's fault— all his carelessness)" (pp. 118–19). The shocking attribution of blame is only ostensibly discounted by parentheses: recall Woolf's parenthetical accounts of human tragedy in the "Time Passes" section of *To the Lighthouse*. The deliberate decision to indict the father contrasts with the earlier story, "Mrs. Dalloway in Bond Street," where Sylvia's death is depicted as a tranquil, vague event absorbed by nature's cyclical benevolence: "It used, thought Clarissa, to be so simple. . . . When Sylvia died, hundreds of years ago, the yew hedges looked so lovely with the diamond webs in the mist before early church."[18] The violence of Sylvia's death in the novel and the very incongruity between the magnitude of the charge against her father and its parenthetical presentation suggest a story intentionally withheld, forcibly deprived of its legitimate proportions, deliberately excised from the narrative yet provoca-

---

[18]"Mrs. Dalloway in Bond Street," in *Mrs. Dalloway's Party*, ed. Stella McNichol (New York: Harcourt Brace Jovanovich, 1975), p. 27.

tively implied in it, written both into and out of the text. This self-consciously inscribed narrative gap echoes the gap in Clarissa's own narrative, as the dramatic severance of Sylvia's life at the moment of maturity echoes the split in her sister's development. The pastoral resonance of Sylvia's name also implies a larger female story of natural existence abruptly curtailed.[19] A related narrative exclusion suggests a crucial untold tale about Clarissa's relation to her mother, remarkably unremembered and unmentioned in the novel except by a casual party guest whose brief comparison of Clarissa to her mother brings sudden tears to Clarissa's eyes. The story of the pain entailed in this loss is signaled by but placed outside the narrative in the double gesture of inclusion and exclusion that structures Woolf's narration of her heroine's development. By locating the clues to this discontinuous narrative in the marginal moments of her text, Woolf creates an inconspicuous subtext perceptible only to an altered vision.

Woolf's discrete suggestion of an intermittent plot is politically astute and aesthetically adept. Her insight into the trauma of female development does subvert the notion of organic, even growth culminating for women in marriage and motherhood, and she prudently conceals her implications of a violent adaptation. The narrative gaps also challenge the conventions of linear plot and suggest its distorted regimentation of experience, particularly the subjective experience of women. These gaps, moreover, are mimetically precise: juxtapositions represent sudden shifts, silence indicates absence and loss. Perhaps Woolf's most striking achievement, however, is her intuition of the "plot" Freud detected in female development. Despite Woolf's obvious familiarity with the popularized aspects of Freudian theory, and despite the close association of the Hogarth press with the Freudian oeuvre, there can be no question of influence here, for Freud first expounded his view of a distinctively female development the year of *Mrs Dalloway's* publication.[20] Rather than influence, *Mrs. Dalloway* demonstrates the common literary prefiguration of psychoanalytic doctrine, which can retroactively articulate patterns implicit in the literary text. The similarities between these fictional and psychoanalytic narratives clarify the structure of Woolf's submerged developmental plot and the power of Freud's submerged demonstration of the loss implicit in female development.

Only late in life did Freud acknowledge the fundamentally different courses of male and female development. Prior to the 1925 essay entitled

[19]Elizabeth Janeway suggests the resonance of this name in an essay entitled "Who Is Sylvia? On the Loss of Sexual Paradigms," *Signs* 5, 4 (Summer 1980), 573–89. She concludes the essay by asking, "Who is Sylvia, whose name carries an edge of wilderness and a hint of unexplored memory? We do not know, but we will surely recognize her when she comes."

[20]The Hogarth Press began publication of Freud's *Collected Papers* in 1924; the first volume of the *Standard Edition*, translated by James Strachey and published in its entirety by Hogarth Press, did not appear until 1948. Woolf's review entitled "Freudian Fiction," in *Times Literary Supplement*, March 25, 1920, reveals that she was familiar with the essentials of Freudian theory, though opposed to a simplistic application of the theory in fiction.

"Some Psychical Consequences of the Anatomical Distinction Between the Sexes," Freud clung, though with increasing reservations, to a view of sexual symmetry in which male and female versions of the Oedipal experience were fundamentally parallel. His growing appreciation of the pre-Oedipal stage in girls, however, finally toppled his view of parallel male and female tracks, inspiring a new formulation of the distinctively female developmental tasks. Female identity is acquired, according to this new theory, by a series of costly repressions from which the male child is exempt. The girl's developmental path is more arduous and bumpy than the boy's smoother linear route. For though the male child must repress his erotic attachment to his mother, he must undergo no change in orientation, since the mother will eventually be replaced by other women with whom he will achieve the status of the father; he suffers an arrest rather than a dislocation. The girl, in contrast, must reverse her course. Like the boy, she begins life erotically bonded with her mother in the symbiotic pre-Oedipal stage, but unlike him she must replace this orientation with a heterosexual attraction to her father. She must change the nature of her desire before renouncing it.

How, Freud repeatedly asks, does the girl accomplish this monumental shift from mother to father? Though the answers he proposes may be dubious, the persistent question indicates the magnitude of the event. The girl's entire sexuality is defined in this transition. She switches not only the object of her erotic interest, but also her erotic zone and mode, relinquishing the active, "masculine," clitoridal sexuality focused on her mother for the passive, receptive, "feminine," vaginal sexuality focused on her father. Freud goes so far as to call this change a "change in her own sex," for prior to this crucial shift, the little girl is a little man."[21] This comprehensive change in sexual object, organ, and attitude, the shift from pre-Oedipal to Oedipal orientation, inserts a profound discontinuity into female development, which contrasts with that of "the more fortunate man [who] has only to continue at the time of his sexual maturity the activity that he has previously carried out at the period of the early efflorescence of his sexuality."[22] The psychosexual shift that occurs in early childhood, moreover, is often reenacted in early adulthood, for marriage typically reinstates a disruption in women's experience, confined until recently to a largely female sphere prior to the heterosexual contract of marriage.[23]

The circuitous route to female identity, Freud acknowledged, is uniquely

---

[21]"Female Sexuality," in Strouse, *Women and Analysis*, p. 42; "Femininity," in Strouse, p. 78.
[22]"Femininity," p. 78.
[23]For an analysis of this female sphere, see Carroll Smith-Rosenberg, "The Female World of Love and Ritual: Relations between Women in Nineteenth-Century America," *Signs*, 1, 1 (Autumn 1975), 1–30. In *The Reproduction of Mothering: Psychoanalysis and the Sociology of Gender* (Berkeley: University of California Press, 1978), Nancy Chodorow argues that the pre-Oedipal orientation is not terminated by the Oedipus complex, but continues as a powerful influence throughout a woman's life, triggering repeated conflicts between allegiances to women and men.

demanding and debilitating: "a comparison with what happens with boys tells us that the development of a little girl into a normal woman is more difficult and more complicated, since it includes two extra tasks [the change of sexual object and organ], to which there is nothing corresponding in the development of a man."[24] No woman completes this difficult process unscathed. Freud outlines three developmental paths for women; all exact a substantial toll. If she follows the first, the girl negotiates the shift from mother to father by accepting the unwelcome "fact" of her castration, detected in comparisons between herself and little boys. Mortified by this discovery of inferiority, aware she can no longer compete for her mother with her better endowed brother, she renounces her active sexual orientation toward her mother, deprived like herself of the valued sexual organ, and accepts a passive orientation toward the superior father. Unfortunately, the girl's renunciation of active sexuality normally entails repressing "a good part of her sexual trends in general," and this route leads to sexual inhibition or neurosis, to "a general revulsion from sexuality."[25] If she chooses the second path, the girl simply refuses this renunciation, clings to her "threatened masculinity," struggles to preserve her active orientation toward her mother, and develops what Freud calls a "masculinity complex," which often finds expression in homosexuality.[26] Only the third "very circuitous" path leads to the "normal female attitude" in which the girl takes her father as the object of her passive eroticism and enters the female Oedipus complex. Curiously, however, Freud never describes this route, which turns out to be only a less damaging version of the first path toward inhibition and neurosis.[27] To the extent that her sexuality survives her "catastrophic" repression of her "masculine" desire for her mother, the girl will be able to complete her turn to her father and seal her femininity by desiring his baby. "Normal" femininity is thus a fragile, tenuous proposition; no unique course is prescribed for its achievement. Freud's most optimistic prognosis assumes a doubly hypothetical, negative form: "If too much is not lost in the course of it [development] through repression, this femininity may turn out to be normal."[28] The achievement of this femininity, moreover, is only the first stage, for the female Oedipus complex, like the male, must itself be overcome, and the hard-won desire for the father renounced and transferred to other men. Female development thus entails a double disappointment in contrast with the single renunciation required of men. No wonder Freud concludes the last of his essays on femininity by contrasting the youthful flexibility of a thirty-year-old male with the psychical rigidity of a woman the same age: "Her libido has taken up final positions and

---

[24]"Femininity," p. 77.
[25]"Femininity," p. 85; "Female Sexuality," p. 43.
[26]"Female Sexuality," p. 43.
[27]This significant fact is also noted by Elizabeth Janeway, "On 'Female Sexuality'," in Strouse, p. 60, and Sarah Kofman, "The Narcissistic Woman: Freud and Girard," *Diacritics*, 10, 3 (Fall 1980), 45.

seems incapable of exchanging them for others. There are no paths open to further development; it is as though the whole process had already run its course and remains thenceforward insusceptible to influence—as though, indeed, the difficult development to femininity had exhausted the possibilities of the person concerned."[29]

In *Mrs. Dalloway*, Woolf suggests the developmental turn that Freud accentuates in his studies of femininity. The narratives they sketch share a radically foreshortened notion of development, condensed for Freud into a few childhood years, focused for Woolf in a single emotional shift. Both narratives eschew the developmental scope traditionally assumed by fiction and psychology, committed to detailing the unfolding of a life, and both stress the discontinuities specific to female development. Woolf, moreover, portrays the sexual and emotional calcification that Freud suggests is the toll of "normal" development. Clarissa is explicit about her unimpassioned response to men, a response she perceives as a failure and a lack, a guarding of virginity through motherhood and marriage. Her emotional and physical self-containment is represented by her narrow attic bed, where she reads Baron Marbot's memoirs of the retreat from Moscow, a victory achieved by icy withdrawal.[30] The association of her bed with a grave—"Narrower and narrower would her bed be" (pp. 45–46)—links her adult sexuality with death. Yet, in a passage of extraordinary erotic writing, Woolf contrasts the description of the narrow bed with Clarissa's passionate responses to women, implying through this juxtaposition the cost of the pivotal developmental choice:

> Yet she could not resist sometimes yielding to the charm of a woman, not a girl, of a woman confessing, as to her they often did, some scrape, some folly. . . she did undoubtedly then feel what men felt. Only for a moment; but it was enough. It was a sudden revelation, a tinge like a blush which one tried to check and then, as it spread, one yielded to its expansion, and rushed to the farthest verge and there quivered and felt the world come closer, swollen with some astonishing significance, some pressure of rapture, which split its thin skin and gushed and poured with an extraordinary alleviation over the cracks and sores! Then, for that moment, she had seen an illumination; a match burning in a crocus; an inner meaning almost expressed. But the close withdrew; the hard softened. It was over—the moment. Against such moments (with women too) there contrasted (as she laid her hat down) the bed and Baron Marbot and the candle half-burnt. [pp. 46–47]

Woolf's language renders a passion that is actively directed toward women, and implicitly "masculine" in attitude and character, yet also receptive and "feminine," epitomized in the image of the match in the crocus, an emblem of active female desire that conflates Freud's sexual dichotomies. The power of

---

[28]"Femininity," p. 87.
[29]"Femininity," p. 92.
[30]Phyllis Rose makes this point about Baron Marbot's *Memoirs* in *Woman of Letters: A Life of Virginia Woolf*, p. 144.

the passage derives in part from the intermeshed male and female imagery, and the interwoven languages of sex and mysticism, a mélange that recurs in Clarissa's memory of Sally Seton's kiss. Fusion—of male and female, active and passive, sacred and profane—is at the heart of this erotic experience. Freud's opposition of active, "masculine," pre-Oedipal sexuality to the passive, "feminine," Oedipal norm denies the basis for this integration. Clarissa's momentary illumination is enabled only by the sexual orientation Freud devalues as (initially) immature and (subsequently) deviant. Woolf's passage suggests the potential completeness Freud denies the pre-Oedipal realm and calls into question the differentiation of normal from aberrant sexuality. The stark contrast between the passionate moment and the narrow bed, another juxtaposition that conceals a schism between two radically different sexual worlds, subverts the opposition normal/abnormal. Woolf here elevates Freud's second developmental path over the costly route toward "normal femininity," as she valorizes a spontaneous homosexual love over the inhibitions of imposed heterosexuality.

As the passage continues, the gap between the sexual options emblematized by the moment and the bed evolves into the familiar split between Sally Seton and Richard Dalloway, the split that structures the developmental plot. The allegorical image of the bed leads to a more concrete description of Clarissa's reaction to her husband's return: "if she raised her head she could just hear the click of the handle released as gently as possible by Richard, who slipped upstairs in his socks and then, as often as not, dropped his hot-water bottle and swore! How she laughed!" (p. 47). The contrast between the passionate moment with women and the narrow marital bed becomes a leap from the sublime to the (affectionately) ridiculous. Opening with the conjunction "But," the next paragraph signals a turn away from mundanity back to "this question of love . . . this falling in love with women" (p. 48), inaugurating Clarissa's lengthy and lyrical reminiscence of Sally Seton. The opposition between Clarissa's relationships with men and women modulates to the split between her present and her past, her orientation and emotional capacities on both sides of the Oedipal divide. Woolf, like Freud, reveals the cost of female development, but she inscribes a far more graphic image of the loss entailed, questions its necessity, and indicates the price of equating female development with acculturation through the rites of passage established by the Oedipus complex.

These are radical claims, and Woolf suggests them indirectly. In addition to her use of juxtaposition as a narrative and rhetorical strategy, Woolf encodes her developmental plot through characters who subtly reflect Clarissa's experience.[31] Perhaps most interesting of these is the infrequently noticed Rezia Warren Smith, wife of Clarissa's acknowledged double who has drawn critical

---

[31]Catharine R. Stimpson implies a parallel between the coding of "aberrant" sexuality in the works of Gertrude Stein and Woolf. See "The Mind, the Body, and Gertrude Stein," *Critical Inquiry*, 3, 3 (Spring 1977), 505.

attention away from the mirroring function of his wife. Rezia's life, like her name, is abbreviated in the novel, yet the course of her "development" suggestively echoes that of the heroine. Like Clarissa, Rezia finds herself plucked by marriage from an Edenic female world with which she preserves no contact. Her memories highlight the exclusively female community of sisters collaboratively making hats in an Italian setting that is pastoral despite the surrounding urban context: "For you should see the Milan gardens!" she later exclaims, when confronted with London's "few ugly flowers stuck in pots!" (p. 34). The cultural shift from Italy to England, like the shift from Bourton to London, locates this idyllic female life in a distant, prelapsarian era—before the war, before industrialization, before marriage. Marriage and war explicitly coalesce for Rezia as agents of expulsion from this female paradise: Septimus comes to Milan as a British soldier and proposes to Rezia to alleviate his war-induced emotional anesthesia. Rezia's memories of Italy, a radiant temporal backdrop to her painful alienation in marriage and a foreign culture, provide a pointed parallel to Clarissa's memories of Bourton. And Rezia's final pastoral vision, inspired by the drug administered after Septimus's suicide, significantly begins with her sense of "opening long windows, stepping out into some garden" (p. 227), thus echoing Clarissa's first recollection of Bourton, where she had "burst open the French windows and plunged . . . into the open air" (p. 3). The death of her husband releases Rezia to return imaginatively to a past she implicitly shares with Clarissa: the female-centered world anterior to heterosexual bonds. After this moment of imaginative release and return, Rezia disappears from the novel, having accomplished the function of delicately echoing the bifurcated structure of the heroine's development.

The relation of Clarissa and Rezia exists only for the reader; the two women know nothing of each other.[32] Woolf employs a different strategy for connecting Clarissa with Septimus, whose death severs the link between these female characters, releasing each to a new developmental stage, Rezia to return imaginatively to the past, Clarissa at last to transcend that past. Septimus's suicide enables Clarissa to resolve the developmental impasse that appears to be one cause of her weakened heart, her constricted vitality. Critics have amply explored Septimus's role as Clarissa's double. As important as this psychological doubling, however, is Woolf's revision of developmental plots, her decision to transfer to Septimus the death she originally imagined for

---

[32]Another parallel between these women is established through the Shakespearean allusions. The recurrent lines from *Cymbeline* associate Clarissa with Imogen; Rezia's name (Lucrezia) recalls Shakespeare's narrative poem, *The Rape of Lucrece*. The situations in these works are remarkably similar: in both, men dispute one another's claims to possess the most chaste and beautiful of women, the dispute prompts one man to observe and/or test the virtue of the other's wife, and this encounter culminates in the real or pretended rape of the woman and eventually her actual or illusory death. The analogy between these Shakespearean heroines more closely allies Clarissa with Lucrezia in a realm external to but signaled by Woolf's text.

Clarissa,[33] to sacrifice male to female development, to preserve her heroine from fictional tradition by substituting a hero for a heroine in the plot of violently thwarted development, a plot that has claimed such heroines as Catharine Linton, Maggie Tulliver, Emma Bovary, Anna Karenina, Tess Durbeyfield, Edna Pontellier, Lily Bart, and Antoinette Cosway Rochester. By making Septimus the hero of a sacrificial plot that enables the heroine's development, Woolf reverses narrative tradition.

It is a critical commonplace that Clarissa receives from Septimus a cathartic, vicarious experience of death that releases her to experience life's pleasures more deeply. Woolf's terms, however, are more precise. The passage describing Clarissa's reaction to Septimus's suicide suggests that he plays a specific role in Clarissa's emotional development. Woolf composes this passage as a subtle but extended parallel to Clarissa's earlier reminiscence of her love for Sally and Bourton.[34] The interplay between the language and structure of these two meditative interludes, the two major sites of the developmental plot, encodes Clarissa's exploration of a conflict more suppressed than resolved. By interpreting Septimus's suicide in her private language of passion and integrity, Clarissa uses the shock of death to probe her unresolved relation to her past. The suicide triggers Clarissa's recurrent preoccupation with this past, providing a perspective that enables her belatedly both to admit and to renounce its hold. On the day in June that encloses the action of *Mrs. Dalloway,* Clarissa completes the developmental turn initiated thirty years before.

Woolf prepares the parallels between the two passages by inaugurating both with Clarissa's withdrawal from her customary social milieu. The emotions prompting Clarissa's first meditation on Sally and the past are initially triggered by her exclusion from Lady Bruton's lunch. Woolf then describes Clarissa's noontime retreat to her solitary attic room as a metaphorical departure from a party: "She began to go slowly upstairs . . . as if she had left a party . . . had shut the door and gone out and stood alone, a single figure against the appalling night"; Clarissa is "like a nun withdrawing" (p. 45). Later that night, when Clarissa hears the news of Septimus's suicide, she does leave her party and retreats to an empty little room where "the party's splendor fell to the floor" (pp. 279–80). The first passage concludes with her preparations for the party, the second with her deliberate return to that party. Within these enclosed narrative and domestic spaces, Clarissa relives through memory the passionate scene with Sally on the terrace at Bourton. The second passage replays in its bifurcated structure the male intervention that curtails the

---

[33]In her "Introduction" to the Modern Library edition of *Mrs. Dalloway* (1928), Woolf explains that "in the first version Septimus, who later is intended to be her double, had no existence. . . . Mrs. Dalloway was originally to kill herself or perhaps merely to die at the end of the party" (p. vi).

[34]Emily Jensen also discusses the relationship between these passages in "Clarissa Dalloway's Respectable Suicide," *New Feminist Essays.*

original scene. In this final version of the female/male juxtaposition, however, the emotional valences are reversed.

Clarissa's meditation on Septimus's death modulates, through her association of passion with death, to a meditation on her relation to her past. Woolf orchestrates the verbal echoes of this passage to evoke with increasing clarity the scene with Sally Seton. Septimus's choice of a violent, early death elicits in Clarissa the notion of a central self preserved: "A thing there was that mattered; a thing, wreathed about with chatter, defaced, obscured in her own life. . . . This he had preserved" (p. 280). The visual image of a vital, central "thing" initiates the link with the earlier description of passion as "something central which permeated" (p. 46). The echoes between these passages develop through their similar representations of passion's ebb: "closeness drew apart; rapture faded, one was alone" (p. 281); "But the close withdrew; the hard softened. It was over—the moment" (p. 47). As Clarissa implies that only death preserves the fading moment of passion, she prepares for her repetition of the *Othello* line that has signified her love for Sally Seton: "If it were now to die, 'twere now to be most happy" (pp. 51, 281). The metaphor of treasure which precedes this explicit allusion to the scene with Sally further connects Clarissa's response to Septimus ("had he plunged holding his treasure?" she wonders) with her memory of Sally's kiss as "a present . . . a diamond, something infinitely precious" (pp. 52–53). Septimus's death evokes in Clarissa the knowledge of what death saves and what she has lost; her grief is not for Septimus, but for herself. Woolf weaves the verbal web between the two passages to summon once again the crucial scene with Sally on the terrace at Bourton, to enable Clarissa to confront her loss. Clarissa's appreciation of this loss, at last fully present to her consciousness, crystallizes in the contrast that concludes this segment of the passage: "She had schemed; she had pilfered. She was never wholly admirable. . . . And once she had walked on the terrace at Bourton" (p. 282).

With this naming of the original scene, Woolf abruptly terminates Clarissa's recollection, replaying with a brilliant stroke Peter Walsh's interruption, the sudden imposition of the granite wall. The masculine intervention this time, though, is enacted not by Peter but by Richard, and not as external imposition but as choice. Clarissa's unexpected thought of Richard abruptly and definitively terminates the memory of Sally, pivoting the scene from past to present, the mood from grief to joy: "It was due to Richard; she had never been so happy" (p. 282). The dramatic and unexplained juxtaposition encapsulates the developmental plot and the dynamics of its central scenes. This final replay of the developmental turn, and final microcosm of Woolf's narrative method, however, represent the abrupt transition positively. The joy inspired by Clarissa's thought of Richard persists as she celebrates "this having done with the triumphs of youth" (p. 282). Woolf does not fill in the gap splitting past from present, grief from joy. We can only speculate that Septimus's sacrificial gift includes a demonstration of Clarissa's alternatives: to preserve the intensity of passion through death, or to accept the changing offerings of life. By recalling to Clarissa the power of her past *and* the only method of eternalizing it, he enables her fully to acknowledge and renounce its hold, to embrace the imperfect pleasures of adulthood more completely. Through Septimus, Woolf recasts the developmental impasse in the general terms of progression or death. In the final act of the developmental plot, she qualifies her challenge to the notion of linear, forward growth.

Woolf signals the shift in Clarissa's orientation by concluding the interlude with Clarissa's reaction to the old lady across the way, an unnamed character who only functions in the novel as an object of Clarissa's awareness. The earlier meditative passage concludes with Clarissa's reflection in the looking glass; this one with an analogous reflection of a future identity. After Clarissa's thoughts shift from Sally and the past to Richard and the present, Woolf turns the angle of vision one notch further to open a perspective on the future. The old lady solemnly prepares for bed, but this intimation of a final repose, recalling Clarissa's earlier ruminations on her narrowing bed, carries no onus for the heroine, excited by the unexpected animation of the sky, the news of Septimus's suicide, the noise from the party in the adjacent room. Release, anticipation, pleasure in change, regardless of its consequences—these are Clarissa's dominant emotions. Her identification with Septimus and pleasure in his suicide indicate her own relief in turning from her past. The gulf between Clarissa and the unknown lady discloses the female intimacy forfeited to growth, yet Clarissa's willingness to contemplate an emblem of age instead of savoring a memory of youth suggests a positive commitment to development—not to any particular course, but to the process of change itself. The vision of the old lady simultaneously concludes the developmental plot and the depiction of Clarissa's consciousness; the rest of the narrative turns to Peter and Sally. The developmental theme resides in the interplay between two interludes in the sequence of the day.

Freud's comparison of the pre-Oedipal stage in women to the Minoan-Mycenean civilization behind that of classical Greece provides a metaphor for the course and textual status of Clarissa's development. It also suggests a broader historical analogue to female development, though not an analogue Freud himself pursues. Freud's psychoanalytic version of ontogeny recapitulating philogeny assumes a genderless (that is, implicitly masculine) norm: personal development repeats the historical progression from "savage" to civilized races.[35] In *Mrs. Dalloway,* Woolf intimates more specifically that *female* development condenses one strand of human history, the progression from matriarchal to patriarchal culture implicit in Freud's archeological trope. Woolf's fascination during the years she was composing *Mrs. Dalloway* with

[35]Freud claims, for example, that "We can thus judge the so-called savage and semi-savage races; their psychic life assumes a peculiar interest for us, for we can recognize in their psychic life a well-preserved, early stage of our own development" (*Totem and Taboo,* trans. A. A. Brill [New York: Random House, 1946], p. 3).

the works of Jane Harrison and the *Oresteia,* which traces precisely the evolution from Mycenean to Athenian culture, may have fostered this concern with the relation of gender to cultural evolution.[36] The developmental plot embedded in *Mrs. Dalloway* traces the outline of a larger historical plot, detached in the novel from its chronological roots and endowed with an uncustomary moral charge.

Woolf assigns the action of *Mrs. Dalloway* a precise date: 1923, shortly after the war that casts its shadow through the novel. Through the experience of Septimus Warren Smith and the descriptions of soldiers marching "as if one will worked legs and arms uniformly, and life, with its varieties, its irreticences, had been laid under a pavement of monuments and wreaths and drugged into a stiff yet staring corpse by discipline" (pp. 76–77), she suggests that the military discipline intended both to manifest and cultivate manliness in fact instills rigor mortis in the living as well as the dead. For women, the masculine war is disruptive in a different way. Woolf's imagery and plot portray the world war as a vast historical counterpart to male intervention in female lives. In one pointed metaphor, the "fingers" of the European war are so "prying and insidious" that they smash a "plaster cast of Ceres" (p. 129), goddess of fertility and mother love, reminder of the force and fragility of the primary female bond. Rezia's female world is shattered by the conjunction of marriage and war. The symbolic association of war with the developmental turn from feminine to masculine orientation will be more clearly marked in *To the Lighthouse,* bisected by the joint ravages of nature and war in the divisive central section. By conflating Mrs. Ramsay's death with the violence of world war, Woolf splits the novel into disjunct portions presided over separately by the mother and the father.

In *Mrs. Dalloway,* Woolf more subtly indicates the masculine tenor of postwar society. The youngest generation in this novel is almost exclusively, and boastfully, male: Sally Seton repeatedly declares her pride in her "five great boys"; the Bradshaws have a son at Eton; "Everyone in the room has six sons at Eton" (p. 289), Peter Walsh observes at Clarissa's party; Rezia Warren Smith mourns the loss of closeness with her sisters but craves a son who would resemble his father. Elizabeth Dalloway is the sole daughter, and she identifies more closely with her father than her mother (the plaster cast of Ceres has been shattered in the war). Male authority, partially incarnate in the relentless chiming of Big Ben, is more ominously embodied in the Doctors Holmes and Bradshaw, the modern officers of coercion. Septimus is

---

36In "*The Years* as Greek Drama, Domestic Novel, and Gotterdämmerung," *Bulletin of the New York Public Library,* 80, 2 (Winter 1977), 276–301, Jane Marcus discusses the influence of Jane Harrison's work on Woolf's fiction. She points out that Woolf's library contained a copy of Harrison's *Ancient Art and Ritual* (1918), inscribed to Woolf by the author on Christmas, 1923. In "*Mrs. Dalloway*: The Communion of Saints," Suzette A. Henke mentions that Woolf's notes for *Mrs. Dalloway* are in a notebook that contains her earlier reflections on Aeschylus' *Choephoroi.* Woolf was reading Greek texts diligently in 1922 and 1923 in preparation for her essay "On Not Knowing Greek."

the dramatic victim of this authority, but Lady Bradshaw's feminine conces-
sion is equally significant: "Fifteen years ago she had gone under . . . there
had been no scene, no snap; only the slow sinking, water-logged, of her will
into his. Sweet was her smile, swift her submission" (p. 152). The loose
connections Woolf suggests between World War I and a bolstered male
authority lack all historical validity, but within the mythology created by the
novel the war assumes a symbolic function dividing a pervasively masculine
present from a mythically female past.

Critics frequently note the elegiac tone permeating *Mrs. Dalloway,* a tone
which allies the novel with the modernist preoccupation with the contrast
between the present and the past.[37] Nostalgia in *Mrs. Dalloway,* however, is
for a specifically female presence and nurturance, drastically diminished in
contemporary life. Woolf suggests this loss primarily in interludes that puncture the narrative, pointing to a loss inadequately recognized by the conventions of developmental tales. The most obvious of these interruptions, the
solitary traveler's archetypal vision, loosely attached to Peter Walsh's dream,
but transcending through its generic formulation the limits of private consciousness, is not, as Reuben Brower asserts, a "beautiful passage . . . which
could be detached with little loss," and which "does not increase or enrich our
knowledge of Peter or of anyone else in the book."[38] Through its vivid
representation of a transpersonal longing for a cosmic female/maternal/natural
presence that might "shower down from her magnificent hands compassion,
comprehension, absolution" (p. 86), the dream/vision names the absence that
haunts *Mrs. Dalloway.* In the mundane present of the novel, the ancient
image of the Goddess, source of life and death, dwindles to the elderly nurse
sleeping next to Peter Walsh, as in another self-contained narrative interlude,
the mythic figure of woman voicing nature's eternal, wordless rhythms con-
tracts, in urban London, to a battered old beggar woman singing for coppers.
The comprehensive, seductive, generative, female powers of the Goddess
split, in the contemporary world, into the purely nurturant energy of Sally
Seton and the social graces of the unmaternal Clarissa, clad as a hostess in a
"silver-green mermaid's dress" (p. 264). The loss of female integration and
power, another echo of the smashed cast of Ceres, is finally suggested in the
contrast between the sequence envisaged by the solitary traveler and the
most intrusive narrative interlude, the lecture on Proportion and Conversion,
where Woolf appears to denounce in her own voice the twin evils of contemporary civilization. Rather than a sign of artistic failure, this interruption calls

[37]See, for example, Maria Di Battista, *Virginia Woolf's Major Novels: The Fables of Anony-
mous* (New Haven: Yale University Press, 1980); Phyllis Rose, *Woman of Letters*; J. Hillis Miller,
"Virginia Woolf's All Souls' Day: The Omniscient Narrator in *Mrs. Dalloway,*" in *The Shaken
Realist: Essays in Honor of Frederick J. Hoffman,* ed. Melvin J. Friedman and John Vickery
(Baton Rouge: Louisiana State University Press, 1970), 100–127.
[38]" 'Something Central which Permeated': Virginia Woolf and Mrs. Dalloway," in *The Fields of
Light* (New York: Oxford University Press, 1951), p. 135. Brower also significantly omits Sally
Seton from his summary of the novel's plot.

attention to itself as a rhetorical as well as ideological antithesis to the solitary traveler's vision. Sir Bradshaw's goddesses of Proportion and Conversion, who serve the ideals of imperialism and patriarchy, renouncing their status as creative female powers, are the contemporary counterpart to the ancient maternal deity, now accessible only in vision and dream. The historical vista intermittently inserted in *Mrs. Dalloway* echoes the developmental progress of the heroine from a nurturing, pastoral, female world to an urban culture governed by men.

One last reverberation of the developmental plot takes as its subject female development in the altered contemporary world. Through the enigmatic figure of Elizabeth, Woolf examines the impact of the new historical context on the course of women's development. Almost the same age as her mother in the earliest recollected scenes at Bourton, Elizabeth has always lived in London; the country to her is an occasional treat she associates specifically with her father. Elizabeth feels a special closeness to her father, a noticeable alienation from her mother. The transition so implicitly traumatic for Clarissa has already been accomplished by her daughter. By structuring the adolescence of mother and daughter as inverse emotional configurations, Woolf reveals the shift that has occurred between these generations. As Clarissa vacillates between two men, while tacitly guarding her special bond with Sally, Elizabeth vacillates between two women, her mother and Miss Kilman, while preserving her special connection with her father. Elizabeth's presence at the final party manifests her independence from Miss Kilman; her impatience for the party to end reveals her differences from her mother. The last scene of the novel highlights Elizabeth's closeness with her father, whose sudden response to his daughter's beauty has drawn her instinctively to his side.

The opposing allegiances of daughter and mother reflect in part the kinds of female nurturance available to each. Elizabeth's relation with the grasping Miss Kilman is the modern counterpart to Clarissa's love for Sally Seton. Specific parallels mark the generational differences. Miss Kilman's possessive desire for Elizabeth parodies the lines that emblazon Clarissa's love for Sally: "If it were now to die, 'twere now to be most happy" becomes, for Elizabeth's hungry tutor, "If she could grasp her, if she could clasp her, if she could make her hers absolutely and forever and then die; that was all she wanted" (pp. 199–200). Sally walks with Clarissa on the terrace at Bourton; Miss Kilman takes Elizabeth to the Army and Navy Stores, a commercial setting that exemplifies the web of social and military ties. Miss Kilman, as her name implies, provides no asylum from this framework. Losing the female sanctuary, however, brings proportionate compensations: Elizabeth assumes she will have a profession, will play some active role in masculine society. Woolf does not evaluate this new developmental course, does not tally losses and gains. If she surrounds the past with an aureole, she points to the future in silence. She offers little access to Elizabeth's consciousness, insisting instead on her status as enigma—her Chinese eyes, "blank, bright, with the staring incredible innocence of sculpture" (p. 206), her Oriental bearing, her "inscrutable mystery" (p. 199). Undecipherable, Elizabeth is "like a hyacinth, sheathed in glossy green, with buds just tinted, a hyacinth which has had no sun" (p. 186); her unfolding is unknown, unknowable. Through the figure of Elizabeth as unopened bud, Woolf encloses in her text the unwritten text of the next developmental narrative.

The silences that punctuate *Mrs. Dalloway* reflect the interruptions and enigmas of female experience and ally the novel with a recent trend in feminist aesthetics. The paradoxical goal of representing women's absence from culture has fostered an emphasis on "blank pages, gaps, borders, spaces and silence, holes in discourse" as the distinctive features of a self-consciously female writing.[39] Since narrative forms normally sanction the patterns of male experience, the woman novelist might signal her exclusion most succinctly by disrupting continuity, accentuating gaps between sequences. "Can the female self be expressed through plot or must it be conceived in resistance to plot? Must it lodge 'between the acts'?" asks Gillian Beer, the allusion to Woolf suggesting the persistence of this issue for a novelist concerned with the links of gender and genre.[40] In her next novel Woolf expands her discrete silence to a gaping hole at the center of her narrative, a hole that divides the action dramatically between two disjunct days. *To the Lighthouse* makes explicit many of the issues latent in *Mrs. Dalloway.* The plot of female bonding, reshaped as the story of a woman's attempts to realize in art her love for an older woman, rises to the surface of the narrative; yet Lily's relationship with Mrs. Ramsay is unrepresented in the emblem Lily fashions for the novel, the painting that manifests a daughter's love for her surrogate mother as a portrait of the mother with her son. Absence is pervasive in *To the Lighthouse.* The gaps in *Mrs. Dalloway* are less conspicuous, yet they make vital and disturbing points about female experience and female plots. The fragmentary form of the developmental plot, where the patterns of experience and art intersect, conceals as insignificance a radical significance. The intervals between events, the stories untold, can remain invisible in *Mrs. Dalloway*—or they can emerge through a sudden shift of vision as the most absorbing features of Woolf's narrative.[41]

[39]Xavière Gauthier, "Is There Such a Thing as Women's Writing?" *New French Feminisms*, ed. Elaine Marks and Isabelle de Courtivron (Amherst: University of Massachusetts Press, 1980), p. 164. The whole project of *écriture féminine* stresses the importance of representing women's silence and absence.

[40]"Beyond Determinism: George Eliot and Virginia Woolf," *Women Writing and Writing about Women*, ed. Mary Jacobus (London: Croom Helm, 1979), p. 80. Beer analyzes Woolf's resistance to plot in *The Waves.*

[41]I would like to thank the coeditors of the anthology in which this essay first appeared (*The Voyage In: Fictions of Female Development*, ed. Elizabeth Abel, Marianne Hirsch, and Elizabeth Langland [Hanover, N.H.: University Press of New England, 1983]), and Diane Middlebrook, Marta Peixoto, Lisa Ruddick, Sanford Schwartz, and Janet Silver for their helpful commentary on this essay.

"Amor Vin—": Modifications of Romance in Woolf

Rachel Blau DuPlessis

The change which has turned the English woman from a nondescript influence, fluctuating and vague, to a voter, a wage-earner, a responsible citizen, has given her both in her life and in her art a turn toward the impersonal. Her relations now are not only emotional; they are intellectual, they are political. The old system which condemned her to squint askance at things through the eyes or through the interests of husband or brother, has given place to the direct and practical interests of one who must act for herself, and not merely influence the acts of others. Hence her attention is being directed away from the personal centre which engaged it exclusively in the past to the impersonal, and her novels naturally become more critical of society, and less analytical of individual lives.

—Virginia Woolf
"Women and Fiction" (1929)

The psychological novelist has been too prone to limit psychology to the psychology of personal intercourse; we long sometimes to escape from the incessant, the remorseless analysis of falling into love and falling out of love, of what Tom feels for Judith and Judith does or does not altogether feel for Tom. We long for some more impersonal relationship. We long for ideas, for dreams, for imaginations, for poetry.

—Virginia Woolf
"The Narrow Bridge of Art" (1927)

Virginia Woolf's career as a novelist makes two great lines crossing on one major problem—the formation of narrative strategies that express a more "impersonal" woman's identity by rupturing the sentences and sequences of romance. Her first two novels both draw on the traditional concerns of love plots—the production of newly joined heterosexual couples—and of quest plots—the *Bildung* of the protagonist. That is, in *The Voyage Out* (1915) and *Night and Day* (1919) Woolf considers the endings of betrothal and death.[1]

Excerpted from *Writing Beyond the Ending: Narrative Strategies of Twentieth-Century Women Writers* (Bloomington: Indiana University Press, 1985). Copyright © 1985 by Rachel Blau DuPlessis. Reprinted with the permission of Rachel Blau DuPlessis and Indiana University Press.

[1]The editions of Woolf's novels used are as follows: *The Voyage Out* (abbreviated in the reading as *VO*) (the 1920 Doran edition; New York: Harcourt, Brace and World, Inc., 1948); *Night and Day* (abbreviated in the reading as *N&D*) (1919; New York: Harcourt Brace Jovanovich, 1973);

After the first two novels, heterosexual romance is displaced from a controlling and privileged position in her work.[2] It will never again appear as the unique center of narrative concern; it will never again appear assumed or unquestioned. *Mrs. Dalloway* (1925) offers thematic and structural debates about romantic love. *To the Lighthouse* (1927) both idealizes and criticizes romance. *Orlando* (1928) and *Flush* (1933) close the issue of heterosexual love by drastic changes in its definition.

In her first set of novels, then, Woolf breaks the sentence by an imbedded critique of heterosexual romantic love, while in the second set, Woolf ruptures the sequence by inventing a narrative center to express postromantic relations among characters. The novels along the second major line of Woolf's career—*The Years* (1937) and *Between the Acts* (1941) as well as *The Waves* (1931)—ask the fundamental ideological and structural question, What desires will empower stories and characters if a writer does not depend on the emphases and motivations of romance? Here Woolf displaces the emotional aura and structural weight of individual quest and of hero and heroine into a communal protagonist. This protagonist—a large family, a group of friends, an audience, containing many close bonds and, not incidentally, including members of all ages and sexual persuasions—creates a structure in which couples, individuals, walls between public and private, polarized sexes, and closures in family houses are subject to strong oppositional formations. In general, Woolf separates *eros* from any forced or conventional bonds, especially such institutions as heterosexuality and marriage.

The possibility for a critique of romance began to be formulated in the earliest days of Bloomsbury, when Woolf felt an enormous liberation at being released from feminine white dresses and the façade of virginal proprieties and correct chatter, all at the service of "love and marriage." This liberation occurred because a number of the "Bloomsberries" were, as Woolf persists in calling them, "buggers"; it was not heterosexual romance and sexuality that fired their imaginations. And their stance on women, for a time refreshingly neutral, was also antimasculinist on principle.[3] So the effect of homosexuality

Mrs. Dalloway (*MD*) (New York: Harcourt, Brace and World, Inc., 1925); *Orlando* (*O*) (New York: The New American Library, 1928); *Flush: A Biography* (New York: Harcourt, Brace and Company, 1933). *Jacob's Room* (1922), which I do not discuss, could be seen as the symbolic death of the male hero, which clears the way for the female hero and her plot.

2Woolf investigates where to put romance even at the absolute beginning of her writing career, in "The Journal of Mistress Joan Martyn" (1906). The narrator escapes marriage by being a scholar; the fifteenth-century heroine dies before a limited marriage; her mother, the nation-builder, survives. The work contrasts the attraction of Tristan and Iseult or Helen of Troy stories as models for romance with the managerial stolidity of marriage as her mother knows it. Although unfinished, the work asks questions that Woolf's whole oeuvre answers. "The Journal of Mistress Joan Martyn," ed. Susan M. Squier and Louise A. DeSalvo, *Twentieth Century Literature* 25, 3/4 (Fall/Winter 1979): 237–69.

3Virginia Woolf, *Moments of Being: Unpublished Autobiographical Writings*, ed. Jeanne Schulkind (New York: Harcourt Brace Jovanovich, 1976), p. 169. Carolyn Heilbrun has analyzed the critique of masculinist values, especially sexual polarization and bellicose phallicism, that distinguished Bloomsbury's ethical vision of androgynous people. *Toward a Recognition of Androgyny* (New York: Harper and Row, Publishers, 1973), p. 126.

in Bloomsbury contributed to Woolf's developing critique of romance, as did, on the other side, what she was rejecting: George Duckworth, keeper of the heterosexual flame, conventional womanhood, and the socially sanctioned "hoops" of romance and advancement. The gift of tolerance, of seeing the many fair erotic possibilities that homosexual relations called forth, thus made a contribution to Woolf's narrative choice not to give priority to heterosexual romance in her oeuvre as a whole.

This is in keeping with Woolf's sense of a change in the status of women, and thus of fiction. Newly achieved legal, economic, and political rights unfixed the modern woman from the limited "personal centre" of "husband and brother." Thus the "incessant and remorseless analysis of falling into love and falling out of love" gives ways to a fiction "more critical of society" precisely because it is more critical of romance.[4] Woolf's major project as a novelist—writing beyond this ending—joins her work to that of other twentieth-century women writers who dispute the social, emotional, and narrative charisma of romance.[5]

In *The Voyage Out*, with Rachel Vinrace, Woolf experiments by placing a mid-nineteenth-century girl heroine in a twentieth-century context. Rachel had begun her quest under the guardianship of characters with banal and limited notions about the education and place of women. In contrast, her aunt Helen Ambrose and her new fiancé, Terence Hewet, are relatively free from conventional ideas of women's duties and interests. "If [women] were properly educated I don't see why they shouldn't be much the same as men—as satisfactory I mean; though, of course, very different."[6]

Terence and Helen agree that women should have the benefit of free, uncensored, wide-ranging talk with men, so that men would stimulate and challenge women as they do each other. This assumption about men as a standard reflects Woolf's early idealization and envy of various schools for English manhood. Helen's plan for Rachel's education, which extends fraternal male bonding to a genial brother-and-sisterhood, attempts, in a flash, to provide a solution to the woman question so commonsensical as to be almost flatfooted: men should treat women as they treat men. While Helen and

---

[4]Woolf speaks of this change in her essay "Women and Fiction," stating that in novels in the future, "men and women will not be observed wholly in relation to each other emotionally, but as they cohere and clash in groups and classes and races." The citations, from the essays cited as epigrams: "The Narrow Bridge of Art" and "Women and Fiction," in *Granite and Rainbow*, (New York: Harcourt Brace and Company, 1958), pp. 19, 83.

[5]The interpretation views the delegitimation of the romance plot as a conscious act of expression; it might be well to note Mark Spilka's analysis. He views the absence of romance as one of the unintended results of unexpressed grief and feels that Woolf longed to uphold a "faith in romantic love" but that her life's circumstances impeded her. *Virginia Woolf's Quarrel with Grieving* (Lincoln: University of Nebraska Press, 1980), pp. 72–73.

[6]This essayistic set piece (*VO*, 96), a letter of Helen's, was troublesome writing for Woolf, who even herself felt it to be "an experiment." Yet she did not solve the compositional problems by cutting this section out (Quentin Bell, *Virginia Woolf: A Biography*, vol. I [London: The Hogarth Press, 1972], p. 211). Quite the contrary; she needed these opinions to be stated by a sympathetic character and not questioned, as they might have been if offered in conversation.

Terence, as well as the acerbic Hirst, repeatedly ponder the gap of sexual difference brought about by differential socialization, they feel that the disability that unmarried women suffer from their prudish and confined upbringing is fairly easily overcome. By means of this novel and Rachel's fate, Woolf confronted herself with the impossibility of straightforward "good faith" solutions to gender asymmetry.

The jungle voyage to a tribal settlement constitutes the central quest of the novel. That journey reverses the relationship of art and nature upon which these cultivated people depend; it tampers with the ethnocentrism that they assume. And on that journey, Terence and Rachel grow more equal and fall in love. Love at that point is consonant with quest and seems experimental, born out of these other critical reversals. Their constant antiphonal echoes of each other ("We sat upon the ground" and "This is happiness") are egalitarian as well as tender. One "You love me?" receives "And you?" "Am I in love—is this being in love—are we to marry each other?" (*VO*, 282, 283, 280, 281). The persistently interrogative mode is not exclusive to the lovers; the central characters use this ethical and rhetorical tactic to show that discourse is opened, judgment is suspended, and fixed answers are eroded. Yet a lovers' dialogue carried out in questions insists on instability and insubstantiality.

The largest question in *The Voyage Out* is asked by its largest narrative fact: the death of Rachel. Woolf shatters conventional hopes for an ending in marriage by introducing not only the dangerous illness of the main character, but a whole new set of emotional pressures, from the alienating hallucinations of Rachel to the paralysis of caretakers faced with doctors. The reader is obliged to confront the issue of death in its most "aimless and cruel" form, the sudden and gratuitous death of a young person, deaths such as Woolf herself endured in the years before her first novel was written.[7]

Using death as "the lash of a random unheeding flail" creates a dramatic rupture with many of the narrative conventions Woolf evoked.[8] Woolf may have meant this closure to be almost unassimilated and unassimilable, placing death at a tangent from all other movements and relationships so that it will never be causally tied to events, but rather will be a thing entirely apart, from another realm of experience. Thus one reads the death of Rachel as the

---

[7]*The Letters of Virginia Woolf, Volume One, 1888–1912 (Virginia Stephen)*, ed. Nigel Nicolson and Joanne Trautmann (New York: Harcourt Brace Jovanovich, 1975), letter #187, 1 Nov. 1904, p. 150. The story of the deaths is harrowing no matter how often it is told. There is no doubt that Woolf is here transposing some of the material and pain from her early family life, including the deaths of Stella Duckworth, her half-sister, three months after her marriage (1897), and of Thoby Stephen, her brother, dead of typhoid contracted on a journey (1906), not to speak of her mother's (1895) and her father's (1904). Each death, save perhaps her father's, was more senseless and unexpected than the last. In three of the illnesses, as Bell points out, there was a strong retrospective sense of a case bungled by the attending physician (Bell, *Biography*, vol. I, p. 110). This, too, enters into *The Voyage Out*; the French doctor, belatedly summoned, could never cure what the hairy Spanish doctor had exacerbated as a spreader of infection.

[8]"A Sketch of the Past," in *Moments of Being: Unpublished Autobiographical Writings*, ed. Jeanne Schulkind (New York: Harcourt Brace Jovanovich, 1976), p. 117.

aggressive act of the author against the hegemonic power of those narrative conventions with which the novel is, in fact, engaged—love and quest—a way of interrupting the plot "tyranny," that avalanche of events moving to "satisfactory solutions."[9] The flail of the author on her novel, the rupture with conventions of love, draws on the gratuitous flail of life on the author, the rupture of normalcy represented by death. Yet Woolf did not have unwobbling control of her critique, because she was only beginning to suspect what she would later enunciate—the relation between sentence, plot, narrative line, and gender-based ideologies and values.

At the same time, all the characters do seem to "earn" the death of Rachel Vinrace. Her death can be connected to a dialectic of rage and repression, critique and its absence, in which all parties are complicit. Rachel has had an education in chastity and avoidance such that any kind of sexual awakening is repulsive and destabilizing. When her first sexual event is the passionate kiss of Richard Dalloway, given as a response to her yearning for education, several levels of trauma and violation are set in motion. The reader feels how Rachel's education has, with a depressing swiftness, been reduce to sexuality. If this reduction—whimsical for Richard, devastating for Rachel—can be severely regarded, so too can the character's response. Because Rachel has no other context in which to put his kiss, and because she feels no other identity but the feminine and passive, it takes on the nightmare proportions of sexual trauma.

In fact, her response is a miniature version of her development in the whole book. First "life seemed to hold infinite possibilities she had never guessed at," for "something wonderful had happened," exactly like her feelings about love for Terence. She then experiences a "pallor" parallel to her whiteness in illness, and a hallucinatory dream of a deformed man, like her later dream of deformed women. Finally, the statement "still and cold as death she lay, not daring to move. . . ." strikingly prefigures her end (*VO*, 76–77).

Even if this is, as Phyllis Rose acutely suggests, a biographical reconstruction of Woolf's own associations, the "yoking of the ideas of death and sex," it may constitute Woolf's cultural criticism as well, attacking that noneducation of women, which makes Rachel so unprepared for life and sexuality that she can only punish her passion with debility and self-annihilation.[10] That mid-nineteenth century ideology of purity, by controlling her "education," has determined her fate.

---

[9]"Tyranny" (actually "tyrant") from "Modern Fiction, in *The Common Reader* (New York: Harcourt, Brace and World, Inc., 1925), p. 153; "satisfactory solutions" from *A Writer's Diary*, ed. Leonard Woolf (New York: Harcourt, Brace and Company, 1953), p. 10. As Woolf viewed the matter soon after completing *Night and Day*, her originality lay in the rejection of the "happy answers" or "satisfactory solutions" of social insertion and successful quest, not answers "one would accept, if one had the least respect for one's soul."

[10]Phyllis Rose, *Woman of Letters: A Life of Virginia Woolf* (New York: Oxford University Press, 1978), p. 15. Rose also points to the nineteenth-century education that Rachel has received.

If she is forced by Dalloway and beset by an internalized ideology, Rachel is also coerced by her "good" mentors. Terence is a character whose opinions on women allow the first expression of Woolf's own; the male persona gives the author permission and cover. Yet when he pursues feminist matters, he receives no response from Rachel but astonished and silent evasion. Terence is sure that Rachel should be concerned with women's status. Rachel, how- ever, just wishes he would quit bothering her. "She was only weary of him and his questions" (*VO*, 215). At no other point but this are questions so blatantly rejected. Yet at no other point does the reader feel Rachel more talked at than in Terence's speeches to Rachel on women's potential and their anger. To break even sympathetic male sentences, women must become speaking subjects of their own discourses.

Rachel's death may accordingly be interpreted as the death of a person who evaded constitutive components of her *Bildung*—rage at her status as a woman, and the seizing of speech for herself. We must consider that Woolf meted out death as Rachel's punishment for her being insufficiently critical and vocal.[11] This death differs precisely from the tragic punishment and affirmation of Maggie Tulliver in *The Mill on the Floss*, to whom death is allotted—the social machinery of the mill dragging her under the flood— because she is too intuitively critical. For the uncritical Rachel, Woolf builds the same ending as in the Victorian novel mixing quest and love, but for an exactly opposite reason.

Woolf continues her critique of the mentors. Terence and Helen—but not Rachel—assume that marriage is the absolute and necessary outcome of the relationship. The first proposal of marriage between Terence and Rachel occurs in the absence of the bride-to-be, and thus, no matter how subtle his discussion, it lacks her informed consent. His meditations put marriage on the defensive, cataloguing the compromises it entails for women, the kinds of dishonesty that can occur when a woman must live in smooth conjunction with a person who has more social power than she.[12] As he imagines it, marriage is precisely opposed to the basic ethics of the book: frankness, honesty, questioning. Yet Terence does not take the logical, if socially drastic, step of separating love and companionship from marriage. Instead, he pursues the question of marriage and concludes that to marry Rachel would be to have a talisman of freedom. At that moment, Rachel passes from being "real" to Terence to being a symbol of Terence's desire for a controlling magnanimity.

It is by no means certain that Rachel is as swift to join love with marriage

---

[11]This aspect of my interpretation—death because of the repressions of patriarchal education, and therefore Rachel's incomplete entrance into critique—should be distinguished from Mitchell Leaska's interpretation of "self-willed death," a suicide of escape from pressures, to protect Rachel's core identity and to avoid sexuality. Mitchell A. Leaska, *The Novels of Virginia Woolf: From Beginning to End* (New York: John Jay Press, 1977), p. 38.

[12]For example, "All the most individual and humane of his friends were bachelors and spinsters; indeed he was surprised to find that the women he most admired and knew best were unmarried women. Marriage seemed to be worse for them than it was for men" (*VO*, 241).

as is Terence. "Marriage?" is Rachel's repeated query to the ending that all would write for her plot. Without answering, Terence and Helen speak of "love and then of marriage" and mark their excitement with a kiss, that quasi-parental embrace over the "speechless," passive, babylike body of Rachel (*VO*, 281, 284, 283). This heavily revised scene has a rather scandalous aura. Learning of their love, Helen harasses Rachel, rolling her in the jungle grass, teasingly but with a good deal of lurid menace. Rachel falls to the ground in an ambiguously rendered excess of erotic violence between women.

Further, at the very moment of heterosexual embrace, Rachel is excluded. Her mentors have agreed on her proper ending. Rachel's death may then be the result of her desire to escape being written into the marriage plot in this cavalier and violent fashion. That Woolf intended something like this sense is clearer when a discarded version of the expedition scene is contrasted with this one. In the Earlier Typescript, it is Rachel who announces her impending marriage to Helen; Woolf once wanted us to feel that Rachel had consented. But not now. The version of this scene we now read ends with the embrace of mentors over the exhausted form of the bride-to-be. In this version, marriage is announced to the powerless Rachel.[13] As they congratulate themselves that their plan for Rachel's education has worked—the Victorian waif is engaged—this moment recapitulates the convention of nineteenth-century fiction in which the quest plot turns into the marriage plot as the energies and potential of the female hero are contained. At this moment romance prefigures death. Death becomes Rachel's protest against marriage and sexuality as her sole aim, against the change of a *Bildung* into a marriage plot, which powerful figures who resemble Woolf's family demand.

For the main characters in this novel are evidently displaced and realigned members of her own family: Terence resembles her brother Thoby, the widowed Jack Hills with his fraternal interest, and her new husband, Leonard Woolf. Helen is a version of her sister Vanessa as well as their dead mother. Richard Dalloway mixes the sexual interests—even abuse—of Gerald and George Duckworth. Rachel is an amalgam at least of Stella Duckworth and Woolf herself. The novelist has brewed herself a potent draught with this mixture of desire, shame, guilt, blocked grief, incest fantasies, ambivalence to marriage, and admissions of anger and despair about women's status. It is therefore likely—this is a first novel after all—that Woolf would want an

---

[13]The composition process, its taxing cost, and its possible meanings are scrupulously traced in Louise DeSalvo, *Virginia Woolf's First Voyage: A Novel in the Making* (Totowa, N.J.: Rowman and Littlefield, 1980). These revisions have received a good deal of forceful comment from both DeSalvo and Leaska. The Earlier Typescript reads: " 'Oh Helen. Helen!' She could hear Rachel gasping as she rolled her, 'Don't! For God sake! Stop! I'll tell you a secret! I'm going—to—be—married!' Helen paused with one hand upon Rachel's throat holding her head down among the grasses. 'You think I didn't know that!' she cried." But the final version (here the 1920 Doran edition) reads, "[Rachel] thought she heard them speak of love and then of marriage" (*VO* 284). The Earlier Typescript cited from Leaska, *The Novels of Virginia Woolf*, pp. 35–36.

escape hatch from the culpability that she had, with difficulty, self-doubt, and mental anguish, assigned to those closest to her.

Woolf accomplishes this by the evocation of spiritual or mystical love, which she puts into the mouth of the only character unoccupied with the toils of complicity that link the central triangle. The otherwise carping St. John Hirst, who earlier in the novel could barely credit female intelligence, undergoes a gratifying, though amazing, conversion to the possibility of equality between men and women in spiritual love. The nonsexual, nonsocial, and impersonal character of that love makes an appealing compromise for the author herself, who apparently cannot decide whether the love of Rachel and Terence is a good or bad thing, whether it is manipulation or equality, whether Rachel's death occurs because she is a victim of her nineteenth-century socialization or because she is resisting being the victim of the "Victorian" ending in marriage that has been reserved for her.

Through St. John, a nimbus from Platonized Christianity comes to settle over the love plot, gives it a peace which passeth understanding, and creates the final ambiguity. One may credit the "peace" and "happiness" that Terence feels as Rachel dies as their only, poignant, and lush consummation, "the union which had been impossible while they lived" (*VO*, 353). Or one may find repulsive the necrophiliac possession of Rachel in a death-marriage about which she herself is finally puzzled: her last look being "fatigue or perplexity."

The death of Rachel expresses Woolf's oscillation between criticism and ambivalence: the criticism of narrative conventions, the shielding of masked family members among her *dramatis personae*. Insofar as Woolf metes out what her characters are owed, Rachel's death announces that they have not investigated deeply enough what they claim to question: marriage, love, gender polarization, the formation of women. Death is the vehicle for affirming the necessity for critique of the conventions governing women and narrative structures, not, as in nineteenth-century fiction, a tragic price exacted for debate and social difference.

From Katherine Mansfield on, readers of *Night and Day* have noted—sometimes in disgusted or apologetic tones—the plain fact that Woolf's second novel carefully recapitulates the "tradition of the English novel." Woolf's purpose was not uncritical homage to that tradition ("drawing from the cast—an academic exercise," she said later); nor was it only the testing of her skills ("to see if she could achieve a perfectly orthodox and conventional novel," Bell explains).[14] Like her first novel, *Night and Day* engages critically with

[14]Katherine Mansfield review, *Athenaeum*, 21 Nov. 1919, reprinted in *Virginia Woolf: The Critical Heritage*, ed. Robin Majumdar and Allen McLaurin (London: Routledge & Kegan Paul, 1975), p. 82. Mansfield concludes, "In the midst of our admiration, it makes us feel old and chill. . . ." Woolf knew the review, was "irritated" by it, and struggled with her jealous but not foolish sense of a quota system for public recognition of the women writers with whom she was most engaged: Mansfield and Dorothy Richardson. *The Diary of Virginia Woolf, Volume One: 1915–1919*, ed. Anne Olivier Bell (New York: Harcourt Brace Jovanovich, 1977), pp. 314–15. Bell citation from the *Biography*, vol. II, p. 42.

nineteenth-century narratives of love, marriage, and quest epitomized here by the works on which Woolf evidently draws: *Emma*, *Pride and Prejudice*, and *Jane Eyre*. This book is a *tour de force*, simultaneously evoking a comic wedlock plot of the Austen variety and the melodramatic and hierogamic quest plot perfected by Charlotte Brontë. *Night and Day* takes up two heroes from two misallied couples, the primal stuff of the comic love plot, yet asserts that they can only affirm mutual passion because of quest. Thus love and quest are joined at narrative resolution, rather than being separated as in the nineteenth-century paradigm.

Katherine has enforced a dishonest but compelling separation in her personality between what she most deeply desires—the vocation of mathematician—and her social role of accommodating daughter and erstwhile fiancée. She has been engaged to William Rodney, a charming boy of letters. Ralph Denham, lawyer and upstart, begins the book involved with Mary Datchet, another serious, intense, independent young woman. But both Katherine and Ralph are embarked on passionless, loveless matches because they are not able to define vocation and bring day in alliance with night, comedy with quest, practicality with fantasy.[15] The night side of each involves their recognition of hidden vocations: the dogged lawyer is really a writer, the dutiful daughter, a mathematician. They yearn toward these vocations; acknowledging their desires for true work frees them for true romance.

Throughout the novel, Ralph visualizes Katherine as something connected "with vague feelings of romance and adventure such as she inspired"; moreover, this will translate into the good news for the intelligentsia that he has quit his job and will write a book (*N&D*, 131). In a precisely parallel way, Katherine, while making preparations for "a perfectly loveless marriage," maintains an interior fantasy life replete with situations from high romance and quest: "the presence of love," the "superb catastrophe in which everything was surrendered," and the possibility of riding off on an adventure with a "magnanimous hero" continually linked to Ralph (*N&D*, 107, 197). By making vocation and love draw equally on a yearning for the ideal, Woolf allows quest and love plots to be united.

This achievement is visible in the love tokens the characters share at the end, when each reads certain secret papers of the other. By the intensity of these tokens, Woolf also confesses that she accepts the narrative emphasis always implicit in heterosexual romance, of the specialness and aura of the central couple. She has not yet moved to the alteration of these established values in her formal and emotional structures.

Woolf balances these plots, and allusions to both love and quest narrative abound. The unity of the Hillbery family banquet, the poignant huff of the

---

[15]Winifred Holtby, an early critic of Woolf, interestingly emphasizes this self-unification at the expense of the marriage plot: "a union not so much of a man with a woman, as of a man with himself, a woman with herself." *Virginia Woolf* (London: Wishart & Co., 1932), p. 93.

patriarch bested, and the mismatched lovers reassigned by an intervening
magic (Mozart and Shakespeare as well as Austen in the background) are all
motifs from a comic tradition.[16] The dark walks through London, the lovers'
fiery excitement, their mutual thralldom, their striving souls, and a visionary
daemonic presence, the mother, are motifs from quest and closely related
hierogamic romance.[17] The final embrace of Katherine and Ralph balances
night and day motifs, for it occurs on the threshold between the blazing light
of the family house and the enchanting darkness of London, with its ideals of
knowledge and achievement. They kiss on the limen between love and
quest.[18]

The Austenian focus of the love plot on choice, involving an acute reading
of social cues, motives, and character, is reiterated in Woolf's emphasis on
honesty. In *Night and Day*, honesty is a torch passed from hand to hand;
truths are spoken at considerable cost, after inner struggles to hide, repress,
and prevaricate. Here, as in Austen, gnosis precedes eros, in the scene where
Mary struggles with her jealousy to tell Katherine that Ralph really loves her,
in the scene where Katherine informs William that he is probably in love with
convenient and charming Cassandra, and in the scene where Ralph, still
under the impression that Katherine is engaged, makes a passionate declara-
tion to her. Jane Austen is matched with *Jane Eyre*, itself one of the more
explosive mixtures of narrative discourses in English fiction, a hierogamic love
plot based on a personal pilgrimage.

About all this, Woolf is soon dubious. As she said, rather tersely, describing
Austen's plots, "A suitable marriage is, after all, the upshot of all this coming
together and drawing apart. A world which so often ends in a suitable
marriage is not a world to wring one's hands over."[19] Similarly, in an earlier
essay on *Jane Eyre*, Woolf assumed a tone of high-handed dismissiveness that

---

[16]Avrom Fleishman has written about the book's abundant allusions to Shakespeare's festive
and romantic comedies. His analysis of "comic vision and imaginative transformation . . . under
the spell of love's illusions" is consistent with this argument. However, for him, love only, and not
vocation, gives meaning. *Virginia Woolf: A Critical Reading* (Baltimore: The Johns Hopkins
University Press, 1975), p. 28. Jane Marcus sees the work in the tradition of *The Magic Flute*, an
"initiation into society, courtship, and marriage," as well as an initiation through quest. "En-
chanted Organs, Magic Bells: *Night and Day* as Comic Opera," in *Virginia Woolf: Revaluation
and Continuity*, ed. Ralph Freedman (Berkeley: University of California Press, 1980), p. 102.

[17]Here as elsewhere my discussion of hierogamic marriage plots draws on Evelyn Hinz,
"Hierogamy versus Wedlock: Types of Marriage Plots and Their Relationship to Genres of Prose
Fiction," *PMLA* 91, 5 (October 1976): 900–913.

[18]Margaret Comstock suggests that *Night and Day* rescripts the novel in a slightly different
fashion, by giving it a double happy ending, marriage in one case, and successful political work in
another, so that the single woman, Mary Datchet, has as happy an ending as the engaged couple.
" 'The current answers don't do': The Comic Form of *Night and Day*," *Women's Studies* 4 (1977):
169.

[19]"Personal relations, we recall, have limits," this passage in "Phases of Fiction" begins. And it
ends, significantly for Woolf's project as a novelist, "Thus, it is possible to ask not that [Austen's]
world shall be improved or altered (that our satisfaction forbids) but that another shall be struck
off, whose constitution shall be different and shall allow of the other relations." *Granite and
Rainbow* pp. 117–18.

hardly accounts for the work. "Always to be a governess and always to be in love is a serious limitation in a world which is full, after all, of people who are neither one nor the other. . . ."[20] Her remarks on her sources gain credibility, if not caritas, in the context of this argument: that Woolf proposed and then struggled to achieve a way of thinking about narratives with women that was not synonymous with thinking about romance for women.

For by the time she had completed *The Voyage Out* and *Night and Day*, Woolf had also begun a critique of her own procedures and a program for another kind of fiction, in the essay "Modern Fiction" (1919). The release from the love plot and from related conventions of production is announced in this manifesto against the well-made novel. "Love interest," the thirty-two chapters, the tyranny of plot, the choices for emphasis, "catastrophe in the accepted style," conventional generic distinctions, and even the solidity of the human soul are alike questioned and challenged.[21] She addresses these conventions using the metaphor of thralldom, as if the expected narrative demands were like a romantic involvement or a spell from which one had to be released, a compelling picture of the woman writer half in love with conventions that she resisted. This tyrant of narrative, as Phyllis Rose observes, has a specifically patriarchal cast.[22] To criticize plots—especially the love-interest plot—was to criticize the cultural and narrative forces that produced women.

The critical rejections that Woolf began in "Modern Fiction" are elaborated a decade later in "Women and Fiction" (1929). Here the sentence, the plot, narrative convention, and subject matter will alike be subjected to revisionary scrutiny by the female novelist, because these narrative forms carry an ideological and interpretive freight about gender. The prevalent values of fiction are androcentric, devaluing or rendering minor and suspect female experiences.

> . . . as men are the arbiters of that [social] convention, as they have established an order of values in life, so too, since fiction is largely based on life, these values prevail there also to a very great extent.
>
> It is probable, however, that both in life and in art, the values of a woman are not the values of a man. Thus, when a woman comes to write a novel, she will find that she is perpetually wishing to alter the established values—to make serious what appears insignificant to a man, and trivial what is to him important.[23]

Therefore, trying to make fiction talk about women and their concerns,

---

[20]*"Jane Eyre* and *Wuthering Heights,"* in *The Common Reader,* p. 161.

[21]"Modern Fiction," in *The Common Reader,* pp. 153–54.

[22]Phyllis Rose discusses the essay as evidence of Woolf's own struggle—visible also in "Professions for Women"—between "a pre-existing (masculine) model of the well-made novel whose norms she has internalized and against whose authority she has begun to rebel." *Woman of Letters* pp. 97–102.

[23]"Women and Fiction," in *Granite and Rainbow,* p. 81.

especially when a woman is the speaking subject, may necessarily lead to a critical transformation of narrative structures.

What allowed Woolf this knowledge of contradictions between dominant and nondominant interpretations of a reality, the revaluing of emphases of the trivial and the serious? One considerable source for this insight was Woolf's early experience of Leslie Stephen's unreasonable demands on his family, incidents not believed by his official biographer.[24] The division between gender and generational interests at the heart of the family and the repression of evidence offered by women marked and defined the presumably neutral, value-free truth that was told. This contradiction between the official and unofficial and the repression of one of the sides of the contradiction helped to form Woolf's project: to examine the lives of the obscure, the stories of the nondominant, the biographies of the quirky (a project accomplished in part in her *Common Reader* essays), and to examine them precisely for differences in value and emphasis. The revelation that "story" was really a product of dominant ideology and interests, and that nondominant views could nonetheless be told in oppositional narrative, helped to structure Woolf's career.

It is not surprising that these issues took shape as a debate on sexualities and on constituted authorities. Among the other structural and emotional changes that distinguish Woolf's writing after "Modern Fiction" and *Night and Day* in 1919, heterosexual romance is displaced from a privileged position in her novels and subjected to much questioning. In *Mrs. Dalloway*, the kinship of a Tory hostess and her "double" Septimus makes Woolf's structural coup, the creation of an unsexual, nonromantic central couple. "The design," she said, "is so queer and so masterful," for its emotional center is the psychic twinship between a man and a woman who never even meet, yet who share a knowledge of coercion and its antonym, ineffable "life."[25] Woolf sets their closeness against Clarissa's other relations with men: with Peter Walsh, who had courted her, and with Richard Dalloway, who married her. The design is queer because neither of the men to whom she is bound in a social, legal, or romantic sense is the man to whom she is bound in the psychic sense. This

---

[24]*Moments of Being*, pp. 124–26, describes a typical scene between father and daughter. Woolf's intense rage and intense muteness constitute a crucial nexus in the formation of a female writer. See also Bell, *Virginia Woolf: A Biography*, vol. I p. 63; my idea was inspired by Berenice A. Carroll, " 'To Crush Him in Our Own Country': The Political Thought of Virginia Woolf," *Feminist Studies* 4, 1 (February 1978): 99–131.

[25]Woolf, *A Writer's Diary* (June 1923), p. 57. The term "double" is also Woolf's, in her brief introduction to the novel, written in 1928, in *Virginia Woolf: A Collection of Criticism*, ed. Thomas S. W. Lewis (New York: McGraw-Hill Book Company, 1975), p. 36. This kind of structural idea had been dormant for years. A letter of 1903 to Violet Dickinson is extraordinarily suggestive of the tensions of *Mrs. Dalloway*, for in that letter Woolf plays with the idea of a couple that never forms, yet that remains the center of narrative attention. "I'm going to have a man and a woman—show them growing up—never meeting—not knowing each other—but all the time you'll feel them come nearer and nearer. This will be the real exciting part (as you'll see)—but when they almost meet—only a door between—you see how they just miss—and go off at a tangent, and never come anywhere near again." Cited in Bell, *Biography*, vol. I, p. 125.

unprecedented treatment of both marriage and sexual desire displaces hetero-sexual love from the narrative center. Indeed, Woolf compares the prescrip-tive treatments for insanity that drive Septinius to suicide with the toils of romantic love in which Clarissa has been caught, constructing an attack in the strongest terms by comparing the passionate coercions of love and the desire to convert, dominate, and compel. Set in contrast are, variously, a valuable irradiating lesbian attachment between Clarissa and Sally (in the past only) and a similarly valued set of connections among people at Clarissa's party.

There are manifold subtly drawn parallels between Clarissa and Septimus, which make their kinship eerily plausible, but the most important is an attitude toward domination, which, Woolf makes quite plain, the characters share with their author.

> Suppose he [Septimus] had had the passion [for rapture], and had gone to Sir William Bradshaw, a great doctor yet to her obscurely evil, without sex or lust, extremely polite to women, but capable of some indescribable outrage—forcing your soul, that was it—if this young man had gone to him, and Sir William had impressed him, like that, with his power, might he not then have said (indeed she felt it now), Life is made intolerable; they make life intolerable, men like that? (MD, 281)

Clarissa interprets the suicide as a symbolic rejection of rapacious power relations. This is his act of resistance to authority, "holding his treasure"—visionary ecstatic terror—intact when the forces of medicine and law are about to possess him (MD, 281). Significantly, her experience with forms of romantic and ideological thralldom allows Clarissa to make this empathetic analysis of Septimus's aims. The allusion to rape is a point of contact between sexual and mental coercion.[26] Woolf prefigures Three Guineas by depicting a continuum between the political and social institutions of imperialism and religion and the imposition of will in personal relations: all versions of that instrumentalism which "offers help, but desires power" (MD, 151). The fact that Woolf links romantic love to social and political compulsions means that she is no longer treating romance uncritically, as she did in Night and Day, but linking it to a general analysis of power and domination.

"Love and religion," represented respectively by Peter Walsh and Miss Kilman, are "the cruelest things in the world, [Clarissa] thought, seeing them clumsy, hot, domineering, hypocritical, eavesdropping, jealous, infinitely cruel and unscrupulous . . . " because they destroyed "the privacy of the soul" (MD, 191, 192). The desire of Miss Kilman for the Dalloway daughter,

---

26Phyllis Rose argues that the name Clarissa alludes to the Richardson heroine, who, after long resistance, suffers sexual violation, and that Clarissa's avoidance of intense sexuality and thralldom in love is a strategy to preserve her "sense of autonomy and selfhood." Woman of Letters, p. 144. Blanche Gelfant has discussed the way coercion and the desire to absorb and dominate are expressed in some of the love bonds in this novel. "Love and Conversion in Mrs. Dalloway," Criticism VIII (Summer 1966): 229–45.

Elizabeth, is one-sided, intolerant, and obsessive. Her sexual and relational frustrations lead her to almost daft behavior. Likewise, in the early courtship of Clarissa, Peter was more sexually and personally demanding of her than was Dalloway. The knife is his sign, as the sugary cake, greedily coveted, is Miss Kilman's. Clarissa's marriage was a resistance to his possessive and jealous love, his sexual and psychic colonization. Peter's demand for total possession, his disrespect for her privacy or aloofness would have been "intolerable" (*MD*, 10). She resists any overinvestment in that romantic love epitomized by the scenes of pursuit, fantasy, and capture in which Peter still relentlessly engages. Such refusal is on the one hand prudish, yet on the other, it is a choice of privacy, whose cost is asexuality. The mutual distance and independence possible in the Dalloway marriage and Dalloway's cool pleasantness are just saved from the vapid because they preserve the self from emotional destruction.

Clarissa and Septimus both experience same-sex love and passionate affection. In Septimus's case, his mourning is incomplete and his war trauma rampant because the doctors protect him from recognizing grief for a dead male companion. Similarly, Peter interrupts Clarissa's wave of joy at being kissed by Sally Seton during that courtship summer. The "infinitely precious" joy of that relationship is summed up at the moment of the kiss; there is no Miss Kilman–style aftermath of anger and frustrated desire, no Peter Walsh's "granite" of jealousy and hostility, not even the "catastrophe" (narrative climax—and damage) of marriage (*MD*, 53, 50). The kiss is able to be "the most exquisite moment of [Clarissa's] whole life," since it is not expressed in a permanent tie, nor does it suffer the temptations of power (*MD*, 52).

In this way Woolf suggests that love of women might mediate between two goods—joyous desire and tolerant privacy (*MD*, 47–48).[27] When Woolf tells of "the purity, the integrity" of Clarissa's feeling for Sally, these words express sterling values (*MD*, 50). But "this falling in love with women," the lesbian element in *Mrs. Dalloway*, has a double position in the text. The bond Clarissa and Sally make is, like the party, a network of pleasurable connec-

---

[27]A number a studies point to the polarization of values by sex. Lee R. Edwards makes a subtle reading in which the feminine is seen as less implicated in the egotistical desire for power and dominance, and is offered not as a new absolute and inflexible standard, but as contributing to a society "in which the having of power is no longer paramount." "War and Roses: The Politics of *Mrs. Dalloway*," in *The Authority of Experience: Essays in Feminist Criticism*, ed. Arlyn Diamond and Lee Edwards (Amherst: University of Massachusetts Press, 1977), p. 163. Jeremy Hawthorn sees that Woolf associates "atomism" and "division and compartmentalisation" with masculinity, authority, and the state, and unity and synthesis with the feminine, expressed in Clarissa's party. *Virginia Woolf's Mrs. Dalloway: A Study in Alienation* (Sussex: Sussex University Press, 1975), p. 88. With the feminine-masculine polarity, Woolf emphasizes the pernicious influence of dominant values and suggests that the marginal and powerless—among these, women and the mad—are the only social repository of countervailing values. This group can be activated, as Alex Zwerdling suggests, because of a historical crisis in the postwar period that finds a complacent governing class in decline, losing hegemony. "*Mrs. Dalloway* and the Social System," *PMLA* 92, 1 (January 1977): 69–81.

tions; the bond between Miss Kilman and Elizabeth is, like heterosexual thralldom, another form of bullying. If lesbianism is a nondominant form of the erotic, Woolf valorizes it; if it is yet another version of power and dominance, she satirizes it.

"Being part" of each other in a network of intense and pleasurable but unpossessive connection, in which ego is "invisible," is the counterforce, just like the kiss, to all the possessive demands criticized by the text, whether romance or power (*MD*, 12, 14). The party suggests communal values that transcend the egos of any single person: risking "one's one little point of view" for that "immeasurable delight" (*MD*, 255, 282). Instead of manipulating, the parties "create," instead of separating, they "combine"; instead of being assertions of one's class and one's power, they have (so Woolf says) no ulterior purpose but are simply "an offering for the sake of offering, perhaps" (*MD*, 185). Thus the party is a rescripting of lesbian desire, and as well solves the issue of romance. The party is like joyous tolerant desire between women extended to a wider community. One climax of the party comes when Clarissa sees her double, a woman, at the window; another comes when she can make Peter, the most pertinacious pursuer of heterosexual romance, see her simply as she is, without the overlay of jealous possessiveness. So Peter, at the very end, feels something of what Sally and Clarissa had felt long ago ("What is this terror? What is this ecstasy?" *MD* 296). Heterosexual romance has been processed and converted into what one might call neo-lesbian joy. And the character Mrs. Dalloway proves herself a switching station for sexualities, bringing all sorts of hot individual desires into humane networks.[28]

In her party, the convergence of multiple centers of sociability and attraction, the many paths pleasurably crossing, the mutual tolerance and the joining of the characters are convincing because they have been stylistically affirmed from the beginning of the novel. The "tunnelling process" that Woolf called one of her great technical discoveries shows each character in an inner alliance with others; the similar ways each will think about leaves, life, and death join them through this "tunnel" or cave behind the surface of manners on which they many never meet or talk seriously.[29] The tunnelling process

---

[28]With a greater Stracheyan emphasis on the satiric reading of *Mrs. Dalloway*, Rachel Brownstein offers two observations that intersect with the argument here. First, the weakness, age, and partial complicity of Mrs. Dalloway in the false virtues of her society occur as Woolf's revisions of the ideal of the heroine. Second, the party at the novel's end is an exact substitute for the marriage of traditional courtship plots: "But unlike a marriage, it is a temporary union of a group, not a couple, sanctioned by no gods, and it changes nothing by occurring." *Becoming a Heroine: Reading About Women in Novels* (New York: The Viking Press, 1982), p. 269.

[29]"Tunnelling process," from *A Writer's Diary*, pp. 59, 60. First, this is "how I dig out beautiful caves behind my characters: I think this gives exactly what I want; humanity, humour, depth. The idea is that the caves shall connect . . . "; it is elaborated as "my tunnelling process, by which I tell the past by installments, as I have need of it." J. Hillis Miller discusses this technique in "Virginia Woolf's All Souls' Day: The Omniscient Narrator in *Mrs. Dalloway*," in *The Shaken Realist: Essays in Modern Literature in Honor of Frederick J. Hoffman*, ed. Melvin J. Friedman and John B. Vickery (Baton Rouge: Louisiana State University Press, 1970), pp. 100–27.

may also mute critique by showing that connections of the heart can occur despite differences in gender and status. In any event, the technique extends the aura of desire, connection, and loyalty, once confined to a couple in formation, to a widening network of characters, and is another way, added to the nonsexual central couple and the use of lesbian desire, to pose the critique of the convention of romance.

To the Lighthouse is able in a different way to express that yearning for a female bond which emerges in the Clarissa-Sally materials, by fashioning a story that displaces the heterosexual love plot in favor of the parent-child tie, a bisexual oscillation between mother and father. The yearning love of Lily for Mrs. Ramsay, which creates vision, the moment of making peace with Mr. Ramsay, which creates sociability, are both formative events, of greater importance than the traces of heterosexual courtship plots in this novel. In the first section of To the Lighthouse, community (the dinner party) depends extensively on couples and the bait of romance: Minta's golden haze of love helps the emotional entanglements of family life; Lily reluctantly attends to the young man whom she has been assigned, after rich meditations on refusal and rebellion. But Woolf supplants the formation of a new couple as a plot center. Lily is deliberately fabricated to avoid the romantic involvements that are proposed, and Mrs. Ramsay is explicitly criticized for proposing them. However, the book offers detailed consideration of an old couple who are always in the process of reformation and reaffirmation. Yet this couple is put in the context of many other networks, communities, and ties, involving, *inter alia*, "geniality, sisterhood, motherhood, brotherhood" (*MD*, 209). And by the death of Mrs. Ramsay at midbook, the affirmation of the romantic, polarized couple is put definitively in the past. In the third section, community and selfhood must be negotiated in the absence of the promise of couple love that once mediated them. This occurs through a concerted use of the preoedipal materials of female identity, to dissolve the purely romantic telos of the oedipal drama. The loop in the Lily plot (a painting untouched for ten years is begun again and finished) expresses the peculiarities of female quest, with its loop back through the family and the psychic stage of preoedipal attachment.

In *Mrs. Dalloway* and then in *To the Lighthouse*, Woolf has expanded the story of romance emotionally and structurally by posing the preoedipal alternatives, lesbian bonding and the mother-child dyad, to rupture the cultural hegemony of the love plot. *Orlando* was inspired by an energizing erotic attachment, and Woolf apparently began it to deal openly with lesbian-ism.[30] One can interpret the drama of androgyny that remains as a socially

[30]The project was then called *Jessamy Brides* (A Writer's Diary, p. 104). It is well established that the book was inspired by Woolf's relationship with Vita Sackville-West. Indeed, Vita Sackville-West teasingly responded to this work, suggesting that Woolf's creation was a rival for Woolf's love: "Also, you have invented a new form of Narcissism,—I confess,—I am in love with Orlando—this is a complication I had not foreseen." *The Letters of Virginia Woolf, Volume Three*, ed. Nigel Nicolson and Joanne Trautmann (New York: Harcourt Brace Jovanovich, 1977), p. 574.

compelled evasion of what Woolf really wanted to address, or as another critical approach to heterosexuality that ruptures the couple by elaborating the sexes. *Orlando* shows that one can have the erotic without the intense and repressive form of gender polarization upon which the romance plot has traditionally been built. As well, the manifold sexualities of the characters construct a cunning attack on contemporaneous theories that denigrate homosexuality.

Orlando is at least a parodic biography, a female history of Britain, a feminist apologue—an insouciant break with conventional norms surrounding gender, sexual identity, and narrative.[31] In this work, the Ages of England have become the Ages of Woman, scrutinized with two questions in mind: whether the protagonist can undertake work and whether she can enjoy love. Until the present, these satisfactions are divided, and love is separated from quest. The hero is originally a man; then in a masquelike event occurring, neatly, after an anticolonial and anti-British uprising, she becomes a woman. With late adolescence, the "he"—a liberated, sensuous child—becomes the skirted, corseted "she"—a change that shocks most women and that Orlando herself views with anger, curiosity, and some calculation. During her early womanhood, she mulls her spent boyish powers and her potential feminine gains, like a naïve visitor to the strange land of femaleness: a satiric voyage in an eighteenth-century mode. This section presents her swift assimilation of the rules concerning sex and gender in her society; since they have to be learned all at once, their social, not biological, character is clear. After a grimly educative phase as a worshipper of a great male poet, she enters the monogamous stolidity of marriage in the Victorian era. This is the normal closure to a plot for a woman in narrative.

This part of *Orlando* begins with the woman's mortifying consciousness, associated with the dampening values of Victorian England, that she is not married. Even her attempt to replace this wallowing yearning with a brisk turn to her vocation proves futile, for she can write insipid verses only. Orlando is thus obliged to put her calling aside and give into a craving for a wedding ring. Her "submission" to the "spirit of the age" is paraded in

Much of the detail of the book is based on Vita's history of the Sackville family and on her personal life. Frank Baldanza, "*Orlando* and the Sackvilles," *PMLA* LXX (1955): 274–79. See also Joanne Trautmann, *The Jessamy Brides: The Friendship of Virginia Woolf and Vita Sackville-West* (University Park, Pa.: The Pennsylvania State University Press, 1973), pp. 41–48.

31John Graham makes an elegant case for the biographical genre parodied ("The 'Caricature Value' of Parody and Fantasy in *Orlando*," *University of Toronto Quarterly* XXX [July 1961]: 345–66). Fleishman sets this "parodic cultural history" in the context of the "encyclopedic" mode of modernism, also considering the work as a mock biography and a *Künstlerroman* (*Virginia Woolf*, pp. x, 139, 148). Trautmann offers a virtually exhaustive list of genres in *Jessamy Brides*: "A parody of biography, an essay in the exotic, a mock-heroic novel of ideas, an imaginative literary and social history of England, and a biography of Vita Sackville-West" (p. 40). J. J. Wilson makes a dashing case for *Orlando* as mainly an antinovel because it is a satire on literary convention (*New Feminist Essays on Virginia Woolf*, ed. Jane Marcus [Lincoln: University of Nebraska Press, 1981], p 174) All are quite correct rambunctious clichés of romance: "It would be a comfort, she felt, to lean; to sit down; yes, to lie down; never, never, never to get up again" (*O*, 160)—a passage that captures the parallel closures of "couverture" in marriage and in death. This sentiment passes to another sublime fancy, reversed but resonant in Charlotte Brontë, and busily at work in Harlequin romances today:

> . . . she saw a man on horseback. He started. The horse stopped.
> "Madam," the man cried, leaping to the ground, "you're hurt!"
> "I'm dead, Sir!" she replied.

> A few minutes later, they became engaged. (*O*, 163)

Yet by a stroke of authorial authority, Orlando has found a man who is a woman, just as she is a man. The institution of marriage, which demands for a fact the legal and social fiction of strict gender polarization (as the lawsuit establishing Orlando's sex reveals), is still flexible enough to accommodate this "ambisexual couple."[32] The marriage ceremony, which caps the Victorian era and forms a baroque and assertive closure before the actual terminus of the book, combines middle-class propriety and romantic critique, as in the clap of thunder that obliterates the word "Obey."

What occurs after that culturally plausible ending is Woolf's swift panorama of the kinds of fiction and values that are now possible, writing beyond the ending. The Hemingway novel of adventure, the Lawrence novel of sexuality are evoked and dismissed (*O*, 175–76). The only kind of writing that might answer is just like *Mrs. Dalloway:* tumbling and porous. Even the innermost threads of narrative, especially ideas of emphasis, have to be reconsidered, for "the truth is that when we write of a woman, everything is out of place— culminations and perorations; the accent never falls where it does with a man" (*O*, 204). Similarly, old mottos ("Amor Vin—," which had been Love Conquers All) are fractured and delegitimated. Sexual norms and narrative strategies are alike the unified subject of Woolf's critical address.

Because Orlando male and Orlando female are nearly the same, so Orlando loving Shel means, at once, men loving men, women loving women, and women and men loving each other. "Androgyny" is Woolf's contemporaneous description for the unconventionally gendered characters. Male and female are not polarized, but fuse and interpenetrate. Androgynous characters cannot be assigned stable places in hierarchies of gender status, nor do they even adhere to physical norms: Shel is both dainty and brawny, for example.

The social constructions called male and female represent, among other features, a logical dichotomy, the dualistic division of things into A and not-A. Although biologically, sex is a spectrum, in mental structures sex is perceived as polarized. Men are men, and women are not-men. This kind of thinking simplifies the world into norm and absence or lack thereof. In *Orlando*, Woolf

---

[32]"Ambisexual" is Blanche Wiesen Cook's useful term in " 'Women Alone Stir My Imagination': Lesbianism and the Cultural Tradition," *Signs* 4, 4 (Summer 1979): 723.

plays with and erodes this powerful model for thought. The Orlando figure is both A and not-A, a logical contradiction, but a narratable prototype of constant heterogeneity.[33]

By proposing androgynous selves, Woolf wants to depict characters who have stepped beyond the sex-gender system as a whole, with its claims to natural, universal status, its manners and morals, its sexual polarization, its gender asymmetry, its devaluation of the female and the homosexual. As if offhandedly, she also undercuts the prime underpinnings of its epistemology.[34] Androgyny is a critical break with ideas about sex and gender, and with interrelated narrative ideas of causality and motivation, of the uniformity of character, of the stability of time, and of the academic rules of the genre: reserve and objectivity.

We also know that by inventing these androgynous characters, Woolf treats by implication the actual bisexuality and homosexuality of key people represented in this *roman à clef*.[35] So not only the domains of gender but also the questions of "deviant" sexual identity are posed by this text. Heterosexual romance and marriage are set aside precisely in being achieved; Orlando's "dexterous deference to the spirit of the age" has let her pass through a socially demanding "customshouse" with subversive "contraband" (*O*, 174). This strategy of overt conformity allows another kind of writing beyond the ending. Orlando is released into a space not only beyond narrative conventions but also beyond sexual norms. Lesbianism is the unspoken contraband desire that marriage liberates and that itself frees writing.[36] The love of women appears with some circumspection, intermingled with the androgynous, ambisexual marriage and the doubled gender identities of Orlando. So lesbianism not only answers but extends and completes the heterosexual couple.

[33]This analysis draws on Nancy Jay, "Gender and Dichotomy," *Feminist Studies* 7, 1 (Spring 1981): 38–56. In a context of argument similar to the general framework I have offered, Mary Jacobus, seeing a woman writer as both critic and inheritor, reads androgyny as "a Utopian vision of undivided consciousness," healing the split brought about by women's dual status. Mary Jacobus, "The Difference of View," in *Women Writing and Writing about Women*, ed. Mary Jacobus (London: Croom Helm, 1979), p. 20.

[34]The utopian and critical hope presented in the idea of androgyny was eloquently presented by Carolyn G. Heilbrun in *Toward a Recognition of Androgyny* (New York: Harper and Row, Publishers, 1973).

[35]Barbara Fassler has argued that the depiction and integration of masculine and feminine traits or any use of "opposite-sex character traits" would imply homosexuality. "Theories of Homosexuality as Sources of Bloomsbury's Androgyny," *Signs* 5, 2 (Winter 1979): 237–51.

[36]The poem cited at the beginning of Woolf's Chapter 6 in the "contraband" section comes from Vita Sackville-West's work *The Land*. If one reads just a few lines beyond the four that Woolf cited, the tempting and exotic imagery alludes to lesbian desire. The foreign girl, "sulky, dark, and quaint" is "Dangerous too, as a girl might sidle up,/An Egyptian girl, with an ancient snaring spell,/Throwing a net, soft round the limbs and heart. . . ." The poem is found in Vita Sackville-West, *Collected Poems*, Vol. I (London: The Hogarth Press, 1933), p. 58. Sackville-West's ambivalent attitude toward the temptations corresponds to her sense of division. Barbara Fassler discusses this passage in the context of Sackville-West's lesbianism, linking it to the allusions in popular and poetic myth to the Southern and Oriental "sotadic zones," where homosexuality is more dominant, according to theories popular since the 1890s. *Signs* 5, 2 (Winter 1979): 244–46.

Given the biographical and narrative designs that make lesbianism a rich part of the discourses in *Orlando*, it is no wonder that Woolf undertakes to correct the interpretation of homosexuality as illness, deviance, or aberration. Structurally, the book presents encoded counterstatements to two current theories, both known to Woolf and her circle, about the nature of the homosexual personality. One is the "trapped soul" theory quite current in the twenties, promulgated by Havelock Ellis and other influential psychologists, and corresponding to the feelings of division and repression with which homosexuals struggled because of social taboos. The "trapped soul" postulated that the sexual container and the thing contained were not congruent—that a person could have a man's spirit and a woman's body, for example, and that one part had to struggle for expression against the other.[37] This kind of thinking could only exacerbate the body-mind dualism also paradigmatic in Western thought. The erotic, zesty tone of Orlando as well as its generic multiplicity generates the counter-idea that mixed or mingled sexual identities could be exhilarating and pleasurable. As well as being a general answer to dichotomous thinking, the androgynous combination answers that depressing notion of a mind-body split in a homosexual personality.

Orlando's perpetual youth—at any rate, her astonishingly slow rate of growth—seems to challenge Freud's idea of the progress of the psyche from bisexual dramas to heterosexual object choice. Any adult still experiencing homosexual desire is, in Freud's terms, suffering from "arrested development," a failed transition to the proper object.[38] What better way to depict, and mock, this "arrest" than by having someone who is a sixteen-year-old in the sixteenth century age only about two decades by 1928? And even more, Woolf makes Orlando's youthfulness be a positive statement of the gay, aggressive verve generated by this situation. The view of Orlando as a quintessentially healthy character, of course, responds to the satanic and lurid cultural images of the lesbian prominent in turn-of-the-century "decadent" works by both Swinburne and Baudelaire.[39] The health of erotic heterogeneity and ambisexuality makes a powerful cultural text. At the midnight stroke with which the book ends, undeclared revelations are implied: of love united with quest, of the end of sexual polarization, of an erotic affirmation of sexualities, and of the critique of all institutions of gender, from unmanageable dresses to narrative conventions.

In *Flush*, the final novel of this line of Woolf's development, numerous narrative and emotional allusions to the nature of romance and thralldom cap

---

[37]H.D.'s companion Winifred Bryher wrote in *Two Selves* (Paris: Contact Editions, 1923) that she was really a "boy" unfortunately caged in the body of a girl.

[38]Sigmund Freud, "The Psychogenesis of a Case of Homosexuality in a Woman" (1920), *Collected Papers*, Vol. II (London: The Hogarth Press, 1957).

[39]Susan Gubar's tracing of culturally different "sapphistries" pointedly reminds us that the lesbian as a cultural and sexual identity has been constructed and utilized in various ways by writers. "Sapphistries," . . . *Signs* [10 (1984), 43–62].

the movement away from heterosexual romance. For in *Flush,* romance has been reduced—no dog lover would say demeaned, just tickled out of all countenance—by emerging in a pooch. With his jealousy, desire, dependence, sublimation, loyalty, and self-sacrifice, Flush's patterns of emotional involvement and levels of pain are closest to the romance plot of *Night and Day* in its early glowering moments of anger, self-doubt, and unspoken passion. The dog is completely enthralled with Elizabeth Barrett; when Robert Browning interrupts their mutual love, the dog is beside himself with jealousy.

The emotions proper to the relation between Mr. Browning and Miss Barrett, which are, of course, the febrile and exciting discovery of mutual love, are displaced by being seen through the point of view of a character whose intense sense of smell, hypersensitivity to all expected tidbits and privileges, and long, fluffy ears are his strongest points. Any attention the reader would have hoped to have given to one of the officially Great Love Stories of English Letters has been baffled by the same emotions of yearning and burning apparent in interspecies desire. In sum, a Woolfean shift of emphasis from person to canine has dramatically ended the readers' and the author's thralldom to the narrative authority of the heterosexual love plot. To achieve this critical stance has been her concerted project in the novels through the central portion of her career.

Out of the Chrysalis:
Female Initiation and Female
Authority in Virginia Woolf's
The Voyage Out

Christine Froula

Virginia Woolf's first novel, depicting the initiation of a female artist-figure, captures the paradoxical relation of female initiation to female authority in the late Victorian culture of Woolf's girlhood.[1] On the one hand, Woolf's story of the semi-autobiographical Rachel Vinrace shows how the paradigms of female initiation encourage the young woman to identify with nature rather than culture and to imagine marriage and maternity as the destiny that will fulfill her life. On the other hand, Woolf endows Rachel with a powerful desire to evade or transcend this culturally determined destiny; in other words, to break out of the female initiation plot that her culture imposes upon women, constituting them not as fully legitimated participants in history and culture but as culture's material support. Neither the strength nor the resources of Rachel's desire are equal to the powerful cultural currents that oppose it, however, and the history of Woolf's heroine ends not in triumph but in death. Rachel's death represents not only the power of female initiation structures to overwhelm female desire when it ventures to imagine a different future, but also the difficulties that Woolf confronted in her first attempt to imagine an alternative to the female initiation plot. If Rachel's death records the failure of Woolf's imaginative project in *The Voyage Out*, it is also a symbolic, initiatory death that precedes the rebirth of Woolf's authority in the more powerful representations of female creativity in her later female *Künstlerromane*. In *The Voyage Out*, Woolf augments the genre of the *failed* female artist-novel.

From *Tulsa Studies in Women's Literature* 5 (1986): 63–90. © 1986 The University of Tulsa.

[1]For a study of the autobiographical dimension of Woolf's first novel, see Louise DeSalvo's *Virginia Woolf's First Voyage: A Novel in the Making* (Totowa, N.J.: Rowman and Littlefield, 1980). Although my interpretations often diverge widely from DeSalvo's, I have found her scholarship very useful. For a discussion of the novel as an initiation (but not a specifically female initiation), see Avrom Fleishman, *Virginia Woolf: A Critical Reading* (Baltimore: Johns Hopkins University Press, 1975), chap. 1. For a wide-ranging collection of essays on the female *Bildungs-roman* that uses *The Voyage Out* to raise general questions about female development, see *The Voyage In: Fictions of Female Development*, ed. Elizabeth Abel, Marianne Hirsch, and Elizabeth Langland (Hanover, N.H.: University Press of New England, 1983).

Although her career might have ended here, it did not, and the existence of Woolf's later female artist-novels enables us to interpret her representation of female initiation and female authority in *The Voyage Out* not as an ultimate failure but as a challenging and transforming critique, and further, as an allegorical measure of the very great odds that Woolf herself conquered in forging her own powerful artistic authority.

Initiation Paradigms and the Female Artist-Novel

In preliterate cultures, according to Mircea Eliade and others, male and female initiation are not two variants of a single process but two radically different processes that symbolically institute the roles accorded to males and females within the culture even as they constitute the historical subjects who fill those roles. Male initiation accomplishes the boy's separation from the mother and his dwellingplace and inducts him into the culture of his fathers. The initiatory rite is conceived as a symbolic death followed by a rebirth, through revelation of the culture's sacred myths, into knowledge of the origins and history of the cosmos. The male rites of passage are performed collectively, and the ages of the initiates may therefore vary widely. Female initiation, by contrast, is associated with the menarche, a biological event in each girl's history; hence female initiation rites are less widespread, less elaborately developed, and individual rather than collective because they are tied to each girl's physical maturation. The education that the rites bestow upon the girl consists not in privileged cultural knowledge but, Eliade notes, in "a revelation of the sacrality of women" bound up with "the mystery of blood" which the rites commemorate.[2] This education confirms the girl's likeness to her mother and prepares her for the domestic and reproductive roles of wife and mother, in contrast to the male initiate's education, which prepares him to participate in the public domains of history and culture.

The different patterns of initiation for males and females elaborate sexual difference into a dichotomy between nature and culture manifest in gender roles. Male initiation, Eliade concludes, "represents an introduction to a world that is not immediate—the world of spirit and culture. For girls, on the contrary, initiation involves a series of revelations concerning the secret meaning of . . . the visible sign of their sexual maturity" (47). The pattern of female initiation that held sway in the late Victorian period resembles Eliade's model in the exclusion of all but a few women from higher education and the most prestigious professions and in the idealization of marriage and motherhood as a daughter's highest calling. Deborah Gorham notes that the Victorians cherished the separate spheres of domesticity and commerce, which permitted the conflicting moral values of Christianity and capitalism to coexist. Prescriptive writings for women describe the daughter as "an immortal creature," a family's "crowning grace," while the mother/wife, possessing an

---

[2]Mircea Eliade, *Rites and Symbols of Initiation: The Mysteries of Birth and Rebirth*, trans. Willard R. Trask (New York: Harper & Row, 1958), 42.

oxymoronic "majestic childishness," is the Angel in the House.[3] For the Victorians, as for Eliade's preliterate cultures, the daughter's transformation from an unsexed but female-gendered "sunbeam" to sacred vessel and angel was tied to the menarche, which was thought to bring not only physiological but emotional and behavioral changes: "She is no longer wayward, romping and careless, but becomes reserved and modest in her deportment. In short, she is now a woman, prepared to love and be loved, and capable of performing the highest and most important functions of her sex."[4] Still, the conviction that female anatomy was destiny was equivocal enough to require vigorous reinforcement through detailed prescription of behavior and priorities. In the late-Victorian period, when serious education was beginning to become available to women, strictures as to the dangers of intellectual work to the female body were frequently reiterated: women were instructed not to strain themselves with work during their periods and were encouraged to think that the purpose of their educations was to prepare them to be better listeners, better wives and mothers, makers of more genteel homes, and more attractive adornments to civilization.[5]

Rather than simply being *perceived* as closer to nature than men, women were *instituted* as subjects who are closer to nature by means of an initiation/education that excluded them from symbolic activity except in the domestic arena.[6] Bruce Lincoln describes female initiation as a three-stage process of "enclosure, metamorphosis (or magnification), and emergence"—a "chrysalis pattern"—and he notes that this pattern, rather than separating the girl from the dwellingplace, confines her within it.[7] Thus female initiation institutes women's *absence* from the culture of the public sphere, which becomes "male" insofar as the male and female rites of passage succeed in preserving a dichotomy between "male" culture and "female" nature. Insofar as women's priorities must be home, husband, and children, public culture becomes a male domain; and insofar as culture is a male domain, the woman artist or culture-maker becomes a contradiction in terms.

Although the educational reforms of late nineteenth century England began to make the public sphere more accessible to women and to widen the social roles available for them, both the male-authored cultural tradition and women's own socialization worked to sustain the nature/culture dichotomy. In her 1925 story "The Introduction," Woolf plays the still-dominant chrysalis

---

[3]Deborah Gorham, *The Victorian Girl and the Feminine Ideal* (London: Croom Helm, 1982), 4–6.

[4]A. Reeves Jackson, "Diseases Peculiar to Women," *Wood's Household Practice*, Vol. 2, 539; cited in Gorham, 86.

[5]See Gorham, chap. 6, particularly the case of Molly Hughes.

[6]See Sherry B. Ortner, "Is Female to Male as Nature Is to Culture?" in *Women, Culture, and Society*, ed. Michelle Zimbalist Rosaldo and Louise Lamphere (Stanford: Stanford University Press, 1974), 67–87.

[7]Bruce Lincoln, *Emerging from the Chrysalis: Studies in Rituals of Women's Initiation* (Cambridge: Harvard University Press, 1981), 101.

pattern of female initiation against her heroine Lily Everit's passion for
learning, her gift for writing, and the possibility of cultural authority that her
education ostensibly makes available to her. Entering Clarissa Dalloway's
drawingroom to attend her first evening party, Lily crosses not only from the
freedom of childhood to the constraints of womanhood but from the imaginative freedom of her writing self to woman's limited sphere. Finding herself in
"the famous place: the world," Lily feels her pleased pride in her essay on
Dean Swift, marked with three stars by her professor, dissolving, though she
clutches it "as a drowning man might hug a spar in the sea."[8] Her "introduction," to society in general and to the literary Oxonian Mr. Brinsley in
particular, is an initiatory ordeal; she feels "flung into a whirlpool where she
would either perish or be saved," a current composed of:

> Westminster Abbey; the sense of enormously high solemn buildings surrounding
> them; grow[ing] up; being a woman . . . the dress, and all the little chivalries and
> respects of the drawing-room . . . she had come out of her chrysalis and was being
> proclaimed what in the long comfortable darkness of childhood she had never
> been—this frail and beautiful creature, this limited and circumscribed creature
> who could not do what she liked, this butterfly with a thousand facets to its eyes,
> and delicate fine plumage, and difficulties and sensibilities and sadnesses innumer-
> able: a woman. (*MDP*, 39)

Lily's intellectual identity (figured, significantly, as a *man*) "drowns" as she
learns that "it was not hers to dominate, or to assert; rather to air and
embellish this orderly life where all was done already" (*MDP*, 40). She feels
her claim to cultural authority fade to insignificance beside Mr. Brinsley's:
whereas he assumes that she writes poetry, not essays—that is, that her genre
is the private one of lyric rather than the public one of the essay—his own
authority is, figuratively speaking, "in direct descent from Shakespeare"
(*MDP*, 41). Something in Lily wants to "be a butterfly," but she discovers that
she cannot be both a butterfly *and* an essayist, both an adornment of
civilization—like Clarissa—and its critic. Although she tries to talk herself
into compliance with the world she has entered in order to stave off the
"terror, this suspicion of something different" that threatens to "drive her out
into loneliness," Lily fails: "In spite of all she could do her essay upon the
character of Swift became more and more obtrusive and the three stars burnt
quite bright again, only with a terrible lustre, no longer clear and brilliant,
but troubled and bloodstained." Woolf metamorphoses Lily not into a butterfly but into something like a warrior, one who thinks "of the towers and
civilisation with horror," and who understands "that there are no sanctuaries,
or butterflies, and this civilisation, said Lily to herself . . . depends on me"
(*MDP*, 42–43). Refiguring female initiation as a battle between women's desire
to be subjects in history and culture and a social world that "depends" upon

---

[8]Virginia Woolf, *Mrs Dalloway's Party: A Short Story Sequence*, ed. Stella McNichol (New
York: Harcourt Brace Jovanovich, 1973), 39; hereafter cited in the text as *MDP*.

their compliant silence, Lily's story reveals some ways in which society, while not excluding its daughters from education in the public sphere, still limited the social and cultural roles available to them in the late Victorian period and the early twentieth century.

Woolf's comparatively late and brief treatment of female initiation in "The Introduction" sheds much light on Rachel's initiation in *The Voyage Out*. Begun in 1908 and published in 1915, the novel traces Woolf's own first voyage toward artistic authority, which she appears to have conceived as a *reformed* female initiation plot that would lead her heroine not only toward love and marriage but also to an identity in history and culture. Early on, when she was still searching for a name for her heroine, who was first Rose, then Cynthia, then Rachel, Woolf rejected a suggestion of Clive Bell's in terms that bespeak both her ambitions and her fears for her heroine: "Belinda is perhaps a little too dainty for my woman, and what I conceive of her destiny. But I talk grandly, feeling in my heart some doubt that she will ever have a destiny."[9] It is doubtful that Woolf would have referred to Rachel's *death* as a *grand* destiny or that she would have feared her never reaching it; much likelier, she did not in 1908 foresee it at all. Rather, Woolf's first gropings toward her novel suggest her ambition not to create a heroine whose individual life story would make her an exception to the rule but rather to create a fictional world in which the plot of marriage and motherhood governing female destiny might itself be challenged and changed.

This greater ambition underlies Woolf's creation of a *colony* in *The Voyage Out*. A passage in the 1910 draft, titled *Melymbrosia*, explains that its fictional colony was founded because the "English were dissatisfied with their own civilisation," from which neither Cornwall nor Italy nor Greece allowed them any escape: "the South Seas being very distant, South America did instead."[10] Woolf's very early writings both anticipate and interpret her founding of a fictional colony. At nineteen, when most young women of her upbringing would have been dreaming of marriage as their own happy end, Virginia Stephen forecast her first novel in a letter: "The only thing in this world is music—music and books and one or two pictures. I am going to found a colony where there shall be no marrying—unless you happen to fall in love with a symphony of Beethoven—no human element at all, except what comes through Art" (*L*, 1: 42–43). A year later, she wrote jokily of her scheme for a play with a marriage counterplot: "Im going to have a man and a woman— show them growing up—never meeting—not knowing each other—but all the time you'll feel them come nearer and nearer. This will be the real exciting part (as you see)—but when they almost meet—only a door

⁹*The Letters of Virginia Woolf*, ed. Nigel Nicolson and Joanne Trautmann, 6 vols. (New York: Harcourt Brace Jovanovich, 1975–1980), Vol. 1, 345; hereafter cited in the text as *L* with volume and page number following.
¹⁰Virginia Woolf, *Melymbrosia: An Early Version of The Voyage Out*, ed. Louise A. DeSalvo (New York: New York Public Library, 1982), 70–71; hereafter cited in the text as *M*.

between—you see how they just miss—and go off at a tangent, and never come anywhere near again. There'll be oceans of talk and emotions without end" (*L*, 1: 60). Woolf imagined the colony of *The Voyage Out*, then, as an escape from that "civilisation" that Lily Everit would say "depends on me." But Rachel too discovers that there are no sanctuaries (or colonies), and that she can claim authority only by a terrible battle of bloodstained words—a battle that the situation of her colony on the Amazon seems to anticipate. An avid reader of Elizabethan voyages of exploration and discovery, Woolf perhaps knew the sixteenth century explorer Francisco de Orellana's tale of encountering "fighting women" on the Amazon river, from which its name may have come.[11] In Greek art, some classicists have argued, the Amazon myth projects male fear of women who challenge their subordinate status in marriage and so escape the bounds within which Greek culture, specifically the marriage structure, strives to contain female desire.[12] In *The Voyage Out*, too, the colony on the Amazon signals hostility to patriarchal marriage. When Hirst derides Rachel's ignorance of Gibbon at Susan and Arthur's engagement dance, she counterposes to his presumption of the superiority of himself and his culture a fleeting vision of a women's colony and culture: "She would be a Persian princess far from civilisation, riding her horse upon the mountains alone, and making her women sing to her in the evening, far from . . . the strife and men and women."[13] Like Lily, Rachel finds that she can become herself only by becoming a warrior, and her journey to this symbolic "Amazon"—in other words, to the double frontier of nature and of women's history—allegorizes her search for symbolic "arms," a language and culture with which to create and defend her destiny.

Such a battle is far more easily lost than won; and in fact, the old chrysalis/ marriage plot overtakes *The Voyage Out* to vanquish Woolf's heroine and repeal her different destiny. In a further reflection of the mutual mirroring of life and art, Rachel's end comes very close to becoming Woolf's own. DeSalvo correlates Woolf's writing and rewriting of Rachel's delirium and death scene with several of Woolf's mental breakdowns and one of her suicide attempts. In larger terms, the failure of Woolf's plan to create a female subject who, away from the laws that govern female destiny in "civilisation," could speak her own ends into being threatened the success, perhaps even the apparent possibility, of Woolf's attempt to bring into being a self who did not yet exist, her own

---

[11]For a study of Elizabethan themes in *The Voyage Out*, see Alice Fox, "Virginia Woolf at Work: The Elizabethan *Voyage Out*," *Bulletin of Research in the Humanities* 84 (Spring 1981), 65–84.

[12]See Page duBois, *Centaurs and Amazons: Women and the Pre-History of the Great Chain of Being* (Ann Arbor: University of Michigan Press, 1982), esp. 41, where she notes that marriage, "in Lévi-Strauss' sense, the exchange of women between men of the same kind, was culture for the Greeks"; and William Blake Tyrrell, *Amazons: A Study in Athenian Mythmaking* (Baltimore: Johns Hopkins University Press, 1984), esp. 65, 83.

[13]Virginia Woolf, *The Voyage Out* (New York: Harcourt Brace Jovanovich, 1948), 155; hereafter cited in the text as *VO*.

artist-self. But the resemblance between the autobiographical fiction and life was broken when Woolf published the novel, lived through its first launching, and went on to create the female artist-novels in which her women artists both speak and survive. In these later works, Woolf places her women artists outside the marriage plot that overcomes Rachel—a decision foreshadowed in her earlier name, Cynthia, in Rachel's repeated insistence that she will never marry and even in Rachel's name.[14] Woolf's later female artists—*Lily* Everit, *Lily* Briscoe, and *Lilian* LaTrobe—all stand outside marriage. In creating these characters, Woolf founded a tiny colony that did not yet exist when she wrote *The Voyage Out*, a work that both represents and transcends the paradigms of female initiation.[15]

Rachel's "Great War": The Marriage Plot

Our first close scrutiny of the twenty-four-year-old Rachel, through Helen's eyes, is not promising. Her face seems:

> weak rather than decided, saved from insipidity by the large enquiring eyes. . . . Moreover, a hesitation in speaking, or rather a tendency to use the wrong words, made her seem more than normally incompetent for her years. . . . how clear it was that she would be vacillating, emotional, and when you said something to her it would make no more lasting impression than the stroke of a stick upon water. There was nothing to take hold of in girls—nothing hard, permanent, satisfactory. (*VO*, 20)

To Helen, Rachel seems unformed and unformable, a watery being that culture, language, writing leave no mark upon. Helen's impressions prove true in some respects, but Rachel surprises her expectation of interminable damp confidences by keeping to herself on the voyage until Helen actually becomes curious about her. Further, in this early scene Woolf subtly heightens Rachel's interest by means of a conversation between her father Willoughby and his old friend Mr. Pepper, who expresses surprise that Willoughby has dedicated none of his ships to investigating "the great white monsters of the lower waters" (*VO*, 22):

> "No, no," laughed Willoughby, "the monsters of the earth are too many for me!" Rachel was heard to sigh, "Poor little goats!"

---

[14]This name alludes not only to the Rachel of Genesis, outside marriage against her will, but also to the French actress Rachel Félix, with whose lament that she had to live the lives of others rather than her own Woolf did not sympathize. What, Woolf asked, is "one's 'Own Life'? . . . It is when we feel most that we live most; and we cannot believe that Rachel, married to a real man, bearing real children, and adding up real butcher's bills, would have lived more truly than Rachel imagining the passions of women who never existed" ("Rachel," *Times Literary Supplement*, 20 April 1911, 155; cited by DeSalvo, 69). For extensive discussion of Woolf's names for her heroine, see DeSalvo, chap. 2.

[15]For Lilian LaTrobe, see *Pointz Hall: The Earlier and Later Typescripts of Between the Acts*, ed. Mitchell A. Leaska (New York: University Publications, 1983), 78.

"If it weren't for the goats there'd be no music, my dear; music depends upon goats," said her father rather sharply, and Mr. Pepper went on to describe the white, hairless, blind monsters lying curled on the ridges of sand at the bottom of the sea, which would explode if you brought them to the surface, their sides bursting asunder and scattering entrails to the winds. . . . (*VO*, 23)

Woolf had earlier described Willoughby as "a sentimental man who imported goats for the sake of the empire" (*M*, 8); and, as DeSalvo notes, the veiled allusion to Woolf's nickname, "Goat," makes Rachel too her father's property. The final text associates her not only with the helpless cargo but also with the monsters of the deep, and the plot of *The Voyage Out* interprets Pepper's image of deepsea beings so accustomed to high pressure that to surface is to explode as an image of female authority. The image of Rachel as sea-monster exemplifies the buried lives that women lead in male culture, resonating with James Joyce's Lily Dale, Henrik Ibsen's deathwalking Irene, Hélène Cixous' repressed women who have lived underground and underwater in male culture, "in dreams, in bodies (though muted), in silences," even as it expresses the mortal danger that surfacing into language and culture poses to a woman thus repressed. Lacking a language, lacking social identity, she is monstrous; raised to consciousness without the words to express herself, she may explode.[16]

Rachel lives her underwater life alone in her rooms, first on the ship and later at Helen's villa, where she practices and reads, falls asleep and day-dreams, lives an elaborate, solitary fantasy life vividly captured in *Melymbrosia*:

"Come, Spirits" she murmured; and was instantly fortified by a sense of the presence of the things that aren't there. . . . Her quarrel with the living was that they did not realise the existence of drowned statues, undiscovered places, the birth of the world, the final darkness, and death. To the one man who had yet asked her to marry him, she had said that it seemed to her ridiculous. Why, she half expected to come up next year as a bed of white flowers. Since she had been conscious at all, she had been conscious of what with her love of vague phrases, she called, "The Great War." It was a war waged on behalf of things like stones, jars, wreckage at the bottom of the sea, trees stars and music, against the people who believe in what they see. (*M*, 21)[17]

16Hélène Cixous, "The Laugh of the Medusa," *New French Feminisms*, ed. Elaine Marks and Isabelle de Courtivron (New York: Schocken, 1981), 256.

17*Melymbrosia* is the extant draft B, begun about 1910 and revised in 1912; Woolf's use of the phrase "Great War," in a passage cut from *The Voyage Out*, thus precedes the beginning of World War I. DeSalvo discusses Woolf's revisions in chaps. 2–4, and I agree with her view that much valuable material was submerged in the transformation of *Melymbrosia* into *The Voyage Out*. In my discussion, therefore, I treat the two versions as a single composite text, citing *The Voyage Out* when possible and *Melymbrosia* when necessary.

For comparison of the two texts, see also Elizabeth Heine, "The Earlier *Voyage Out*: Virginia Woolf's First Novel," *Bulletin of Research in the Humanities* 84 (Spring 1981), 294–316, and Beverly Ann Schlack, "The Novelist's Voyage from Manuscripts to Text: Revisions of Literary Allusions in *The Voyage Out*," *Bulletin of Research in the Humanities* 84 (Spring 1981), 317–27.

Rachel's "Great War" for the remembrance of drowned things is a vigil for what has been repressed from language, history, and consciousness, and in particular, for lost origins: her dead mother, the "birth of the world," the sources of her own musical art. In a curious association, Rachel opposes her bond with these drowned things that exist outside language "until a note of music, or a sentence or a sight, joined hands with them" to the marriage proposal that she has received, as though marriage and her communion with this buried life were somehow mutually exclusive. Rachel's image of her future as "a bed of white flowers" combines the nuptial bed and the grave; whereas her identification with drowned things represents an alternative to human culture as structured by the marriage plot, marriage would, it seems, "drown" her buried life more finally than death itself. To marry, for Rachel, would be to lose the life she lives so vividly outside language. Thus her "Great War" on behalf of drowned things is also a war against the human culture and language that deny their existence.

Rachel repeatedly insists in the early chapters of *The Voyage Out* that she will never marry but this embattled position is attacked on all sides. The novel's opening scene—in which Helen, walking on the Strand, weeps at leaving her children behind while her husband stalks along stoically intoning heroic poetry and street urchins shriek, "Bluebeard!"—precedes Rachel's own introduction; and this portrait of a marriage and of men's and women's separate spheres is reinforced by many others that together form an implicit initiation scenario for Rachel. Although her mother, Theresa, is dead, everyone compares Rachel with her, and the comparison assumes a sameness that it constantly tries to uncover (*VO*, 15, 25, 60, 85–86; *M*, 45). The aura that survives Theresa seems at times more vivid than her living daughter. The double refrain, "She's like her mother/She's not like her mother," signals an undifferentiated condition that lies deeper than resemblance and makes a danger of Rachel's desire for her lost mother. For, if Rachel needs her mother's image in order both to recognize and to differentiate her own, she also risks resembling her too much, of losing her own identity in her mother's, reproducing her in motherhood and in death. Thus, as Rachel associates marriage with death in the "Great War" passage, so the thought of motherhood brings with it the thought of death by drowning:

> "If I thought that by dying I could give birth to twenty—no thirty—children, all beautiful and very charming, I'd die for that. . . . Perhaps." Candour forced her to consider the extreme horror of feeling the water give under her, of losing her head, splashing wildly, sinking again with every vein smarting and bursting, an enormous weight sealing her mouth, and pressing salt water down her lungs when she breathed. (*M*, 179)

Woolf writes that Rachel was born to play the piano, unlike women born "for a thousand other reasons; to marry, to nurse, to ride, to fill the world" (*M*, 41). Yet the idea and the fact of marriage seem to surround Rachel and shut the life she was born for from view.

Rachel resists with irony enough her aged aunts' concern that she should marry, but the seductive and imposing Dalloways, who come on board in Lisbon, embody the marriage plot in a fashion the more dangerous because it nearly disarms her. Clarissa and Richard play a very special role in Rachel's education. Clarissa invites Rachel into conventional womanhood as she will later invite Lily Everit; playing mother to the motherless girl, she makes Rachel desire to follow her example. Shortly after meeting Clarissa, Rachel gazes with dissatisfaction into her mirror, seeing a face quite unlike Clarissa's exquisite one; when the glittering, worldly Dalloways enter, Rachel's "mermaids, caves, the unseen things suddenly deserted her; she was disrobed, an incompetent, unattractive, insignificant girl" (*M*, 28). "Tell me—everything," Rachel wants to say to the adults at dinner. Yet when they do, she finds that she does not agree. If the "unseen things" desert her, she cannot desert them. Thus when Clarissa, with characteristic hyperbole, says, "I really couldn't exist without the Brontës! Don't you love them? Still, on the whole, I'd rather live without them than without Jane Austen," Rachel answers, "Jane Austen? I don't like Jane Austen."

> "You monster!" Clarissa exclaimed. "I can only just forgive you. Tell me why?"
> "She's so—so—well, so like a tight plait," Rachel floundered. (*VO*, 57–58)

For Rachel, Austen's novels, for all their sharpness, wit, and irony, signify the education that "plaits" or plots young girls tightly into femininity, marriage, and motherhood. Uneducated, curious, and impressionable, she is also unteachable in some ways, unknowingly loyal to feelings to which literature gives no voice.

Rachel is also slow to grasp the idea of separate spheres so crucial to the marriage plot as the Dalloways and the other couples around her embody it. Bemused, she watches Richard first praise Austen as "incomparably the greatest female writer we possess" because "she does not attempt to write like a man," then doze off as his wife reads him the first page of *Persuasion*; and she thinks "Poor Jane Austen! She was impotent beside this body. She talked of unreal things" (*VO*, 62). Richard makes Rachel feel not only Austen's weakness but her own: comparing her hand and his, she "realised the unimportance of her life. 'I should have to give you what you asked', she reflected, 'because—because—' The reason was not found, for Richard woke" (*M*, 46–47). When Rachel tries to learn from Richard what his political views are, he confuses rather than enlightens her. He opposes women's suffrage with his very body: "May I be in my grave before a woman has the right to vote in England!" (*VO*, 43). And he silences Rachel's questions by explaining:

> "I never allow my wife to talk politics. . . . It is impossible for human beings, constituted as they are, both to fight and to have ideals. If I have preserved mine . . . it is due to the fact that I have been able to come home to my wife in the evening and to find that she has spent her day in calling, music, play with the children, domestic duties, what you will; her illusions have not been destroyed. She gives me courage to go on." (*VO*, 65)

With his enforced separate spheres and his sequestered Angel in the House, Richard is the male defender of the marriage plot as Clarissa is the female. Rachel responds by instinctively invoking an outsider figure, a widow whose mind and affections Richard's politics of "unity" leaves out of account. In their talk, Rachel is worsted, not only because Richard cannot listen to her seriously but because she lacks a language (*VO*, 67). But the difference in strength between his language and hers, like that between their two hands, makes Rachel feel not, as Clarissa does, a claim upon his protection but the dangerous inadequacy of her symbolic arms for the "war" that she is fighting, "waged chiefly at meals, when one had to keep on knowing that the things that were said were all misfits for ideas, or did not try to fit anything" (*M*, 23).

Rachel's frustrated conversation with Richard foreshadows the scene of his kiss, a very important event in Rachel's initiation. Driven Dido-and-Aeneaslike into Rachel's stateroom by a tempest, the two enact a comic, and very English, version of that catastrophe. Richard, sitting down on a Bach score left lying in a chair, asks Rachel about her "interests and occupations," and she answers simply, with comic irony: "You see, I'm a woman." Richard comments sententiously, "How strange to be a woman! A young and beautiful woman . . . has the whole world at her feet. . . . You have inestimable power—for good or for evil—what couldn't you do—' he broke off." "What?" Rachel asks blankly; the ship lurches and Richard kisses her. Richard's sudden kiss—which for Rachel unveils "infinite possibilities she had never guessed at" (*VO*, 76)—recalls Lincoln's discussion of the Kore myth as a paradigm for female initiation in "a number of male-centered, misogynistically inclined cultures, and strongly suggested in numerous Greek myths" (Lincoln, 78). The Kore paradigm signals the young woman's violent abduction into male culture, where her place is in the underworld. Defining women not as free, desiring subjects but as objects of desire and exchange among men, it takes as its goal not the girl's introduction to procreative sexuality but "the forcible subjugation of women to male control." Replacing the menarche, a natural and exclusively female event, with "defloration," rape represents a male appropriation of female initiation that overwrites the natural event with a violent male act (Lincoln, citing La Fontaine, 78–79).

Richard's kiss is not a rape, but it is nonetheless a violent sexual act in its Edwardian degree, and Rachel responds both positively, to its awakening of her own sexuality, and negatively, to its enactment of male privilege in the socially constructed economy of desire. She feels that "something wonderful had happened"; she tells Helen, "I liked him, and I liked being kissed" (*VO*, 77, 82). But she also feels terror, and she connects Richard's kiss with the prostitutes in Piccadilly and more subtly with marriage as Helen, here evoking Helen of Troy, urges complicity, expresses mock-jealousy that Richard has kissed Rachel and not herself, and advises Rachel to "think no more about it" (*VO*, 80). Rachel, loyal to drowned things, replies, "I shall think about it all day and all night until I find out exactly what it does mean." The first meaning that she finds is that of her own sexual vulnerability: "So that's why I can't walk alone!" she expostulates. "Because men are brutes! I hate men!" She suddenly sees her life as "a creeping hedged-in thing, driven cautiously between high walls, here turned aside, there plunged in darkness, made dull and crippled for ever—her life that was the only chance she had—the short season between two silences" (*VO*, 82). This image of enforced enclosure recurs in Rachel's nightmare, a freehand revision of Christina Rossetti's "Goblin Market" with its differentiation between enclosed domestic space in which women are safe and the great world outside where men threaten to "ruin" them:

> She dreamt that she was walking down a long tunnel, which grew so narrow by degrees that she could touch the damp bricks on either side. At length the tunnel opened and became a vault; she found herself trapped in it, bricks meeting her wherever she turned, along with a little deformed man who squatted on the floor gibbering, with long nails. His face was pitted and like the face of an animal. The wall behind him oozed with damp, which collected into drops and slid down. Still and cold as death she lay, not daring to move, until she broke the agony by tossing herself across the bed, and woke crying "Oh!" . . .
>
> She felt herself pursued, so that she got up and actually locked her door. A voice moaned for her; eyes desired her. All night long barbarian men harrassed the ship; they came scuffling down the passages, and stopped to snuffle at her door (*VO*, 77)

Rossetti's Laura is redeemed by her sister's love into the female domestic community of sisters, mothers, and daughters that protects her from the goblin men's ravaging temptations. Rossetti thus resolves the crisis of female initiation with a utopian scenario, for although marriage seems implicit in the existence of mothers and daughters, the only males in the poem are the goblins whom this domestic solution evades. In Rachel's dream, Woolf makes explicit the skeptical treatment of marriage that Rossetti's fantasy implies: the domestic enclosure becomes not a haven but a deadly, tomblike, manmade place—the woman a sequestered treasure, the goblin man her jailer. The barbarian men who harass the ship all night ironically recall the earlier description of the ship as "a bride going forth to her husband unattended" (*M*, 19). Given its instigation in Richard Dalloway, pillar of the Empire and ex-M.P., Rachel's dream, far more directly than Rossetti's poem, grotesquely mirrors that "civilisation" from which her voyage departs.

As her nightmare shows, Rachel resists the initiation that the Dalloways and Helen, who assures her that nothing at all out of the ordinary has happened, together encourage. To Rachel, the virgin, the prostitute, and the wife seem inescapably linked and all damned. "You're doomed, Rachel. There's no escape," Helen says, intending lightness (*M*, 66). "It *is* terrifying— it *is* disgusting," Rachel asserts, "as if she included Helen in her hatred" (*VO*, 81). As the Dalloways depart, Clarissa bestows upon Rachel an inscribed copy of *Persuasion*, closing a chapter of her education that has worked by persuasion (Clarissa), complicity (Helen), and force (Richard). "Why do people marry?" Rachel has asked Clarissa. "That's what you're going to find out,"

Clarissa answers (*VO*, 60). Leaving Rachel, she places the answer—or one form of it—in her hand, a gesture that subtly links the marriage plot that will undo Rachel with the plots of the female literary tradition that cannot well support the ambitions of Woolf's voyage out.

The Book of the World: Cultural Initiation

When the ship reaches Santa Marina, Willoughby agrees to Helen's plan to have Rachel stay at the Ambroses' villa for several months while Willoughby concludes his business on the river. Willoughby hopes that Helen will help educate the motherless Rachel and "make a woman of her, the kind of woman her mother would have liked her to be" (*VO*, 86). Helen does concern herself with educating Rachel, but her ideas of what kind of woman Rachel should be differ from Willoughby's. She thinks Rachel's ignorance of the simple facts of life "not merely foolish but criminal" and enlightens her. For the rest, Helen sees no reason why women should not be as "satisfactory" as men if properly educated, and to that end she gives Rachel a room of her own: "She desired that Rachel should think, and for this reason offered books and discouraged too entire a dependence upon Bach and Beethoven and Wagner" (*VO*, 124).

Rachel's room at the villa, the scene of her self-education, is "a fortress as well as a sanctuary" from which she can "defy the world" (*VO*, 123). There she can defend and preserve that which she is and is choosing to become, away from persuasion and force. Rachel chooses her own books, and in one scene she concludes an Ibsen play and asks aloud:

> "What is the truth? What's the truth of it all?" She was speaking partly as herself and partly as the heroine of the play she had just read. The landscape outside . . . now appeared amazingly solid and clear . . . for the moment she herself was the most vivid thing in it—an heroic statue in the middle of the foreground, dominating the view. Ibsen's plays always left her in that condition. She acted them for days at a time, greatly to Helen's amusement; and then it would be Meredith's turn and she became Diana of the Crossways. (*VO*, 123–24)

The "heroic statue" that Rachel resembles after reading Ibsen recalls the "beautiful drowned statues" of her underwater world, as though reading him had brought her to the surface, drawn her out of her buried life. As though her reading has stripped her world of convention, Rachel sees the daily familiar surfaces dissolve; things stand forth bare of human meaning:

> after a moment or two she began to raise her first finger to let it fall on the arm of her chair so as to bring back to herself some consciousness of her own existence. She was next overcome by the unspeakable queerness of the fact that she should be sitting in an arm-chair, in the morning, in the middle of the world. . . . life, what was that? It was only a light passing over the surface and vanishing, as in time she would vanish, though the furniture in the room would remain. Her dissolution became so complete that she could not raise her finger any more, and sat perfectly

still, listening and looking always at the same spot. It became stranger and stranger. She was overcome with awe that things should exist at all. . . . She forgot that she had any fingers to raise. . . . The things that existed were so immense and so desolate. She continued to be conscious of these vast masses of substance for a long stretch of time, the clock still ticking in the midst of the universal silence. (*VO*, 125)

The intrusion of a "moment of being" upon Rachel's education marks a radical gap between language and the world, between the books of the world and the "book of the world." This moment evokes Rachel's awareness of what lies outside language, but even as it gestures toward Rachel's own authority, born of loyalty to things people do not say, it signals the great danger that her loyalty, her "war," poses to her. As Ibsen's art moves Rachel beyond conventional ideas about the world, Rachel's "What's the truth of it all?" moves beyond Ibsen's play to blank, unworded being as such. It is as though Rachel/ Woolf were clearing the way for this reality to come into language—creating a space, in other words, for her own "truth of it all," her own words, to come. But Rachel seems in danger of losing herself in wordlessness, and when Helen breaks in, entering with Terence's invitation to the picnic, Rachel responds with relief and decision: "We must go" (*VO*, 126). As Rachel says "yes," the old plots rush into the vacuum her reading and thinking have created, for with Terence the female "destiny" of love and marriage re-enters her life.

But the marriage plot does not immediately prevail. Rather, Rachel is caught between the old plot and a new one as Helen, Rachel, and the two young Oxford men, Hirst and Hewet, form a tiny colony within the colony, one that assumes, against the current, that women ought to be educated. While Susan Warrington and Arthur Venning, whose bliss Rachel secretly scorns, act out the conventional courtship-and-marriage plot, Hewet, Hirst, and Helen undertake to educate Rachel. At Arthur's and Susan's engagement party, Hirst infuriates Rachel by patronizing her. "Have you got a mind, or are you like the rest of your sex?" he asks; and he wonders whether she will be able to appreciate the Gibbon he is going to lend her: "He's the test, of course. It's awfully difficult to tell about women . . . how much, I mean, is due to lack of training, and how much is native incapacity" (*VO*, 154). Rachel is angry that Hirst should patronize her because she has not had his education, yet she resents her own haphazard one. In this she both identifies with and, in her self-consciousness, diverges from Hirst's sister, of whom Terence says: "No one takes her seriously, poor dear. She feeds the rabbits." Rachel answers, "I've fed rabbits for twenty-four years; it seems odd now" (*VO*, 211).[18]

---

[18]This feminine rabbit-feeding alludes to *The Mill on the Floss*, in which Maggie Tulliver fails to feed Tom's rabbits while he's away at school so that they die; and it had a wider currency in popular literature for children, for example, Maria E. Budden's *Always Happy!! Anecdotes of Felix and his Sister Serena. A tale. Written for her Children, by a Mother* (4th ed.; London, 1820), which remarks of Serena that "in feeding his rabbits, and arranging his garden, she felt she was preparing a pleasure for her dear brother" (90; cited in Gorham, 45). The scene between

Hirst, who tells Helen shortly after leaving Rachel that "few things at the present time mattered more than the enlightenment of women" (*VO*, 164), sends Rachel the first volume of Gibbon the next day, and she takes it, along with Balzac's *La cousine Bette*, borrowed from her uncle, outdoors to read. In this initiatory scene, Woolf poises Rachel at the threshold between nature and culture. Rachel walks away from the villa, for in "this country . . . it was possible to lose sight of civilisation in a very short time" (*VO*, 173). In the early draft, before opening Gibbon, Rachel touches a tree, picks a flower, and performs a solitary "rite," as though she were taking leave of these natural things (*M*, 130). In the final text, she performs a similar rite, laying side by side red flowers that "brought back the feelings of a child to whom they were companions." Gibbon and Balzac, meanwhile, lie in the grass, more like bodies than minds: "a tall stem bending over and tickling the smooth brown cover of Gibbon, while the mottled blue Balzac lay naked in the sun" (*VO*, 174).

Her rites of farewell done, Rachel opens Gibbon and reads four sentences that concern, significantly, resistance to colonization: the hot climate that prevented "the reduction of Aethiopia and Arabia Felix," repelling the invaders and protecting "the unwarlike natives of those sequestered regions"; and the northern European countries that "scarcely deserved the expense and labour of conquest," being "filled with a hardy race of barbarians, who despised life when it was separated from freedom" (*VO*, 174–75). Rachel responds not only to the beautiful sentences and to the specific facts that the historian sets out but to the immense possibilities that the idea of history opens to her imagination:

> Never had any words been so vivid and so beautiful—Arabia Felix—Aethiopia. But those were not more noble than the others, hardy barbarians, forests, and morasses. They seemed to drive roads back to the very beginning of the world, on either side of which the populations of all times and countries stood in avenues, and by passing down them all knowledge would be hers, and the book of the world turned back to the very first page. Such was her excitement at the possibilities of knowledge now opening before her that she ceased to read, and a breeze turning the page, the covers of Gibbon gently ruffled and closed together. (*VO*, 175)

Gibbon's book again reverts to matter as Rachel, excited by the prospect of reading "the book of the world," ceases to read this more limited one; its

---

Hirst and Rachel gains yet more ironic resonance in light of Woolf's naming the ship on which Rachel voyages the *Euphrosyne*, after the muse of Joy and also after a collection of uninspired poetry that her brother Thoby and his friends produced while at Cambridge. The young Woolf wrote a devastating "review" in which she mocks these pretentiously melancholy fruits of male education and suggests ironically that "there is much to be said surely for that respectable custom which allows the daughter to educate herself at home . . . preser[ving] her from the omniscience, the early satiety, the melancholy self-satisfaction which a training at either of our great universities produces in her brothers." See Quentin Bell, *Virginia Woolf: A Biography* (New York: Harcourt Brace Jovanovich, 1971), Vol. 1, 205. See also *L*, 1: 245.

butterfly-like body signifies not Gibbon's ideas but the newly unveiled possibility of her own. Later, disturbed by Mr. Bax's sermon as if by bad music badly played, Rachel will struggle to grasp "an idea like a butterfly" that floats out of reach, an idea not "in" Gibbon, but whose potential existence in language Gibbon's words confirm (*VO*, 228). In both these passages, the butterfly image transforms the chrysalis plot of female initiation by representing not Rachel's metamorphosis but the possibility of a different destiny.

Scarcely does Rachel's exhilaration rise than it passes, replaced by a "suspicion" that she is "reluctant to face." Here again Woolf makes the butterfly an object of Rachel's thoughts and gaze, no clear portent but an uncertain image of possibility:

> Unconsciously she had been walking faster and faster, her body trying to outrun her mind; but she was now on the summit of a little hillock of earth which rose above the river and displayed the valley. . . . a kind of melancholy replaced her excitement. She sank down on to the earth, clasping her knees together and looking blankly in front of her. For some time she observed a great yellow butterfly, which was opening and closing its wings very slowly on a little flat stone.
>
> "What is it to be in love?" she demanded, after a long silence; each word as it came into being seemed to shove itself out into an unknown sea. Hypnotized by the wings of the butterfly, and awed by the discovery of a terrible possibility in life, she sat for some time longer. When the butterfly flew away, she rose, and with her two books beneath her arm returned home again, much as a soldier prepared for battle. (*VO*, 175–76)

Although Woolf uses chrysalis imagery in this initiatory scene, she also puts it radically in question by superimposing love and danger, discovery and terrible possibility, Rachel metamorphosing into a butterfly and Rachel metamorphosing into a soldier. The structure of the Gibbon scene creates a highly complex and self-reflexive representation of female initiation, for it compounds the chrysalis metaphor of female initiation with the image of Rachel *reading*, and not only reading but, in her not-reading, potentially *writing* into history what Gibbon—his style spinning smoothly like "a roll of oilcloth" (*VO*, 201)—has left out: among other things, women's history. The scene thus represents not a single woman's initiation but the prospect of Rachel/Woolf's augmenting the books of the world. Rachel's war on behalf of drowned and buried things is also Woolf's: into her newly educated Rachel, a determined soldier setting off in the direction of civilization, Woolf projected the writer she herself wished to become.

Genesis Revisited: Rachel's Version of the Fall

Rachel/Woolf's "war" must be fought on the battlefield not only of experience but of consciousness and language; her project too is aptly described by Stephen Dedalus's figure of forging "the uncreated conscience of his race."

The very word *conscience*—"knowing-with"—implies a form of awareness that is social rather than individual.[19] In order to forge a conscience, Rachel must forge a language to mediate it, words to bring that experience of drowned things that she has known all alone into being as things people can know and speak about together. In her old dream of "a colony where there should be no marrying," the young Virginia Stephen had fantasized a human society to transcend language as difference, as distance and strife: "nothing but ideal peace and endless meditation." In the "real" world of her novel, however, to marry is to "fight" a battle that can only be fought with words.

As a "soldier," Rachel appears doubly endangered, first, because she lacks a language, and second, because she is a musician and as such is always tending to retire into music as a transcendent language that says everything at once, better than words can do. "Why do you write novels?" she asks Terence. "You ought to write music" (*VO*, 212). In this scene, Terence and Rachel become two different selves of Woolf: he the writer, she the woman. Terence tells Rachel of his desire to write "a novel about Silence . . . the things people don't say. But the difficulty is immense" (*VO*, 216, 220). When he tries to make Rachel his subject, she resists: "'Doesn't it make your blood boil? . . .' he asked suddenly, turning upon her. 'If I were a woman I'd blow someone's brains out.' " Rachel thinks, "No, she would not consent to be pinned down by any second person in the whole world" (*VO*, 215). *The Voyage Out* is itself a novel about the things people don't say, but Rachel's silence and weary gesture toward the sea imperil Woolf's voyage of discovery as they imperil Rachel herself. Yet her silence is hard to break; to speak what people do not say requires new words, and these are not easy to find. In love with Terence, Rachel has no words for her feelings: "none of the books she read, from *Wuthering Heights* to *Man and Superman*, and the plays of Ibsen, suggested from their analysis of love that what their heroines felt was what she was feeling now. It seemed to her that her sensations had no name" (*VO*, 223). As Rachel, and Woolf, struggle toward new words, the burden of the past weighs them down, not as a wealth of words in which everything worth saying is found to have been said, but as a terrifying silence which seems to mirror Rachel's experience and to withhold from it all authority.

Woolf dramatizes this burden in the strange scene in which Rachel and Terence become engaged, without ever uttering the words, during an interlude in the boat trip up the Amazon when they leave the rest of the party and walk some distance into the jungle together. Reading Gibbon, Rachel has imagined with excitement the book of the world turned back to the very first page; this scene acts out that fantasy in a grim repetition of the Fall. Even before setting out on the river journey, Helen is uneasy about Rachel: "great

---

[19]The root of *conscience* is the Latin *conscientia*, "privity of knowledge, consciousness," from *conscire*, "to know or be privy with (another or oneself)." I am drawing in this discussion upon Marie Balmary, *Psychoanalyzing Psychoanalysis: Freud and the Hidden Fault of the Father*, trans. Ned Lukacher (1979; Baltimore: Johns Hopkins University Press, 1982), 159ff.

things were happening—terrible things, because they were so great. Her sense of safety was shaken, as if beneath twigs and dead leaves she had seen the movement of a snake." Human desire, she fears, has only "a moment's respite . . . and then again the profound and reasonless law asserted itself, moulding them all to its liking" (*VO*, 263). As Rachel and Terence set off into the jungle, Hirst warns, "Beware of snakes!" (*VO*, 270). They enter a world that Henri Rousseau might have painted: larger than life, their solitary figures move through great spaces full of strange light, vast and green, in which butterflies circle and settle. The creaking and sighing sounds that surround them make them feel as though they are "walking at the bottom of the sea" (*VO*, 270). Strangest of all is the silence, not the jungle silence but the silence between them which weighs them down:

> they were both unable to frame any thoughts. There was something between them which had to be spoken of. One of them had to begin, but which of them was it to be? Then Hewet picked up a red fruit and threw it as high as he could. When it dropped, he would speak. They heard the flapping of great wings; they heard the fruit go pattering through the leaves and eventually fall with a thud. The silence was again profound. (*VO*, 271)

Woolf sets the stage to reclaim that drowned history which Rachel knows. That words should have left the scene might seem a hopeful sign, a sign of a new genesis, since Woolf is so clearly turning the page back not to reread but to rewrite it. But the words that her characters find are bare and few, so much so that their conversation sustains itself as though by echo:

> "Does this frighten you?" Terence asked. . . .
> "No," she answered, "I like it." . . . There was another pause.
> "You like being with me?" Terence asked.
> "Yes, with you," she replied.
> He was silent for a moment. Silence seemed to have fallen upon the world.
> "This is what I have felt ever since I knew you," he replied. "We are happy together." He did not seem to be speaking, or she to be hearing.
> "Very happy," she answered.
> They continued to walk for some time in silence. . . .
> "We love each other," Terence said.
> "We love each other," she repeated.
> The silence was then broken by their voices which joined in tones of strange unfamiliar sound which formed no words. . . . Sounds stood out from the background making a bridge across their silence. . . .
> "We love each other," Terence repeated. . . . She said "Terence" once; he answered "Rachel."
> "Terrible—terrible," she murmured after another pause. . . . (*VO*, 271)

The heavy silence that has fallen upon the world seems itself to constitute this Fall. "To find the sources of the river," Woolf had written, "you must be the first to cut through the thongs of creepers; the first who has ever trodden upon the mosses by the river side, or seen trees which have stood since the beginning of the world" (*M*, 193). But Rachel and Terence are unable to find that source, a fountainhead of words from which to create their life together. Searching for a beginning, they find only silence, a silence that terrifies Rachel and makes Terence weep. In the weight of this silence, Woolf represents speech and story—authority—as a burden heavy with terrors: of leaving the past behind, of groping without words in the silences of an unwritten world, of a tongue burdened by the past, and, most of all, of the old words returning in spite of all effort to keep them at bay. "I don't want to be late," says Terence. "We're so late—so late—so horribly late," he repeats, "as if he were talking in his sleep," as the two make their way back to the broad path that resembles "the drive in an English forest" (*VO*, 272). Cutting through thongs of creepers in search of an early language, Rachel/Woolf confronts both the danger of old words that encroach upon and limit life and the immense difficulty of forging new ones, a language or conscience for her colony.

In a similarly surreal scene, Rachel undergoes an actual fall at Helen's hands. Back with the others, Rachel hardly knows that she is "engaged"; the words were never spoken. "Are we to marry each other?" she asks. "Marriage?" she repeats, and "It will be a fight" (*VO*, 281, 282). While she and Terence are walking ahead of the others, Helen comes up unheard and knocks Rachel to the ground:

> A hand dropped abruptly as iron on Rachel's shoulder; it might have been a bolt from heaven. She fell beneath it, and the grass whipped across her eyes and filled her mouth and ears. Through the waving stems she saw a figure, large and shapeless against the sky. Helen was upon her. Rolled this way and that, now seeing only forests of green and now the high blue heaven, she was speechless and almost without sense. At last she lay still, all the grasses shaken round her and before her by her panting. Over her loomed the two great heads, the heads of a man and woman, of Terence and Helen. (*VO*, 283)

Rachel does not fall but *is felled* in a scene dense with allusions to women and falling. Rachel—who tells Terence, "Loving you is like having iron thrust through one" (*M*, 212) and who is felled by an iron hand that might have been a bolt from heaven—resembles a hero slain in battle. Falling "in love" with Terence and in doing so into misery and dispossession, she is the Eve of *Genesis* and *Paradise Lost*. Rolled round with grass, earth, and trees, speechless and almost senseless, she is Wordsworth's Lucy, sealed into the silent grave of earth. Against all these male texts, Helen, Rachel's mock-adversary, becomes a type of Homer's Helen, and her blow signals first, women's complicity with these texts, and second, the lack of "mother" texts with which Rachel might arm herself for her battle. Recalling their exchange after Richard's kiss—Helen telling Rachel not to think, Rachel replying that she would think until she understood "exactly what it does mean" (*VO*, 80)— Helen's blow suggests that Rachel, lacking the support of a language that no mothers have given her, can do nothing *but* fall.

Voyaging back to a metaphorical beginning, Rachel discovers not what things mean but images of meaningless repetition. In the river village to which Mr. Flushing leads the party, Rachel listens in vain for the women's words, but "if they spoke, it was to cry some harsh unintelligible cry" (*VO*, 285). Rachel discovers that what she desires cannot be discovered; the enabling words and history that she seeks to defend herself against the things people say and do not say are not to be found, but must instead be created, carved out of terrible silences by the seeker herself. There is, then, no place of safety for Rachel, as Helen—feeling "presentiments of disaster," imagining "a boat upset on the river in England, at midday"—seems to know (*VO*, 285–86). Like Maggie Tulliver, whom her author drowns in a boat upset on a flooding river at midday for want of a plot that can carry her toward a grander destiny, Rachel/Woolf repeats the Fall in words that are different and yet also somehow the same. "Cynthia [Rachel] will not speak and my ship is like to sink," Woolf had written in 1908 (*L*, 1: 241); and what is at stake is precisely the *conscience* that her speech must forge, a language to float her silenced world of drowned things into the conscience of her race. Not yet having forged such a language, Rachel, in Woolf's rewriting of the Fall, is condemned to repeat it.

The Death and Life of the Moth

After the engagement scene the struggle between Terence and Rachel, the writer and the woman in Woolf, continues. Terence's book *Silence* will, he thinks, be different now, and he prods Rachel to address herself to the lists of female characteristics that he is compiling. Rachel, however, remains silent, rapt in her music: "Up and up the steep spiral of a very late Beethoven sonata she climbed, like a person ascending a ruined staircase" (*VO*, 291). Terence's intrusive questions signal the fact that literature does not yet provide for the life Rachel would lead. Like the young Woolf, she would retreat to a colony where the plot of her life might unwind from the moment of falling in love with a symphony of Beethoven, but Terence recalls her to the "realist" novel, which must validate itself not in life but in literature.[20] Terence interrupts Rachel's playing, telling her that she should be answering the congratulatory letters of their friends; and while she writes, he reads aloud from a bad Meredithian novel about a modern marriage: "Lord, Rachel," he concludes, "will it be like that when we're married?" Rachel answers, "Why don't people write about the things they do feel?" (*VO*, 296). But, while Rachel scorns the novel's so-called realism, she, a literary character, cannot "live" without a script; and the plot she is pursuing, one that transcends the constraints of tradition upon the individual talent, has no script, no author, no authority.

[20]See Nancy K. Miller's brilliant theoretical argument concerning criteria for "verisimilitude" in the realist novel in "Emphasis Added: Plots and Plausibilities in Women's Fiction," *PMLA* 96 (January 1981), 36–47.

When Terence asks, "Well, then, what will it be like when we're married? What are the things people do feel?" the languageless Rachel seems "doubtful" (*VO*, 297).

Terence attempts to goad Rachel into speech: "'what I like about your face is it makes me wonder what the devil you're thinking about—it makes me want to do that—' He clenched his fist and shook it so near her that she started back, 'because now you look as if you'd blow my brains out. There are moments . . . when if we stood on a rock together, you'd throw me into the sea' " (*VO*, 298). Then they struggle together, and their mock-violence acts out Rachel's feeling that marriage is a "fight":

> To be flung into the sea, to be washed hither and thither, and driven about the roots of the world—the idea was incoherently delightful. She sprang up and began moving about the room . . . as if she were indeed striking through the waters. . . . she seemed to be cleaving a passage for herself, and dealing triumphantly with the obstacles which would hinder their passage through life.
>
> "It does seem possible!" he exclaimed, " . . . our marriage will be the most exciting thing that's ever been done! . . . " He caught her in his arms as she passed him, and they fought for mastery, imagining a rock, and the sea heaving beneath them. At last she was thrown to the floor, where she lay gasping and crying for mercy.
>
> "I'm a mermaid! I can swim," she cried, "so the game's up." (*VO*, 298)

Rachel loses this mock-marriage fight, but she claims victory anyway in terms that recall her earlier life of communion with the world of drowned things. In light of the dangers of that buried life which the narrative has revealed, however, Rachel's reversion to mermaid cannot be a triumph. Helen, Terence, and Hirst had roused her from her sea-creaturely life, but now she is flung back into the sea, to her former watery existence.

Rachel's fantasy of triumph is dispelled a few pages later when she and Terence gaze together into a looking-glass: "it chilled them to see themselves in the glass, for instead of being vast and indivisible they were really very small and separate, the size of the glass leaving a large space for the reflection of other things" (*VO*, 303). As though the mirror-image were a prophecy, the world of grim realities, which was finely represented at the novel's beginning but has receded behind the love-plot of Rachel and Terence, begins to press in again. In particular, episodes of women and violence intrude. Hirst receives a letter from home about the suicide of the parlormaid, while Mr. Thornbury and Mr. Elliott join forces to hound out of the hotel a woman accused of prostitution. "It's monstrous," Helen comments. "A man who's made a fortune in trade as Mr. Thornbury has is bound to be twice as bad as any prostitute" (*VO*, 308). As the "real world" encroaches upon the lovers' sphere, the stage is gradually set for Rachel's "destiny." Neither the transcendence of music nor the comforts of fantasy shield her from the plot that governs the lives of the parlormaid and the prostitute. The fates of these women prepare the way for her own.

The fever that causes Rachel's death is traced to her voyage up the river, and the Eden-like scene of her engagement to Terence is recalled in the scene in which her illness first makes itself felt. Rachel and Terence sit outdoors in the extreme heat, hearing waves that sound "like the repeated sigh of some exhausted creature." They are too hot to talk, and they have dropped one by one the books they have been trying to read, finding them unable to "withstand the power of the sun." Terence now tries *Comus* "because he said the words of Milton had substance and shape, so that it was not necessary to understand what he was saying; one could merely listen to his words; one could almost handle them" (*VO*, 326). Rachel, however, cannot escape from meaning: "The words, in spite of what Terence had said, seemed to be laden with meaning, and perhaps it was for this reason that it was painful to listen to them." Terence reads the song to Sabrina, the drowned virgin of Spenser's *Faerie Queene* whom Milton brings back to "life" as a water-goddess with power to undo the Lady's enchantment:

> Sabrina fair,
>   Listen where thou art sitting
> Under the glassy, cool, translucent wave,
>   In twisted braids of lilies knitting
> The loose train of thy amber dropping hair,
> Listen for dear honour's sake,
>   Goddess of the silver lake,
>   Listen and save!
>
>   (11.859–66)

How Milton's lines can be the cause of Rachel's illness is clear enough in light of Woolf's exploration of female initiation in *The Voyage Out*. Although the mythical Sabrina is not "dead," her underwater existence—initiated in flight from a rape, and from which she is called back to preserve a lady's chastity—signals the female destiny given by the marriage plot that occasions Milton's poem, enlists Sabrina's protective service, forms Jane Austen's tight plots/plaits (recalled in Sabrina's twisting braids), and becomes the agent of Rachel's own symbolic death. As Terence reads, Rachel falls ill: her head aches "whichever way she turned it" (*VO*, 327). Milton's words are fatal to Rachel, not because no nymph arrives to save her but because they represent a tradition in which bound, endangered "ladies," drowned nymphs, and the marriage plot with its tightwoven construction of female sexuality as virginity, domesticity, and maternity, figure woman's "destiny." Woolf's allusion to Milton's Mask figures female "destiny" in terms of impossible alternatives: a forking path that leads to virginity, marriage, and maternity on one side and to rape, fallenness, and death on the other. Earlier, as we saw, Rachel has associated both marriage and maternity with her own death; now, Woolf's desire for a new plot, figured in the colony where one might "marry" a symphony of Beethoven, collides with that "real" world in which parlormaids commit suicide and hypocrites expend their virtue upon prostitutes. The lines from *Comus*, strong enough to withstand the sun, are also strong enough to kill Rachel; they represent to her a fate that she embraces like a death.

The distinction between actual death and the symbolic death-in-life that Rachel enters is crucial to *The Voyage Out* as a representation of female initiation.[21] From the novel's beginning, Woolf has figured Rachel as an underwater creature, the drowned daughter who "is like her mother, as the image in a pool on a still summer's day is like the vivid flushed face that hangs over it" (*VO*, 25). Rachel's death-scenes also represent the perils that she confronts on her voyage of discovery in water imagery. The song to Sabrina runs in Rachel's feverish head, though the adjectives get out of place, and by the second day of her illness, the "glassy, cool, translucent wave" is "almost visible before her, curling up at the end of the bed, and as it was refreshingly cool she tried to keep her mind fixed upon it" (*VO*, 329). Against Milton's deadly, beautiful wave of words, Rachel is defenseless because she herself has no language: "She was completely cut off, and unable to communicate with the rest of the world, isolated alone with her body" (*VO*, 330). Upon the woman who nurses her, playing cards by candlelight in Rachel's room, Rachel projects the female fate of underwater existence, fearfully seeing women playing cards in archways "in a tunnel under a river" (*VO*, 331).

All these images express not death from fever but that symbolic death which is Rachel's, and often woman's, fate; indeed, it is Rachel herself who pictures her own death not as bodily and final but as a watery death-in-life:

> she fell into a deep pool of sticky water, which eventually closed over her head. She saw nothing and heard nothing but a faint booming sound, which was the sound of the sea rolling over her head. While all her tormentors thought that she was dead, she was not dead, but curled up at the bottom of the sea. There she lay, sometimes seeing darkness, sometimes light, while every now and then some one turned her over at the bottom of the sea. (*VO*, 341)

Here Rachel represents herself as a half-conscious creature, thought to be dead but in fact only silent, fathoms down on the ocean floor. Her images recall Mr. Pepper's evocation of the "white, hairless, blind monsters lying curled on the ridges of sand at the bottom of the sea" (*VO*, 23). Dr. Lesage tells Terence, "She has a chance of life" (*VO*, 347); but when Rachel again surfaces, it is without will and without desire: "She had come to the surface of the dark, sticky pool, and a wave seemed to bear her up and down with it; she had ceased to have any will of her own" (*VO*, 346). When Lesage speaks of having been called in "to ascertain, by severing a vein, that an old lady of eighty-five was really dead" because "she had a horror of being buried alive"

---

[21]Many critics have understood Rachel's death as "psychogenic," but they have tended to seek its causes in the personal inadequacies of Hewet, the "curious" circumstances of Rachel's own life, or "laws governing human nature"; see, for example, Mitchell Leaska's "The Death of Rachel Vinrace," *Bulletin of Research in the Humanities* 84 (Spring 1981), 328–37. I am arguing for a wider and more complex range of causes to be sought not in Rachel's psyche but in the culture that suppresses female authority.

(*VO*, 350), it is Rachel whose death-in-life this detail highlights: "curled up at the bottom of the sea," she awaits the speech, the script, the plot, that would make of hers an *initiatory* death, redeeming it by a rebirth into a new language. In these scenes, Woolf advances the plot of the female artist-novel, representing not the death of the body but the symbolic death that her heroine undergoes when she finds no language in which to live.

Woolf could not write a plot, a script, to resurrect Rachel from her symbolic death, for reasons that have to do not only with literary plots and literary history, as Nancy K. Miller has argued [see note 20], but with a further turn of the screw that finds Woolf's own life imitating the plot of her fiction. Paul de Man notes with respect to autobiography that it is not literature that imitates life but life that shapes itself according to the possibilities sought and found in the mirrors of literary texts.[22] When Woolf represents her heroine infected by Milton's Mask and dying a symbolic death, she represents not "life" but the inescapable interweaving of life and literature; and when we remember that Woolf herself almost took her life while composing this fiction whose plot she was unable to reform, the reversibility of "verisimilitude" becomes all too vivid.[23] *The Voyage Out*, Woolf's first exploration of female authority, discovers the perils that the woman artist must pass: deeps of silence that may swallow her ship, social and sexual dangers that entangle the bridelike vessel, and the wandering rocks of texts like *Comus* that threaten to wreck it. These perils, and the fact that Woolf could not save her heroine, attest to the courage that her autobiographical voyage demanded, for in seeking Rachel's fortune she was also seeking her own.

Although she could not give Rachel a grand destiny, Woolf wrote an image of her own survival into her text, in the figure of the moth that hovers like a signature at the very end of the novel. Tracing this image in Woolf's writing, Harvena Richter observes that over the years Woolf made it a symbol for herself as a writer and for the creative imagination.[24] The moth images of *The Voyage Out* already suggest this identification, and the moth that survives Rachel's death carries forward the possibility, if not the implication, that Rachel's death will prove initiatory and symbolic, preceding the birth of a new self, stronger now in armor forged by her own pen in the writing of this novel: Virginia Woolf. The moth that flies over the heads of the hotel guests after the storm following Rachel's death portends this rebirth: a young woman exclaims, " 'Poor creature! it would be kinder to kill it.' But nobody seemed disposed to rouse himself in order to kill the moth. They watched it dash from lamp to lamp, because they were comfortable, and had nothing to do" (*VO*,

[22]Paul de Man, "Autobiography as De-facement," *MLN* 94 (1979), 926.

[23]See Bell, vol. 2, 10ff. See also DeSalvo, *passim*, and Stephen Trombley, *All That Summer She Was Mad: Virginia Woolf and Her Doctors* (London: Junction, 1981), chapter 1.

[24]Harvena Richter, "Hunting the Moth: Virginia Woolf and the Creative Imagination," in *Virginia Woolf: Revaluation and Continuity*, ed. Ralph Freedman (Berkeley: University of California Press, 1980), 13–28.

370). The image exactly repeats an after-dinner scene at the hotel some months earlier, in which the "only disturbance in the bright placid room was caused by a large moth which shot from light to light . . . causing several young women to raise their hands nervously and exclaim, 'Some one ought to kill it!' " (*VO*, 183). Again, reminiscing about reading Gibbon by a nightlight in her girlhood—"some of the happiest hours of my life"—Mrs. Flushing remembers the moths: "Louisa, my sister, would have the window open. I wanted it shut. We fought every night of our lives over that window. Have you ever seen a moth dyin' in a night-light?" (*VO*, 200). All three images gloss Rachel/Woolf's attraction to the lamps of a "civilisation" that proves dangerous, and the last glosses Rachel's reading of Gibbon, her flight toward the lamp of learning at the risk of being consumed.

But as Rachel is "not dead, but curled up at the bottom of the sea," so Woolf's moth is not consumed but survives her trial by fire. The moth and the lamp recur fleetingly in *Jacob's Room*, in Woolf's essay "Reading" (undated, which Leonard Woolf places between 1921 and 1941), in her diaries, in *Orlando*, and, of course, in *The Waves*. In light of the female initiation plot of *The Voyage Out*, what is especially interesting in these images is that the moth symbol recalls the butterfly that Rachel does not become even as it translates that image into the fragile, endangered ("Some one ought to kill it"), but genuine possibility of a different female "destiny." In "Reading" the moth is a complex image of authority as the theme moves from reading the Elizabethans to a hunt for the moth in the forest at night.[25] When the tree falls with a sound like a shot at the moment the moth is caught, we are reminded of the jungle scene of Rachel and Terence's engagement, for both represent reading and language as at once violent and necessary. Again, Woolf writes in her diary of "tapping my antennae in the air vaguely" each morning before settling down to work, and a later entry develops this metaphor of her creative process:

> Once or twice I have felt that odd whirr of wings in the head which comes when I am ill so often. . . . Something happens in my mind. It refuses to go on registering impressions. It becomes chrysalis. I lie quite torpid, often with acute physical pain. . . . Then suddenly something springs . . . and this is I believe the moth shaking its wings in me. I then begin to make up my story whatever it is.[26]

Woolf describes her creative process as painful, violent, and mysterious. The transformative and creative acts of her art, like nature's transformations, are not willed acts but miraculous "somethings" that happen to her. By 1930, the date of this diary entry, Woolf has fully transformed the chrysalis plot that

[25]Virginia Woolf, "Reading," *The Captain's Death Bed and Other Essays* (New York: Harcourt Brace Jovanovich, 1950), 168–69.
[26]*The Diary of Virginia Woolf*, ed. Anne Olivier Bell, 5 vols. (New York: Harcourt Brace Jovanovich, 1977–1984), vol. 3: 106, 286–87.

threatens her young female artists in *The Voyage Out* and "The Introduction" into an image of herself *as a writer.* Her chrysalis figure describes not the sexual maturity of a woman's body but the miraculous births of her own creative imagination, transformations no less wonderful than those of natural procreation. For Woolf, natural and symbolic creativity mirror each other. Thus, in a sublime turn on this theme in *Orlando*, Woolf precedes the birth of Orlando's child with an image drawn from the birth of her own imaginative forms: "sleep, sleep . . . water of dimness inscrutable, and there, folded, shrouded, like a mummy, like a moth, prone let us lie on the sand at the bottom of sleep."[27] All these moths in her later writings figure the artist-self to which Woolf gave birth through the painful labor of her first novel, in an image that recalls not only the origins of female authority but its history of perils passed. In her essay "The Death of the Moth," Woolf reflects upon the tiny moth's struggle against its great antagonist death; upon how, "when there was nobody to care or to know, this gigantic effort on the part of an insignificant little moth, against a power of such magnitude, to retain what no one else values or desires to keep, moved one strangely."[28] This image, too, is autobiography. The continuing life of the moth in Woolf's writing makes legible Woolf's own great battle against that powerful antagonist, the literary and cultural tradition, to find words for the life of the female imagination, to enlarge its plots and scripts.

---

[27]Virginia Woolf, *Orlando* (New York: Harcourt Brace Jovanovich, 1956), 295.
[28]Virginia Woolf, "The Death of the Moth," *The Death of the Moth and Other Essays* (New York: Harcourt Brace Jovanovich, 1942), 6.

The Interrupted Moment:
A View of Virginia Woolf's Novels

Lucio P. Ruotolo

For interruptions there will always be.[1]

—Virginia Woolf

On a morning toward the end of 1940, Virginia Woolf records finishing the first draft of *Between the Acts* and how at "this moment" her thoughts have shifted to consider her next book: "Anon, it will be called." The explanation for the inspiration, she adds somewhat enigmatically, "should refer to Louie's interruption, holding a glass jar, in whose thin milk was a pat of butter." Characteristically, Woolf works this intrusion into her own preceding speculations: "I am a little triumphant about the book. I think its an interesting attempt in a new method. I think its more quintessential than the others. More milk skimmed off. A richer pat."[2]

Throughout the novelist's life and fiction, interruptions arouse inventive impulses. At times the event is more dramatic than her cook's domestic intrusion. The storm that strikes the *Euphrosyne* in *The Voyage Out*, for example, upsets and reforms narrative relationships. Most frequently these disruptions occur subtly, as when Ralph Denham appears at tea toward the opening of *Night and Day*. The deployment of such disorienting moments in the eight novels under consideration[3] constitutes, in the view of this study, an important aspect of Woolf's experimental intention.[4]

[1]Woolf, *A Room of One's Own* (1929; New York: Harcourt Brace, 1963), p. 81. Hereafter abbreviated as *AROO*.

[2]*The Diary of Virginia Woolf*, ed. Anne Olivier Bell with Andrew McNeillie, 5 vols. (New York: Harcourt Brace Jovanovich, 1977–1984), V, 340. Here as elsewhere, I retain such idiosyncrasies as Woolf's "its" for the contraction. However, for expository purposes, I have freely changed punctuation and initial capping in omitting sentences or sentence fragments from quoted material.

[3]I take seriously Woolf's designation of *Orlando* as "A Biography" and so do not include it for discussion here. Along with *Flush*, *Roger Fry*, and Woolf's shorter biographical essays, it deserves and will continue to receive fuller treatment under a different experimental rubric.

[4]Many critics have discussed the theme of narrative interruption. In regard to Woolf, let me call attention particularly to Reuben Brower's "Something Central Which Permeated," reprinted in Claire Sprague, ed., *Virginia Woolf: Twentieth Century Views* (Englewood Cliffs, N.J. 1971), pp. 51–62. . . . Among more recent discussions on the subject is Peggy Kamuf, "Penelope at Work: Interruptions in *A Room of One's Own*," *Novel*, Fall 1982, pp. 5–18.

A choreography for Woolf's fiction inevitably develops from the rhythm of broken sequence. Those characters who join the dance create a new and constantly shifting pattern, sustained and nourished, I would argue, by a succession of interruptions. To be open to life in Woolf's fictional world is to remain open to an aesthetic of disjunction situated at the heart of human interplay. Those who allow the often-random intrusion of others to reshape their lives emerge at times heroically. Those who voice distaste for interruption fall back, invariably it seems, into self-supporting insularity. Septimus Smith, a victim of shell shock in *Mrs. Dalloway*, complains that his wife Rezia "was always interrupting." Struggling to maintain the continuity of his inward world, with one important exception he resists her intervention. The confident Mr. Bankes in *To the Lighthouse* prefers dining alone to enduring the discomfort of "interruptions" at Mrs. Ramsay's dinner table. Mrs. Ramsay, in turn, derives most pleasure from those moments when, free of other people, she can simply "be herself, by herself." Alone, free of attachments, she employs her imagination to transcend "the fret, the hurry, the stir" of a persistently impinging world.

However much Woolf relishes such cloistered moments of solitude, they tempt her most memorable heroines to ignore political as well as aesthetic realities. To withdraw from an abrasive external world presumes for women in particular an excessive reliance on the protection of men, what Woolf, in describing her own inheritance, terms "a legacy of dependence."[5] Sheltered by ruling patriarchs throughout history, women understandably have looked toward men to support such moments of leisure. The fluctuations Woolf discerns in modern life make this need for governance and direction increasingly more attractive. Lucy Swithin, who resists her brother's masterly overtures in *Between the Acts* and responds intuitively to the village pageant, is nonetheless moved like Mrs. Ramsay to accept a final order of values, to reduce life's unnerving multiplicity to harmonious singularity. It follows that the favorite time for each is evening, "when nothing interrupted."

In a most relevant essay Woolf compares the experience of modern times with the impact of being ill. What characterizes each, in her view, is an "unending procession of changes" inevitably undermining "the doings of the mind." Urging her reader to relinquish for the moment the time-honored safeguards of Western thought and literature, she advocates, however playfully, "a new hierarchy of the passions." In illness, with reason unmoored, "undiscovered countries" emerge mysteriously from the "wastes and deserts of the soul" to interrupt all semblance of order and stability. Her invitation to explore the ensuing "anarchy and newness" is not made casually.[6] Aware of the

[5]Woolf, "A Sketch of the Past," in *Moments of Being: Unpublished Autobiographical Writings*, ed. Jeanne Schulkind (New York: Harcourt Brace Jovanovich, (1976), p. 114, hereafter abbreviated as *Moments*.

[6]Woolf, "On Being Ill," in *Collected Essays*, ed. Leonard Woolf, 4 vols. (New York: Harcourt Brace and World, 1967), IV, 193–95.

risks—unguarded moments occasion blows from a world at best impervious to human needs—Woolf understandably regards such voyages with some misgiving.

In the autobiographical essay "A Sketch of the Past," Woolf recalls her childish presumption that the "sudden shocks" she received from the external world were "simply a blow from an enemy hidden behind the cotton wool of daily life." Each such recollection involved an interruption of her own expectations. In one disorienting instance the memory of seven brothers and sisters competing for their mother's attention evokes a familiar lament: "Can I remember ever being alone with her for more than a few minutes? Someone was always interrupting" (*Moments*, 83). As an adult Woolf recognizes the value of these early blows: "They are now always welcome; after the first surprise, I always feel instantly that they are particularly valuable. And I go on to suppose that the shock receiving capacity is what makes me a writer" (*Moments*, 72).

Under the impact of interruption she will grow increasingly less confident in the authority of others to supply centrality for her life. Thrown back on her own resources, Woolf, in company with the characters of her fiction, comes to entertain a world demanding incessant readjustment, a world, as she describes her own childhood, in which "nothing remained stable long" (*Moments*, 79).

Woolf's first published story, "The Mark on the Wall" (1917), reflects the ambivalence with which interruption moves the writer, in this case her narrator, toward an unmediated world of "movement and change." Seated in front of the fireplace, her eyes fixed on burning coals, she finds her imagination rather sluggishly contriving an old fancy: a flag; a castle; a cavalcade of red knights riding up a black rock. Then, unexpectedly, "for the first time," an object emerges into sight. "Rather to my relief the sight of the mark interrupted the fancy, for it is an old fancy, an automatic fancy, made as a child perhaps."[7] Inspired by this fresh intrusion, her thoughts spring into the future. Newly animated, her mind expands to include a world where nothing is predetermined or constricted, where each perception seems grounded in a continually shifting landscape. The result is both a story and the compensating authorial desire for regained equilibrium.

Artistically, the barrage of objects that follows sweeps the viewer along with frightening rapidity—"if one wants to compare life to anything, one must liken it to being blown through the Tube at fifty miles an hour"—evoking the customary need for mediating distance: "I want to think quietly, calmly, spaciously, never to be interrupted, never to have to rise from my chair, to slip easily from one thing to another, without any sense of hostility, or obstacle. I want to sink deeper and deeper, away from the surface, with its

---

[7]Woolf, "The Mark on the Wall," in *The Haunted House and Other Short Stories* (New York: Harcourt Brace, 1944), p. 37.

hard separate facts. To steady myself, let me catch hold of the first idea that passes . . . Shakespeare" ("The Mark on the Wall," 38–40).

The realization of a distinctively external dimension of time and space motivates her in two forms of evasion: psychologically, to retreat like Septimus in madness back into herself; intellectually, to fix on an incontestably honored literary model. Avoiding contradiction with its inevitable friction would appear to induce a peace of mind Woolf prizes. *A Room of One's Own* illustrates how even the smallest sense of grievance distorts a woman's art: "at war with her lot," Charlotte Brontë could not "write calmly" (*AROO*, 73).

The fact that women, subject "to all kinds of casual interruptions," were forced to live more discontinuous lives, particularly if they aspired to some form of artistic achievement, proves an unexpected advantage. Ironically, *A Room of One's Own* links women's historical deprivation of separate space— "kept in one room, and to one occupation"—with the fictional Mary Carmichael's capacity to tamper with traditional literary sequence. Reading Mary's prose, Woolf half complains in a tone that recalls the narrator of "The Mark," "was like being out at sea in an open boat."

Woolf initially expresses "certain grievances against" Mary for interrupting her own rhetorical expectations. Plunged into this baffling fluidity where the basis for all preference seems obscured, she is transformed in her consciousness of literature and of life: "For whenever I was about to feel the usual things in the usual places, about love, about death, the annoying creature twitched me away, as if the important point were just a little further on. And thus she made it impossible for me to roll out my sonorous phrases about 'elemental feelings,' the 'common stuff of humanity,' 'depths of the human heart,' and all those other phrases which support us in our belief" (*AROO*, 95).[8] Freed simultaneously from "the expected order" and from her "grievance," she recognizes and censures the inertia that has made her "lazy minded and conventional into the bargain."

Tolerance for interruption is all but synonymous in Woolf with the quality of comprehension itself. The presumption describes her relationship to literary texts as well as to the world at large. The very talent of good reading means indulging a world not necessarily one's own. "If you open your mind as widely as possible, then signs and hints of almost imperceptible fineness, from the twist and turn of the first sentences, will bring you into the presence of a human being unlike any other." She compares the act of reading to the act of seeing, and enjoins her reader to turn and break away: "Is there not an open window on the right hand of the bookcase? How delightful to stop reading and look out! How stimulating the scene is, in its unconsciousness, its irrelevance, its perpetual movement."[9]

---

[8]Woolf's diaries acknowledge an aversion to as well as a fascination with interruption.

[9]Woolf, "How Should One Read a Book?," in *Collected Essays*, II, 2, 5. Ruth Gruber argues that throughout Woolf's fiction the room represents reality, and the view from the window illusion. *Virginia Woolf—A Study* (Leipzig, 1936), p. 78.

Where every reader or writer entertains similar inclinations as a necessary break from concentrated effort, Woolf allows these disruptive pauses to affect the basis of her thinking. Stepping outside the given, she looks for inspiration in that genderless no-man's-land between the acts of human intervention. The defining intention of her narrative strategy is to loosen the hold we are disposed to establish both on the world and, as readers, on the text before us.[10] If this seems a choice for indeterminacy, the alternative signifies a reductive neglect of an inscrutably larger external world. It is the very hierarchical attitude of mind, what Mikhail Bakhtin terms "the valorized-hierarchical category of the past," that Woolf too finds inapplicable to modern life.[11] Her critique of education, most evident in *Three Guineas*, assaults the representatives of culture who, privileged to classify phenomena, dispense truth from the height of an unquestioned authority. One notes in this regard her invitation to the university lecturer to step down from his podium to discourse more genuinely from the floor. Woolf's medium, like Bakhtin's, remains dialogical.

In the diary entry immediately preceding her cook's interruption, Woolf characterizes four distinguished contemporaries writing their books as "little boys making sand castles. This refers to H. Read; Tom Eliot; Santayana; Wells. Each is weathertight & gives shelter to the occupant" (*Diary*, V, 340). By contrast, she continues, "I am the sea which demolishes these castles." While Herbert Read's criticism of Roger Fry motivates this attack, it is the pontificating tone of his recently published autobiography that moves her for the second time in several months to employ the phrase "tower dwellers." However much she may admire the authors praised in Read's new book, his propensity to wall certain writers in and "others out" suggests an architecture of closure. Woolf encourages the overseers of the world—novelists and professors as well as political leaders—to step down into the tumult of a "classless and towerless society," and she affirms an alternate "common ground."[12]

. . . Woolf's evolving aesthetics encompass both existentialist and anarchist presumptions. In this light, it is ironic to find her diary critique of hierarchy motivated by the autobiography of a writer whose predilection for both anarchism and existentialism was well known. Herbert Read's offending criticism of Fry expresses, moreover, that same distaste for closure Woolf's diary turns back on him. Claiming "Fry's deepest instinct was not adventurous," Read complains specifically of Fry's preference for "the protectiveness of the Ivory Tower."

---

[10]A similar intention describes Sören Kierkegaard's Knight of Faith lounging by "an open window" in *Fear and Trembling*. Observing the breadth of everything going on, no longer cowed by processes or training, "he does not lack courage to make trial of everything and to venture everything." *Fear and Trembling* (New York, 1954), pp. 51–53.

[11]Mikhail Bakhtin, *The Dialogic Imagination*, ed. Michael Holquist (Austin, Tex., 1983), p. 20.

[12]Woolf, "The Leaning Tower," in *Collected Essays*, II, 170–81.

Woolf's own culturally derived disposition to create "weathertight" castles, art forms that stand above refutation, moves her to collaborate in undercutting her own design. Only when existing structures lose centrality and become, in her idiom, porous and transparent, does nature in some mysterious way inspire experimental ventures. For Woolf the incautious freedom to pursue such options grows proportionately with her willingness to confront disorder. In his autobiography the anarchist Read marks the line from Nietzsche—"one must have chaos within one to give birth to a dancing star"—as an early source of his philosophical inspiration.[13] Woolf's diary image of herself as the demolishing sea reflects something of this impulse to begin through an act of radical disengagement from an education that has stressed, in her mind, competitive rather than cooperative values. In each case the goal is not chaos but mutuality, the effort to reconstitute social intercourse on more communal grounds.

Not all structures stand condemned through her sand-castle simile, but only an architecture she conceives to be misapplied to the aesthetics of the novel. Had Woolf read Bakhtin she would no doubt have added his strictures on the outdated poetics of an epic past to the Russian criteria she praised so highly. He echoes her language in a phrase he employs frequently in his essay "Epic and Novel" to describe the "language of tradition." It appears in a particularly relevant passage of *The Dialogic Imagination:* "Precisely because it is walled off from all subsequent times, the epic past is absolute and complete. It is as closed as a circle; inside it everything is finished, already over. There is no place in the epic world for any openendedness, indecision, indeterminacy. There are no loopholes in it through which we glimpse the future."[14]

Windows in Woolf's novels form an important medium through which interruption is manifest. Their function, metaphorically at least, remains suspect if not irrelevant to the tower dweller. Once formulated, his or her overarching vision requires little if any emendation, indeed depends, in a manner of speaking, on the exclusion of an ever-fluctuating external world. Avoiding the haphazard multiplicity of life, tower dwellers, Woolf points out with self-incriminating honesty, fall prey to a familiar desire to retain what D. H. Lawrence aptly termed "the old stable ego":[15] "They have been great egotists. That too was forced upon them by their circumstances. When everything is rocking round one, the only person who remains comparatively stable is oneself. When all faces are changing and obscured, the only face one can see clearly is one's own. So they wrote about themselves" (*Collected Essays*, II, 177).

[13]Herbert Read, *Annals of Innocence and Experience* (London, 1940), p. 82.
[14]Bakhtin, *Dialogic Imagination*, p. 16.
[15]Lawrence employs the phrase in a letter to Edward Garnett dated June 5, 1914. *The Letters of D. H. Lawrence*, ed. Aldous Huxley (New York, 1932), p. 200.

Woolf's recollection of her mother and nursery, "the most important of all my memories," conveys a sense of undisturbed protectiveness, but the corresponding image of a window emerging in the midst of enclosure supplants this first memory. She remembers "lying half asleep, half awake" in her nursery at St. Ives, and the ecstasy of the subsequent moment as associated in some way with the widening dissolution of self: "It is of hearing the blind draw its little acorn across the floor as the wind blew the blind out. It is of lying and hearing this splash and seeing this light, and feeling, it is almost impossible that I should be here" (*Moments*, 64–65).

She is tempted to express the moment in terms of a large canvas abounding with color, the light showing through, the edges blurred as in a Rothko painting.[16] Instead she pursues and renders a different ambience. At the center of every picture, "very definite; very upright," stands her mother, filling so authoritatively that dimensionless space of childhood. Unlike the world at large, this center requires no alteration. For Woolf, "living so completely in her atmosphere," everything external seems at best irrelevant. "She was the whole thing" (*Moments*, 83).

Two conflicting images emerge from Woolf's earliest recollections of childhood, one of the wind and sea beyond the protective walls of her nursery, the other of her mother Julia Stephen, a model for that wholeness and perfection she desires to attain. Through Woolf's autobiographical recounting, the healthy sense of protectiveness associated with her mother expands into a pervasive metaphysical principle of order and centrality. Controlling, as it were, the confusion of the world, her mother comes easily to personify those classical decorums that have allowed Western culture to survive each threat of vagrancy.

In terms of art, such intentions include, as Bakhtin understood, an outdated expectation of artistic fulfillment. From Aristotle and Horace to Boileau, the Russian critic found a poetics "permeated with a deep sense of the wholeness of literature," a wholeness that he considered anathema to all notions of the novel; "it is characteristic of the novel that it never enters into this whole, it does not participate in any harmony of the genres."[17]

One cannot overemphasize the degree to which the appeal of this tradition tempts Woolf to fall back on exemplary artistic strategies of her own patriarchal heritage. "The great writer," she reminds herself in "Robinson Crusoe," who triumphs over the external world, "brings order from chaos; he plants his tree there, and his man here; he makes the figure of his deity remote or present as he wills. In masterpieces—books, that is, where the vision is clear

---

[16]Mark Rothko's familiar rectangles, with their varying horizontal lines so suggestive of uncurtained windows, inspire similarly a bewildering vision of time and space. One critic describes the experience of viewing his paintings as being "drawn . . . into vast spaces that threaten to dissolve both the viewer and his world." Irving Sandler, *The Triumph of American Painting: A History of Abstract Expressionism* (New York, 1970), p. 183.

[17]Bakhtin, *Dialogic Imagination*, pp. 4–5.

and order has been achieved—he inflicts his own perspective upon us."[18]

Even though a Hardy or a Proust is commended for wrenching old supports from readers, for imposing a different sense of structure—"our vanity is injured because our order is upset"—Woolf is inclined at such times to become artistically less adventuresome. Although her aesthetic of the novel invites comparison with Bakhtin's, it is easy to understand why so many of her best-known passages are often employed to support an opposing aesthetic of wholeness. In the very passage where she affirms the shock-receiving capacity, we find her adopting a defensively omniscient view of her art: "I make it real by putting it into words. It is only by putting it into words that I make it whole; this wholeness means that it has lost its power to hurt me" (*Moments*, 72). Art at such moments too easily becomes a method of avoiding nature's admonition to confront unending change.

Woolf's letters and diaries reveal how fully a compulsive need for authority affected and constricted her closest relationships. Her sister Vanessa, her husband Leonard, and, perhaps more than either, her close friend Vita Sackville-West assume the role of protective guardians. Aware of her own fears about life, she describes Vita as lavishing on her "the maternal protection which, for some reason, is what I have always most wished from everyone" (*Diary*, III, 52). Recalling Mrs. Ramsay's presiding influence on Lily Briscoe, Vita's strong presence, "like a lampost, straight, glowing" (*Diary*, III, 204), interposes an old way of seeing and doing.[19] The fault, of course, is not Vita's. Virginia seems aware of the need to move on her own behalf without the constancy of a defining center, be it Julia or Vita, Vanessa or Leonard.

To move outside the boundaries of a familiar world occasions for all Woolf's heroines anxieties that tempt them back into postures of dependence. Clarissa Dalloway, shaken by an "awful fear" of experience—"one's parents giving it into one's hands, this life to be lived to the end"—finds reassurance in the recurring presence of her husband "reading the *Times*" at breakfast. Fearful that "nothing persists," Rhoda stumbles in *The Waves* because she finds no one to lead her. Tied to an old script, fearful of the very space her play has created, Miss La Trobe in *Between the Acts* feels enslaved by her audience.

From my perspective, Woolf's novels form the arena of her own struggle to resist that wholesome proportion the doctors of her fiction, among others, are quick to prescribe—witness her strenuous effort to resist seduction by Mrs. Ramsay's "party around a table." The promise of wholeness, designed to oppose "fluidity out there," invites what has already been described as an architecture of closure.

---

[18]Woolf, "Robinson Crusoe," in *Collected Essays*, I, 71. P. K. Joplin's fine analysis of Terence Hewet's recitation of *Comus* and its effect on Woolf's first heroine conveys this appeal: "Milton's words seem to possess poetic authority approaching that of the divine author whose performative utterances transformed 'words' into 'things.' " "The Art of Resistance: Authority and Violence in the Work of Virginia Woolf," Ph.D. dissertation, Stanford University, 1984, p. 66.

[19]These words echo Julia Stephen's last words to Virginia: "Hold yourself straight, my little Goat" (*Moments*, p. 84).

The mediating artist, rising above "the spasmodic, the obscure, the fragmentary, the failure," is inclined from this privileged ground to become a soldier "in the army of the upright," descending imperially "to civilize, to share, to cultivate the desert, educate the native." However sensible this course of action may at times seem to her, Woolf clearly urges noncompliance: "We become deserters. They march to battle. We float with sticks on the stream; helter-skelter with the dead leaves on the lawn, irresponsible and disinterested and able, perhaps for the first time for years, to look round, to look up—to look for example at the sky" (*Collected Essays*, IV, 196).

Avoiding the unexpected, choosing the security of prescribed actions, her characters repeatedly decline such invitations to disengage. Under the influence of Mrs. Ramsay, Lily Briscoe is tempted to contemplate and reproduce an object of art complete in itself. Bernard, despite his delight in the confusion of the moment, at the end of *The Waves* comes to regard people and experience outside his own well-framed narratives as the enemy. If Woolf makes their respective incantations so appealing, indeed invites us to share a world immune from interruption and change, it is because she would have us confront and hopefully resist our own largely educated predilections.

Innumerable readers and critics have been moved, and I suspect misled, by the poignancy with which Woolf's language arouses a comforting sense of artistic wholeness. However fulfilling scenes such as the Boeuf en Daube dinner in *To the Lighthouse* may be, they create a disposition for stasis Woolf compels us, as she must herself, unremittingly to question and oppose. "Like Clarissa Dalloway (and Terence Hewet), Mrs. Ramsay can create moments of unity that remain intact in the memory," as one of Woolf's best early critics puts it.[20] Yet to stress this virtue is surely misleading. Ideas that remain "intact" are ideas ill-disposed to change. We may recall in this light Leonard Woolf's response to the absolutism of totalitarian ideology in *Quack, Quack!*: "A true belief is little more than a stepping stone to something else; it keeps the mind fluid, volatile; it sets it riding off on new adventures."[21]

Even though Virginia Woolf longed to find some sustaining pattern above or behind the jumble of human experience, she suspected transcendental truth as she suspected the hierarchical claims of Whitaker's Table of Precedency: "The Archbishop of Canterbury is followed by the Lord High Chancellor; the Lord High Chancellor is followed by the Archbishop of York. Everybody follows somebody, such is the philosophy of Whitaker; and the great thing is to know who follows whom" (*Haunted House*, 44).

Far less fixed and absolute, her characters' deepest convictions appear, much like their author's, consistently open to influence and change. To read her well, we must try similarly to suspend some derived expectations. Even the best of her commentators have not always found this easy to accomplish.

---

[20]James Hafley, *The Glass Roof: Virginia Woolf as Novelist* (Berkeley, Calif., 1954), p. 80.
[21]Leonard Woolf, *Quack, Quack!* (New York, 1935), p. 14.

Applying the very values of hierarchy she repudiates, more than a few critics view her first heroine as a woman who has failed to take heed of proper models: neither aunt nor fiancé can save Rachel Vinrace from a chaos of her own making. Since her fiancé's poetics follow Proust's, it seems reasonable to presume "that Rachel's attitude is wrong and Terence's right."[22] The "few perfect moments" that redeem *The Voyage Out* (such critics, it seems, long for perfection) occur as Rachel, in accord with society's intentions as they apply to a young unmarried woman lucky enough to be chosen by an honorable and attractive young man, submits to social decorum. Rachel's existential doubts about marriage are often read from this perspective as symptomatic of Virginia Stephen's own unhealthy state of mind while composing the novel.

The promise of leadership reappearing in Woolf's work represents a fulfillment that proves, more often than not, destructive of life and art. The advice, first of Helen and Terence, subsequently of Jacob, Mrs. Ramsay, and Bernard-become-Percival, fosters, I suggest, closure and bad faith. However beloved and magnanimous these figures may be to their author as well as to her readers, they all, dutifully conventional, share a common disinclination to experiment.[23] Jacob may well be "an exemplar of all the other young men whose promise the war destroyed,"[24] and for this reason we regret his untimely death, but for Woolf such promise merely perpetuates reactionary values.

In the 1970's Mitchell Leaska and Carolyn Heilbrun questioned the assumption that Mrs. Ramsay represented an ideal sort of woman.[25] Most subsequent criticism evidently remains unconvinced. Restating earlier assumptions that the novel's chief purpose was "to capture and render stable and permanent the essence of Mrs. Ramsay," critics continue to affirm its celebration of marital love while applauding Mrs. Ramsay's role at the center of the family, "the foundation of social life" in the words of one commentator.[26] It follows that the problem lies with those like Lily (and before her, Rachel) whose will to experiment threatens unanimity. Unable to respond to Mr. Ramsay's plea for sympathy—"it is to her immense discredit sexually"—Lily is marked as the deficient one. To regard Lily as the heroine of *To the Lighthouse*, rather than as "the child who communicates [Mrs. Ramsay's] light to the world," may offend readers who find pleasure in Mrs. Ramsay's gifts.[27]

[22]Hafley, *Glass Roof*, p. 18.

[23]Hermione Lee makes this point repeatedly in *The Novels of Virginia Woolf* (New York, 1977), pp. 1–30.

[24]Bernard Blackstone, *Virginia Woolf: A Commentary* (New York, 1949), p. 65.

[25]See Carolyn G. Heilbrun, *Toward a Recognition of Androgyny* (New York, 1973), pp. 155–63; and Mitchell A. Leaska, *Virginia Woolf's Lighthouse: A Study in Critical Method* (New York, 1970). One of the earliest "negative" treatments of Mrs. Ramsay is Glenn Pederson's "Vision in *To the Lighthouse*," *PMLA*, 73 (1958), pp. 585–600.

[26]Maria DiBattista, *Virginia Woolf's Major Novels: The Fables of Anon* (New Haven, Conn., 1980), p. 76. The first quotation is from Hafley, p. 89. For a similar emphasis, see Alice van Buren Kelley, *The Novels of Virginia Woolf: Fact and Vision* (Chicago, 1973), p. 118.

[27]DiBattista, *Fables of Anon*, pp. 69, 103–4.

The merging of Bernard with Percival in *The Waves* conveys an acceptance of that same wholeness Mrs. Ramsay would pass on to those who follow, a legacy Lily emphatically declines by refusing Mr. Ramsay accord. The present study submits that *The Waves*, far from simply an honoring of Thoby Stephen or an impulse to revive a legacy of romance,[28] commemorates art's tenuous struggle to resist the appeal of closure. Most critics see Bernard at the conclusion of this novel as the ideal artist, intent on creating unity, struggling "to conquer chaos and give form to the vision."[29] Such analyses presume, perhaps too confidently, that Bernard is Woolf's spokesman. The story Bernard shapes and sets down before the stranger in the restaurant is, much like Mrs. Ramsay's dish, "a complete thing," a coherent object of art, insusceptible to change. Woolf suggests in *A Room of One's Own* that such a work, requiring no collaboration, is "doomed to death. It ceases to be fertilised" (*AROO*, 108). In this context the transcendence one critic identifies with the traditional leap of poets—the final ride suggests a "leap at immortality"[30]—may appear, antithetically, a return to patriarchal omniscience.

At the end of *The Years* Eleanor Pargiter, close to eighty years old, returning to the family circle, hollows her hands as if "to enclose the present moment," perhaps for one last time. Rather than a return to pattern,[31] such a contraction, I argue, involves for Woolf a rejection of human potentiality.

It is in Woolf's last novel, *Between the Acts* (1941), that the consolation both of wholeness and of governance receives its most compelling critique. The survival of the human species, much less art, appears contingent on society's willingness to question, like the audience of Miss La Trobe's play, what it takes mostly for granted. The future after the defeat of fascism envisioned in the *Times* is prophetically insufficient. Its prediction of everyone in a new flat filled with the latest appliances builds to an ironic "all liberated; made whole."

As *Three Guineas* suggests, Woolf has in mind different alternatives that must inevitably offend a culture nourished on virtues of acquisition. We the readers, in company with Colonel Mayhew, seated impatiently as the action of the play flags, resist the invitation to do nothing, an advice that sounds particularly naïve and suicidal at times when military preparedness seems the only course for survival.[32]

Those who seek models of wholeness in the novel point to the figures of Lucy Swithin and Mrs. Manresa for unifying paradigms, to the former for the spirit, to the latter for the body. But surely it is Isa and Miss La Trobe, in

---

[28]Ibid., p. 153.

[29]Kelley, *Fact and Vision*, p. 199.

[30]Avrom Fleishman, *Virginia Woolf: A Critical Reading* (Baltimore, 1975), p. 171.

[31]Kelley, *Fact and Vision*, p. 221.

[32]Phyllis Rose points out that this was an especially desperate period for Woolf, a time when her personal need for order must have been most strident. *Woman of Letters: A Life of Virginia Woolf* (New York, 1978), p. 231.

similar states of disarray, who prompt our deepest admiration. *Between the Acts* postulates a series of temptations for the author and her readers, from the consolation of art to the nostalgia for rural England, only to leave us all without a center, equally dispersed, equally open to the impact of interruption.

The uncertainty with which Woolf ends her first novel will become a conscious strategy through which to disrupt more traditional modes of narration and thereby allow the advent of something radically new. With the center vacant, the text itself becomes the medium of revelation, though of a nature different from that of pointedly religious epics. Where an informing vision emerges for Dante Alighieri through the figure of Beatrice or structurally through the number nine, for Woolf the idea of the holy resides quite literally in those "chasms" the narrator of *Jacob's Room* points to within "the continuity of our ways." Whether such intrusions signify the "loopholes" Bakhtin describes or the rejuvenating pause through which a mysterious sense of shared experience inspires renewal, they mark in Woolf's fiction moments of profound possibility. However brief the human life span—Woolf describes it in her first novel as that "short season between two silences"—the most mundane particularities of existence continue to startle and arouse her heroines, once, that is, they have resisted the enticements of patriarchal generosity.

. . . Central to all her thinking is the revelation of interruption, heralding change, and the growing expectation that society is on the verge of radical transformation. . . . [For example,] *Night and Day*, if the most traditional of her novels, saw her break with literary conventions and her reception of those upheavals that describe the new Georgian age. Katharine and Ralph can be said to mature in proportion to their capacity to indulge interruption. . . . The expansion and confusion of narrative boundaries informs Woolf's attack on patriarchal hierarchy. . . . Though of thoroughly different backgrounds and persuasions, Clarissa Dalloway and Lily Briscoe both create art forms whose vitality does not depend on continued omniscient intervention. Each steps back from the center to allow her creation to take on a discernibly eccentric life of its own. Woolf's last three novels develop this theme. *The Waves*, dispensing entirely with an omniscient narrator, confronts the impact of a world in which the very concept of centrality collapses. The absence of Percival, like the sudden departure of Mrs. Ramsay in "Time Passes," introduces a world without authenticating rulers. The subversion of omniscience moves her finally with *The Years* and *Between the Acts* to envision an egalitarian society without constricting hierarchies or patriarchal leaders, where each new interruption emerges, however anarchically, with a promise of renewal. .

The Trained Mind: *A Room of One's Own*

Rachel Bowlby

I am almost sure, I said to myself, that Mary Carmichael is playing a trick on us. For I feel as one feels on a switchback railway when the car, instead of sinking, as one had been led to expect, swerves up again. Mary is tampering with the expected sequence. First she broke the sentence; now she has broken the sequence.

—(*A Room of One's Own*)[1]

'But' is the first word of *A Room of One's Own:* a beginning against the conventions of 'what one had been led to expect' for Woolf the invited lecturer on 'Women and Fiction', as much as for the hypothetical new woman novelist, Mary Carmichael. Starting *in medias res*, as if a conversation had been going on already, Woolf's 'but' indicates, first of all, that the topic cannot be addressed from some place of absolute innocence: a story involving women and fiction in various complicated ways has been under way for quite some time (for the duration of written history, at least), and it would be utopian to imagine that it might be possible to discuss such a matter in abstract or ideal terms. Hence, as in 'Mr Bennett and Mrs Brown,' a general question immediately takes a narrative turn, as Woolf moves—or is she just 'playing a trick'?— from theory to the fictional ramble through 'Oxbridge,' London, the British Museum and through many byways of literary history, in an exploration where ' "I" is only a convenient term for somebody who has no real being' (*AROO*, 6).

Secondly, the unconventional opening represents a provocative interruption of the discourse in progress. Like Mary Carmichael's 'tampering with the expected sequence' and with the norms of syntax, it represents a kind of 'butting in.' This has ramifications or branch lines throughout the text, as we shall see. On what, exactly, does 'Woolf' butt in, and does she do so only in so far as she is excluded from it? If it is as a woman that she interrupts something conceived as occupied or dominated by men, does she anticipate a future alteration of the terms on which that differential—between men and women, between the insiders and the outsiders —has operated so far?

[1]Virginia Woolf, *A Room of One's Own* (1929; London: Granada), p. 78. Subsequent quotations will be identified in the text by *AROO* and page number(s).

Many different suggestions appear in the course of *A Room* for what is, or what makes, the difference between men and women, and the differences of men's and women's writing. Though Woolf (or rather Woolf's narrator, her 'convenient' I) settles for none in particular, some of them are now influential models for thinking about women and writing—or about Woolf— in their own right. While they can be broadly subsumed under the headings of 'historical' and 'psychological'—as having to do with social constraints or with possibly universal forms of psychic organization—part of their interest lies in the ways that in Woolf's analyses such divisions are themselves rendered more complicated, and altered by the ways that they turn out to impinge upon each other.

Materials

In an overtly historical mode, Woolf alludes to what she calls the 'material' conditions of writing. It is fallacious, she says, to think of Shakespeare as if he dropped from the sky: great works of literature

> are not spun in mid-air by incorporeal creatures, but are the work of suffering human beings, and are attached to grossly material things, like health and money and the houses we live in. (*AROO*, 41)

Owing to their lack of property and education, as well as to constraints on their freedom of movement and to demands on their time for other purposes, women have not been in a position to spin the particular substance of which Shakespeare's *oeuvre* is Woolf's favourite example: and Woolf cites the imaginary representative case of 'Shakespeare's sister' endowed with gifts equal to her brother's but unable, because of the position of women at the time, to make anything of them.[2]

But as compared with other professions, the material resources for writing are much easier to obtain. In another of her lectures of this period, 'Professions for Women,' Woolf matter-of-factly points out that 'for ten and sixpence one can buy paper enough to write all the plays of Shakespeare' (*CE*, II: 284).[3] Joined with the fact that writing could just about be done as it was by Jane Austen, in 'the common sitting-room' (*AROO*, 108), as opposed to a room and time of one's own, this accounts partly for why writing for money should have

---

2See *A Room*, pp. 46–8. *Shakespeare's Sisters* is the title of a collection of essays on women poets edited by Sandra M. Gilbert and Susan Gubar (Bloomington: Indiana University Press, 1979).

3Virginia Woolf, *Collected Essays*, ed. Leonard Woolf, 4 vols. (London: Chatto & Windus, 1967), II, 284. Subsequent quotations will be identified as *CE* with volume and page numbers. As well as in the *Collected Essays*, 'Professions for Women' appears also in a selection of essays by Woolf on *Women and Writing*, ed. with an introduction by Michèle Barrett (New York: Harcourt Brace Jovanovich, 1979), pp. 57–63. An earlier, much longer version is published in *The Pargiters*: the essay was the basis of Woolf's idea for what became *The Pargiters* and then *The Years*

been so widely engaged in by women without material support from the conventional (male) quarters for themselves or for their dependants, once Aphra Behn and her followers had established the precedent.

Outsiders

The apparent simplicity of this factual enumeration of 'material' conditions already implies a further question about why women should have had less money or not have engaged in the same professional activities as men. Here a structural rather than statistical description comes into play. Woolf refers, in this text as in others, to British society as a 'patriarchy'. The use of this term indicates a hierarchical division of ruled and rulers, with 'fathers' providing the pivotal category. Whereas sons will inherit and mothers be honoured, daughters in this arrangement are not easily put in their place, except in that their place is one of exclusion from any position of authority. Woolf's references in *Three Guineas* to the non-place of 'the daughters of educated men' lead to the development of her proposal of a 'Society of Outsiders.' Such a position is adumbrated in *A Room* in the stories of the various exclusions to which the narrator is subjected in her wanderings round 'Oxbridge.' Having been shooed off for trespassing on the grass and debarred from entering the library, 'I thought how unpleasant it is to be locked out; and I thought how it is worse perhaps to be locked in' (*AROO*, 24).

It is thus that a position outside might turn out to hold more possibilities for forms of activity or reasoning ruled out a priori for those who have to maintain the proprieties of the insider group. Woolf's narrator is full of scorn and mockery for the stereotyped personifications of patriarchal conventions who don their gowns and their furs to parade an unswerving conformity to whatever institution it may be: 'As I leant against the wall the University indeed seemed a sanctuary in which are preserved rare types which would soon be obsolete if left to fight for existence on the pavement of the Strand' (10). Elsewhere—in London, in *Three Guineas*, for instance—the 'procession' of masculine tradition is less readily dismissed as a provincial anachronism, and the question becomes that of whether the hitherto excluded woman should want or attempt to join it.[4]

Trespassing

Instantly a man's figure rose to intercept me. Nor did I at first understand that the gesticulations of a curious-looking object, in a cut-away coat and evening shirt, were aimed at me. His face expressed horror and indignation. Instinct rather than reason came to my help; he was a Beadle; I was a woman. This was the turf; there was the path. (*AROO*, 7)

[4]Virginia Woolf, *Three Guineas* (New York: Harcourt Brace, 1938), 60–62.

The walk through 'Oxbridge' approaches an allegory of the banning of women from the citadels of masculine authority, all the more effective for its deployment of the imagery of territorial demarcations. The colleges which do not admit women symbolize the male monopoly on every aspect of cultural authority.[5] In *Three Guineas*, Woolf develops in more detail the arguments around the mutual reinforcement of the social institutions which combine to keep women out, and questions whether theirs is the kind of power in which women would like to participate. In *A Room*, she shows the poverty of the women's college as an inevitable effect of the centuries of patriarchal control of the 'material' supports of such institutions.

> The most transient visitor to this planet, I thought, who picked up this paper could not fail to be aware, even from this scattered testimony, that England is under the rule of a patriarchy. Nobody in their senses could fail to detect the dominance of the professor. His was the power and the money and the influence. He was the proprietor of the paper and its editor and sub-editor. He was the Foreign Secretary and the Judge. He was the cricketer; he owned the racehorses and the yachts. He was the director of the company that pays two hundred per cent to its shareholders. He left millions to charities and colleges that were ruled by himself. (*AROO*, 33–4)

Woolf is thus quite unequivocal about the kind of social power that is at stake in the marking of different values and differential access to the public use of language. The terms are absolutely set out ('His was the power') and absolutely fixed according to the lines of gender: what is 'his' must not be hers.

It is one thing to name this power of exclusion and control 'patriarchy': Woolf can offer no rational explanation for such a thorough separation of functions between the sexes. Hence the exposure of the arbitrariness of the division: the opposition between 'Beadle' and 'woman' is enough to constitute a difference of which Woolf's narrator is in no more doubt than the 'curious-looking object' which rises up to intercept her movements. He, or it, butts in on the rumination about 'women and fiction' she has just begun, as if to call 'Halt!' to an illicit turn of thought. Against his authority she has no appeal; and she recognizes the meaning of his expression in a flash: by 'instinct' rather than reason. Since the law she recognizes is obviously cultural, this underlining of the received understanding of the difference between men's and women's ways of knowing—rationally or intuitively—then operates as its parodic undermining.

Its very pretension to exclusiveness seems to imply that male power is always under threat. The Beadle's response to the woman's presence on the grass is anything but neutral: his 'horror and indignation' show that a woman who fails to abide by the law has roused in him a reaction that itself goes beyond the bounds of reason. Woolf's narrator settles down in the British Museum with an 'avalanche of books' (*AROO*, 28) written by authors with 'no

---

[5]On the first stage of Woolf's writing against masculine cultural authority, see Christine Froula, 'Out of the Chrysalis: Female Initiation and Female Authority in Virginia Woolf's *The Voyage Out*', *Tulsa Studies in Women's Literature*, 5, 1 (Spring 1986), pp. 63–90, reprinted in this volume.

qualification save that they were not women' (*AROO*, 29). It is as if there is a continuous and never completed effort on the part of man to keep woman in the place assigned to her by him: outside the precincts of representational power, defined, bounded, in a proliferation of heterogeneous characteristics which the narrator lists for her readers in a parody of the books' pseudo-scholarly procedures (*AROO*, 29).

Impediments

Following the historical line of reasoning, the differential access to sites of social authority and prestige gives rise to different kinds of thinking. His 'training' (*AROO*, 29) means that the middle- or upper-class male learns to regulate and organize his writing in a way that a Dorothy Osborne or a Duchess of Newcastle could not; while its institutional back-up means that 'the freedom of the mind' (*AROO*, 61) is not constrained for him by the need to attend to 'material' concerns. It is this difference of material and educational means which accounts for the contrast between the culinary amenities of the men's and women's colleges at the start of *A Room*, the amply or meagerly nourished bodies of their respective inmates providing food for Woolf's thoughts about the 'two pictures, disjointed and disconnected' (*AROO*, 20) of the history of their respective endowments: munificent and age-old in one case, lacking and barely begun in the other. Reproductive differences are cited as one major reason why women have been confined within the limits of the private sphere, and later on the childlessness of many of the women who have been successful writers is noted as significant.[6]

Describing the writing of nineteenth-century women novelists, Woolf's narrator identifies flaws which she attributes to this arbitrary and historically contingent state of affairs. Charlotte Brontë's achievement is marred because: 'She will write in a rage where she should write calmly. . . . She is at war with her lot. How could she help but die young, cramped and thwarted?' (*AROO*, 67). Such 'impediments' (*AROO*, 65) in the writing—shared, for example, by a Lady Winchilsea 'bursting out' in her much earlier poetry 'in indignation against the position of women' (*AROO*, 56)—are seen as socially induced: her 'defects' are 'those of her sex at the time' (*AROO*, 67): 'It is clear that anger was tampering with the integrity of Charlotte Brontë the novelist. . . . She remembered that she had been starved of her proper due of experience—she had been made to stagnate in a parsonage mending stockings when she wanted to wander free over the world' (*AROO*, 70). These quotations imply that a novel and a writer should have 'integrity' and be free of 'anger' or 'indignation.' There is a horizon of wholeness and healthy development according to a given 'nature', in relation to which the failed novel or novelist will be dull ('stagnate') or 'cramped.' . . .

[6]See *A Room*, pp. 59 and 63.

The Difference of Value

It is obvious that the values of women differ very often from the values which have been made by the other sex; naturally, this is so. Yet it is the masculine values that prevail. Speaking crudely, football and sport are 'important;' the worship of fashion, the buying of clothes 'trivial.' And these values are inevitably transferred from life to fiction. This is an important book, the critic assumes, because it deals with war. This is an insignificant book because it deals with the feelings of women in a drawing-room. A scene in a battlefield is more important than a scene in a shop—everywhere and much more subtly the difference of value persists. (*AROO*, 70–1)

'Naturally,' each sex has its own values; yet once this is granted, it is not clear how or why the values 'made' by one come to take precedence over those of the other. The passage assumes a fundamental and natural difference between the sexes. It does not ask whether the distinction of 'important' from 'trivial,' the inverted commas signalling a question as to their respective priority, is itself part of what 'the other sex' has made.

Given that there is a difference, but that one set of values succeeds in establishing a priority, it is only right, the passage implies, that the 'fair' sex should be given a hearing, and that women should come to be granted their different but equal place. Under the prevailing system, the nineteenth-century woman writer was deflected from her natural values, 'pulled from the straight . . . in deference to external authority' (*AROO*, 71): 'she was admitting that she was "only a woman," or protesting that she was "as good as a man"' (*AROO*, 71). But again, Woolf's narrator singles out exceptions—Jane Austen and Emily Brontë: 'They wrote as women write, not as men write' (*AROO*, 71).

The implied destination here is a situation where women will both catch up with men and cease to be deflected by them from their own path. There is a full and natural state, with its own set of values, proper to each sex. In themselves these values do not intrude upon or interfere with one another; each is the other's outside, and the 'impediment' that needs to be removed is the hierarchy that has established the one as superior to the other. In the meantime, women's writing can be identified as not yet women's writing, or as women's writing *manquée*, when it manifests the qualities of feminine self-abnegation (' "only a woman" ') or masculine protestation (' "as good as a man" '), each of which complies with the dominant order by accepting that womanly values are less than men's.

Recovering a Female Tradition

We think back through our mothers if we are women. It is useless to go to the great men writers for help, however much one may go to them for pleasure. (*AROO*, 72–3)

It is implicit in Woolf's assertion here that women writers need women writers as examples: if they are to write 'as women,' they need to see that women have written (and not, for example, that men have written or simply that there has been writing). And Woolf has herself become foremother to a generation of feminists who 'think back through our mothers.' She pioneered the work of making known the writing of women whose existence had previously been obscured, covered over, by the weight of the masculine canon, and this enterprise has since become an industry on a large scale in both publishing and criticism. . . .

Those who challenge the mainstream patriarchal 'canon' generally try to avoid setting up what only turns out to be another definitive list of the best and the greatest. In Woolf's discussion of what women's writing is, she usually draws on the names that are already known and already in print. For the nineteenth century, for instance, her examples are Eliot and the Brontës, the same women singled out habitually as having produced work worthy of a place in the 'common' canon or the 'great tradition' of English literature. In her programmatic statements, however, she suggests more that it is 'obscure' writing, the works of 'Anon'—who, she says, was probably most often a woman—that need to be brought to notice.[7]

On the other side of this, she also hints that some of the best-known women writers have been 'overdone':

> And, after all, we have lives enough of Jane Austen; it scarcely seems necessary to consider again the influence of the tragedies of Joanna Baillie upon the poetry of Edgar Allan Poe; as for myself, I should not mind if the homes and the haunts of Mary Russell Mitford were closed to the public for a century at least. (*AROO*, 45)

It is another uncanny anticipation of the destiny of the name 'Virginia Woolf': as part of the coffee-table book cult of 'Bloomsbury', as the object of a feminist cult of the 'great foremother'; and—to modify Mrs Ramsay's explanation of Charles Tansley's thesis topic[8]—as the object of numerous critical studies about 'the influence of something' upon her.

Another turn to the process of thinking back through our mothers is suggested by Woolf's fable of Shakespeare's hypothetical sister Judith, unable because of her sex to fulfil theatrical gifts equal to her brother's. The fictional reconstruction highlights the fact that it is impossible to know whether such a sister did or did not exist, since what it relates is nothing else than how she

---

[7]'Indeed, I would venture to guess that Anon, who wrote so many poems without signing them, was often a woman' (*AROO*, 48). In the Granada edition, 'signing' is misprinted as 'singing', which suggests an inverse relationship between the two: even more anonymous than Anon, who wrote without signing, are the women who sang without writing, even anonymously. The very next sentence continues: 'It was a woman Edward Fitzgerald, I think, suggested who made the ballads and the folk-songs, crooning them to her children, beguiling her spinning with them, or the length of the winter's night' (*AROO*, 48). Maria DiBattista interprets the folksongs of Anon in Woolf as her vision of a maternal poetry anterior to the polemical forms of masculine history and literature. See *Virginia Woolf's Major Novels: The Fables of Anon* (New Haven: Yale University Press, 1980), especially pp. 228–34.

[8]Virginia Woolf, *To the Lighthouse* (New York: Harcourt Brace and World, 1927) p. 22.

would have been prevented from doing anything worthy of historical 'note:' 'Let me imagine, since facts are so hard to come by' (*AROO*, 46). Women also think back, perhaps, through the very fact of having 'no tradition behind them' (*AROO*, 72): think back through the *absence* of mothers.

Sentences

> The sentence that was current at the beginning of the nineteenth century ran something like this perhaps: 'The grandeur of their works was an argument with them, not to stop short, but to proceed. They could have no higher excitement or satisfaction than in the exercise of their art and endless generations of truth and beauty. Success prompted to exertion; and habit facilitates success.' That is a man's sentence: behind it one can see Johnson, Gibbon and the rest. It was a sentence that was unsuited for a woman's use. (*AROO*, 73)

The last two sentences of this passage are two of the most often quoted among Virginia Woolf's many thousands; the previous three, while described as one—'That'—are identified as 'a man's,' though written by the same woman. Many questions are broached here about the possibility of recognizing a difference of linguistic style according to the writer's sex, or that of determining the sex of the writer on the basis of stylistic evidence.

The passage proposes that there is a definite connection between sexual difference and language, but that its form is historically variable. Different sentences, it is implied, will be suitable for a man and a woman. Their identity as one or the other precedes the language they put to 'use' as a medium of expression, and the luck of historical accident decides whether or not the woman (or, by extension, the man) will find an appropriate sort of sentence available. One type of sentence only was 'current' at the beginning of the nineteenth century, and it was 'a man's'; a woman could write it (Woolf does so) but only, apparently, by taking up a man's materials or a man's identity: 'such a lack of tradition, such a scarcity and inadequacy of tools, must have told enormously upon the writing of women' (*AROO*, 73).

But the seeming asymmetry between the grammatical situation of the two sexes deserves a closer look. 'A man's sentence' is at first sight possessive: the man with a sentence of his own, forged by himself and suitable for his use. The sentence belongs to him and not to the woman. She, by contrast, is passively placed in relation to the only available sentence (his), which is unsuited 'for' her use. This discrepancy between the genitive and the dative, between the sentence 'of' the man and the sentence 'for' the woman, indicates a differential access to the medium of language use: we are dealing with quite different cases, grammatically and judicially. Something about the man's sentence causes it to take precedence, to take control, while the woman's sentence simply does not exist, is nowhere 'current' or available for use.

But then it turns out that though there was no woman's sentence, some women might be exempt from the man's sentence: Jane Austen looked at it and laughed at it and devised a perfectly natural, shapely sentence proper for her own use and never departed from it' (*AROO*, 73). Here we return to the question of the exceptional writer, the exceptional woman. If Jane Austen is a woman and is capable of pronouncing her own sentence, that seems to throw doubt upon the general powerlessness attributed to women suffering from 'such a scarcity and inadequacy of tools' (*AROO*, 73). What is the relation of what is 'proper' to the individual writer, woman or man, and what is general to their sex (or their class, or their race, or their historical provenance, for that matter)? What could it mean to 'devise' what is 'natural'? If 'a' Jane Austen, or indeed 'a' Virginia Woolf, can successfully fabricate a sentence suited to her use, then there must be some uncertainty as to the universality of the claim for the sexual division of sentences. The special case both disproves the rule and points to a different model of stylistic analysis. Man's sentence/woman's sentence divides the linguistic universe in two: a writer is one or the other, man or woman, and the sentence is adequate evidence as to the gender of its writer. Jane Austen's sentence/George Eliot's sentence (the latter 'committed atrocities with it that beggar description' [*AROO*,73]) suggests a degree of agency and idiosyncrasy denied by the initial model of women's forced compliance with a linguistic state of affairs which offers them no place. Read retrospectively, 'a man's sentence' might then seem to imply, as for the woman, the sentence available for the man, and the decisive distinction would in this case be not between the sexes, equally subject to the currency of suitable sentences, but between creative writers who make their own sentences, and the rest.

New Regions of Literature

'Chloe liked Olivia,' I read. And then it struck me how immense a change was there. Chloe liked Olivia perhaps for the first time in literature. (*AROO*, 78)

The hypothesis of a man's and a woman's sentence suggests that there is a difference in the form of the language suitable to each sex. Another of the models of gendered writing considered by Woolf's narrator focuses rather on the subject matter of women's fiction. Turning literature in the direction of women's values may produce quite new spaces and possibilities for fiction. The lectures which make up *A Room of One's Own* were delivered just before the trial of Radclyffe Hall's novel *The Well of Loneliness* (1928), which was prosecuted (and eventually suppressed) for its lesbian content. Though she privately regarded it as a 'meritorious dull book,' Woolf was willing to speak on its behalf.[9] The pushing back of the frontiers of literary representation to open up new areas of women's experience was a cause worth defending.

[9]*The Diary of Virginia Woolf*, ed. Anne Olivier Bell with Andrew McNeillie, 5 vols. (London: Hogarth, 1977–1984) III, 193. Subsequent quotations will be identified by *D* with volume and page numbers.

In the passage above, Woolf claims that the novel of 'Mary Carmichael' is not just the first novel to treat of a lesbian relationship, but the first to allow the existence of friendship between women—their relations hitherto regarded, as with Cleopatra contemplating Octavia, with patriarchal eyes, as the jealous contention for men's favours. The expansion of the field of writing about women is thus at the same time bound to upset or transform the norms of masculine and feminine values. In regard to values, Woolf's example 'speaking crudely' was the different importance accorded to football and shopping (*AROO*, 70). Just as she celebrates the extension of legitimate literary fields to the area of relationships between women, so she envisages the literary possibilities that might be offered by giving a place in literature to the 'feminine' shop:

> Mary Carmichael might well have a look at that in passing, I thought, for it is a sight that would lend itself to the pen as fittingly as any snowy peak or rocky gorge in the Andes. And there is the girl behind the counter too—I would as soon have her true history as the hundred and fiftieth life of Napoleon or seventieth study of Keats and his use of Miltonic inversion which old professor Z and his like are now inditing. (*AROO*, 86)

The exploration of new literary countries is thus no neutral addition: it is also a challenge to the priority and interest of the mountain peaks of the present empire, preoccupied only with dramatic exploits and the lives of great men. While it is implied that the new fields of feminine literature are there to start with, only waiting for the pen to come along and borrow them, there is also the possibility that they might in some way be of a different, not just devalorized, order:

> For if Chloe likes Olivia and Mary Carmichael knows how to express it she will light a torch in that vast chamber where nobody has yet been. It is all half lights and profound shadows like those serpentine caves where one goes with a candle peering up and down, not knowing where one is stepping. (*AROO*, 80)

The hygienic and thoroughly well-lighted laboratory where the two women work has now been transformed into a much more mysterious space: a dark 'chamber,' even a 'serpentine' cave. Is this buried region of unrepresented femininity enigmatic only until it is brought up into the bright lights of the modern novel? Is it a place, or a topic, like any other, only obscure until the torch is turned its way? Or is there something qualitatively different about it, something which will always give it this half-lit atmosphere of a place not so readily put on the general map?

The subterranean, shadowy imagery of this passage recalls the frequent allusions in one region of contemporary feminist theory to two of Freud's metaphors for femininity. In his essay on 'Female Sexuality' (1931), Freud compares the discovery of the significance of 'the early, pre-Oedipus, phase in girls' to that 'in another field, of the Minoan-Mycenaean civilization behind the civilization of Greece' And in *The Question of Lay Analysis* (1926), he says: 'the sexual life of adult women is a "dark continent" for psychology.'[10] The conflation of historical and spatial obscurity in the archaeological analogy suggests that femininity in some way eludes or precedes the parameters of rationalistic representation; the ' "dark continent" ' suggests a vast expanse awaiting its enlightenment, but also the enigma of a space which cannot be assimilated to the norms of 'civilized' thought.

Exponents of what is called *écriture féminine*, notably Hélène Cixous, associate the 'dark continent' of femininity with both the unconscious and the body; feminine writing (which is not exclusively the province of women, since male artists are precisely those men who have not repressed the bisexual aspect of their own pre-Oedipal phase) is writing in which the body and the unconscious are expressed, are put into text, without the intervention of patriarchal codings and compartmentalizations ('Instantly a man's figure rose to intercept me . . .'. [*AROO*, 7]). In this view, feminine writing, by whichever sex, is writing which breaks up, or is somehow antecedent to, the conventions and boundaries of 'civilized' representation. It is not just one more new literary field, but that form of writing which throws into question the status of all the rest.

Writing the Body

I want you to figure to yourselves a girl sitting with a pen in her hand, which for minutes, and indeed for hours, she never dips into the inkpot. The image that comes into my mind when I think of this girl is the image of a fisherman lying sunk in dreams on the verge of a deep lake with a rod held out over the water. She was letting her imagination sweep unchecked round every rock and cranny of the world that lies submerged in the depths of our unconscious being. Now came the experience that I believe to be far commoner with women writers than with men. The line raced through the girl's fingers. Her imagination had rushed away. It had sought the pools, the depths, the dark places where the largest fish slumber. And then there was a smash. There was an explosion. There was foam and confusion. The imagination had dashed itself against something hard. The girl was roused from her dream. . . . To speak without figure she had thought of something, something about the body, about the passions which it was unfitting for her as a woman to say. Men, her reason told her, would be shocked. ('Professions for Women,' *CE*, II: 287–8)

Like the advocates of *écriture féminine*, Woolf also regarded the lack of representation of the body in literature as something which needed to be remedied; Jinny in *The Waves* declares ardently that 'My imagination is the body's'.[11] In the passage above, Woolf further implies that the body's present

[10]See *The Pelican Freud Library* (Harmondsworth: Penguin, 1973–87), 'Female Sexuality' (1931), vol. 7, p. 372, and *The Question of Lay Analysis* (1926), vol. 15, p. 313.
[11]Virginia Woolf, *The Waves* (1931; London: Granada) p. 199.

absence is an effect of suppression (of men as well as of women) on the part of men.

This passage closely parallels the mental angling episode near the beginning of *A Room*. The narrator has just settled down by the banks of the river to fish for her idea ('thought . . . had let its line down' [*AROO*, 7]), when she is reprimanded, interrupted, by the Beadle. What the 'unchecked' imagination explores here has to do with both the body and the unconscious; it is figured as hidden in a submerged depth, like the buried civilization or the 'dark' continent; bringing it to the surface is shocking for men and provokes the rock-like resistance of 'something hard' in contrast to its own fluidity. Cixous uses a similar fishing image when she says: 'The truth, which lives only sheltered by silence, is forced to give evidence, and so it is in the same state as a fish pulled out of the water, thinking of the sea in a last convulsion, then, the end.'[12] It is as if the relational structure of language necessarily spells the end of the feminine 'truth,' sentencing it to death. And this then raises a question as to the possibility of *écriture féminine* as such. For if it is defined as precisely that which cannot be represented, put into words, it must remain, like the woman's sentence, always elsewhere than in the 'current': always submerged in a region prior to or beyond that of language, from which it can only be brought into the light of representation at the price of assimilation and thus by the loss of what makes it different. *Écriture féminine* thus flounders somewhere between the invisibility of what lies hidden in the waves and the killing consistencies of the upper world. And this is perhaps why it is more difficult to catch the thing itself than to advocate or allude to it as that which cannot be fitted into the forms of language.[13]

Rewriting History

It would be ambitious beyond my daring, I thought, looking about the shelves for books that were not there, to suggest to the students of those famous colleges that they should rewrite history, though I own that it often seems a little queer as it is, unreal, lop-sided; but why should they not add a supplement to history, calling it, of course, by some inconspicuous name so that women might figure there without

---

[12]Hélène Cixous, 'Tancrède continue' (1983), in *Entre l'écriture* (Paris: éditions des femmes, 1986), p. 165. Short extracts from the work of Cixous and others, including Luce Irigaray and Julia Kristeva, are translated in Elaine Marks and Isabelle de Courtivron, eds., *New French Feminisms* (Amherst: University of Massachussetts Press, 1980). *La Jeune née* (1975), a joint text written with Catherine Clément, has now been translated by Betsy Wing as *The Newly Born Woman* (Manchester: Manchester University Press, 1986).

[13]Makiko Minow-Pinkney analyses the implications and possibilities of this dilemma in a book which draws fully on the theoretical insights of French feminist theory. In *Virginia Woolf and the Problem of the Subject* (Brighton: Harvester Press, 1987), she reads Woolf's *oeuvre* as an anticipation of Julia Kristeva's theorization of the possible emergence of a new, 'post-individualist' subjectivity from the greater openness of the maternal/feminine 'semiotic,' prior to the imposition of the symbolic order.

impropriety? For one often catches a glimpse of them in the lives of the great, whisking away into the background, concealing, I sometimes think, a wink, a laugh, perhaps a tear. (*AROO*, 44–5)

At several points in the course of *A Room*, Woolf's narrator suggests lines for future research that her female student audience might like to pursue: an 'elaborate study of the psychology of women by a woman' (*AROO*, 75); a study of the reasons for men's opposition to women's emancipation (*AROO*, 54); research into the lives of ordinary women in different historical periods (*AROO*, 44); 'the value that men set upon women's chastity' (*AROO*, 61), for example. Like the extension of literature to accommodate women's writing about women, such projects will be more than mere addenda to the lines of volumes already existing in the British Museum and the university libraries: they will rewrite history in the sense indicated by the passage above, shifting the criteria for what is considered to count as relevant; revealing as 'lop-sided' what was taken as straight and true; and challenging the standard histories of wars and campaigns which formerly stood in splendid isolation.

Other kinds of event will occupy the foreground, and it is significant that the one Woolf's narrator singles out in her adumbration of a rewritten history has to do with women and writing: 'Thus, towards the end of the eighteenth century a change came about which, if I were rewriting history, I should describe more fully and think of greater importance than the Crusades or the Wars of the Roses. The middle-class woman began to write' (*AROO*, 62–3). Not only is fictional writing considered historically important, but 'rewriting' history now appears not so much as a rectification in the light of new evidence but as the telling of a different story, elicited by new questions asked of the evidence.

This suggests further a possible disturbance of conventional generic boundaries, a disturbance to which Woolf's own writing constantly aspires. In her essays she turns away from formal exposition to tell a story, and in her novels she attempts to shift the conventions that lay down the received distinctions of the factual and the poetical and the frequently correlated 'masculine' and 'feminine.' Woolf shied away from standard generic categories and experimented with new possibilities: *The Pargiters* was to be an 'Essay—Novel' (*D*, 4: 129), and *The Waves* 'a playpoem' (*D*, 3: 203). She even speculated on the possibility of abandoning such categories altogether: 'I have an idea that I will invent a new name for my books to supplant "novel." A new—by Virginia Woolf' (*D*, 3: 34).

The new writing of women is to have effects on both literature and history, equally subject hitherto to the dominance of the man's divisions. And the placing of both under one parasol may perhaps redress the balance of a monstrous division from which, Woolf stresses, it is women, not men, who have suffered: entirely ignored in the one, and blown up to excessive proportions in the other:

A very queer, composite being thus emerges. Imaginatively she is of the highest importance; practically she is completely insignificant. She pervades poetry from cover to cover; she is all but absent from history. . . .

It was certainly an odd monster that one made up by reading the historians first and the poets afterwards—a worm winged like an eagle; the spirit of beauty in a kitchen chopping up suet. But these monsters, however amusing to the imagination, have no existence in fact. What one must do to bring her to life was to think poetically and prosaically at one and the same moment. (*AROO*, 43)

The living woman is to be found in neither literature nor history; she might, however, be invented by some new combination of the two. That is not to say that she would be any more a creature of nature, since it is a new kind of writing which will bring her to 'life.'

Woolf's challenge to what she identifies as a masculine history (great wars, great nations, great men) anticipates the principles and practices of explicitly feminist history and the related development of the study of social history. If social history reveals the 'lop-sided' nature of what now appears as an old-fashioned, narrow focus on national history, feminist history in its turn has pointed out the specifically masculine tilt of such assumptions as to what is to constitute the hypothetical 'whole picture' of history. It makes a nice coincidence that the turn towards modern social history could be marked as having occurred 'in or about' the year of the publication of *A Room of One's Own*, with the founding of the French journal *Annales* in 1929.

New fields of research imply new premises, then, about what is to count as history. But Woolf's emphasis on the dichotomy between poetic and historical representations of women points also to a question of style. The first passage quoted above wryly suggests that the radical 'supplement' to history should slip in as if by the back door, using 'some inconspicuous name' to avoid an overt breach of decorum, and apparently maintaining the acceptable supporting roles of the women just glimpsed 'whisking away into the background' in the pages of 'the lives of the great.' The new history will make use of devices of indirection, simulating a perfect conformity to masculine prescriptions for proper feminine comportment while in the act of radically undermining them. The wink, the laugh and the tear of the women not quite hidden from history serve as models for strategies of feminist subversion—by mocking, upsetting and looking askance at the paternal proprieties and turning the practice of history-writing away from their appearance of sublime scholarly indifference and neutrality.

Margins and Mirrors

Wherever one looked men thought about women and thought differently. It was impossible to make head or tail of it all, I decided, glancing with envy at the reader next door who was making the neatest abstracts, headed often with an A or a B or a

C, while my own notebook rioted with the wildest scribble of contradictory jottings. (*AROO*, 30–1)

Women's exclusion from access to the means of being 'trained' (*AROO*, 28) as a qualified scholar can also be read in a different way: as an openness to kinds of thinking ruled out by pedantic discipline. The stubborn insistence on reducing everything automatically to alphabetical order obscures the 'contradictory' matter which might otherwise become the basis of a less formulaic and less artificially consistent sequence of points.

'Woman,' it seems, is the exemplary instance of what the trained masculine mind has to bring into line, to put in order. The 'woman' reader does not recognize herself in the assorted representations the books provide of this personage she abbreviates to 'W'.; and making a list, in an attempted imitation of her neighbour's methods, only brings her to a dead end: 'And if I could not grasp the truth about W. (as for brevity's sake I had come to call her) in the past, why bother about W. in the future?' (*AROO*, 31). It is here, with the failure of the alphabetical procedure ('W' = ?), that the 'contradictory jottings' come into their own, and a lack of lists becomes the punning advantage of absent-mindedness:

> But while I pondered I had unconsciously, in my listlessness, in my desperation, been drawing a picture where I should, like my neighbour, have been writing a conclusion. . . . It was the face and the figure of Professor von X engaged in writing his monumental work entitled *The Mental, Moral, and Physical Inferiority of the Female Sex*. He was not in my picture a man attractive to women. . . . His expression suggested that he was labouring under some emotion that made him jab his pen on the paper as if he were killing some noxious insect as he wrote, but even when he killed it that did not satisfy him; he must go on killing it; and even so, some cause for anger and irritation remained. (*AROO*, 31)

The picture reveals to this 'W'. both her own anger at the man's representation of 'W'. and 'X''s own anger at 'W.': 'unconsciously' departing from the given terms of scholarly reference, her 'listlessness' results in a further question and reveals the professor's supposedly rational inventory to have been made in 'the red light of emotion' (*AROO*, 33).

Doodling in the margins, against the main line of thought, proves to be a fruitful figure for the undirected speculations of Woolf's narrator. 'Drawing cart-wheels on the slips of paper provided by the British taxpayer for other purposes' (*AROO*, 28) already hints at a mildly subversive activity; then 'my mind wandered' (*AROO*, 28) in directions other than those of the man who knows where he is going:

> The student who has been trained in research at Oxbridge has no doubt some method of shepherding his question past all distractions till it runs into his answer as a sheep runs into its pen. (*AROO*, 28)

The 'trained' as opposed to the wandering, cartwheeling mind is here firmly snubbed, as reducing every question to fit its ready-made answer. And in the same gesture, the 'pen'—for Gilbert and Gubar the instrument and symbol *par excellence* of masculine literary authority—is punned into nothing more threatening than a tame retreat to which the sheep returns in blind obedience.[14] The trained mind's pretensions are cut down to sheer conformity, with 'all distractions' holding far more interesting possibilities. Where he proceeds and processes along rigidly defined lines, the female narrator has the liberty, as well as the difficulty, of being without a fixed enclosure for writing—a pen of her own. And this contains the same ambivalence as the 'money and a room of her own' (6) declared as prerequisites for women to write: at once the necessity and the over-protection of a 'stable' situation, the source of an 'insider's' dumb security. Beadle or woman? Sheep or Woolf? The relative positions and identities become ever more difficult to sustain.

The jottings of 'W'. cast doubt on the plausibility and coherence of Professor X's lists, and suggest unsuspected interpretations for 'some of those psychological puzzles that one notes in the margin of daily life' (*AROO*, 35). In particular, the revelation of the anger behind the professor's writing leads the narrator to a hypothesis about the structure of patriarchal thought:

> Women have served all these centuries as looking-glasses possessing the magic and delicious power of reflecting the figure of man at twice its natural size. Without that power probably the earth would still be swamp and jungle. . . . Mirrors are essential to all violent and heroic action. That is why Napoleon and Mussolini both insist so emphatically upon the inferiority of women, for if they were not inferior, they would cease to enlarge. (*AROO*, 35–6)

In a deft redrawing of conventional 'images' of the woman as narcissistic, Woolf here exposes a self-aggrandizing image of man as prior. Far from having any image of her own, or even functioning as an image for man to look at, women have only 'served' as the means of him seeing himself. But Woolf also suggests that such a looking-glass effect is perhaps essential: without it, 'the earth would still be swamp.' Implicitly, the solution would not be in a return to the 'natural' size, but in an alteration of the hierarchized sexual terms on which 'the looking-glass vision' presently rests. It is by means of the seemingly peripheral 'puzzles that one notes in the margin of daily life' that the ubiquitous mirroring function comes to be seen for what it is.

Luce Irigaray works with the same double identification of margins and mirrors in her analysis of texts from the tradition of western philosophy, beginning with Plato. In *Speculum: de l'autre femme*, she shows the complicity of intellectual and narcissistic ways of looking: men's discourse is forever seeking to represent, to 'speculate' upon 'woman,' in his own image. She also practises a technique of 'marginal' writing, inserting her commentary literally between the lines of men's philosophical texts, including Freud's 1933 lecture

---

[14]Sandra M. Gilbert and Susan Gubar, *The Madwoman in the Attic: The Woman Writer and the Nineteenth-Century Literary Imagination* (New Haven: Yale University Press, 1979).

on femininity.[15] Woolf suggests a similar strategy here. Just as *writing* includes a silent 'w,' so 'W.' is endlessly represented, and misrepresented, in 'phallogocentric' writing, and so the woman reader can begin to break down the apparent coherence of that writing by questioning it on its own terms, by writing her own marginal comments, revealing the limits of logic there all the time but never before shown up.

At every point, *A Room of One's Own* insists on the possibilities of the 'wandering' over the 'trained' mind running on preconceived lines. This occurs partly by thematic hints: the opposition or the rigid austerity of the grounds of the men's college at Oxbridge and the 'wild, unkempt grasses' (*AROO*, 20) of the women's. It is also effected through the structure of the lecture as a whole, which is cast in the form of a long digression—literally, a wandering off the main path—or indeed a 'pre-amble,' describing the narrator's mental and physical strollings before she began to write. It is as if the topic of 'Women and Fiction,' if it is not to consist in platitudes equivalent to those in the books of the British Museum, can only be approached indirectly, under the guise of merely leading up to it.

The strategy of marginal writing is not, however, to be taken as a licence for anarchy. The 'riot' of contradictory jottings is useful only if it turns out to switch back round to some further 'train of thought' (*AROO*, 6, 104), or if it works as an implicit criticism of the masculine line to which it is juxtaposed. Woolf's narrator is firm in her reproof of the enthusiastic excesses of the Duchess of Newcastle, one of the early women writers she discusses: 'What a vision of loneliness and riot the thought of Margaret Cavendish brings to mind! as if some giant cucumber had spread itself over all the roses and carnations in the garden and choked them to death.' (*AROO*, 59–60). Here, the 'riot' has gone too far, so out-naturing nature in its grotesque profusion as to be beyond any possible connection with, or criticism of, more cultivated lines of thought.

The Androgynous Mind

Of all the models or what constitutes the relation between 'women' and 'writing' in *A Room*, androgyny has provoked some of the wildest outbursts of indignation and celebration, and also some of the best-trained academic criticism. It thus seems worth quoting the principal offending or inspiring passage at some length.

> The sight of the two people getting into the taxi and the satisfaction it gave me made me also ask whether there are two sexes in the mind corresponding to the two sexes in the body, and whether they also require to be united in order to get

---

[15]*Speculum of the Other Woman* has been translated by Gillian C. Gill (Ithaca: Cornell University Press, 1985).

complete satisfaction and happiness? And I went on amateurishly to sketch a plan of the soul so that in each of us two powers preside, one male, one female; and in the man's brain the man predominates over the woman, and in the woman's brain the woman predominates over the man. . . . If one is a man, still the woman part of his brain must have effect; and a woman also must have intercourse with the man in her. Coleridge perhaps meant this when he said that a great mind is androgynous. It is when this fusion takes place that the mind is fully fertilized and uses all its faculties. Perhaps a mind that is purely masculine cannot create, any more than a mind that is purely feminine, I thought. (*AROO*, 94)

'Man,' 'woman,' 'masculine' and 'feminine' are all known quantities or qualities, with each pair forming a complementary whole. The man and woman get into the taxi together, the masculine and feminine (or male and female) parts of the mind (of the woman or the man) are fused together. There is no apparent hierarchical order between them: the only dominance is of the feminine part in the woman's brain, and vice versa for the man. We are thus not dealing with anything like the hypothesis according to which 'W.' is a contradictory figment of the patriarchal imagination. Nor are we dealing with the hypothesis which says that men and women are entirely different animals, each with the right and the capacity for their own form of maturation and autonomy (though what androgyny has in common with this model is an endorsement of harmony and unity as the ideal state of the mind and of writing). Nor is this a historical hypothesis, indicating differing conditions for the social production of masculinity and femininity in various kinds of body. The two terms in each pair are offered without qualification, and as invariables.

Advocates of androgyny have found in the theory a model for a harmonious personality, wholesomely balancing two eternal sides of the human psyche usually stuck apart in different bodies. Nancy Topping Bazin, for instance, begins her book on *Virginia Woolf and the Androgynous Vision* as follows:

> Virginia Woolf would have agreed with D. H. Lawrence that human beings have two ways of knowing, 'knowing in terms of apartness, which is mental, rational, scientific, and knowing in terms of togetherness, which is religious and poetic.' Virginia Woolf associated these two ways with the two sexes.[16]

The passage first of all raises the question of whether, given these definitions of masculinity and feminity, androgyny is not inconceivable. For the fusion of the 'two ways of knowing' would itself have to be considered as an example of feminine 'togetherness'. Masculinity as 'apartness', would necessarily lose its separate identity in being brought together with femininity as 'togetherness'.

---

[16]Nancy Topping Bazin, *Virginia Woolf and the Androgynous Vision* (New Brunswick: Rutgers University Press, 1973), p. 3. Other books which deal with the notion of androgyny in Woolf include Carolyn G. Heilbrun, *Towards Androgyny: Aspects of Male and Female in Literature* (1964; rpt. London: Victor Gollancz, 1973); Herbert Marder, *Feminism and Art: A Study of Virginia Woolf* (Chicago: University of Chicago Press, 1968); and Phyllis Rose, *Woman of Letters: A Life of Virginia Woolf* (London: Routledge & Kegan Paul, 1978).

There is also a circularity to the argument: having stated what features are associated with each sex, it is a simple matter for Bazin to designate as androgynous those characters in the novels who are biologically of one sex but manifest features of the other. In the Woolf passage, bodily sex does indeed seem to determine the predominance of one or other mental sex, even though the traits to be associated with 'manly' and 'womanly' are not specified. Mental qualities are therefore less flexible than they may look at first sight: to say that male minds can be 'feminine' only reinforces the dualism according to which the difference between the two sexes is known in advance.

Ironically, then, one of the implications of this model of androgyny might be a reinforcement rather than an undoing of the habitual separation of sexual characters. But it has also come in for criticism from another angle: as seeming to reject the specificity of female subjectivity, effacing a difference which should rather be emphasized and valorized. Woolf's narrator later states categorically that 'it is fatal for anyone who writes to think of their sex' (*AROO*, 99). That creative writers, of all people, should be singled out as those for whom their sex should not figure seems to constitute a denial of the necessity of asserting women's difference, whether psychological or in terms of their access to forms of literary expression. This is Elaine Showalter's principal objection to what she calls Woolf's 'flight into androgyny'; and Showalter also criticizes the erotic imagery of this passage which occurs further on:

> Some marriage of opposites has to be consummated. The whole of the mind must lie wide open if we are to get the sense that the writer is communicating his experience with perfect fullness. . . . Not a wheel must grate, not a light glimmer. The curtains must be close drawn. The writer, I thought, once his experience is over, must lie back and let his mind celebrate its nuptials in darkness. He must not look or question what is being done. (*AROO*, 99)

For Showalter, the slip at this point is to have made the writer not only explicitly male, but 'a male voyeur'.[17] But in fact the triangular structure here, as with the scene of the writer's spying on the couple getting into the taxi, can be taken to complicate the presentation of androgyny. The harmonious 'man-womanly' couple, in the street, in the room, in the writer's mind, is put at the distance of a satisfying scene for the narrator looking on. It is thus not simply represented as completeness, but set in the form of a *fantasy* of completeness and complementarity—between the sexes, within the mind, in the work of literature. The apparently simple duality of masculine and feminine is disrupted in this superimposition of the third element, the spectator.

The writer seems in fact to be placed in two different, equally ambiguous positions. In the first passage, s/he is a voyeur, actively looking and in control, seeing but unseen by the objects of his or her gaze. In the second passage,

---

[17]Showalter, *A Literature of Their Own: British Women Novelists from Brontë to Lessing* (London: Virago, 1977), p. 288.

s/he is passive ('lie back and let his mind . . .'), as not understanding something that is going on elsewhere. In view of the sexual charge of the scenes, this seems to resemble the situation of the ignorant child, secretly witnessing or imagining what is not yet understood ('he must not look or question'). The first passage, on the other hand, like a film with a happy ending, suggests the adult's need for reassurance that all is well and normal out there, that nothing need threaten the wish to believe in the naturalness of a comfortable complementarity of masculine and feminine.

Both these positions suggested in the presentation of androgyny can be seen to figure in the explorations of sexual relations in Virginia Woolf's work; they transfer the issues of androgyny away from the hypothesis of gendered personality traits onto a terrain which is more concerned with the implied sexual structure of looking, and its relation to the practice of writing—'as a woman', or indeed 'as a man'.

Showalter's pointing out that the 'darkened chamber' passage implies a male voyeur highlights a question about the significance of women writing that has been implicit in this discussion of Woolf's many approaches to the issue. Is the identification of writing as a male activity (the man's sentence, the male professional) to be taken as only a contingent, social restriction ('the sentence that was current at the beginning of the nineteenth century', for instance), or is there a more profound structure of enclosure and exclusion which makes of writing a practice which implies taking up a position identified as masculine?

When Woolf's narrator announces categorically that 'it is fatal for anyone who writes to think of their sex,' there is something excessive about the forcefulness, and the threat, of the assertion. It occurs in a passage towards the end of *A Room* which is heavily underlined as representing the approach to a definite conclusion:

> Even so, the very first sentence that I would write here, I said, crossing over to the writing-table and taking up the page headed Women and Fiction, is that it is fatal for anyone who writes to think of their sex. It is fatal to be a man or woman pure and simple; one must be woman-manly or man-womanly. It is fatal for a woman to lay the least stress on any grievance; to plead even with justice any cause; in any way to speak consciously as a woman. And fatal is no figure of speech; for anything written with that conscious bias is doomed to death. It ceases to be fertilized. (*AROO*, 99)

It seems here that the man-woman is protesting too much the dangers of protestation: there is a grievance in the denunciation of grievance and a programmatic insistence in the censuring of 'any cause' as being unsuited to writing. After a hundred pages of meandering exploration of the different ways of thinking about the relationship of women and fiction, suddenly some force of censorship rises up like the Beadle himself to intercept such freedom, to sentence to death, a priori ('the very first sentence'), all the possibilities that the preamble has opened up.

There is also a curious slippage between the first and second parts of the passage. Initially, it is 'fatal for anyone,' man or woman presumably, to think of his or her sex; then, it is 'fatal for a woman' to plead her case. This seems to prescribe asymmetrical rules for the two sexes, and to leave the adjudication of such matters entirely in male hands, in the time-honoured manner. This would leave Mrs Brown, for instance, back where she started and without the right of 'protesting that she was different, quite different from what they made out' (*CE*, I: 333). By claiming that men and women should act indifferently with respect to writing, Woolf's narrator rules out the possibility that language may already be differentiating between them, and offers no means whereby a woman could utter her difference as a woman. (And this may indeed be precisely the problem which it would be 'fatal' for the woman writer to acknowledge.) Ironically, then, the passage reinforces the existing differences in the very act of asserting their irrelevance.

The discrepancy noted here is paralleled in the first passage quoted on the androgynous writers: 'If one is a man, still the woman part of his brain must have effect; and a woman also must have intercourse with the man in her' (*AROO*, 94). For the man, there is only a 'woman part' of his brain, whereas the woman has 'the man' entire in her. This again would seem to suggest that the man-womanly combination in the ideal writer is not a union of two separate, equal and qualitatively different elements. Rather, the masculine dominates as whole to part, and we have returned to another version of the patriarchal structure.

Angel, Mother, Baby, Book

> Moreover, I thought, looking at the four famous names, what had George Eliot in common with Emily Brontë? Did not Charlotte Brontë fail entirely to understand Jane Austen? Save for the possibly relevant fact that not one of them had a child, four more incongruous characters could not have met together in a room . . . (*AROO*, 63–4)

Woolf's narrator hints at some relation between women's writing and childlessness. Considered socially, this might mean the incompatibility of the two activities, one consuming the time and emotional investment that would otherwise be used for the other. But there is also the possibility of a more complex symbolic connection. Traditionally, men's writing is represented as creation, on the analogy of childbearing; and in one version of this myth, the book is not just the equivalent but the substitute for the baby the man cannot literally produce. 'Natural' reproduction is thus taken as primary and enviable: the man seeks to make in another sphere what the woman is able spontaneously to produce in hers. In Woolf's case, the same analogy of writing and childbearing (or nurturing) figures, often enough, but with resonances that reveal a somewhat different symbolic structure.

In *A Room*, as we have seen, Woolf emphasizes that 'we think back through our mothers if we are women.' These are metaphorical mothers, or mothers of metaphorical invention. What happens to a different mother figure of the would-be woman writer is quite the opposite. In 'Professions for Women,' Woolf deals summarily with a character she identifies as 'the Angel in the House':

> You who come of a younger and happier generation may not have heard of her . . . She was intensely sympathetic. She was immensely charming. She was utterly unselfish. . . . She sacrificed herself daily. . . . And when I came to write I encountered her with the very first words. . . . Directly, that is to say, I took my pen in my hand to review that novel by a famous man, she slipped behind me and whispered: 'My dear, you are a young woman. You are writing about a book that has been written by a man. Be sympathetic; be tender; flatter; deceive; use all the arts and wiles of our sex. Never let anybody guess that you have a mind of your own. Above all, be pure.' And she made as if to guide my pen. I now record the one act for which I take some credit to myself . . . I turned upon her and caught her by the throat. I did my best to kill her. My excuse, if I were to be had up in a court of law, would be that I acted in self-defence. Had I not killed her she would have killed me. (*CE*, II: 285–6)

The 'Angel' is quite explicitly a fictional rather than a real person: the phrase comes from the title of Coventry Patmore's bestselling nineteenth-century poem, so what is being represented here is the woman writer's need to do away with the standard images of femininity current in men's literature:

> She died hard. Her fictitious nature was of great assistance to her. It is far harder to kill a phantom than reality. . . . But it was a real experience. It was an experience that was found to befall all women writers at that time. Killing the Angel in the House was part of the occupation of the woman writer. (*CE*, II: 286)

But the reference to the potency of a distorted, man-made figure of femininity is placed rather differently from the demand for a fairer treatment for Mrs Brown. Here, the literary representation of woman proves to be an inhibition to the prospective woman writer: changing the current appearance of the sex is not some routine task no sooner seen than done, but rather involves the removal of what is understood to be a ban. And here the agent of that censorship is not 'the figure of a man,' but the Angel herself, whose fictional, phantom-like status proves to be all the more insidious.

The 'real experience' of killing the fictitious angel archly makes manifest the difficulty of treating matters of sexual identification with the supposed objectivity and neutrality of the court of law where the woman writer hypothetically offers her defence. And this 'real experience' reveals another side to the notion that we 'think back through our mothers,' one which involves not the assumption but the putting away of a femininity taken to be not only incompatible with but actively censorious of a woman writing. Woolf's 'Angel' explicitly identifies writing as an unwomanly manner of behaving; her own sacrificial femininity is itself over-represented in Woolf's parody in order to render the murder all the more justifiable. . . .

The Darkest Plots:
Narration and Compulsory
Heterosexuality

Marianne Hirsch

The turning-away from her mother is an extremely important step in the course of a little girl's development.

—Sigmund Freud

Again if one is a woman one is often surprised by a sudden splitting off of consciousness, say in walking down Whitehall, when from being the natural inheritor of that civilization, she becomes, on the contrary, outside of it, alien and critical.

—Virginia Woolf

I am inclined to believe that there is no such thing as repetition.

—Gertrude Stein

Parables of Exclusion

In 1928, at the request of one of the women's colleges at Cambridge, Virginia Woolf gave the talks on women and fiction that later became A *Room of One's Own*, perhaps the most famous essay in feminist literary theory. Woolf's tone in this text is as modest as her argument is tentative: "All I could do was to offer you an opinion upon one minor point—a woman must have money and a room of her own if she is to write fiction. . . . I have shirked the duty of coming to a conclusion upon these two questions—women and fiction remain . . . unsolved problems."[1] At most, Woolf insists, she can show us how she arrives at her "opinion," thereby offering us not an essay but a narrative about her own involvement in the question of women's relation to fiction. The subject of that narrative, the speaking "I," moreover, is not Virginia Woolf, but "only a convenient term for somebody who has no real being" (p. 4).

[1]Virginia Woolf, A *Room of One's Own* (New York: Harcourt Brace Jovanovich, 1929), p. 4.

Beginning with a walk through Oxbridge University, her trajectory is full of interruptions and false turns, one of which provides a convenient starting point for my own analysis of gender, writing, and modernism. Near the beginning, totally focused on her thoughts, Woolf finds herself walking across a college lawn. "Instantly," she tells us, "a man's figure rose to intercept me. Nor did I at first understand that the gesticulations of a curious-looking object, in a cut-away coat and evening shirt, were aimed at me. His face expressed horror and indignation. Instinct rather than reason came to my help; he was a Beadle; I was a woman. This was the turf; there was the path. Only the fellows and Scholars are allowed here; the gravel is the place for me" (p. 6).[2] Woolf's narrator does not complain about her exclusion from the turf here—the only harm done, she remarks ironically, is that the Beadle's intervention caused her to forget her thought. When the exclusion is repeated, however, this time at the door of the library, the narrator reacts more directly—"Never will I ask for hospitality again, I vowed, as I descended the steps in anger" (p. 8). Resolved nevertheless to admire the famous buildings from the outside, the narrator resumes her meditation on her status as a woman writer and scholar, on what it means to tell the story of women's lives *as a woman*. Woolf's parable of interruption, exclusion, and writing—her marginal position in Oxbridge—illuminates the locus of femininity and women's discourse at the particular moment of her narration, the 1920s.

A Room of One's Own, like a number of women's *Künstlerromane* of the twenties, defines the liminal discourse of a female artist who stands both inside and outside of the library, both inside and outside of the structures of tradition, representation, and the symbolic. They do so by means of a particularly female and very private thematics—the mother-daughter relationship. . . .

The difficulties Woolf's narrator encounters in *A Room of One's Own* can serve as parables for understanding the peculiar strategies devised in women's writing of the period. Faced with totally contradictory representations of "woman" in the books of male "experts" and forced to come up with some answers of her own, she oscillates, in her exploration, between the shelves of the British Museum and the dining rooms of a women's college. The same oscillation marks her thinking.[3] On the one hand, Woolf's text insists on a female difference which is and must be inscribed into women's writing: the sentence available is unsuited for a woman's use, she tells us, and must be

[2]In *Alice Doesn't: Feminism, Semiotics, Cinema* (Bloomington: Indiana University Press, 1984), Teresa de Laurentis uses Woolf's distinction between *instinct* and *reason* to develop an extremely useful way of theorizing female *experience*. See esp. pp. 158–160, 182–186.

[3]*Oscillation* is a term also used by Rachel Blau DuPlessis in relation to Woolf and other modernist writers. See her *Writing beyond the Ending: Narrative Strategies of Twentieth-Century Women Writers* (Bloomington: Indiana University Press, 1985), excerpted in this volume, and "For the Etruscans: Sexual Difference and Artistic Production—The Debate Over a Female Aesthetic," in *The Future of Difference*, ed. Hester Eisenstein and Alice Jardine (Boston: G. K. Hall & Co., 1980).

transformed, adapted to the female body and to women's ways of working, which will always be subject to interruption and to inadequate concentration. On the other hand, she says that "it is fatal for anyone who writes to think of their sex" (p. 108). Criticizing Charlotte Brontë for letting a female anger contaminate her writing, she advocates the androgynous consummation of "some marriage of opposites": "It is fatal to be a man or a woman pure and simple; one must be woman-manly or man-womanly" (p. 108).

Critical assessments of these obvious contradictions in Woolf's text have varied. Jane Marcus, for example, asks: "How can she hold both views at once? . . . She is biased in favor of women."[4] Peggy Kamuf, on the other hand, sees Woolf's interruptions as providing her with a means to unravel the sexual opposition which has been the root of women's oppression and exclusion.[5] In contrast to both of these views, I see Woolf's text as offering her a way to address the contradictions of her gendered position within academic and literary convention. I would argue that Woolf's is a strategy of inconclusiveness—embracing rather than denying contradiction, lingering on process rather than rushing toward conclusion, zigzagging around Oxbridge and London rather than directly pursuing a destination—a strategy appropriate to someone who, having been represented as object, strains to define herself as subject. Woolf does so neither by insisting on a separate female culture nor by deconstructing gender dichotomies, but rather by walking both paths simultaneously, by affirming difference and undoing it at the same time.[6] The dialogic form of her essay/lecture, a dialogue not only with the "mothers" of past tradition and the "daughters" at Girton, but also with the fathers, brothers, and sons who, as Adrienne Rich suggests in her reading of the essay, are always eavesdropping, serves as a model of discourse available to the woman who is turned away from the steps of the library.[7] If Woolf's insights into women and writing are valuable, then, it is precisely because they subvert each other and lead, as one recent critic deploringly observes, to "a thicket of self-refutation."[8] This chapter argues that Woolf's oscillations in *A Room* ultimately do become her mark of gendered specificity, characteristic of the circuitous strategies of female modernism.

One of the protagonists of Woolf's narrative in *A Room* is Judith Shake-

---

[4]Jane Marcus, *Virginia Woolf and the Languages of Patriarchy* (Bloomington: Indiana University Press, 1987), p. 184.

[5]Peggy Kamuf, "Penelope at Work: Interruptions in *A Room of One's Own*," *Novel* 16, 1(Fall 1982): 5–18; see also Toril Moi, *Sexual/Textual Politics: Feminist Literary Theory* (London: Methuen, 1985) for a deconstructive reading of Woolf and a strong argument in favor of the exclusive validity of such readings.

[6]See Naomi Schor's "Reading Double: Sand's Difference," in *The Poetics of Gender*, ed. Nancy K. Miller (New York: Columbia University Press, 1986), for a suggestive exposition of this feminist strategy.

[7]Adrienne Rich, "When We Dead Awaken: Writing as Re-Vision," in *On Lies, Secrets and Silence* (New York: Norton, 1979), p. 37.

[8]John Burt, "Irreconcilable Habits of Thought in *A Room of One's Own* and *To the Lighthouse*," *English Literary History* 49(1982): 893.

speare, the imaginary sister of William, and Woolf's emblem for the woman artist. Judith's story reveals a sexual division of labor which has disastrous results for women's artistic aspirations. Shakespeare's sister does not write, of course; her talents remain undeveloped, her hopes unfulfilled. Typically for a woman who is also an artist, she flees an arranged marriage, but ends up committing suicide as a result of an unwanted pregnancy by the man who had offered to aid her in her career. Woolf never suggests that William could have offered Judith access to his masculine creative world; she is less than sanguine about the fraternal fantasies that marked female family romances in the Victorian period. As Sara Ruddick suggests: "No matter how good a brother Shakespeare might have been, he could not have offered his world to his sister. . . . there would have been no place in his world for a person with a woman's body who wished to practise a man's art" (p. 191).[9] And yet *A Room,* locating itself at a different moment from that in which Judith Shakespeare was thwarted, does propose the solution of androgyny in fraternal terms.

After engaging in painful thoughts about the separate realm of femininity, and after puzzling through Mary Carmichael's revolutionary female sentence and broken sequence, Woolf's narrator finds refuge in the idea of androgyny.[10] When she arrives at her emblematic vision of the young girl and young man getting into the taxicab, she finds the "natural" quality of the image of heterosexuality to be a great relief: "perhaps to think, as I had been thinking these two days, of one sex as distinct from the other is an effort. It interferes with the unity of the mind. . . . some of these states of mind seem, even if adopted spontaneously, to be less comfortable than others. In order to keep oneself continuing in them one is unconsciously holding something back, and gradually the repression becomes an effort" (pp. 100–101). The idea of androgyny, of the "natural" cooperation of the sexes, emerges for Woolf as one state of mind that requires no effort. And the mind that emerges as most fully androgynous and, at the same time, most clearly exemplary of the dangers of androgyny is the mind of Shakespeare himself. But there is a cost: his very androgyny may be what prevents him from thinking of women, his sister for example. His lack of thoughtfulness, Woolf's narrator maintains, takes on disastrous proportions in the modern era. If Shakespeare's sister is to be born in the twentieth century, she tentatively concludes, it will be not as a result of

---

[9]On brothers and sisters in Woolf see Sara Ruddick, "Private Brother, Public World," in *New Feminist Essays on Virginia Woolf,* ed. Jane Marcus (Lincoln: University of Nebraska Press, 1981). In *The Years* and *The Pargiters,* Woolf does a more devastating critique of the gender arrangements which train brothers for war and sisters for domestic life.

[10]For readings of androgyny in Woolf, see Carolyn Heilbrun, *Toward a Recognition of Androgyny* (New York: Norton, 1964) and Nancy Topping Bazin, *Virginia Woolf and the Androgynous Vision* (New Brunswick: Rutgers University Press, 1973). I disagree here with Elaine Showalter, *A Literature of Their Own: British Women Novelists from Brontë to Lessing* (Princeton: Princeton University Press, 1977), who describes Woolf's stance as a "flight" into androgyny. Rather than a flight, I prefer to see it as a momentary solution, not granted any ultimate validity. See also Jane Marcus's discussion of this moment in *A Room,* in her *Virginia Woolf and the Languages of Patriarchy,* pp. 159–162.

her brother's help, but instead with that of her sisters and mothers: "she would come if we worked for her" (p. 117). Here Woolf reinforces the female line of literary inheritance she refers to as "thinking back through our mothers": "for masterpieces are not single and solitary births; they are the outcome of many years of thinking in common, of thinking by the body of the people, so that the experience of the mass is behind the single voice" (p. 69).

Just like androgyny, however, female assistance has its own grave limitations. When Woolf's narrator compares the modest dinner in the women's college with the elegant and filling meal at Oxbridge, we notice the beginnings of her resentment against the mothers whose nurturing of their daughters leaves much to be desired:[11] "What had our mothers been doing then that they had no wealth to leave us?" (p. 21). Beyond failing to provide the financial inheritance that would foster female education and creativity, however, mothers have actively impeded the daughters' freedom to write. Woolf explains this most clearly with the figure of the angel in the house in her 1931 essay "Professions for Women."[12] The maternal angel is the figure who encourages the woman writer to "be sympathetic; be tender; flatter; deceive; use all the arts and wiles of your sex. Never let anybody guess that you have a mind of your own. Above all, be pure" (p. 59), and who must be killed if women are to continue to create. "Killing the Angel in the House was part of the occupation of the woman writer" (p. 60), Woolf insists, in a tone that does not succeed in concealing her rage.

Both solutions—androgyny and male identification, on the one hand, and the act of "thinking back through our mothers," on the other—are fraught with contradiction and ambivalence. I would argue that the process of oscillating between them, however, is attractive not only because it is the only course to take but because it suggests the possibility of a different construction of femininity and of narrative. In speaking about the split consciousness Woolf's narrator discovers in herself in the passage that serves as an epigram to this chapter, Mary Jacobus says: "To recognize both the split and the means by which it is constituted, to challenge its terms while necessarily working within them—that is the hidden narrative of the trespass on the grass."[13] . . .

For Virginia Woolf, . . . writing involved a dual origin and a dual destination, both paternal and maternal. . . . Woolf's father . . . left [her] the text of patriarchal tradition itself.[14] It was he who initiated her into reading and writing, he who gave her books to read, and he who inspired her description of herself as "an educated man's daughter." Woolf first saw *To the Lighthouse* as a book about her father; only later does she clearly identify it with the

---

[11]See Elizabeth Abel's brilliant analysis of hunger and food in *A Room*, in her *Virginia Woolf and the Fictions of Psychoanalysis* (Chicago: University of Chicago Press, 1989).

[12]Reprinted in Michèle Barrett, ed., *Women and Writing* (New York: Harcourt Brace Jovanovich, 1979).

[13]Mary Jacobus, *Reading Woman: Essays in Feminist Criticism* (New York: Columbia University Press, 1986), p. 39.

[14]Jane Marcus, *Virginia Woolf and the Languages of Patriarchy*, p. 8.

memory of her mother. In a 1925 diary entry Woolf writes: "This is going to be fairly short, to have father's character done complete in it; and mother's; St. Ives; and childhood; and all the usual things I try to put in—life, death, etc. But in the centre is father's character, sitting in a boat, reciting, we perished, each alone, while he crushes a dying mackerel."[15] But when she writes about *To the Lighthouse* in retrospect, in "A Sketch of the Past," it is the figure of her mother which stands at the center of the entire project: "Until I was in the forties . . . the presence of my mother obsessed me. I could hear her voice, see her, imagine what she would do or say as I went about my day's doings."[16] It is *To the Lighthouse* that frees Woolf from this obsession: "I wrote the book very quickly; and when it was written, I ceased to be obsessed by my mother. I no longer hear her voice; I do not see her. I suppose that I did for myself what psycho-analysts do for their patients. I expressed some very long and deeply felt emotion. And in expressing it I explained it and then laid it to rest" (*Moments of Being*, p. 81). In the complicated genesis of this novel, then, the story of the mother displaces a projected story featuring the father. Later in "A Sketch of the Past," Woolf reevaluates yet again her father's role in relation to her mother and finds it to be more central than she had been willing to admit earlier: "Just as I rubbed out a great deal of the force of my mother's memory by writing about her in *To the Lighthouse*, so I rubbed out much of his memory there too. Yet he too obsessed me for years. Until I wrote it out, I would find my lips moving; I would be arguing with him; raging against him; saying to myself all that I had never said to him. How deep they drove themselves into me, the things it was impossible to say aloud. . . . But in me . . . rage alternated with love. It was only the other day when I read Freud for the first time, that I discovered that this violently disturbing conflict between love and hate is a common feeling; and is called ambivalence" (*Moments of Being*, p. 108). Woolf's novel acts out this alternation and ambivalence, this dual allegiance to mother and father, in its very structure and form. It thereby creates a distinctively modernist version of the female family romance. Although father, mother, brothers, and sisters all play archetypal roles, this family romance is capacious enough to include the mother in a position of centrality, to focus on her presence as well as her absence. . . . It offers feminist critics a central text through which to explore the representation of mother-daughter relationships.[17]

[15]*The Diary of Virginia Woolf*, vol. 3, ed. Anne Olivier Bell (New York: Harcourt Brace Jovanovich, 1980), May 14, 1925.

[16]Virginia Woolf, *Moments of Being*, 2d edition, ed. Jeanne Schulkind (New York: Harcourt Brace Jovanovich, 1985), p. 80.

[17]To write about *To the Lighthouse* as a mother-daughter text is to situate oneself within a ten-year tradition of feminist readings which have featured this novel as the central mother-daughter text in women's writing and have featured the mother-daughter thematics as central to any understanding of the text. Among these readings, see esp. Sara Ruddick, "Learning to Live with the Angel in the House," *Women's Studies* 4(1977): 181–200; Jane Lilienfield, "The Deceptiveness of Beauty: Mother Love and Mother Hate in *To the Lighthouse*," *Twentieth-Century Literature* 23(1977): 345–376; Elizabeth Abel's chapters on *To the Lighthouse* in *Virginia Woolf and the*

To the Lighthouse is propelled by a desire for understanding, by a series of question which fit Peter Brooks's schema of the novel as explanatory narrative.[18] The novel begins with Mrs. Ramsay's answer to James's implied question about the trip to the lighthouse: "Yes, of course, if it's fine. . . ."[19] Other questions, posed by different characters at different moments structure the novel's progression: "What was there behind . . . [Mrs. Ramsay's] beauty and splendor?" (p. 46); "But after Q? What comes next?" (p. 53); "What did it all mean?" (p. 159); "Would they go to the Lighthouse tomorrow?" (p. 173); "What does it mean then, what can it all mean?" (p. 217); "What's the use of going now?" (p. 218); "D'you remember?" (p. 254); "What does it mean, how do you explain it all?" (p. 266). The primary enigma in the novel is the figure of the mother—the beautiful and mysterious Mrs. Ramsay. Repeated, rephrased, reformulated throughout the text, the questions about Mrs. Ramsay, her life, and the lives of those who surround her are not answered but are confronted with a series of oppositions. Male and female, father and mother, life and death, light and darkness, affirmation and destruction, enclosure and separation, lighthouse and window—all appear to find in the text a third term of resolution. At the end of the novel, a form of closure and discovery seems to redeem the pervasive destruction of the novel's second part, "Time Passes." Critics often focus their analyses on Woolf's strategies for resolving opposites, for finding that "razor-edge of balance between two opposite forces," for creating in Lily the figure of the artist who is "woman-manly and man-womanly" (*A Room of One's Own*, 108). They discuss the novel in terms of "equilibrium" (Corsa), "balance of forms" (Proudfit), the triumph of art over the "powers of darkness, dissolution and chaos" (Love); the process of maturation which depends on the integration of a male principle which will resist the engulfment that the maternal will commands (di Battista).[20]

Fictions of Psychoanalysis; Ellen Bayuk Rosenman, *The Invisible Presence: Virginia Woolf and the Mother-Daughter Relationship* (Baton Rouge: Louisiana State University Press, 1986); Joan Lidoff, "Virginia Woolf's Feminine Sentence: The Mother-Daughter World of *To the Lighthouse*," *Literature and Psychology* 32, 3(1986): 43–59; Claire Kahane, "The Nuptials of Metaphor: Self and Other in Virginia Woolf," *Literature and Psychology* 30, 2(1980): 72–82; Susan Squier, "Mirroring and Mothering: Reflections on the Mirror Encounter Metaphor in Virginia Woolf's Works," *Twentieth-Century Literature* 27, 3(Fall 1981): 272–288; Gayatri Spivak, "Making and Unmaking in *To the Lighthouse*," in *Women and Language in Literature and Society*, ed. Sally McConnell-Ginet, Ruth Borker, and Nelly Furman (New York: Praeger, 1980), pp. 310–327; Carolyn Williams, "Virginia Woolf's Rhetoric of Enclosure," *Denver Quarterly* 18, 4(Winter 1984): 43–61; Carolyn Heilbrun, "Virginia Woolf's *To the Lighthouse*," paper delivered at the 1986 MLA [Modern Language Association] Convention.

[18]Peter Brooks, *Reading for the Plot: Design and Intention in Narrative* (New York: Knopf, 1984).

[19]Virginia Woolf, *To the Lighthouse* (New York: Harcourt Brace Jovanovich, 1927), p. 9. Subsequent quotations will be cited by page number in the text.

[20]Helen Storm Corsa, "*To the Lighthouse*: Death, Mourning and Transfiguration," *Literature and Psychology* 21, 3(1971): 115–132; Sharon Wood Proudfit, "Lily Briscoe's Painting: A Key to Personal Relationships in *To the Lighthouse*," *Criticism* 13, 1(1971): 26–38; Jean O. Love, *Virginia Woolf: Sources of Madness and Art* (Berkeley: University of California Press, 1977); Maria di Battista, *Virginia Woolf's Major Novels: The Fables of Anon* (New Haven: Yale University Press, 1980).

Loss and longing mark the novel's very substance. We cannot deny that the trip happens too late, that nothing can compensate for the loss of Mrs. Ramsay, that the annihilation wrought by the war is impossible to redeem. Yet the economy of loss and recovery still operates in much of the novel, as the reader is repeatedly seduced by moments of harmonious resolution, moments which are implicit in the text's oppositional structure. Brooks emphasizes the necessity for delays and false turns on the road to healing and culmination, and it is precisely such a pattern that the novel at first seems to enact.

However seductive this sort of reading might be, it is my contention that the economy of loss and recovery and the aesthetic conceptions that accompany it are actually revised in the course of *To the Lighthouse.* I do not mean that the apparent resolution is simply ironic, but that it is left behind in favor of a different economy. My argument centers on the figure of Lily and on the relation between her work on her painting and her connection with Mrs. Ramsay.[21] In my reading, Lily's strategy is not the adoption of an androgynous artistic identity, but of a dual, perhaps duplicitous posture which, instead of resolving the differences between opposite forces, embraces contradiction as the only stance which allows the woman artist to produce.[22]

In the first section of the novel, Lily is unable to finish her painting or even to work on it productively. She is hindered both by Mrs. Ramsay's injunction that she should marry and by Charles Tansley's repeated judgement that "Women can't paint, women can't write . . . " (p. 75). In this period, painting is a very personal act for Lily: she describes it as a birth process in which the "passage from conception to work [is] as dreadful as any down a dark passage for a child" (p. 32). In this analogy, painting is both a way out of what she experienced as the wish for childhood fusion—during the dinner she can protect herself from the lure of the "we" by thinking about the picture and moving the salt-cellar on the tablecloth—and a way back into it, but differently, a way to know Mrs. Ramsay, to "spell out" the secret she locks up inside her, like "treasures in the tombs of kings, bearing sacred inscriptions." Sitting in the bedroom with Mrs. Ramsay, putting her head on Mrs. Ramsay's knee, Lily wonders how she can get closer, how she can know more about Mrs. Ramsay: "What art was there, known to love or cunning, by which one pressed into those secret chambers? What device for becoming, like waters poured into one jar, inextricably the same, one with the object one adored? . . . Could loving, as people called it, make her and Mrs. Ramsay one? [F]or it was not knowledge but unity that she desired, not inscriptions on tablets, nothing that could be written in any language known to men, but

<hr>

21Jane Lilienfeld aptly points out that Lily is the figure of the Victorian orphan reframed as surrogate daughter, passionately attached to the mother.

22In his study of Lily's painting in relation to contemporary artistic conventions, Thomas Matro also argues against the achievement of balance in the novel; see his "Only Relations: Vision and Achievement in *To the Lighthouse*," *PMLA* 99, 2(March 1984): 212–224.

intimacy itself, which is knowledge . . . " (p. 79).[23] Critics have read this passage as an indication of Lily's immature and self-annihilating desire for fusion with the mother, a desire she must outgrow, resolve, and reframe so as to separate from Mrs. Ramsay and finish the painting. Freudian telos would, indeed, emphasize the necessity for separation as a measure of maturity and would present Mrs. Ramsay's death as the essential rupture which occasions the mourning that allows Lily to grow.

The novel itself supports such a sense of progression. The moments between Lily and Mrs. Ramsay move gradually outward from the bedroom to the dining room and finally to the beach, which occasions a return to the steps and Lily's vision. Yet this spatial progression is not clearly mirrored in Lily's thoughts and feelings. In fact, she describes the process of painting not as an externalization but as a progressive movement inward, back into the past, back beyond the "illuminated zone" into the earliest feelings of longing and desire: "She went on tunneling her way into her picture, into the past" (p. 258); "She was not inventing; she was only trying to smooth out something she had been given years ago folded up; something she had seen" (p. 295). Lily's movement into (or out of) the picture, Lily's process of painting it, is a complicated one and cannot be encompassed by either a linear or a dialectical image. In fact, it does not conform to the conceptions and images of art and the artistic process on which the other characters agree. This may well be the source of Lily's problem, that in telling or painting the story of Mrs. Ramsay, the scene of mother and child, she must redefine the forms and the expectations of art: "for it was not knowledge but unity that she desired, not inscriptions on tablets, *nothing that could be written in any language known to men, but intimacy itself, which is knowledge . . .*" (my italics). If we read "men" not for its generic but for its specific meaning, we see that Lily searches for a different language, one that will not oppose knowledge and intimacy, but will allow for what we might call their tautological interrelation. In so doing, she refines the notion of modernist art, struggling painfully and against her own sense of culture and tradition, to introduce a mark of female difference.

Art, the characters agree, must last, a requirement which is distinguished from momentary enjoyment. Art must create order and understanding through its form. Like the sonnet it must be "beautiful and reasonable, clear and complete, the essence sucked out of life and held rounded here" (p. 181); "If only she could put them together, she felt, write them out in some sentence, then she would have got at the truth of things" (p. 219). More than anything, perhaps, art creates unity and harmony where before there was chaos, fragmentation, hostility and destruction. This could be the key to the

---

[23]In *Moments of Being*, Woolf describes her parents' bedroom: "the bedroom—the double bedded bedroom on the first floor was the sexual centre; the birth centre, the death centre of the house" (p. 118).

success of Mr. Carmichael's poetry during the war. It is also the key to Mrs. Ramsay's very particular artistic creation: "That woman . . . made out of that miserable silliness and spite . . . something . . . which survived . . . like a work of art. . . . In the midst of chaos there was shape; this eternal passing and flowing . . . was struck into stability" (pp. 239–41). As Lily sees and remembers it, Mrs. Ramsay creates harmony, Mrs. Ramsay brings people together and forms a communion which will survive her. This is what art must do, Lily thinks, recognizing Mrs. Ramsay as an artist, even though her media are food and community.[24]

When Lily works on her own painting, then, she too aspires to the criteria of permanence, harmony, and aesthetic balance as the measure of success. "It was a question . . . how to connect this mass on the right hand with that on the left" (pp. 82–83); "the question was of some relation between those masses" (p. 221). She feels that her painting must achieve a particularly difficult kind of artistic equilibrium: "the light of a butterfly's wing lying upon the arches of a cathedral" (p. 75). Where are her models for such a task? Lily does not work within a tradition; she does not benefit from the discussion about art and philosophy shared by Mr. Ramsay and Charles Tansley. Her talks with Mr. Bankes demonstrate how little encouragement she actually receives: he shakes his head with incomprehension at her irreverent interpretation of the mother and child theme. And Mr. Carmichael offers no more than a silent presence. Surrounded by a community of scholars and artists, Lily acutely experiences her distance from their exchanges.

. . . Mrs. Ramsay's stance as artist is, for women, a dangerous one to live up to because her aesthetic perfection is bought at the expense of her life. Her success at establishing harmony, permanence, and order, at resolving opposite forces, causes in Mrs. Ramsay a strain she cannot survive, precisely because her medium is interpersonal and not aesthetic. Her art of matchmaking, knitting, storytelling, cooking, and community building is a form of plotting not unlike Emma's; her plots are as ingenious and her solutions as creative. Yet while Woolf's novel validates the activity more than Austen's, it also clearly measures its costs. During the dinner and at the beach, the guests only come together because Mrs. Ramsay wills them to, because she can hide from them, and from herself, the irredeemable areas of contradiction and disconnection. She can do so, however, only by absorbing that discord, just as she absorbs the disagreements between herself and her husband.[25] Only later do we find out how provisional and fragile, how momentary and how costly the community and the marriage she creates really are. Mrs. Ramsay literally spends herself in order to sustain husband, children, and guests: "There was

---

[24]See Lilienfeld's analysis of food and ritual in the novel in "Deceptiveness."

[25]On the novel's critique of the Victorian ideology of marriage, see Joseph A. Boone, *Tradition Counter Tradition: Love and the Form of Fiction* (Chicago: University of Chicago Press, 1987), pp. 201–214.

scarcely a shell of herself left for her to know herself by; all was so lavished and spent" (p. 60). "She often felt she was nothing but a sponge sopped full of human emotions" (p. 51). Even in the moments when she is alone and sees herself as a "wedge-shaped core of darkness" relating only to the beam of the lighthouse, we realize that the archetypal mother, presiding over the archetypal family, can claim for herself only silence, emptiness, and darkness, not presence and plenitude.[26] Mrs. Ramsay exists to reflect Mr. Ramsay's sterility, her son's anger, her daughters' desire, the existence of inanimate things. Her only moment of triumph is her ability *not* to speak—*not* to say to Mr. Ramsay that she loves him.

In substituting Lily's art for Mrs. Ramsay's, Woolf is not only substituting a woman's independent unmarried life for Mrs. Ramsay's compulsive and fatal life of "giving, giving, giving," but she is also calling into question the traditional standards of female artistic achievement represented by Mrs. Ramsay, those that are dependent on sacrifice and subordination, on a cruel "consent . . . to femininity."[27] Woolf speaks of this lack of full cooperation in *A Room of One's Own*, remarking on the anger of the gentlemen who are used to seeing themselves reflected in the female looking-glass at twice their natural size. Lily's refusal of marriage is her refusal of this role and a refusal, as well, of the economic and emotional dependence fostered by the institution of marriage. Yet her rejection of the course Mrs. Ramsay has taken cannot be total; against her will, Lily finds herself being nice to Charles and comforting Mr. Ramsay.

I see Lily's solution to what art should be and her completion of the painting as being made possible by yet another partial, modulated refusal. Presenting only a very provisional form of closure, one that can be read from within the pattern of Sido and Colette or of Demeter and Persephone, the painting itself ultimately refuses a notion of artistic permanence. In fact, in a clear reversal of the myth, Lily envisions the dead Mrs. Ramsay and Prue, the married women, walking through fields of flowers, just as Persephone does *before* her rape and marriage. For Lily, this repeated and dream-like vision gives rise to another vision—the apparition of an approving Mrs. Ramsay on the steps. The timeless vision of Mrs. Ramsay and Prue is a vision of death. Both married, mother and daughter are both dead. The married mother cannot offer a refuge from the underworld of marriage and the triangular structure of the nuclear family, represented in the vision by the third mysterious figure that accompanies them. Death, the novel implies, might result if Lily's desire for unity and intimacy could be fulfilled or, conversely, if she were willing to participate in Mr. Ramsay's and Mr. Tansley's male

[26]In "Making and Unmaking," Gayatri Spivak argues that Mrs. Ramsay is in the position of predicate rather than subject; she sees Lily's creation as a form of uterine plenitude developing a thematics of womb-envy in the novel, but one in which Mrs. Ramsay cannot participate.

[27]Teresa de Laurentis, *Alice Doesn't: Feminism, Semiotics, Cinema* (Bloomington: Indiana University Press, 1984), p. 10.

plot. Although there is no third option for Lily, she chooses neither of the two debilitating ones, or both.

The contradiction between the two options is not resolved in the novel, but its two sides are maintained in a state of perpetual tension. Thus the parallel plot of Part III, the male oedipal story of the trip to the lighthouse, offsets the threat of female dissolution, just as the female plot of mother-daughter reunification offsets the threat of marriage and appropriation. Gayatri Spivak has argued that Lily uses the men in the novel as instruments, to further her work—Charles Tansley's nasty comments are actually productive, and Mr. Ramsay's trip enables her to see Mrs. Ramsay [see note 17]. Charles Tansley is in fact the "brother" who, in *this* text, has become a useful antagonist: in the scene on the beach, for example, Lily and Charles act like a brother and a sister whose relationship is mediated and controlled by a tolerant and maternal Mrs. Ramsay. Again, as we have seen in *A Room* . . . , male presence provides a mediating space which clarifies the liminal position of women's discourse and of female relationships in the realm of the father, thereby making possible the representation of mother-daughter love.

Significantly, the novel does not end triumphantly with the vision of Mrs. Ramsay come back to life. After the vision on the steps, Lily and the narrator turn to Mr. Ramsay's landing at the lighthouse and to Mr. Carmichael. Only then does Lily go back to the painting, only then can she think about how to complete it: "There it was—her picture. . . . It would be hung in the attics, she thought; it would be destroyed. But what did that matter? she asked herself, taking up her brush again. She looked at the steps; they were empty; she looked at her canvas; it was blurred. With a sudden intensity, as if she saw it clear for a second, she drew a line there, in the centre. It was done; it was finished. Yes, she thought, laying down her brush in extreme fatigue, I have had my vision" (pp. 309–310).

What does the painting, what does this line look like and what does it mean? Critics have assumed that the line is the textual equivalent of the lighthouse which connects the two disparate parts of the painting, but that assumption needs to be reexamined. Is the line horizontal, we might ask, connecting the masses on the right and left? Is it vertical, suggesting not unity but separation? Or does it radiate in different directions like the rays of the lighthouse? I would argue that the novel chooses not to interpret this crucial moment, but rather supports contradictory readings of it. This very undecidability makes it a rejection, or at least a revision of the aesthetic requirements to which modernist art still adheres and to which Lily has been trying to live up throughout the novel. Here is an acknowledgment that the masses on the right and left can neither be connected nor remain disconnected, but must be both. This reading is only possible, of course, because we have a verbal description of a visual image—it would not be possible were the image represented for us. This explains Woolf's choice of a visual rather than a verbal artist for the protagonist of this novel. The line is drawn in the space

where Lily can be productive—between mother and father, between feminine and masculine; not meant as a connection, it marks the perpetual
boundary of Lily's difference.[28] In this sense, Lily's solution—the line at the
center—could be read as the equivalent of Mrs. Ramsay's shawl, instead of as
a repetition of the lighthouse. When Cam is afraid of the skull on the wall and
unable to go to sleep, whereas James refuses to go to sleep if the skull is
removed, Mrs. Ramsay decides, brilliantly I think, to cover the skull with her
shawl so that it can be present for James and absent for Cam. Similarly, the
line can mean presence and absence, connection and disconnection for Lily,
and the bodily gesture of painting it can both connect and separate her from
the model of Mrs. Ramsay. Unlike Cam, who continues to deal with the
father's demand for sympathy, hating him, admiring him, relying on him to
save her from drowning, and who continues to subordinate her own feelings to
those of her brother James, Lily succeeds in breaking her own silence in the
novel. The possibility of expression comes with her decisive drawing of the
line, her acceptance of contradiction and of the boundary.

Woolf's modernist style, with its violent interruptions and alternations
demonstrates the implications of such an aesthetic choice. The culmination of
Part I—the dinner party, the silent expression of love between the Ramsays—
is followed by the violent and devastating intervention of Part II—the destruction of the war, the dissolution of the house, the breaking of the mirror,
the devastating effects of maternal death. This "Time Passes" section is itself
full of shocking stylistic breaks and cuts, not the least of which is the
parenthetical mention of the deaths of Mrs. Ramsay herself, of Prue in
childbirth, and of Andrew in the war. This experiment with an impersonal
representation of loss and mourning itself illustrates the aesthetic of "both/
and": there is no writing without loss, and writing cannot quite constitute
recovery. Loss is the pretext for a fictional attempt at recovery. Similarly,
Lily's longing cry for "Mrs. Ramsay, Mrs. Ramsay," which eventually results in
the vision, is immediately followed not by that vision but by the brief and
bracketed chapter about fishing: "(Macalister's boy took one of the fish and cut
a square out of its side to bait his hook with. The mutilated body (it was alive
still) was thrown back into the sea.)" (p. 268). The reader, like Lily, must learn
to adjust to such shocking cuts, to recognize and maintain contradictions
rather than trying to subsume them into a false synthesis. At the end of Part
III, Mr. Ramsay compliments James, they land at the lighthouse, Lily completes her painting. Yet the double plot does not merge and oppositions
remain. Mrs. Ramsay remains potentially present (she did appear on the steps

28This is what Spivak calls the copula, identified in her argument with the "Time Passes"
section, which, like the line, occupies the space in the center. She reads "Time Passes" as the
discourse of madness, war, and undecidability. See also Matro's focus in "Only Relations" on effort
rather than achievement and his emphasis on the "to" in the novel's title. [For a parallel analysis
of Lily's painting and its role in her relationship to Mrs. Ramsay, see Abel, *Virginia Woolf and the
Fictions of Psychoanalysis*, Chapter 4, "Spatial Relations: Lily Briscoe's Painting," pp. 68–83. Abel
also speculates about the shape of the line.]

for a moment), but now the steps are empty. Cam, as Elizabeth Abel has pointed out, remains the silent victim of paternal filiation who can only "gesture toward a story she cannot tell."[29] Lily herself has learned to relinquish her demand for unity and permanence. Her "It would be hung in the attics, she thought; it would be destroyed," echoes Woolf's own predictions of the reception of *A Room of One's Own*: "I am afraid it will not be taken seriously. . . . I doubt that I mind very much. . . . It is a trifle, I shall say; so it is; but I wrote it with ardour and conviction."[30] Similarly Lily feels, "I have had my vision." The process of writing, the ardour put into it, and not the product or the response are the bases of Lily's and of Woolf's own aesthetic.

As she strolls through Oxbridge, Woolf muses about Milton's *Lycidas,* an elegy like *To the Lighthouse*, rethinking it as a work which is not venerable and whole like a religious object but the result of a process of creation and alteration. Such is Lily's painting: it need not last like Mr. Carmichael's poetry; she is content to see it "clear for a second," content to accept that "the vision must be perpetually remade" (p. 270). She is content to have had her vision, because it is the concrete and *bodily* process of having it that is important, and not the vision itself. In this conception of her art, Lily is not far removed from Mrs. Ramsay whose creative act is the "boeuf en daube," quickly consumed yet remembered by those who were present. In her new borderline language unknown to men, but in which men are also involved, intimacy redefines knowledge and constitutes art: not possession, it becomes a form of momentary contact, continually in need of being remade.[31]

[29]Abel's reading of Cam's silence diverges radically from Homans's. For Homans, Cam is not the silent sister and paternal daughter, but the representative of a different, non-figurative, mother-daughter language of presence. See the last chapter in Margaret Homans, *Bearing the Word: Language and Female Experience in Nineteenth-Century Women's Writing* (Chicago: University of Chicago Press, 1986).

[30]1929 *Diary*, cited in *Women and Writing*, ed. Michèle Barrett, p. 3.

[31]Spivak defines the novel as "an attempt to articulate, by using man as an instrument, a woman's vision of a woman" ("Making and Unmaking," p. 326).

The Authority of Illusion:
Feminism and Fascism
in Virginia Woolf's *Between the Acts*

Patricia Klindienst Joplin

"We are not passive spectators doomed to unresisting obedience," Woolf wrote at the close of *Three Guineas*, "but by our thoughts and actions" we can change the figure who "is called in German and Italian Führer or Duce; in our own language Tyrant or Dictator."[1] In June of 1938 the book written in response to the question a distinguished public official was said to have addressed to Woolf—"How in your opinion are we to prevent war?"—allowed her to say all that had been building in her during the thirties, as she collected newspaper clippings of Hitler's speeches and Nazi political rallies which she had an opportunity to observe firsthand in 1935 when she and her husband Leonard traveled through Germany and saw written on a banner stretched across a street in Bonn: "The Jew is our enemy" and "There is no place for Jews in _____ ."[2] When, at the close of *Three Guineas* Woolf argues that art reminds us of "the capacity of the human spirit to overflow boundaries and make unity out of multiplicity," she emphasizes the role of the artist whose work is necessary in a crisis to keep alive "the recurring dream that has haunted the human mind since the beginning of time; the dream of peace, the dream of freedom" (143).

These two concerns preoccupied Virginia Woolf in the last decade of her life: the nature of her own narrative authority and its relation to the external crisis in social and political authority as she saw it—patriarchy at home and its extreme form abroad, fascism. These two concerns meet not only in *Three Guineas*, her most radical feminist pamphlet, but in her posthumous novel, *Between the Acts*, where she creates in the lesbian playwright, Miss La Trobe, a female artist who in key moments of crisis—most notably when the power of her artistic illusions fails—bears a striking resemblance to a petty dictator in her will to re-impose unity on her fragile, dispersed, uncontrollable work of

From *South Central Review* 6 (2, Summer 1989): 88–104. Copyright 1989 The South Central Modern Language Association.

[1] *Three Guineas* (New York: Harcourt, Brace & World, 1938, reprinted 1963) 142.
[2] *The Diary of Virginia Woolf, Volume Four, 1931–1935*, ed. Anne Olivier Bell with Andrew McNeillie (New York: Harcourt Brace Jovanovich, 1982) 311. Hereafter cited as *D* followed by volume and page numbers.

art, a pageant of English social life which disintegrates as soon as it reaches the "present day."[3]

La Trobe takes command of a strip of what the narrator tells us is naturally "hallowed" high ground above Pointz Hall (which is built in a "hollow"), as the outdoor stage for the village's yearly pageant. The narrative of family life in the troubled Oliver house where the aging brother and sister, Bart and Lucy, live with the estranged middle-aged couple, Isa and Giles, is continually interrupted by the pageant which brings the playwright and actors—all marginal people, the "riffraff"—to this genteel country home. But the pageant, too, is continually interrupted. La Trobe plans for formal intervals between the acts of her play, with each act representing an epoch. But even in mid-act, her play is interrupted, both by nature (the wind separates shopkeeper Eliza from her costume as Queen Elizabeth and blows the actors' words away) and by human will (sometimes neither the actors nor the audience know how to play their parts).

This year—1939—La Trobe has decided to present a pageant of English history enacted as a series of social occasions laced with witty and sardonic references to England's great writers. But both the history of England as a place and as a people proves terrifyingly elusive: as Lucy Swithin, the comic elderly woman in the novel, learns from an *Outline of History*, England the island was once part of Europe, the continent presently blistering with war.[4] The English channel represents a fragile physical gap between barbarism and civilization, between slavery and freedom; one, furthermore, which we learn is an accident of nature. The fear of invasion by Hitler is embodied in the fiction in the eerie knowledge that the geographical gap opened by natural force might, at any moment, be closed by modern technological force wielded by a tyrant.[5] For the first time in Woolf's career, she seizes hold of the gap, the distance, the interval, and the interrupted structure not as a terrible defeat of the will to continuity or aesthetic unity. Rather, she elevates the interrupted structure to a positive formal and metaphysical principle.

In *Between the Acts*, Woolf celebrates rather than mourns the impossibility of final meaning. She cultivates the generative ground of language and being, more clearly distinguishing among kinds of silence that have always concerned her. In contrast to the silence which provokes a *horror vacui*, the silence marking a cut-off voice, a violently abrupted moment, or death, the end of all language, Woolf muses over the silence akin to the white space on a blank canvas (the staring whiteness that transfixes Lily Briscoe in *To the Lighthouse*) or the music of the world Septimus Smith perceives as a series of meaningful intervals of sound and silence, the very "pattern" of nature: "Sounds made

---

[3]*Between the Acts* (New York: Harcourt, Brace & World, 1941).

[4]Though the title of Lucy's book suggests H. G. Wells' *Outline of History*, the actual source of her paraphrase is G. M. Trevelyan's *History of England* (London: Longmans, Green, 1929) 3.

[5]See *D* 5: 291–309. See, too, Churchill's account of Hitler's Operation Sea Lion, Chapters 14 and 15 of *Their Finest Hour* (New York: Houghton Mifflin, 1949).

harmonies with premeditation; the spaces between them were as significant as the sounds."[6] Even the physical properties of her book reflect this concern. Woolf creates no chapter headings. She uses only large blank spaces between narrative acts. Visually, *Between the Acts* evokes the unstructured or *anti-structure*, what Victor Turner has identified and named as the occasion for an irruption of new, potentially subversive meanings.[7]

In both theme and structure, Woolf's last work becomes a meditation on the proximity of artist to dictator—of author to authoritarian ruler—when language is used as if there were no gap between sound and meaning, sign and referent. But this deep puzzling over words and their nature was not an ahistorical, apolitical enterprise for Virginia Woolf. Rather, it was a struggle of life against death, of meaning against annihilation. For Virginia Woolf, when words collapse out of meaning, when speech or writing becomes private and self-referential, we have the beginning of totalitarianism. In *Between the Acts*, Woolf forces the likeness of woman playwright to fascist dictator to press her recognition of her own will to power as practicing author, a will to unify, to find or to make—by force of imaginative skill—a principle of continuity. At its inception, this will to unity is a life-affirming impulse. For Woolf, art was a primary means of resistance to all that would violate the individual. Virginia Woolf saw that even in the hands of a powerful feminist author (and she was at the height of her powers in the thirties), narrative bears within it a temptation to bend the reader/audience to the author's will.

To appreciate Woolf's understanding of the relationship between narrative and political authority we must remember that the word commonly used for the fascist tyrants—dictators—derives from a fundamental perception of the relationship between an abuse of language and the will to dominate by force, to dictate rather than to communicate meaning. Communication necessarily entails recognition of the physical and spiritual distance or difference between speaker and listener. Woolf exploits this distance between the "I" and the "you" of every speech-act both within her work and between herself and her reader. In *Between the Acts*, La Trobe embodies the author-as-tyrant when she succumbs to the temptation to treat meaning as "hers," finished when written, complete as she has conceived it. At times, she would urgently impose upon her audience, whose freedom feels damnable when it threatens her play's performance. But in her finer moments, Woolf's playwright becomes the author as anti-fascist. Then La Trobe celebrates the intrusion of nature's wild and uncontrollable whims to counter the fixity of social behavior. When La Trobe stops resisting the freedom of the wind, the rain, the instincts of the grazing animals, she treats meaning as shared, as mutually generated by author, players, and audience. Then meaning is fragile and free, and it is a

---

6*To the Lighthouse* (New York: Harcourt Brace & Co., 1927) 234. Septimus' musing occurs during the skywriting scene in *Mrs. Dalloway* (New York: Harcourt, Brace Jovanovich, 1925, 1953) 33.
7*The Ritual Process: Structure and Anti-Structure* (Ithaca: Cornell UP, 1969) chapters 3 and 4.

struggle to bring it into being, and then an even riskier struggle to communicate it.

In the novel, as in the play within it, every attempt to speak is interrupted; every word becomes a gesture, provisional, in process. Indeed, the audience of La Trobe's pageant is our primary concern, the drama of their lives occurring during the intervals. Shocked and frightened by the effect upon her inner life of the loss of her audience to the general panic and suffering of war, Woolf was moved to make a work of art that openly explored the artist's need for her audience:

> A kind of growl behind the cuckoo & t'other birds: a furnace behind the sky. It struck me that one curious feeling is, that the writing 'I', has vanished. No audience. No Echo. Thats [sic] part of one's death. (*D* 5: 293)

The most extreme threat to civilization revealed to the modernist who was also an ardent feminist her dependence upon the listening, reading "you." Ill at ease in exile in Lewes, Woolf's snobbery was assaulted by the more rustic life of the country; her intellect was outraged by the resurgence of misogynist and anti-intellectual rhetoric in the press.

Still, Woolf remained passionately devoted to England and its literature and felt that she could best express these two great loyalties only by writing. But unlike many of her male contemporaries, such as George Orwell, whose argument was that the popular slogan to rally the people of England faced with the threat of invasion by Hitler should be "Arm the people," Woolf refused to make unequivocal patriotic gestures. England was not her country "right or left."[8] "As a woman I have no country," she argued in *Three Guineas*, "As a woman I want no country" (109). Her defiance must be read in the context of the muscular patriotism of the day, just as her last fiction must be read as a confession of a deep and perhaps helpless love of England—an England whose history and hope lay, for Woolf, primarily in literature. Comic hope characterizes Woolf's early vision of her last novel in April of 1938:

> But to amuse myself, let me note: Why not Poyntzet Hall: a centre: all lit. discussed in connection with real little incongruous living humour; & anything that comes into my head; but "I" rejected: 'We' substituted: to whom at the end there shall be an invocation? "We" . . . composed of many different things . . . we all life, all art, all waifs & strays—a rambling capricious but somehow unified whole—the present state of my mind? And English country; & a scenic old house—& a terrace where nursemaids walk? & people passing—& a perpetual variety & change from intensity to prose. & facts—& notes; &—but eno'. (*D* 5: 135)

From the beginning, then, apparent discontinuity (the incongruous, random, and capricious) was to reveal achieved unity, aesthetic and social. Aesthetically, unity is a product of the artist's act of imagination: the power to disclose

---

[8]George Orwell, *My Country Right or Left, 1940–1943*, ed. Sonia Orwell and Ian Angus (New York: Harcourt, Brace & World, 1968) 27–28

how all things radiate *to* a center. Socially, it is a process of substitution—"we" for "I." In the published novel, as the audience departs from Miss La Trobe's pageant, though they have all just been transformed from disparate "I's" into a unified "we," one of them is heard to say: "What we need is a centre. Something to bring us all together." The shifts in Woolf's title, like the character's observation that the community *lacks* the articulated center that Pointz Hall was originally meant to provide, suggests an important transformation in Woolf's idea of "the center" from which all things radiate.

"*Poynzet Hall:* a centre," a name borrowed from Thackeray's *Pendennis* (also the source of Arthur's Education Fund, so central to Woolf's arguments in *Three Guineas*), became *Pointz Hall* by May 5th, 1938, and then became *The Pageant* some time in late 1940. Only in its final stages in early 1941 did the book become *Between the Acts*: "Finished Pointz Hall, the Pageant: the Play—finally Between the Acts this morning" (26 February 1941; *D* 5: 356). The first substitution represents a shift in focus from place to performance, from the domestic to the dramatic. But then Woolf makes another substitution, moving from a center to an interstice, from a concrete place (Pointz Hall) to a radically indeterminate time—indeed, to a time which is also a figural space, nameable only with the periphrasis "*between* the acts." Between the Spring of 1938 (before the Munich Crisis) and the late Winter of 1941 (during the bombing of London) Woolf's concept of her fiction underwent a decisive change. To attend to this change is necessarily to raise a second, related question: why did Woolf choose to fix the time of the action as mid-day, mid-June, 1939 when she began to write the fiction more than a year earlier and completed it more than six months later? The question necessarily engages us with the political events of the moment and their implications for art.

Mid-Summer, 1939, the moment Woolf's fiction represents, was the last interval of "normal" life before Britain ceased to be a spectator and became an actor in the war. Both her narrative and La Trobe's pageant dramatize the "mental tension" which was "rapidly approaching the breaking-point" in Britain between Hitler's occupation of Czechoslovakia in March and his invasion of Poland in September of 1939, when Britain unilaterally declared war against Germany.[9]

The summer of 1939 was also the last moment when the radical Left in Britain could believe that Stalin's communist regime offered a real alternative to Hitler's fascism. The signing of a non-aggression pact between Germany and Russia in August, 1939 marked the "complete reversal of the grand battle between Communism and Fascism which Spain had been supposed to be about."[10] The extremes had met, and through Stalin's treachery, the symmetry of Right and Left was manifest. But for Woolf, who remained anti-ideological,

---

[9]From H. G. Wells, *The Fate of Homo Sapiens*, (London, 1939) quoted in Robert Hewison, *Under Siege: Literary Life in London, 1939–1945* (New York: Oxford UP, 1977) 5.
[10]Hewison 6.

the likeness of enemies had been visible for some time, and the infection of art with propaganda—even if it was anti-fascist propaganda—represented a dangerous weakening of art's true power to represent the deep, hidden structures of culture.

In *Between the Acts*, the threat of collapsed distance without—the fear that Hitler was powerful enough to decisively rupture if not destroy Britain's national boundaries—has its counterpart within Britain. The culture's internal violence (which persists during periods of both "war" and "peace") is represented in sexual terms in a newspaper story about an English girl raped by soldiers of the prestigious Horse Guards at Whitehall. Rape undermines the officially defined difference between "ourselves," the decent English, and "them," the brutal Germans. War against the common enemy is a form of false community which obscures internal differences (violence against the vulnerable victim) not by transcending them, but rather by suppressing them in the name of a falsely construed unity, the false transcendence of the state.

For Virginia Woolf, as for most of her peers, the outbreak of war on the continent and the agonizing moral and political question of England's r le as an ally meant not only that the artist could no longer expect to live by the old "contract" of reciprocal dissociation from the state, but that the meaning of art—and even the possibility of continuing to produce it—was called into question.[11]

As early as 1936 Walter Benjamin had observed the double truth of Nazi culture. Fascism made great art impossible. Instead, Benjamin observed, Hitler had succeeded in the "aesthetization of political life."[12] As Joseph Goebbels, Hitler's Minister of Propaganda, declared publicly,

> Politics, too, is an art, perhaps the highest and most far-reaching one of all, and we who shape modern German politics feel ourselves to be artistic people, entrusted with the great responsibility of forming out of the raw material of the masses a solid, well-wrought structure of a Volk.[13]

To achieve the goal of creating this folk community (identified with *structure*), the Third Reich redefined every occasion which used to offer the people a taste of *communitas*, or release from official structure: folk celebration, religious ritual, and art. For every major event in both the religious and secular calendar, the Nazis substituted "artificially created customs and staged folklore." In addition to Hitler's party day rallies, mass events were staged for the Volk. More than 400 theatres were built on "historically consecrated

---

11"The Artist and Politics," *The Moment and Other Essays* (New York: Harcourt Brace Jovanovich, 1948, repr. 1974).

12Walter Benjamin, "The Work of Art in the Age of Mechanical Reproduction," *Illuminations*, ed. with intro. by Hannah Arendt, trans. Harry Zohn (New York: Schocken Books, 1964) 241.

13[Quoted in] Ranier Stollman, "Fascist Politics as a Total Work of Art: Tendencies of Aesthetization of Political Life in National Socialism," *New German Critique*, 14 (Spring, 1978): 47.

ground" for ideological performances produced as part of *Thingspiel*, state sponsored drama. For playwrights and audiences alike, participation in these "celebrations" (which were performed for up to 60,000 at a time) was mandatory.[14]

In Germany, the extreme Right violently exploited the human need for art and ritual while reifying the state. In England, the radical Left also used theatre and performance to create a unified community of "the people" but to the end of revolutionizing the state. In 1938, The Left Book Club helped sponsor an alternative professional theatre whose name—Unity—signaled the decision among the splintered Left to form a popular, united front against fascism. Their theatre was overtly political in form and content, a synthesis of the avant-garde performance of the politically motivated amateur theatre groups, including agitprop theatre (inspired by anti-fascist German and Russian models from the early thirties) and The Worker's Theatre Movement.[15] Unity softened the confrontational tactics of the theatres of resistance, which had been criticized for being "too much agit and not enough prop." However, in moving away from the excesses of "agitation," Unity moved more toward overt propaganda, as the sympathetic review of Unity's opening night performance (itself a piece of propaganda) demonstrates:

> Here before an audience representing a cross-section of London's cultural and social forces, Unity, built by workers, was to give its first vital message through the medium of drama. . . .
>
> The theatre programme opened with five songs by the London Labour Choral Union. These songs were put over with terrific vigor, and evoked an equally vigorous applause.
>
> The Workers' Propaganda Dance Group then gave a performance of *A Comrade Has Died*. Here we saw the brutality and inhumanity of fascism and the inevitability of its overthrow in the workers' revolution. . . .
>
> Unity's opening night was in every way a triumph. The audience told us so, and what is far more important, the building itself showed that the workers for Unity had achieved all that they had striven for.[16]

In its self-deluded rhetoric of "inevitability" and its appeal to externalized, material structure as the ultimate sign of community, the Left sounds like a bad parody of the extreme Right. The Nazis, too, claimed that externalized structure expressed the highest attainment of unity, as Hitler claimed in a public address celebrating the opening of a new piece of monumental architecture:

---

[14]Stollman 42–44.

[15]Andre van Gyseghem, "British Theatre in the Thirties: An Autobiographical Record," Jon Clark et al., *Culture and Crisis in Britain in the Thirties* (London: Lawrence & Wishart, 1979) 212–15.

[16]Jon Clark, "Agitprop & Unity Theatre: Socialist Theatre in the Thirties," *Culture and Crisis* 223–27.

These works will become for the Germans a part of a feeling of proud togetherness. They will prove how ludicrous our petty differences are in face of these mighty, gigantic evidences of our community.[17]

Despite its apparently different end, Unity Theatre's means resembled those of its opposite number, *Thingspiel*, in several crucial ways. Both employ a rhetoric of community which suppresses internal differences by transforming an audience into a mob. Both exploit what Le Bon and Freud observed about the psychology of groups: the loss of individual will and discernment, the emergence of a "collective mind" bent to the will of the leader who, by exploiting the group's susceptibility to "the truly magical power of words," can either rouse or calm "the most formidable tempests in the group mind." Groups not only "demand illusions and cannot do without them,"[18] but as Adorno and his colleagues in the Frankfurt School were also to find in studying the characteristics of the mind susceptible to authoritarianism, the individual in a group has an extreme passion for authority.[19] Woolf, who was avidly reading Freud's *Group Psychology and the Analysis of the Ego* while writing *Between the Acts*, worries about Freud's premise that "Just as primitive man survives potentially in every individual, so the primal horde may arise once more out of any random collection," including the audience at a play.

Shouting the same word together becomes the sign of solidarity, whether in Nazi Germany where the audience was required to shout "Heil Hitler!" in unison, or in London's Unity Theatre where the regularly staged performances of Clifford Odets's *Waiting for Lefty* culminated in the moment the actors on the stage turned to the audience and roused them to join in shouting "Strike!" Both fascist aesthetized politics and anti-fascist politicized theatre justified war, for both generated community by suppressing internal differences in the name of union against a common enemy. Both Left and Right exploited the performative power of art to transform an audience, a group of unaligned and self-interested spectators, into a group which submits to authority and could be roused to violence.

As a woman and a feminist, Woolf had excellent reason for distrusting most expressions of mass solidarity, for the falling birth rate, the high level of unemployment, and general social unrest had led in England, as in Germany, to a resurgence of virulent anti-feminist sentiment and suggestions (in England) and enactment (in Germany) of laws to enforce the gender status quo.[20]

[17]Quoted in Stollman 46.

[18]Here Freud quotes Le Bon in *Group Psychology and the Analysis of the Ego*, trans. James Strachey (New York: Bantam Books, 1960) 7, 16. For Woolf's reflections on Freud's text see *D* 5: 244–52.

[19]Theodor W. Adorno, "Freudian Theory and the Pattern of Fascist Propaganda," ed. Andrew Arato and Eike Gebhardt, *The Essential Frankfurt School Reader* (New York: Continuum Press, 1982) 118–37.

[20]Dr. E. Woermann, Counsellor of the German Embassy to the Royal United Service

In the name of the state, the "natural law" of male dominance was invoked to quell social unrest and unify the people terrified by the prospect of Nazi invasion.[21] The call that "we" should "forget our differences," meant that women were asked to abandon the luxury (or, as E. M. Forster was to declare on behalf of several of Woolf's uncomprehending male friends among the Bloomsbury Group, the *irrelevance*) of feminist activism and unite with men in the name of their common identity. The incendiary tactics of *Three Guineas* expose and destroy this "oneness" while *Between the Acts* explores the fragile hope that art can, even in a crisis—perhaps especially in a crisis—mediate moments of authentic community.

Despite their famous (or notorious, depending upon one's position) intimacy, the members of the Bloomsbury Group were not in agreement about the relationship between art and politics in this period. I believe Woolf was so extraordinarily isolated in her views that her friends, and even Leonard, did not comprehend the meaning of her work. As much as she respected Leonard, Virginia Woolf did not share his view of fascism. While she was working on *Three Guineas* and *Between the Acts* Leonard wrote and published his own work on the "clear and present danger": *Barbarians at the Gates* was published by the Left Book Club in 1939 (see *D* 5: 248). In contrast to Leonard, Virginia Woolf nursed no easy sense that England represented the forces of civilization over against Germany. To her mind, the crisis was at once less clear and more sinister: fascism was not alien to England or to any culture. "We must attack Hitler in England," she wrote in her diary during May of 1938 (*D* 6: 142). And while she recognized that British culture was patriarchal, she was honest enough to search out and name the impulse to dominate and destroy within herself, an impulse she explored with frightening originality in that much misunderstood work, *The Waves* (1931). Woolf's fiction, far more than her essays (including her feminist essays) moves deeper and deeper into the question of whether it is possible to constitute an identity, whether as individual or group, except at the expense of an other who is at once model, rival, authoritarian persecutor, and ultimately, victim to the self.

The Waves undermines the ostensible difference between those, like Louis, who openly crave authority and those, like Neville, who think they scorn it. When they enter chapel at their boys' school for the first time, Louis takes refuge in the Headmaster's "bulk, in his authority" while Neville, sitting nearby, thinks the Headmaster "menaces my liberty when he prays."[22] We may take Neville's angry resistance to the Headmaster's authority as a clue to

Institution in London, December, 1927: "To believe that a woman's principal work was family life and bringing up the younger generation was simply a return to natural and eternal law." *Virginia Woolf's Reading Notebooks*, ed. Brenda Silver (Princeton: Princeton UP, 1977) 310–11.

[21] "Homes are the real places of the women who are now compelling men to be idle. It is time the Government insisted upon employers giving work to more men, thus enabling them to marry the women they cannot now approach." Quoted from *The Daily Telegraph* (22 January 1936), *Three Guineas* 51.

[22] *The Waves* (New York: Harcourt Brace Jovanovich, 1931, 1959) 34, 35.

the central paradox of the fiction. Though he asserts that "The words of authority are corrupted by those who speak them" it is he who later confesses that he must preserve his "absurd and violent passion" for Percival from misunderstanding. Silently, Neville lives in a constant state of anguished desire: "Nobody guessed the need I had to offer my being to one god; and perish, and disappear" (52). Neither Neville nor most critics see the profound contradiction between his outward posture of defiance and his inward passion to submit to the authority of another. Critics have been slow to wrestle with the nature of desire in Woolf and its relation to authority, the sacred, and violence. It may feel outrageous to read Percival as a figure for the blond ideal of Hitler's aryan dream, but his apotheosis in the minds of his friends is described in rhetoric chillingly like fascist propaganda in this era.[23]

Slavish submission to authority in *The Waves* is accomplished by no external dictator. It is not the Headmaster, representative of established patriarchal institutions, who dominates and vitiates the inner lives of Rhoda, Jinny, Susan, Louis, Neville, and Bernard. It is the secret Master within— blond, beautiful, and brutish Percival, a peer, a friend—who is thought to possess transcendent, "monolithic" Being. Percival is experienced as so autonomous, spontaneous, and powerful that, as Neville confesses, he cannot help offering himself up totally, as if in ritual slaughter of his innermost being. The six characters in this novel are not rebels against authority. Nor is Bernard a model of positive narrative authority; his last gesture is a feeble imitation of Percival, a ride toward death and silence. In truth, the six friends crave authority, they suffer for it, they do symbolic violence to others and to themselves in the name of it—but always blindly. Theirs is a negative passion, a dark twin of the transcendence so badly represented by the corpulent and verbose Headmaster. All differences (gender, class, sexuality) are subsumed by this profound likeness: all six are deluded in their desire for Percival. So far from being a hero, Percival is both tyrant and, as the ritual sacrifice Rhoda and Louis imagine during his farewell dinner suggests, victim of his friends' desire to substitute him for the divine Author they have evicted from the center of their lives. *The Waves* is perhaps Woolf's most profound exploration of the origins of totalitarianism in the individual. What is glimpsed in *The Waves* is enacted between La Trobe and her audience: the rejection of authority conceals within it a deep craving to be dominated into meaning, a temptation no less fatal to the writer than to her audience.

The crisis *Between the Acts* commemorates is at once literary and political: precisely what choice of meaningful action could the writer take to resist Nazi aggression, to rouse an audience to relinquish the stance of "unresisting obedience" to authority so necessary to the triumph of a dictator? For Woolf,

---

[23]See Bernard's vision of Percival in India which concludes, "He rides on, the multitude cluster round him, regarding him as if he were—what indeed he is—a God" (136), and his "We are creators" peroration (146).

as for the German intellectuals who opposed Hitler and became known as members of the Frankfurt School, fascism was not new, was not accidental or surprising. As Adorno put it, "The true horror of Fascism is that it represents a slow end-product of the concentration of social power." Any art that refuses to make this visible, Adorno added, "conjures away the true threat."[24] For Virginia Woolf the "old plot" of love and hate finds its most common expression in the transformation of desire into violence, its smallest social unit in the pair: man and woman. And Woolf, like Benjamin, believed that art must "expose what is present" and move the audience to *reflection* because "events are alterable not at their climaxes, not by virtue and resolution, but only in their strictly habitual course, by reason and practice."[25]

The habitual relations at Pointz Hall breed violence, a suppressed war that comes to light on the day of the pageant when a flagrantly nonconforming artist decides to strip her audience of protection—to denature the role of spectator and to lay bare the suspense and terror of the present by emptying her stage. "Time Present" is made available to the senses as an unacted possibility, the time and place between the official acts of history when meaning is suspended and members of the audience can no longer enjoy their anonymity and false safety. Words are cut in two by the "distant music" which turns out to be no voice from the sky but twelve war planes droning by overhead (193). What rouses La Trobe's audience to rage and ridicule, what brings out their well-buried terror of the impending war and their withdrawal from the scapegoat—"But what about the Jews? . . . people like ourselves?"— is not agitprop theatre (121). It is a scriptless act, a staged confrontation with "life itself," a pastoral with no poetry. The unmediated and unendurably mute physical plenitude of the earth is what La Trobe's audience must see behind her stage, a primitive substitute for the ritual space of early drama. The English audience that finds it impossible to complete the thought that the Nazis' victims might really be "people like ourselves" is finally forced to see when La Trobe abandons her experiment with ten minutes of unmediated reality ("Reality too strong" she notes in the margins of her text) and has the actors confront the audience with "hand glasses, tin cans, scraps of scullery glass, harness room glass, and heavily embossed silver mirrors"; "Anything that's bright enough to reflect, presumably, ourselves?" (*BA* 183, 185).

Woolf's readers no less than the audience within the fiction are asked to submit to "The mirror bearers," who ask us to consider how "scraps, orts and fragments" may be transformed not into a herd moved by bestial instinct to unite against a victim/enemy, but into a community conscious of its internal differences but momentarily united and at peace.

In *Between the Acts* the author's loss of control marks the birth of meaning. The urgent, if not desperate, need for a final, finalizing affirmative gesture

24[Theodor W. Adorno,] "Commitment," Arato and Gebhardt 308, 302.
25"The Author as Producer," *Reflections*, ed. with intro. Peter Demetz (New York: Harcourt Brace Jovanovich, 1978) 235–36.

like that of Woolf's earlier artist-hero, Lily Briscoe, is renounced. In contrast to Lily's private victory over her violent desire to become "one" with Mrs. Ramsay ("I have had my vision"), in *Between the Acts* words "put on meaning" only when each speaks as part of a community, "as one of the audience" (191). In Woolf's last work, the artist not only has no subject, she *is* subject to her audience and the perpetual need to renew the play. Woolf intentionally contrasts while uniting the action of the pub, or Public House where La Trobe drinks and muses in a smoke-wrapped crowd as she hears the first words of her new play, and "real life" in the Private House, Pointz Hall, where Isa and Giles renew their struggle with only the slimmest suggestion of an open ending.

Meaning cannot be one or the product of one mind in *Between the Acts*; the focus is not the individual, nor the artist, not "I" but "we," the group. Communication and community, dialogue rather than monologue, shared meaning rather than autonomy and originality are at issue, and Woolf was never more sophisticated and terrifying a writer than in this work.

From the very beginning of her career, Woolf envisioned authority as operating along a continuum reaching from the private house to the highest position of power in the public state. What is argued from the biographies of Victorian women in *Three Guineas* is incarnated in a contemporary woman in *Between the Acts*: Isa's suffering is an expression of "the fear which forbids freedom in the private house" which is connected "with the other fear, the public fear" of the dictator "which is neither small nor insignificant" (*Three Guineas* 142). Like Horkheimer and his colleagues of the Frankfurt Institut who produced the study "Authority and the Family" in 1935,[26] Woolf understood that the turn-of-the-century family, so far from proving a locus of resistance to dehumanizing social structure, initiated children into the politics of dominance and submission. It is only as the audience leaves La Trobe's performance and Bart looks back to Pointz Hall that we find the "end" of the pageant articulated: "The house emerged; the house that had been obliterated" (204).

In *Between the Acts* the practices of art, the production of a work of literature and a public performance, are scrutinized for relations of power, both the danger of inciting people to violence and the hope of destroying reified structure in order to generate peace. But La Trobe's creative violence, unlike a German bomb, leaves the beautiful house and setting intact—and attacks only the static violence, the little, local acts of domination it represents.

But in order for art to function as both process and performance, as both metaphor and metamorphosis, it must violate the conventions which have made it possible for people no longer to feel threatened by great art's power

---

[26]*Critical Theory*, trans. Matthew J. O'Connell et al. (New York: Herder & Herder, 1972) 47–128.

to estrange them from their daily lives. And in this "making strange" (a term Benjamin invented for Brecht's theatre)[27] the artist first appeals to individuals, who, if she succeeds, will begin to feel their habitual alienation in order that they may desire community for its own sake.

Insofar as *Between the Acts* legitimates the use of violence to achieve desired unity, the only enemy it is justifiable and *necessary* to oppose with the full force of intentional violence is the dead letter. And the only victim the serious play marks for ritual sacrifice is the passive, falsely neutral self—whether petty dictator like Giles or self-destructive victim like Isa—who refuses to give up being a member of the audience in order to become one of the actors. But in what drama? Woolf had already sketched it out in *Three Guineas*. When she issued a provocative call to "cremate the corpse" of the word "feminist," because it had become obsolete, since women had earned the "only right, the right to earn a living . . . and a word without meaning is a dead word, a corrupt word" (101). This shocking idea (would that the word "feminist" really had become obsolete) has a positive motive: "The word 'feminist' is destroyed; the air is cleared; and in that clearer air what do we see? Men and women working together for the same cause" (102). The cause is peace, and the enemy is fascism at home and abroad: "The whole iniquity of dictatorship, whether in Oxford or Cambridge, in Whitehall or Downing Street, against Jews or against women, in England, or in Germany, in Italy or in Spain is now apparent to you. But now we are fighting together" (103). This was a hope; the events of ensuing years complicated this hope as Woolf renounced direct discourse and returned to the indirection of fiction. Woolf's own shift from the direct discourse of *Three Guineas* to the subtleties of *Between the Acts* is replicated in the fiction when La Trobe puts down her megaphone (and renounces its 'infernal bray') and abandons her script, letting the actors run freely among the audience.

Miss La Trobe's pageant moves toward the ensuing momentary but powerful achievement of "the essential 'We' " by an inversion of the characters' process of domesticating language.[28] On the day of her pageant language becomes strange again:

> "We remain seated"—"We are the audience." Words this afternoon ceased to lie flat in the sentence. They rose, became menacing and shook their fists at you. (59)
> "The nursery," said Mrs. Swithin.
> Words raised themselves and became symbolical. "The cradle of our race," she seemed to say. (71)

And just as words rise up from the sentence as it is spoken, sometimes with power and meaning independent of the speaker's motives, so all those at the pageant are at once not themselves (estranged from their habitual ways of being) and more essentially themselves than ever. For Giles, who is unwilling

---

27"What is Epic Theatre?" *Illuminations* 150.
28*The Ritual Process* 137.

to say "we" except as an interrogative ("*We?*"), sitting in the audience as a spectator makes his actual status as passive observer of the war too plain:

> This afternoon he wasn't Giles Oliver come to see the villagers act their annual pageant; manacled to a rock he was, and forced passively to behold indescribable horror. (60)

Enforced passivity is the hallmark of daily life at Pointz Hall, where people live in a constant state of undeclared war. With a real war threatened, the pageant makes Giles' status as spectator and the force bred by his enraged helplessness painfully obvious by exaggerating it, by formalizing it as his definitive role.

The violations of literary genre and social manners in La Trobe's pageant and Woolf's narrative are calculated to realize the unarticulated middle: "the third emotion," clearly identified as "peace" (91–92). Significantly, the third term Isa can only envision, until the final moment, as the last of a string of separate feelings—"Love. Hate. Peace." (215)—is intimated in the mysterious issuing forth of "another voice . . . a third voice . . . saying something simple" (115). This is described as the antithesis of the Dictator's force-backed utterance. Because it is "the voice that was no one's voice" this newly articulated presence, a ghostly echo of the ancient voice of Anon, may well be "the voice that is *everyone's* voice."

Both Woolf's prose and La Trobe's play reflect what Bakhtin has called the "carnivalisation" of literature. As a celebration of "change itself," the carnival celebrates "the very process of replaceability . . . rather than that which is replaced."[29] In other words, this is a refusal to "absolutize" anything—a subversion of the univocal or "single leveled" expressions of political authority. When Carnival moves from the town square to the literary text it becomes a revolt not only against the absolutizing of political power, but also a revolt against "literary finalization."[30]

Like Bakhtin, Adorno and Benjamin also attempted to distinguish between literature that participated in the hidden violence of false knowing and objectifying naming and that which resisted such foreclosures of language and experience. Isa's wordless interpretation of Giles' clenched fist as he sums up Dodge ("homosexual," he concludes, using a word which, like "lesbian" is unspeakable in this world), like Dodge's revulsion (and Bart's condescension) for what Lucy's cross signifies, are only a few of the reified words or ideas in circulation in proper English society. The violence of easy interpretation of other people has its counterpart in the hacked up bits and pieces of literature Woolf's characters quote to their own private ends. Her late formal experiments offer a meaningful revolt against these tendencies.

Woolf understood, as did Benjamin, that fascism has a counterpart in degraded art, specifically art that reproduces a relationship of dominance and

---

[29]Mikhail Bakhtin, *Problems of Dostoevsky's Poetics* (Ann Arbor: Ardis Press, 1973) 107, 103.
[30]Bakhtin 47.

submission between author and reader (or audience). Like Nazi politics, such art represents a corruption of a means of producing community, an abuse of "an apparatus which is pressed into the production of ritual values" to violent ends: politically, Benjamin argued, the "*Führer* cult," artistically, the cult of the author.[31]

Woolf's last work becomes a fiction formally and thematically dedicated to the carnivalesque. Her narrative as well as La Trobe's performance celebrates the re-doubling of language. Both the figure of the local worker— big strong Eliza for great Elizabeth, Monarch—and the very word "monarch" are carnivalized in *Between the Acts*, where the important Monarchs and Admirals are not figures of political and military authority. Instead, they are either butterflies—Red Admirals—that come and feed, with delight, on the actor's glittering costumes strewn in lovely profusion on the grass behind the bushes; or they are artists:

> Miss La Trobe was pacing to and fro between the leaning birch trees. One hand was deep stuck in her jacket pocket; the other held a foolscap sheet. She was reading what was written there. She had the look of a commander pacing his deck. The leaning graceful trees with black bracelets circling the silver bark were distant about a ship's length.
>
> Wet would it be, or fine? Out came the sun; and shading her eyes in the attitude proper to an Admiral on his quarter-deck, she decided to risk the engagement out of doors. Doubts were over. All stage properties, she commanded, must be moved from the Barn to the bushes. It was done. And the actors, while she paced, taking all responsibility and plumping for fine, not wet, dressed among the brambles. Hence the laughter. (62)

As the word-play in the narrator's description suggests, the dramatic "properties" of life on La Trobe's side of the bushes include comic resistance to violently closed structures of thought and representation. La Trobe cannot bring the audience back there with her, but she can struggle to transport her vision across the fragile yet active threshold dividing them. The "mobbed" bushes represent a necessary division between audience and author, one meant not to mystify the author's stature, but to keep attention on the play. The bushes also seem active in protecting her from the possibility that the audience, once roused to see their prejudices and ignorance exposed, once they realize that the object of La Trobe's artistic playful violence is their own rigid dedication to convention, might become a mob and turn against her, stranger that she is.

La Trobe is herself a comically mixed form, and in her martial strutting she inspires not fear but laughter. In this lesbian artist, a female outsider detached from and therefore better able to see the nature of social and political fictions which protect official structure, Woolf makes the substance as well as the illusion of the author's power obvious. The actors may laugh, but they also

31"The Work of Art in the Age of Mechanical Reproduction," *Illuminations* 241.

obey. La Trobe speaks and her subjects, in response to the artist-as-monarch or admiral, perform: "It was done." But La Trobe's dominion is ephemeral, and it is only by the consent of actors and audience alike that she has even these brief moments of rule. Her glory is fitful and agonizingly incomplete. She has no authority but the power of illusion: art. Outside the boundaries of the play, she would do nothing to intercede with her audience, to interrupt or to obstruct them should they rise to leave. La Trobe uses no physical force, no overt coercion on anyone. Her "whip" is entirely symbolic, never coming into play except as a sign of her self-restrained will to power.

In *Between the Acts* the authority of illusion unmasks the illusion of authority. To the audience's anxious questions, "Whom to thank? . . . Whom to *make responsible*?" (194–95, my emphasis), La Trobe and Woolf respond by remaining "invisible" (191). Insofar as there *is* a work of art anymore in Woolf, it is no longer represented by the bound book, but by the script—a text which must be performed—and which only then binds author, actors, and audience together as an authentic community. Miss La Trobe's momentary desire to be author of "the play without an audience—*the play*" (180) and the consequent momentary sacrificial death she experiences when her will to power is frustrated, represent a retreat from the acted production with its collective, public audience, to the bound book with private reader. As the comic violence behind the "mobbed" bushes suggests, the artist becomes both tyrant and victim when she misappropriates language's free play to her own ends: "Panic seized her. Blood seemed to pour from her shoes. This is death, death, death, she noted in the margin of her mind; when illusion fails" (180).

The fiction ends with a simultaneous arrival at a new beginning for the artist, the central couple, and the reader. Isa and Giles appear to act out the drama La Trobe is that moment dreaming up, a drama of cultural regression, a return to origins: "There was the high ground at midnight; there the rock; and two scarcely perceptible figures. . . . She set down her glass. She heard the first words" (212). As La Trobe opens herself to the inspiration of a new play in the public house, Isa and Giles prepare for the scene they have avoided all day, not a fight to the death between predator and prey. This private war— from which new life might be born—is figured as a necessary struggle between creatures of the same species. Fox and vixen, male and female, suggest the perpetual 'war at home' whose players must move past enmity to peace and renewed hope. In a farewell gesture to her audience, Woolf removes our gaze from the author with finality, leaving us, her readers, poised on a threshold.

> Left alone together for the first time that day, they were silent. Alone, enmity was bared; also love. Before they slept, they must fight; after they had fought, they would embrace. From that embrace another life might be born. But first they must fight, as the dog fox fights with the vixen, in the heart of darkness, in the fields of night.
> . . . The house had lost its shelter. It was night before roads were made, or

houses. It was the night that dwellers in caves had watched from some high place among rocks.

Then the curtain rose. They spoke. (219)

Like Woolf's characters, we her readers are asked to move from being spectators to becoming actors, to name accurately the violence loose in the world as originating within and between us. And like La Trobe, Woolf the author withdraws. Now we, too, are left before a lifted curtain, on the threshold of meaning, with no words except the ones we choose to utter ourselves.[32]

[32]Vanessa Bell's original cover for the novel depicted an empty stage with outer curtains lifted.

Britannia Rules *The Waves*

Jane Marcus

What has made it impossible for us to live in time like fish in water, like birds in air, like children? It is the fault of Empire! Empire has created the time of history. Empire has located its existence not in the smooth recurrent spinning time of the cycle of the seasons but in the jagged time of rise and fall, of beginning and end, of catastrophe. Empire dooms itself to live in history and plot against history. One thought alone preoccupies the submerged mind of Empire: how not to end, how not to die, how to prolong its era. By day it pursues its enemies. . . . By night it feeds on images of disaster.

> —J. M. Coetzee, *Waiting for the Barbarians*

The waves drummed on the shore, like turbaned warriors, like turbaned men with poisoned assegais who, whirling their arms on high, advance upon the feeding flocks, the white sheep.

> —Virginia Woolf, *The Waves*

Rise and Fall

Canon building is Empire building. Canon defense is national defense. Canon debate, whatever the terrain, nature and range (of criticism, of history, of the history of knowledge, of the definition of language, the universality of aesthetic principles, the sociology of art, the humanist imagination), is the clash of cultures. And *all* of the interests are vested.

> —Toni Morrison, "Unspeakable Things Unspoken"

From *Decolonizing Tradition: New Views of Twentieth-Century "British" Literary Canons*, ed. Karen R. Lawrence (Urbana: University of Illinois Press, 1992), pp. 136–62. Copyright 1992 by the Board of Trustees of the University of Illinois.

My thanks to Louise Yelin, Mary Mathis, Patricia Laurence, and Mary Ann Caws for their comments on an early draft; to Karen Lawrence for her rigorous critique and her editorial skills in shaping this essay; to James Haule and his and Philip Smith's *Concordance*; to Regina Barreca's seminar at the University of Connecticut; and to Ruth Perry for pointing out the connection between my argument about white ideology and Toni Morrison's essay, when I read an earlier version of this essay at Harvard in 1988. Thanks also to audiences at CUNY Graduate Center, SUNY Purchase, the University of Hawaii, Texas A & M, SUNY Stony Brook, and Emory University. My deepest debt is to my student Mary Mathis, who inspired this essay by asking if *The Waves* could be recuperated for feminism and by discussing questions about the death of the author and the influence of Shelley. My thanks also to the M.A. students at City College in fall 1987, where this reading of *The Waves* was first worked out.

Virginia Woolf's novel *The Waves* (1931) has consistently been read critically as a work of High Modernism, a novel of the thirties that is not a thirties novel. Its canonical status has been based on a series of misreadings of this poetic text and of Woolf herself as synonymous with and celebratory of upper-class genteel British culture. My reading claims that *The Waves* is the story of "the submerged mind of empire." Woolf has, to use Coetzee's terms (133), set her experimental antinovel in "the jagged time of rise and fall," explicitly repeating the words "rise and fall and rise again" throughout the text. But this text (roman in typeface as opposed to the italics recording the rise and setting of the sun) of humans making their life history (plotting against history?) is surrounded by an italicized text of "spinning time" in the cycle of the seasons. These italicized interludes take the form of a set of Hindu prayers to the sun, called Gayatri, marking its course during a single day. These (Eastern) episodes surround a (Western) narrative of the fall of British imperialism. Imperialist history is divided into chapters called "the rise of . . . " or "the fall of . . . . " *The Waves* explores the way in which the cultural narrative "England" is created by an Eton/Cambridge elite who (re)produce the national epic (the rise of . . .) and elegy (the fall of . . .) in praise of the hero. The poetic language and experimental structure of this modernist classic are vehicles for a radical politics that is both anti-imperialist and anticanonical.[1]

Woolf dramatizes the death of the white male Western author, Bernard, his fixation with "how not to die," while exposing the writer's collusion in keeping alive the myth of individualism and selfhood that fuels English patriotism and nationalism. This violent homosocial narrative of English national identity, in its simple-minded racism (and sexism) and nostalgia for class bias, which Woolf mercilessly parodies in an infantilized fictional focalization of "he said" and "she said," is nevertheless so powerful in its intertextuality with hundreds of lines from familiar Romantic poems that readers for five decades have been taught to read Percival and Bernard as Hero and Poet, without recognizing Woolf's fictional prophecy of fascist characters. *The Waves* quotes (and misquotes) Shelley, not to praise him but to bury him. Woolf is infusing her discourse about Orientalism in England at the beginning of the postcolonial period with Shelley's Orientalism, exposing the implications of race and gender in the still-living English Romantic quest for a self and definition of the (white male) self against the racial or sexual Other. There has been so much critical resistance to Woolf's politics that her anti-imperialist effort of enclosing a Western narrative in an Eastern narrative in order to critique Western philosophy and politics in *The Waves* may have seemed too radical for a descendant of Anglo-Indian policymakers. But as a socialist, feminist, and pacifist, Woolf had far more reason to explore Indian history and religion than T. S. Eliot did, for example, whose references to the great Indian texts

---

[1]It is ironic that *The Waves*, a novel that critiques the canon-making process itself, should have been among the first four volumes in the Cambridge University Press Landmarks of World Literature series, begun in 1986 with *The Iliad, The Divine Comedy,* and *Faust.*

are taken seriously. It is my contention that Woolf uses Shelley's poems, specifically "The Indian Girl's Song," to create a discourse for an alienated Western woman like Rhoda to have a "heroic death," like Indian widows in sati.

In creating Rhoda's internal speech out of the texts of Shelley's poems, Woolf participates in and exposes at least two historical Orientalisms that force us to look at race and gender in relation to colonialism. Shelley's visions of Indian love/death come from his readings of Sydney Owenson's (Lady Morgan's) novel *The Missionary* (1811), as hers came from reading Sir William Jones, an early English "Orientalist." The abjection of Rhoda's suicide is politicized by mirroring the acts of Shelley's Indian maidens, though her Western sati is death by water, not by fire. Rhoda's silence invokes the silence of the Indian woman (Gramsci and Spivak's "subaltern"?), so verbal and intellectual a figure in Owenson but transformed in Shelley into a Romantic suicide, thereafter speechless, absent, or dead in Western texts. Shelley's Romanticization of sati recalls British colonial chivalry, arguing that colonialism would free Indian women from such "barbaric" practices, as one patriarchy invokes its superiority to another patriarchy, in the same way that the overturned bullock cart, righted by Percival, recalls the throngs of worshipers run over and killed by Krishna's cart at religious celebrations, another excuse for English intervention.

The history of the reception of the text, particularly its rejection by those leftist critics whose ideology it presumably shares, exposes an awkward gender and class bias, a certain paternalism in British Left criticism from Leavis to Williams, which cannot come to terms with a marxist novel that is not realist, an anti-imperialist novel that is not (I am sorry to say) written by a man.[2] The failure of the text to reach its contemporary intended audience, and its subsequent status as "difficult" or only available to an elite, have ensured its relegation to the unread, except in formalist or philosophical terms, and have operated as a cultural imperative that continues to deprive Virginia Woolf of readers of color or of the working class. Left-wing guardians of English culture steered such readers to Lawrence and Orwell for their moral and political heritage, rather than to the radicalism of Woolf. What a different narrative of modernism might have emerged if Jameson had read *The Waves* with Conrad's *Lord Jim* as exposing the ideology of the British ruling class. Perhaps he would have been forced to question his privileging of *Lord Jim.*

Said's praise of *Kim* and Jameson's exploration of fascist modernism are moves that seem deliberately to avoid reading or acknowledgment of the

---

[2]See the appendix in Raymond William's *Politics of Modernism* for the responses of Said and Williams to the question of gender. Williams's well-known attacks on Bloomsbury reveal a need to maintain a muscular macho modernism of the working class. As late as 1965 Leonard Woolf answered Queenie Leavis's claim that Virginia Woolf's novels were not *popular* with sales figures to show that they were (*TLS*, Mar. 2–8, 1990, 211).

profound critique of imperialism and the class system in Virginia Woolf's work. Some very astute critics are unable to accept Woolf's irony about an author figure so like herself in the portrait of Bernard; they ignore the antipatriotic and anti-imperialist outbursts in the text because they are inconsistent with these critics' notion of the author's politics, based on her gender and class. The interpretive history of *The Waves* for a socialist feminist critic, then, is largely a negative burden, for *The Waves* simply does not exist as a cultural icon of the 1930s, as part of the discourse about (the rise of . . .) fascism, war, and imperialism in which it participated. The critical act of replacing it in this discourse is an aggressive cultural move made possible now, I would argue, by the legitimation of cultural studies and the combined methodologies of feminism, marxism, revisionist Orientalism, and the recognition of certain postmodern characteristics in some modernist texts.

The rescue of the text, which I here attempt, is addressed to those deeply indoctrinated by the Leavisite legacy of a mythical "Virginia Woolf," created to stand for that elite, effete English culture against which the democratic Great Tradition strenuously struggled. Adena Rosmarin has theorized the cultural process of recuperative reading: "the argument that best accounts for the work is coincident with the argument that best accounts for the manifold histories of its reworkings" (21), an idea that moves me to say it is the project of cultural studies that now allows one to read *The Waves* as a narrative about culture making. Exploring the relations between race, class, and gender in the text *and* in the history of its production allows us to see those forces at work in criticism as well. Bernard in *The Waves* authorizes his role as inheritor of civilization by summoning a recurring vision of a "lady at a table writing, the gardeners with their great brooms sweeping" (192). This is a vision in which English culture is represented as an aristocratic female figure in a grand country house called Elvedon, leisure for creativity provided by the security of the fixed class position of servants. Bernard insists that the two figures are inseparable, that you cannot have one without the other. As inheritor of culture, he will always have a Mrs. Moffat to "sweep it all up." The figure of the lady represents the gentleman artist; once the reader pries apart Bernard's pairing of the writing classes and the sweeping classes and questions the inevitability of Elvedon as a figure for art, it is possible to read the novel as a critique of the culture-making process, and especially as Woolf's feminist exploration of the patriarchal representation of Woman as Culture, a representation that nevertheless silences and intimidates women like Rhoda. Bernard's fetishized Portrait of the Artist as a Lady has more to do with his own image as a ruling-class writer than the possibility of women's producing culture. (Desmond MacCarthy, the model for Bernard, would never concede that there were any great women writers.)

Marina Warner, in *Monuments and Maidens: The Allegory of the Female Form*, discusses the allegorical use of female figures for national and imperial projects. She wittily points out the irony in the history of the symbolism of

Britannia, in recent years portentously figuring official state power in cartoons of Mrs. Thatcher as the armed warrior woman when, in fact, Britannia was originally a figure on coins struck by the Roman emperors Hadrian and Antoninus Pius to celebrate the colonization of Britain. In the seventeenth century Britannia was mythologized as the British constitution and the triumphant naval nation, and engraved with Neptune yielding his scepter to her. In 1740 James Thomson's poem "Rule, Britannia!" with music by Thomas Arne, was sung as the finale of his masque *Alfred*; it did not become a popular unofficial national anthem until the next century. Thomson's text reflects the tension between free democracy and the dread ruler of subject nations: Britannia is commanded to rule as if in fearful memory of Roman subjection; other nations are joyfully given over to tyrants while Britons shout their determination never, never to be slaves. This is a fitting anthem for imperialists.

As nineteenth-century figures of Britannia began to impersonate Athena, the democratic persona gave way to the figure of might and power. Warner writes: "It is noteworthy that Britannia appears more frequently on the stamps of subject nations than on the stamps of Great Britain herself, revealing her shift from personification of a free people to symbol of the authority which endorses it" (49). My calling upon the figure of Britannia in the title of this essay is meant to convey the national anxiety of the former colony about the colonizing process itself, as if there were no other role but colonizer or colonized. The Lady at a Table Writing serves as a "Britannia" figure and an allegory for Bernard. But in order to read it this way, one has to be open to irony in Woolf's voice, particularly toward Bernard, the writer figure, and be aware of and open to Woolf's critique of class and empire. Bernard is a parody of authorship; his words are a postmodern pastiche of quotation from the master texts of English literature.

Woolf's "biographeme," her model for the character of Bernard, is Desmond MacCarthy, the man of letters, editor of *Life and Letters*, prominent reviewer and arbiter of taste, writing as "Affable Hawk" a series of judgments of literary value in which he claims that there is no such thing as a "great" woman artist (Woolf argued the point with him in "The Intellectual Status of Women," but he never wavered). This process by which the actual Desmond and the fictional Bernard figure Woman as Culture while denying either women or the working class the possibility of creating culture, to follow Rosmarin again, can be plotted both in formalist and materialist readings of *The Waves* and in the problematic scapegoating of Virginia Woolf herself. She may represent culture, but she may not create it. Insofar as Elvedon *is* Bloomsbury in the novel and Bloomsbury/Virginia Woolf is an enormous inflated straw woman against whom both the Left and Right may fulminate (and did; and still do?) from the 1930s to the present, we notice that the figure of Woman as Culture in *The Waves* is constructed as demanding the continued oppression of the working class, a move that allows certain marxists to continue their misreading. Such interpretations of the author's class and gender as "lady" denied feminism a founding place in modernism or in English Left criticism by insisting on its inability to ally itself with the working class. This deprived socialist women of a model critic and founding mother and foreclosed the possibility of inserting, at an earlier historical date, gender (and race) into a predominantly class-centered oppositional narrative.

Other cultural narratives about Virginia Woolf were invented and circulated around this master narrative of the lady: Quentin Bell's biography was constructed backward from the suicide and produced versions of madwoman and victim; feminist narratives of the survivor of child abuse were fashioned; American feminists revived *A Room of One's Own* as a founding text for women's studies as a field, a practice that sometimes ignored the class narrative in the text. Also problematic was the explicit rejection of Woolf as the origin of modern socialist feminist critical practice by American empiricist feminists, responding, it appears, to the demand of English Left cultural authority. Woolf alienated a contemporary leftist audience in "The Leaning Tower" by exposing the way leftist intellectuals romanticized the working class and neglected the political education of their own class. (Their heroizing of Lawrence is as problematic as the demonizing of Woolf.) Her fiction relentlessly connects imperialism to patriarchy; *Three Guineas*, for example, insists that the origin of fascism is in the patriarchal family, not in Italian or German nationalism, a politics recuperated by certain 1970s feminisms but certainly not by the British Left.

It is not my purpose to claim subaltern status for Woolf or for *The Waves*, or even to claim that my reading of its politics is a restoration of a lost original text. But what becomes apparent in reading *The Waves* with the benefit of recent cultural methodologies is that the text itself provides strategies for readers excluded from the cultural inheritance it represents. Woolf provides such strategies through Bernard's demand as an artist for an audience of "other people's eyes" (I's, ayes). Bernard's is an act of literary hegemony; he absorbs the voices of his marginalized peers into his own voice—he needs "other people's eyes" to read him and other people's I's, their lives and selves, to make his stories. As Bernard's audience, however, we are made to see this act of appropriation. The text as a whole thus invokes a reader who can read as a barbarian or outsider, not just as a Greek or inheritor of the tradition. As readers, prying open the difference between the two positions allows us to enter into the racial/colonial narrative in the way that opening the lady/ sweeper pairing assists in the interrogation of class.

I argue here that *The Waves* is a thirties novel and that it is concerned with race, class, colonialism, and the cultural politics of canonicity itself. In *The Waves* Woolf interrogates the color problem, setting a metropolitan "whiteness" against the colored colonial world as a vast desert against which an intellectual elite like the Bloomsbury Group creates itself as culture. *The Waves* might have been called *Waiting for the Barbarians* because of its emotional evocation of white fear and guilt for colonial and class oppression, the national dream of being assailed by the assegais of the savage enemy as "white sheep." But fifty years of readings are difficult to displace—just as readers of Edith Sitwell's *Façade* have been prevented from hearing its profound critique of British naval power because of a narrow notion that the political is foreign to a performative aesthetic emphasizing sound, dance, and nonsense children's rhymes. Postmodern performance art may allow us to recuperate Sitwell's text, music, and megaphone, as well as the mockery of English maritime power she shared with Woolf. We might think of Woolf's rehearsal for *The Waves* in her youthful participation in the "Dreadnought Hoax" in 1910, a prank in which she and her friends, posing as the emperor of Abyssinia and his court, successfully boarded a formidable secret man-of-war of which her cousin, William Fisher, was flag commander.

Consistent with the socialist politics and antifascist ethics of *The Years* and *Three Guineas*, which explore the relation of the patriarchal family and state institutions to fascism, *The Waves* investigates the origin of cultural power in the generation or group formed by the British public school and in its values. Woolf mocks snobbish, eternally adolescent male bonding around the ethos of "the playing fields of Eton" and she exposes the cult of the hero and the complicity of the poet in the making of culture as he excudes cultural glue (in the form of an elegy for the dead hero) as a source of social cohesion, the grounding for nationalism, war, and eventually fascism. I claim here that in 1931, despite her personal privilege in class terms, Woolf prophesized the doom of the insular civilization that produced her by specifically problematizing whiteness as an issue. If, as I have argued, *A Room of One's Own* is an elegy for all the lives of women left out of history, then *The Waves* deconstructs the politics of the elegy as an instrument of social control. In the process of inventing a new name for her fictions, Woolf thought "elegy" might do. But in exploring its function, she revealed the ethical problems to be faced in using this patriarchal genre. Bernard's production of culture is authorized by the politics of the elegy in the history of poetry; his writing mourns the death of Percival in India: "He was thrown, riding in a race, and when I came along Shaftesbury Avenue tonight, those insignificant and scarcely formulated faces that bubble up out of the doors of the Tube, and many obscure Indians, and people dying of famine and disease, and women who have been cheated, and whipped dogs and crying children—all these seemed to me bereft. He would have done justice. He would have protected. . . . No lullaby has ever occurred to me capable of singing him to rest" (243).

The Waves insists that the modernist epic-elegy is a melodrama for beset imperialists. (*The Waste Land, Ulysses*, etc., might be read in the same way.) It marks the end of empire, but to read it this way, as part of what I call the "postcolonial carnivalesque," one must be willing to read the comic and ironic and perhaps even regard with relief the death of the author which it enacts.

The study of the silenced colonial other and the search for the subaltern voice, while not articulated in Woolf's text, do lead us to recognize the power of the white woman's critique of herself and her social system, and of the complicity of English literature with imperialism and class oppression, especially when such a critique is not to be found in the writing of modernist men. The gardeners and the natives do not speak in *The Waves*; they are pictures taken under Bernard's imaginary Western eyes. But their presence, and that of Mrs. Moffat, the charwoman, and Bernard's nanny-muse, suggests that we ask whose interest was served by marking this text apolitical for five decades.

Virginia Woolf self-consciously creates here a literature of color, and that color is white, a literature written under the protection of the "white arm" of imperialism and defining itself by the brown and black of colonized peoples, ideologically asserting itself even in the unconscious of oppressed and silenced women in Rhoda's fantasy of her white flower fleet. The Haule-Smith concordance reports 117 instances of "white" or "whiteness" in this very short text, evidence of Woolf's effort to interrogate the color problem of whiteness as ideology. A barbarian reading notices *The Waves* as a white book, as Toni Morrison's provocative reading of Melville recalls the moment in American history "when whiteness became ideology. . . . And if the white whale is the ideology of race, what Ahab has lost to it is personal dismemberment and family and society and his own place as a human in the world. The trauma of racism is, for the racist and the victim, the severe fragmentation of self" (15–16). Bernard's "world without a self" is the white postcolonial world. The fragmented selves of the "civilized" characters in *The Waves* are directly related to the politics of British imperialism. If Bernard is an Ahab figure, then the vision of a "fin in a waste of waters" may belong to his own white whale, his obsession with Percival and India. (We know that Woolf read *Moby Dick* on February 14, 1922, and again on September 10, 1928; her centenary article on Melville, for which she read all his works, appeared in *TLS* on August 7, 1919. Her diary mentions *Moby Dick* in connection with Desmond MacCarthy [Diary III, 195], and she also jokes about Moby Dick's whiteness.)

This Occidental tribe of alienated characters, so often read as figures in a roman à clef of Bloomsbury intellectuals, collectively inscribe their class and race superiority only by imagining a world of the Savage Other in India and Africa, where their representative, Percival (a Siegfried, a Superman, the strong silent bully who will by the end of the decade be a fascist idol), secures their privilege by violent exertions of brute force. As *Orlando* writes the history of English literature based on a founding gesture of violence and conquest, Orlando slicing at the shrunken head of a Moor, the trophy of a violent British adventure against African blacks, *The Waves* reveals that the primal narrative of British culture is the (imperialist) quest. Bernard and his friends idolize Percival, the violent last of the British imperialists, as his (imagined) life and death in India become the story of their generation. Percival embodies their history, and Bernard, the man of letters, ensures by his elegies to Percival that this tale, the romance of the dead brother/lover in India, is inscribed as *the story* of modern Britain. My reading of the novel goes against the grain of its reception as ahistorical and abstract by insisting that it records a precise historical moment—the postcolonial carnivalesque— in Percival's quixotic ride on a fleabitten mare and his fall from a donkey, of England's fall from imperial glory and the upper-class angst of the intellectu- als, their primal terror in imagining the assegais of subject peoples turned against them, their agony at contact with the masses and the classes at home, who threaten the order of their whiteness with blood and dirt. The success of Woolf's postmodern practice is evident in her ambivalence about the "fall," unless she was joking when she wrote to Quentin Bell in 1935 that she shed a tear at the film *Bengal Lancers* ("that's what comes of being one generation nearer to Uncle Fitzy" [*Letters* V, 383]).

The Waves is about the ideology of white British colonialism and the Romantic literature that sustains it. Its parody and irony mock the complicity of the hero and the poet in the creation of a collective national subject through an elegy for imperialism. In its loving misquotation and textual appropriation of Romantic poetry, *The Waves* may participate more fully in postmodernism as Linda Hutcheon defines it than it does in that modernism where its tenuous canonical place is earned by praise for technical difficulty and apparent antirealism as a representation of consciousness. *The Waves* undermines humanistic faith in the individual coherent subject while exposing the role writing plays in shoring up *national* subjectivity; it challenges the idea of the artist's integrity. In its allusion to Romantic poetry, and, specifi- cally, to Shelley's earlier Orientalism, Woolf's text recalls another historical moment of English fetishization of selfhood and individualism as the struggle against death. It questions the white man's anxiety about identity as universal. Woolf mocks the Western valorization of individual selfhood in her exhaustion of the form of soliloquy, and she disposes of the notion of individual literary genius by an overdetermined intertextuality with Romantic poetry, which simultaneously pokes fun at Romantic diction and ideology and demonstrates how powerful certain phrases and images are in the invocation of patriotism and nationalist claims for English genius. Harold Bloom completely misses this aspect of Woolf's cultural critique when he interprets *The Waves* as belated Romanticism and calls Bernard's last speech a "feminization of the Paterian aesthetic stance" (5). This canonical move denies the politics of Woolf's parody of the English culture-making machinery in which one genius succeeds another. *The Waves* is the swan song of the white Western male author with his Romantic notions of individual genius, and his Cartesian confidence in the unitary self. Byronic man, the Romantic artist-hero, sings his last aria against death.[3]

---

[3]The classic essay on Romanticism and *The Waves* is McConnell's " 'Death among the Apple Trees.' " Also relevant is J. H. McGavran, "Alone Seeking the Visible World," and J. W. Graham, "MSS Revision and the Heroic Theme of *The Waves*."

The waves that interest me in this essay are the waves called up in the English national anthem, "Britannia Rules the . . . ," waves that surround an island imperialist culture defining itself as civilization against the perceived savagery of those whom it has conquered across the seas, specifically, in this text, India. The children of empire, the British ruling class of the 1930s, six characters lacking patronymics and fixed forever in their first names by an absent authority, fixate on the seventh, Percival, the hero, the man of action, the figure whose body they all identify with England. (Since they address only themselves and not each other, and the women don't even call themselves by name, Woolf enacts a discursive infantilization that she emphasizes by the use of the pure present—"I come; I go.") Her authorial hand had torn these characters from the bosoms of their families as if to isolate for scientific study the peer group as carrier of ideology. While *To the Lighthouse* and *The Years* provide acute social critiques of marriage and the family, *The Waves* examines the role of childhood friendships and schooling in the formation of individual, group, and national identity, and the group's production of the figures of hero and poet in the consolidation of cultural hegemony. The school scenes are in fact an indictment of the British public school systems, exposing the barbarism and cruelty by which upper-class boys learn to be "Greeks," inheritors of culture, what Woolf's cousin J. K. Stephen first called "the intellectual aristocracy."

Woolf exposes as well the way that white women are implicated in, rather than exempt from, this imperialistic project. Correctly, I think, she reveals the way each of the white women in their Foucauldian roles as sexualized social beings—Rhoda the hysteric, Ginny the prostitute, and Susan the mother—collaborates in Bernard's plot to canonize the physical and verbal brutality, class arrogance, and racial intolerance of Percival. Feminist readings often argue that Bernard's fluency depends upon the suppression of Rhoda, that her silence is necessary for his speech. But in their roles as victims, silenced subjects, the women still participate in imperialist practice. . . .

India and the Makers of Ideology

In writing *The Waves*, Woolf critiqued the system from within, acknowledging her own role as inheritor of class privilege and Stephen family history, her concern for the sins of the fathers as makers of imperialism and patriarchy. As I have argued in "Liberty, Sorority, Misogyny," Stephen family members in the nineteenth century were the great professionalizers who consolidated the power of the rising middle class in British institutions. They were also great reformers. The Stephen dynasty escaped its poor Scottish origins and began with the first James Stephen writing his way out of debtors' prison by claiming that such imprisonment was against the Magna Carta. James's son was educated courtesy of money earned by his uncle in the West Indies, and the second James Stephen was made into an abolitionist by witnessing a slave auction on St. Kitts in 1783 and joined Wilberforce and the Claphan Sect on his return from the West Indies. Beginning with Woolf's great-grandfather, who wrote the Anti-Slavery Bill (though it was her paternal grandfather, James Stephen, permanent undersecretary for the Colonies, who got it passed), the Stephen family shaped British ideology, especially in relation to colonial policy in India. A patriarchal tyrant at home, Mr. Mother-Country-Stephen, as he was called by the press, brilliantly invented the family metaphors that locked colonial subjects into the roles of infantilized bad children in relation to a benevolent "Mother Country."

All the Stephens were conscious makers of ideology, but the mother-country metaphor made an impact in shaping colonialism British style in behind-the-scenes bureaucracy by creating the colonial subject as a child and displacing the patriarchal power that fueled colonialism onto a less-threatening female figure. It ensured that any revolt of the colonized could be constituted as a crime against the sacred institution of motherhood. Queen Victoria grew into the role of imperial mother as the century progressed. My argument is that the Stephens invested the philosophy of imperialism with the theology of the patriarchal family, rewarding their complicitous women with power over servants in a replication of the master-servant relationship that James Fitzjames Stephen argued as a political philosophy was the model for a man's relation to his wife and children. James Stephen implemented a policy of making the conquered colonies British, members of a family. His son Fitzjames was one of the chief codifiers of Indian law, a major feat of cultural hegemony, for it was through the rigorous application of law and a system of courts and judges that the British were able to govern and to create a native governing class. This classification and centralizing of disparate systems of law served as a rehearsal for similar work in England, a centralizing and profes-sionalizing activity that standardized the law according to an Old Testament evangelical obsession with punishment. Often the colonies served as practice grounds for policies later implemented at home. It is clear that this codifica-tion of disparate practices into a single system laid the groundwork for certain narratives of nationalism in both India and England. Leslie Stephen, in his monumental *Dictionary of National Biography*, created a master cultural narrative of England as a history of the lives of Great Men, and in her youth his sister Caroline wrote a history of sisterhoods, nuns, and nurses that argued all such separate organizations of women were a threat to the patriar-chal family.

Fitzjames's daughter Katherine was principal of Newnham College, and her sister Dorothea spent many years in India studying Indian religions, publish-ing *Studies in Early Indian Thought* in 1918. This work done by the Stephen family was all cultural anthropology—classifying information. Katherine and Dorothea's brother J. K. Stephen, the model for Percival in *The Waves*, "bard of Eton and of boyhood," misogynist poet and parodist, studied law and edited

a journal called *The Reflector* before his strange death at age thirty-three
related to a fall from his horse (the origin of the tragic and culturally unifying
scene in *The Waves*). Julia Stephen, Woolf's mother, wrote on two subjects,
the power of the nurse over her patient and the responsibility of upper-class
women to discipline and control their servants. Woolf's insistence in her work
on the relation of patriarchy to imperialism and of both to class and fascism
comes from careful study of her family's legacy and her guilty refusal to be the
inheritor of the class privilege and power over servants with which such
women were bribed to serve the interests of patriarchal state institutions and
colonialism.

Imperialism in India and the exploitation of servants in England thus fused
in Woolf's imagination with her own revolt as a feminist; and, as I argue
elsewhere, the charwoman appears as a major figure in each novel, marking
Woolf's concern with class, along with barbed references to India and other
colonies, marking her concern with race. Middle-class white women in
England traded their own freedom for power over servants (or natives in the
colonies) which replicated the master/slave relationship of husbands and
wives. That these markers in Woolf's writing have generally been ignored or
misread by critics does not diminish their signifying power. Even that classic
text of feminist emancipatory literature, *A Room of One's Own*, clearly
indicates that literary freedom for the white middle-class English woman
writer is bought at the expense of complicity in colonialism. The narrator
dissociates herself from the racism of her family and class by announcing that
she could pass even a "very fine Negress" without wanting to "make an
Englishwoman of her." She will not participate in the social mission of
"civilizing" the natives in the manner of her family. Yet the word "fine"
suggests that she is not wholly free, for it is a word used to describe an object,
not a fellow subject, as if the Negress were an exotic work of art displayed for
a collector. (Here, of course, one may see Woolf's part in the Orientalism of
modernism, from Picasso's appropriation of African sculpture for his painting
to the cult of black American jazz and dance in Paris and other European
capitals.) Woolf had a double legacy regarding race. While her great-
grandfather had devoted his life to the emancipation of slaves (in recognition
that his own rise in status had been paid for by exploitation of the colonies),
her grandfather had introduced a different system of exploitation by creating
the bureaucracy that governed the Empire.

The narrator of *A Room of One's Own* owes her freedom and £500 a year to
a legacy from an aunt who died in Bombay from a fall from her horse. This fall
recurs in Woolf's writing as the sign of the sins of the fathers. It anticipates
Percival's carnivalized fall from a donkey while racing in India (obviously also a
reference to Forster's *Passage to India*), the move from horse to donkey
signifying the decline of the raj in the comic end of British colonialism.
Woolf's cousin's quixotic fall from a horse and his early death, the various
versions of this event that circulated as family mythology, and Desmond

MacCarthy's elegy for this ferocious figure in *Portraits,* invest this fall with literary and political resonance in Woolf's work. She often uses figures of horses and donkeys to describe her own work as an artist. Neville, in *The Waves,* constructs his whole worldview around the opposition between the rider and the reader, the hero and the poet, marking again the complicity between culture and colonialism. In *The Waves* Woolf criticizes the twentieth-century colonial and postcolonial discourse that replaced her grandfather's nineteenth-century myth of the Mother Country and her childish colonies as Imperial Family Romance. The new myth for twentieth-century colonialism was an imperialist Boy's Own Story, the Adventure of Brotherly Love, a homoerotic adoration of the strong, silent, violent hero conquering the desert alone. All the characters in *The Waves* participate in this drama of Percival's riding against the spears of the enemy, and they gain a national identity by mythologizing the hero. Reflecting on their common feeling, one may begin to understand the rise of fascism.

Leonard Woolf, Virginia Woolf's husband, veteran of seven years in the Ceylon Civil Service, and author of *The Village in the Jungle* (1913), reprinted by the Hogarth Press in 1931, the year of publication of *The Waves,* always associated his years in Hambantota with the image of himself on horseback among natives on foot. In his letters to Lytton Strachey (housed in the Harry Ransome Humanities Research Center at the University of Texas) he reveals his desire on coming down from Cambridge to teach in a British public school. When he found that Jews were never hired for these positions, he chose the civil service but agonized at length to Strachey about his difficulties learning to ride, a necessity for such a post. His memoirs trace the "innocent, unconscious imperialist" to his rejection of the role of "imperial proconsul." Accused by a native lawyer of whipping him in the street, Woolf rejected the accusation as false on the literal level though symbolically true, for he realized that the people of Jaffna were "right in feeling that my sitting on a horse arrogantly in the main street of their town was as good as a slap in the face" (*Growing* 113–14). Later, as secretary of the Labour party's Advisory Committee on Imperial Affairs, he advocated self-government for India, espousing advanced but not revolutionary views. His novel is bold in its narrative rejection of the notion of the possibility of justice in the application of British law in Ceylon, but its diction participates in the portrayal of the jungle and its people as savage, cruel, and sinister by the repetition of the words "evil" and "obscene."

In *The Waves* the scene of the hero's fall from his donkey is mythologized by Bernard as the death of the Christian knight in pursuit of the Holy Grail, as part of Bernard's vision of the "rise and fall and fall and rise again" of the narrative of colonialism. Neville opposes the rider to the reader, sees Percival as Alcibiades, Ajax, and Hector. His fall from a donkey while racing becomes History. Critics have remarked here on Virginia Woolf's memorial to her dead brother, Thoby. But the mention of Ajax and the ignominious nature of his fall reminds me of Woolf's cousin J. K. Stephen, whom she compares to Ajax, and the strange and contradictory reports of his fall, which led to madness and early death. Leslie Stephen and Quentin Bell tell of a stone thrown from a train that hit J. K. Stephen's head and knocked him off his horse, and again of his riding into a windmill. The stuff of legends, J. K. Stephen was a violent man made into a hero by all the Cambridge men who wrote about him.

Indeed, Woolf's cousin, whose violent, misogynistic poetry and strange early death play a part in some contemporary claims that he was Jack the Ripper, either alone or with the Duke of Clarence, whose tutor he was at Cambridge, makes an interesting source, not only for Percival, but for the whole hero-poet narrative that is British culture. As I show elsewhere, Woolf read Wortham's 1927 biography of Oscar Browning, which describes her cousin as a hero, and, more important, Desmond MacCarthy's sketch of him in *Portraits*. Woolf saw, I believe, the Bernard-Percival relationship acted out in Desmond's memoir of J. K. Stephen in *Portraits* as "our real laureate," mooning, as Neville and Bernard do about Percival, over the giant who was "violently masculine, a lover of law and abstract argument," the "Philistine," the "Bard of Eton and of boyhood." MacCarthy praises the "prowess of that wild-looking man with rolling but abstracted eye and path-clearing gait, whom I can just remember, hatless and slovenly, mouching round the Playing Fields" (249). This is the origin of Woolf's Eton scenes in *The Waves*, where Percival "mouches" around the same playing fields. . . .

. . . All these apostrophes to the dead hero add up to "culture," what Bernard does to re-create England by memorializing Percival. MacCarthy moans about being a failure and overpraises his male peers while ignoring or despising women artists. He does create J. K. Stephen as Percival. His book of portraits, dedicated to himself at age twenty-two, is the tidal wave that never breaks, which Woolf parodies in *The Waves*.[4] "It is curious," MacCarthy writes, "how nearly every group of young men, some of whom afterwards became famous, has had its inconspicuous hero to whom, while the world was looking up at them, they looked up to." Bernard is Desmond and Percival is J. K. Stephen, the patriarchal imperialist makers of British culture.

Bernard's memories of Percival repeat the figure of oscillation ("rise and fall and fall and rise again") of the force of cultural inheritance as a wave that drowns alternative voices. The story of Percival's fall is countered by the story of how he raised the bullock cart and imposed his Western values on the lazy and incompetent natives. ("I see India. . . . I see a pair of bullocks who drag a low cart along the sun-baked road. The cart sways incompetently from side to side" [*The Waves* 135].) For Woolf this recurring fall is a primal scene of the Fall, England's fall from heroic history, her family's fall from ethical purity, her culture's fall into colonialism and its angst. In *The Waves* Woolf uses the

---

4Woolf writes of MacCarthy as "a wave that never breaks, but lollops one this way & that way & the sail hangs on one's mast & the sun beats down" (Diary III, 27).

case of her cousin (conflated with her dead brother, Thoby, who was said to look like Jem) to explain the deadlock embrace of violence and poetry in the English male cultural script. Her version of the fall and the poet's mythologizing of violence is a critique of family history as well as cultural history.

Mrs. Moffat Will Sweep It All Up

The most powerful undertow in *The Waves* is class. The ruling-class characters define themselves as clean, free, and dominant against the dirt and ugly squalor of the masses. Bernard is bound to the big house by strong narrative ties. Elvedon and its *lady at a table writing, its gardeners with their great brooms sweeping,* the haunting memory that fuels his sense of himself as a writer, is *not* a fixed and eternal figure for writing. Not only do the characters imagine their racial superiority by conjuring up Asia and Africa as the enemy whose assegais are poised against them, but they build their class superiority by hating and despising the working class.[5] Rhoda is afraid of the "squalid" people in the Tube; Neville "cannot endure" that shopgirls should exist next to beautiful buildings; Susan sees country folk living like animals on a dungheap; and even Bernard composes little stories that betray his class and gender bias. He plots the greengrocer's Saturday night dream as an oscillation between thoughts of having posted his letter to the lottery and killing a rabbit, a projection of his own obsessions with chance and violent death onto Mrs. Thatcher's parents' class. This story makes life "tolerable" for him. The lady/gardener aesthetic is surely being mocked by the author of "The Leaning Tower," who urged the thirties poets to convert members of their own class to divest themselves of privilege, rather than become missionaries to the lower classes. This aesthetic, which figures English culture as a lady, not a woman, and insists on the unalterable relationship between the gardener and the lady, the working class and the writing class, is historically specific to Bernard in England in the early 1930s and certainly not in any way an aesthetic Woolf endorses. If those readers who despise Woolf for her supposed class loyalty and snobby membership in the Bloomsbury Group were to read the novel without its critical history as a canonical text, they might see that it deconstructs the idea of the cultural elite, showing that their power is derived from sex, class, and racial privilege.

The Corpse of the Canon

The boundaries between self and other, between classes and sexes, between the colonizers and the colonized that Woolf maps here are perhaps best

---

[5]Louise De Salvo points out that the drafts of *The Waves* originally mentioned working-class children who were "washing up plates" as the upper-class children sat at their desks, and "Florrie" who went out as a kitchenmaid when the others went off to school in Switzerland (183).

expressed in Neville's appalling vision of "death among the apple trees," the doom of the "unintelligible obstacle," his version of the "immitigable" Wordsworthian tree (24), which literally stops him in his tracks and figures the dilemma of the postwar intellectual dealing with the pastoral myth of England's green and pleasant land. The origin of the "story" for which Bernard and his friends search is in the burbling of blood from a cut throat, the wars and imperialist adventures on which their power was built. The violence of Woolf's subject, the dominance of monologic male voices over culture, is clear in the language of blood which she uses in discussing revisions in her diary— "And I am getting my blood up." She wants to avoid chapters and run all her scenes together "so as to make the blood run like a torrent from end to end." She views her achievement as if she had created in the novel a living body "done without spilling a drop" (343). The body of her text, *The Waves*, is the corpse of the literary canon, the mausoleum of white male English culture.

Bernard figures himself as the "continuer" of a dead tradition with a "devastating sense of grey ashes in a burnt-out grate" (80). In this modernist wasteland the poet, like T. S. Eliot, "is he who now takes the poker and rattles the cinders so that they fall in showers through the grate" (81). The ashes and cinders that haunt this novel as aftermath of World War I and as prophecy of the Holocaust for the modern reader invoke dirt and disorder as the artist's inspiration, marking his own urban civilized dependence on the slum. The ash-grey dawn of the opening prelude pictures the canvas of sea and sky as a wrinkled grey blanket, a smoky woolen cloth over a bonfire, a kind of blank page "barred with thick strokes moving" (7) where birds sing "their blank melody." Like Bernard's "dead fire" in a burnt-out grate, this ominous opening scene suggests the end of writing and the end of a certain kind of culture—Bernard's dependence on servants like Mrs. Moffat to reinforce his image of himself as "chosen."

In this opening scene the arm of the lady with the lamp clarifies the light until "the dark stripes were almost wiped out" (7), recalling the traditional representation of Britannia ruling the waves. It seems to me that this opening passage as a hymn to Dawn also invokes the Indian text, the *Rig Veda*, as Virginia Woolf's cousin Dorothea Stephen explained it in *Studies in Early Indian Thought*, to call up Indian philosophy and its emphasis on astronomy and the randomness of the universe, a major subject of *The Waves*, which incorporates relativity theory and the new physics into fiction.[6] Stephen

---

[6]Throughout December 1930, when she was revising *The Waves*, Woolf was reading and discussing Sir James Jeans's books and listening to his lectures on the radio (Diary 3, 337–40). Readers can find some of these brilliant and readable essays in Jeans's *Mysterious Universe* (1930), Alfred North Whitehead's *Science and the Modern World* (1925), and Sir Arthur Eddington's *Stars and Atoms* (1927). Imagine Woolf listening to the broadcasts that aided her in recording the atoms as they fell and fictionally mirroring nature as flux, the randomness of a universe without cause and effect, the intersections of time and space. The monologues are full of waves and loops, literary versions of the new science of her time, as she heard it on the radio.

argues that Indian thought emphasizes that personal character is not important in the scheme of the universe: "In early Indian thought we have the
boldest and the most consistent effort that the human mind has ever made to
show that it is nothing" (172). Is it too much to suppose that Woolf used an
Indian religious text to write the death of a particular form of white Western
culture? When she called *The Waves* "mystical," did she mean Eastern
mysticism? (The Vedas are in fact mentioned on page 186 as texts Bernard will
never read, though Louis, the T. S. Eliot figure and the white colonial
returned to the mother country, is familiar with them.) The specific uncanni-
ness of the poetic language of *The Waves*, its ecstasies of apostrophe, are
common both to the Romantic lyric of Shelley and Keats and to prayer—in
this case, the mode of Hindu religious texts. While popular sentiment might
declare that the sun never sets on the British Empire, *The Waves* emphatically dramatizes the very historical moment in which the sun does set. By
making the sun set on the British Empire in her novel Woolf enacts the possibility of writing as liberation rather than collaboration. If we read the opening sections, the interludes, as a Western imitation or homage to the Hindu
Gayatri, or as prayers on the course of the sun, we may see that Woolf surrounds the text of the decline and fall of the West (the transcendental self
striving and struggling against death) with the text of the East, random natural
recurrence.

But the narrative of violent struggle bleeds into the interludes; they are not
entirely passive and innocent—assegais appear even here (though the text is
not sure how to spell these African interlopers in Woolf's Indian novel). While
no native of the subcontinent actually speaks in *The Waves*, Hindu philosophy
embracing death is invoked at the ending in an ironic reading of Bernard's
famous ride against Death as "the enemy." Bernard sees himself "with . . .
spear couched and . . . hair flying back like a young man's, like Percival's"
(297), galloping in India. In fact Percival was riding a donkey, not galloping,
and this long-haired rider seems to be not Percival but a reincarnation of
Shiva, in what may be read as a new dawn "kindling" in the East, as Western
"civilization is burnt out" (296). (This Eastern dawn also ends *The Years*.)
W. B. Yeats recognized Woolf's incorporation of Eastern philosophy into her
text, linking it with *Ulysses* and Pound's *Cantos*, which "suggest a philosophy
like that of the Samkara school of ancient India, mental and physical objects
alike material, a deluge of experience breaking over us and within us, melting
limits whether of line or tint; man no hard bright mirror dawdling by the dry
sticks of a hedge, but a swimmer, or rather the waves themselves" (Yeats 64–
65).

Woolf wrote in her diary: "Talk about the riddle of the universe (Jeans's book) whether it will be
known; not by us; found out suddenly: about rhythm in prose" [Diary III, Dec. 18, 1930, 337].
The connection between *The Waves* and relativity and wave mechanics was first suggested to me
several years ago in an unpublished paper by Carol Donley (Hiram College) in which she graphed
the spatial and temporal movements of the characters alone and together as wave patterns.

"Our English past—one inch of light" (*The Waves* 227), Bernard's vision, is more pessimistically viewed by Louis, the Australian T. S. Eliot figure who thinks "the lighted strip of history is past and our Kings and Queens; we are gone; our civilization; the Nile; and all life . . . we are extinct" (225). As a former colonial subject, Louis is most afraid of the dissolution of empire. He hears the great beast of revolution stamping on the shore. He commutes between a garret room, where he can observe sordid sights of poverty and degradation, and a mahogany desk in a posh office, where he plans for swimming pools on luxury liners: "I pick my way over broken glass, among blistered tiles, and see only vile and famished faces" (202). (Doubtless, it is on one of his company's ships going to Africa and ruling the waves that Bernard met the unnamed person to whom he tells his life story in the last section of the book, the only "dialogue," such as it is, when the Other is a reluctant listener, in this deliberately monologic text.) In Louis's soliloquy, Woolf connects the British businessman, spreading commerce and colonialism, militarism and patriarchy, with Napoleon, Plato, and Sir Robert Peel: "I like to hear . . . the heavy male tread of responsible feet down the corridors. . . . The weight of the world is on our shoulders" (169). Louis's identity is so insecure that he needs continual reinforcement of his class position from walking the slums. He participates in what Stallybrass and White call the nineteenth-century "construction of subjectivity through totally ambivalent internalizations of the city slum" (21).

Bernard constructs his subjectivity by internalizing the second of the figures pointed out by Stallybrass and White—the nurse or the nanny. Using the work of Jim Swan and Jane Gallop, Stallybrass and White look at Freud's obsession with his own and his patients' nurses or nannies during the time that he was working on the theory of the Oedipus complex. The critical role of the nurse in initiating the child sexually while engaged in hygiene (by bathing children of the middle and upper classes) is displaced when Freud claims this role for the mother of the male child. Both mothers and fathers are absent in *The Waves*, but Bernard remembers his nurse, Mrs. Constable, for his whole life. She is his muse, and the primal scene of writing is for him the memory of her turning over the pages of a picture book and naming the objects. But his recurrent dream of her squeezing the sponge over his naked body, releasing "arrows of sensation" (239), is so fearful a moment that he wishes to save other newborns from the experience. Are we to see that his rigid Tory politics, imperialistic hero-worship, and barely repressed homosexuality are all derived from this childhood experience? He does have an image of his appetitive self as a "hairy ape" who lives inside his body, a self he despises and also projects onto the "savages" Percival is taming in India. One could say that his life is circumscribed by his nurse and his charwoman, Mrs. Constable and Mrs. Moffat. Woolf is laying out a psychological trail to explain Bernard's origin as the self-appointed arbiter of British culture.

The clearest exposition of the politics of the novel is in the scene at an expensive restaurant, where the six young white inheritors, sleek and well fed, eat roast duck and think of themselves as the center of civilization. They create themselves as civilized only by imagining Britain's colonies as savage. The Greeks define themselves against the barbarians. (There are nineteen direct references to India in the novel and several indirect ones.) And they each fantasize India as dark, dirty, disordered, and directly threatening their own deaths. The language of their dreams of Percival in India is thoroughly racist and colonialist—"incompetent," "natives in loincloths," "strange sour smells," "remote provinces are fetched out of darkness," "muddy roads," "twisted jungle," "the vulture that feeds on some bloated carcass," "the dancing and drumming of naked men with assegais," "ruthless," "flapping bladders," "painted faces," "bleeding limbs which they have torn from the living body" (136, 137, 140). India silently becomes Africa; the "Oriental problem" becomes the "African problem." Woolf's white British characters see the colonized as cannibals. Neville says, "We are walled in here. But India lies outside" (135). The following passage, with its mythologizing of Percival as a hero in his righting of the bullock cart (a rewriting of the classic scene with a bullock cart in Kipling's *Kim*), exposes Bernard's complicity with imperialism—how necessary his myth-making capacity is to the maintenance of domination and submission, master and slave:

> "I see India," said Bernard. "I see the low, long shore; I see the tortuous lanes of stamped mud that lead in and out among ramshackle pagodas; I see the gilt and crenellated buildings which have an air of fragility and decay as if they were temporarily run up buildings in some Oriental exhibition. I see a pair of bullocks who drag a low cart along the sun-baked road. The cart sways incompetently from side to side. Now one wheel sticks in the rut, and at once innumerable natives in loin-cloths swarm around it, chattering excitedly. But they do nothing. Time seems endless, ambition vain. Over all broods a sense of the uselessness of human exertion. There are strange sour smells. An old man in a ditch continues to chew betel and to contemplate his navel. But now, behold, Percival advances; Percival rides a flea-bitten mare, and wears a sun-helmet. By applying the standards of the West, by using the violent language that is natural to him, the bullock-cart is righted in less than five minutes. The Oriental problem is solved. He rides on; the multitude cluster round him, regarding him as if he were—what indeed he is—a God." (135–36)

This scene is a carnivalization of racism's master plot, a scene created again in film and fiction—the white man brings order and reason to the natives and is made a god. Woolf's grammar is strangely off-kilter here—the incompetent cart, the absent Percival as the subject of the bullock-cart-righting—why is there a passive construction? Bernard's colonialist fantasy contains all the elements of a textbook study of the operations of racism, imperialism, and colonialism—and yet there is something comic in the flea-bitten mare, the sun-helmet. (This resembles a scene from a colonial exhibition or a film like *The African Queen.* There was in fact a Colonial Exhibition in Paris in 1931, and Josephine Baker, the black exotic dancer, was chosen queen until it was pointed out that she was in fact an American.) It seems possible also that Woolf's image of the overturned cart invokes in some readers the figure of the juggernaut, Krishna's cart under whose wheels the faithful would throw themselves—to the British, along with sati, evidence of the savagery of India. Rhoda sees "beyond India," imagining "pilgrimages" from her peers into a landscape where a "white arm" "makes no sign, it does not beckon, it does not see us" (139). One could imagine that Rhoda alone sees the white arm of the mysterious woman with a lamp who brings the dawn, a Britannia in endless surveillance of conquerable lands. But it seems important that the arm is white and that it forms a triangle when resting upon the figure's knee, then a column, then a fountain. The mighty white arm of empire and civilization.

Andreas Huyssen argues that the mark of modernism is fear of contamination. This is Bernard's fear (Mrs. Moffat will sweep it all up). Rhoda fears the puddle and all human beings; Neville fears the recurrence of murder; Louis fears the "great Beast stamping" in the East; Susan hates Ginny all her life for having kissed Louis. The contamination of kisses and classes, the fear of dirt, disorder, and dying, the fear of Africa and India, is the recurring theme of the speakers' monologues. Neville says, "We must oppose the waste and deformity of the world, its crowds eddying round and round disgorged and trampling. One must slip paper-knives, even, exactly through the pages of novels, and tie up packets of letters neatly with green silk, and brush up the cinders and a hearth broom. Everything must be done to rebuke the horror of deformity" (180). If the speakers in *The Waves* are waiting apprehensively for the barbarians, the postcolonial reader may be the barbarian Woolf's text has awaited.

Works Cited

Bakhtin, M. M. *Rabelais and His World.* Trans. H. Iswolsky. Bloomington: Indiana University Press, 1984.

Bell, Quentin. Virginia Woolf: A Biography. New York: Harcourt Brace, 1972.

Bloom, Harold. *Modern Critical Views of Virginia Woolf.* New York: Chelsea House, 1986.

Coetzee, J. M. *Waiting for the Barbarians.* New York: Penguin Books, 1982.

De Salvo, Louise, *Virginia Woolf: The Impact of Childhood Sexual Abuse on Her Life and Work.* Boston: Beacon Press, 1989.

Eddington, Sir Arthur. *Stars and Atoms.* New Haven: Yale University Press, 1927.

———. *The Philosophy of Physical Science.* New York: Macmillan, 1939.

Graham, J. W. "MSS Revision and the Heroic Theme of *The Waves.*" *Twentieth Century Literature* 29 (1983): 312–32.

Haule, James M., and Philip H. Smith. *A Concordance to The Waves.* Ann Arbor: University Microfilms, 1986.

Hutcheon, Linda. *A Poetics of Postmodernism: History, Theory, Fiction.* New York: Routledge, 1988.

Huyssen, Andreas. *After the Great Divide: Modernism, Mass Culture, Postmodernism.* Bloomington: Indiana University Press, 1986.

Jeans, Sir James. *The Mysterious Universe.* Cambridge: Cambridge University Press, 1930.

MacCarthy, Desmond. *Portraits.* New York: Macmillan, 1932.

McConnell, Frank. " 'Death among the Apple Trees': *The Waves* and the World of Things." *Bucknell Review* 16 (1968): 23–29.

McGavran, J. H. "Alone Seeking the Visible World." *MLQ* [Modern Language Quarterly] 42 (1981): 265–91.

Marcus, Jane. *Virginia Woolf and the Languages of Patriarchy.* Bloomington: Indiana University Press, 1986.

———. "Liberty, Sorority, Misogyny." In *The Representation of Women in Fiction.* Ed. Carolyn Heilbrun and Margaret Higonnet. Baltimore: Johns Hopkins University Press, 1983.

Morrison, Toni. "Unspeakable Things Unspoken: The Afro-American Presence in American Literature." *Michigan Quarterly Review* 27, no. 1 (1989): 1–34.

Rosmarin, Adena. "The Narrativity of Interpretive History." In *Reading Narrative: Form, Ethics, Ideology.* Ed. James Phelan. Columbus: Ohio State University Press, 1989, 12–26.

Said, Edward. "*Kim*, the Pleasures of Imperialism." *Raritan* 7 (1987): 27–64.

———. *Orientalism.* New York: Pantheon, 1978.

Schlack, Beverly. *Continuing Presences: Virginia Woolf's Use of Literary Allusion.* University Park: Pennsylvania State University Press, 1979.

Spivak, Gayatri C. *In Other Words: Essays in Cultural Politics.* New York: Routledge, 1988.

Stallybrass, Peter, and Allon White. *The Politics and Poetics of Transgression.* Ithaca: Cornell University Press, 1986.

Stephen, Dorothea Jane. *Studies in Early Indian Thought.* Cambridge: Cambridge University Press, 1918.

Stephen, James Fitzjames. *Liberty, Equality, Fraternity.* Ed. J. R. White. 1873. Cambridge: Cambridge University Press, 1967.

Stephen, J. K. *The Living Languages: A Defense of the Compulsory Study of Greek at Cambridge.* Cambridge: Macmillan and Bowes, 1891.

Warner, Marina. *Monuments and Maidens: The Allegory of the Female Form.* London: Picador, 1985.

Whitehead, Alfred North. *Science and the Modern World.* New York: Macmillan, 1925.

Williams, Raymond. *The Politics of Modernism: Against the New Conformists.* New York: Verso, 1989.

Woolf, Leonard. *Growing.* New York: Harcourt Brace, 1961.

———. *The Village in the Jungle.* 1913. New York: Oxford University Press, 1981.

Woolf, Virginia. *The Waves.* 1931. New York: Harcourt Brace Jovanovich, 1959. [Source for quotations]

———. *The Waves.* New York: Cambridge University Press, 1986.

———. *The Diary of Virginia Woolf.* Vol. 3. Ed. Anne Olivier Bell and Andrew McNeillie. New York: Harcourt Brace Jovanovich, 1980.

————. *The Letters of Virginia Woolf*, Vol. 5. Ed. Nigel Nicholson and Joanne Trautmann. New York: Harcourt Brace Jovanovich, 1979.

Wortham, Hugh Evelyn. *Oscar Browning*. London: Constable and Co., 1927.

Yeats, William Butler. Introduction to "Fighting the Waves," *Wheels and Butterflies*. (New York: Macmillan, 1935), 64–65.

Chronology of Important Dates

1878	Leslie Stephen and Julia Jackson Duckworth marry. From previous marriages, Stephen had a daughter and Duckworth had three children. Together they had four more children: Vanessa, Julian Thoby, Virginia, and Adrian. They settled at 22 Hyde Park Gate, Kensington, London.
1882	Virginia Stephen born on January 25. Leslie Stephen assumes editorship of the *Dictionary of National Biography*. From now until 1894 the family spends every summer at Talland House, Saint Ives, Cornwall.
1883	Julia Stephen publishes *Notes from the Sick Room*.
c. 1888	Gerald Duckworth, Virginia's stepbrother, shows sexual interest in her.
1895	Julia Stephen dies. Virginia's first mental breakdown follows.
1897	Stella Duckworth, Virginia's stepsister, marries Jack Hills in April and dies in July.
1897–1900	Off and on, Virginia attends university classes; otherwise she is educated at home.
1899	Thoby Stephen enters Cambridge University.
1902	Virginia studies Greek with Janet Case. Leslie Stephen knighted.
1904	Leslie Stephen dies. Virginia is the object of sexual attention from her half-brother George Duckworth. Her second breakdown occurs. Virginia, Vanessa, Thoby, and Adrian Stephen move to 46 Gordon Square, Bloomsbury, London. Virginia's first publication, an unsigned review, appears in the *Guardian*; she soon becomes a regular book reviewer for the *Times Literary Supplement*.
1905	Thoby's Cambridge friends start coming to 46 Gordon Square on Thursday evenings: the beginning of the "Bloomsbury group." Virginia teaches at Morley College in London for working men and women.
1906	Virginia visits Greece with her sister and brothers. Thoby and Vanessa become ill. Thoby dies.
1907	Vanessa marries Clive Bell. Virginia and Adrian move to 29 Fitzroy Square, London. Virginia begins working on *The Voyage Out* (originally *Melymbrosia*).

Adapted from *Woman of Letters: A Life of Virginia Woolf*, by Phyllis Rose (Oxford: Oxford University Press, 1978); San Diego, New York, and London: Harcourt Brace Jovanovich, 1987, and other sources.

1909   Lytton Strachey proposes to Virginia and is accepted, but then retracts his offer. Virginia receives a legacy of £2,500 from her aunt Caroline Emilia Stephen.

1910   Virginia participates in the "Dreadnought Hoax," a practical joke against the British Navy. She works for women's suffrage.

1911   Virginia joins a cooperative living arrangement with John Maynard Keynes, Duncan Grant, Leonard Woolf, and Adrian at 38 Brunswick Square, London.

1912   Virginia marries Leonard Woolf in August.

1913   Virginia completes *The Voyage Out*. A breakdown begins that lasts through 1915.

1914   World War I begins.

1915   *The Voyage Out* published by Gerald Duckworth. The Woolfs move into Hogarth House, Richmond, London.

1917   Hogarth Press is founded in the Woolfs' basement in Richmond. Its first publication is Virginia's *The Mark on the Wall*, with a story by Leonard. Virginia begins keeping a regular diary.

1918   World War I ends. Virginia is active as a journalist.

1919   *Night and Day* published by Duckworth. *Kew Gardens* published by Hogarth Press, henceforth her regular publisher. The Woolfs buy Monk's House in Rodmell, Sussex.

1921   *Monday or Tuesday* published.

1922   *Jacob's Room* published.

1924   "Mr. Bennett and Mrs. Brown" published. The Woolfs move to 52 Tavistock Square, London.

1925   *Mrs. Dalloway* and *The Common Reader* published. Beginning of Virginia's romance with Vita Sackville-West. Hogarth Press moves to London.

1927   *To the Lighthouse* published.

1928   *Orlando* published, dedicated to Sackville-West. Originally to be called *The Jessamy Brides* and more directly concerned with lesbianism.

1929   *A Room of One's Own* published, based on Virginia's 1928 lectures.

1931   *The Waves* published.

1932   *The Second Common Reader* and *Letter to a Young Poet* published. Lytton Strachey and Dora Carrington die. First academic studies of Virginia's work published. She is attacked by *Scrutiny* and others and is offered honors (also in 1933 and 1939), which she refuses.

1933   *Flush: A Biography* published.

1935   *Freshwater*, a play, produced for friends.

1936   Completion of *The Years*, originally *The Pargiters*, after three years of writing.

1937   *The Years* published and becomes a popular success. Her nephew Julian Bell is killed in the Spanish Civil War.

1938   *Three Guineas* published. War with Germany seems imminent.

1939   World War II begins. The Woolfs live in Rodmell and only visit London, where their home is now 37 Mecklenburgh Square.

1940   *Roger Fry: A Biography* published. 37 Mecklenburgh Square is bombed in the Battle of Britain.

1941   Virginia is finishing *Between the Acts* (originally *Pointz Hall*). On March 28, at the onset of another breakdown, she commits suicide by drowning.

1969   Leonard Woolf dies.

Bibliography

Critical Studies

Abel, Elizabeth. *Virginia Woolf and the Fictions of Psychoanalysis*. Chicago: University of Chicago Press, 1989.

Beer, Gillian. "The Body of the People in Virginia Woolf." In *Women Reading Women's Writing*, edited by Sue Roe. Brighton: Harvester, 1987.

————. *Arguing with the Past: Essays on Narrative from Woolf to Sidney*. London: Routledge, 1989.

Beja, Morris, ed. *Critical Essays on Virginia Woolf*. Boston: G. K. Hall, 1985.

Caughie, Pamela L. *Virginia Woolf and Postmodernism: Literature in Quest and Question of Itself*. Urbana: University of Illinois Press, 1991.

Clements, Patricia, and Grundy, Isobel, eds. *Virginia Woolf: New Critical Essays*. London: Vision Press, 1983.

DiBattista, Maria. *Virginia Woolf's Major Novels: The Fables of Anon*. New Haven: Yale University Press, 1980.

Fleishman, Avrom. *Virginia Woolf: A Critical Reading*. Baltimore: The Johns Hopkins University Press, 1975.

Freedman, Ralph, ed. *Virginia Woolf: Revaluation and Continuity*. Berkeley: University of California Press, 1980.

Froula, Christine. *Joyce and Woolf: Gender Theory and the Literary Text*. New York: Columbia University Press, 1993.

Gillespie, Diane. *The Sisters' Arts: The Writing and Painting of Virginia Woolf and Vanessa Bell*. Syracuse: Syracuse University Press, 1988.

Ginsburg, Elaine K., and Gottlieb, Laura Moss, eds. *Virginia Woolf: Centennial Essays*. Troy, NY: Whitston, 1983.

Hussey, Mark. *The Singing of the Real World*. Columbus: Ohio State University Press, 1986.

Jacobus, Mary. " 'The Third Stroke': Reading Woolf with Freud." In *Grafts: Feminist Cultural Criticism*. Ed. Susan Sheridan. London: Verso, 1988.

Kamuf, Peggy. "Penelope at Work: Interruptions in *A Room of One's Own*." *Novel* 16, no. 1 (1982): 5–18.

Kelley, Alice van Buren. *The Novels of Virginia Woolf: Fact and Vision*. Chicago: The University of Chicago Press, 1973.

Kiely, Robert. *Beyond Egotism: The Fiction of James Joyce, Virginia Woolf, and D. H. Lawrence*. Cambridge: Harvard University Press, 1980.

Kirkpatrick, B. J. *A Bibliography of Virginia Woolf*, 3rd ed. New York: Oxford University Press, 1980.

Lee, Hermione. *The Novels of Virginia Woolf*. London: Methuen, 1977.

Lilienfield, Jane. " 'The Deceptiveness of Beauty': Mother Love and Mother Hate in *To the Lighthouse.*" *Twentieth Century Literature* 23 (1977): 345–76.

Majumdar, Robin. *Virginia Woolf: An Annotated Bibliography of Criticism.* New York: Garland, 1976.

Majumdar, Robin, and McLaurin, Allen, eds. *Virginia Woolf: The Critical Heritage.* London: Routledge and Kegan Paul, 1975.

Marcus, Jane. *Virginia Woolf and the Languages of Patriarchy.* Bloomington: Indiana University Press, 1987.

———. ed. *New Feminist Essays on Virginia Woolf.* Lincoln: University of Nebraska Press, 1981.

———. ed. *Virginia Woolf: A Feminist Slant.* Lincoln: University of Nebraska Press, 1983.

———. ed. *Virginia Woolf and Bloomsbury: A Centenary Celebration.* Bloomington: Indiana University Press, 1987.

Meisel, Perry. *The Absent Father: Virginia Woolf and Walter Pater.* New Haven: Yale University Press, 1980.

Middleton, Victoria. "*Three Guineas*: Subversion and Survival in the Professions." *Twentieth Century Literature* 28 (1982): 405–17.

Miller, J. Hillis. *Fiction and Repetition.* Cambridge: Harvard University Press, 1982.

Miller, Ruth C. *Virginia Woolf: Frames of Life and Art.* London: Macmillan, 1988.

Minow-Pinkney, Makiko. *Virginia Woolf and the Problems of the Subject.* Brighton: The Harvester Press, and New Brunswick: Rutgers University Press, 1987.

Richter, Harvena. *Virginia Woolf: The Inward Voyage.* Princeton: Princeton University Press, 1970.

Silver, Brenda R. "The Authority of Anger: *Three Guineas* as a Case Study." *Signs* 16 (1991): 340–70.

———. ed. *Virginia Woolf's Reading Notebooks.* Princeton: Princeton University Press, 1983.

Spivak, Gayatri Chakravorty. "Making and Unmaking in *To the Lighthouse.*" In *Women and Language in Literature and Society,* edited by Sally McConnell-Ginet, Ruth Borker, and Nelly Furman. New York: Praeger, 1980.

Sprague, Claire, ed. *Virginia Woolf: A Collection of Critical Essays.* Twentieth Century Views. Englewood Cliffs, NJ: Prentice Hall, 1971.

Squier, Susan. *Virginia Woolf and London.* Chapel Hill: University of North Carolina Press, 1985.

Journals and Special Journal Issues

Bulletin of the New York Public Library 80 (Winter 1977). [On *The Years*]

Bulletin of Research in the Humanities 84 (Spring 1981). [On *The Voyage Out*]

Modern Fiction Studies 38, no. 1 (Spring 1992)

Twentieth Century Literature 25, nos. 3–4 (Fall–Winter 1979)

Virginia Woolf Miscellany

Virginia Woolf Quarterly

Women's Studies: An Interdisciplinary Journal 4, nos. 2–3 (1977)

Biographies

Bell, Quentin. *Virginia Woolf: A Biography.* New York: Harcourt Brace, 1972.
Gordon, Lyndall. *Virginia Woolf: A Writer's Life.* New York: Oxford University Press, 1984.
Rose, Phyllis. *Woman of Letters: A Life of Virginia Woolf.* Oxford: Oxford University Press, 1978.

Notes on Contributors

ELIZABETH ABEL is Associate Professor of English at the University of California at Berkeley. She is the editor of *Writing and Sexual Difference* (1982) and co-editor of *The Voyage In: Fictions of Female Development* (1983) and of *The Signs Reader* (1983). She is the author of *Virginia Woolf and the Fictions of Psychoanalysis* (1989) and, most recently, of essays on race, feminism, and psychoanalysis.

ERICH AUERBACH was Sterling Professor of French and Romance Philology at Yale University. He wrote *Mimesis* (1946) while a professor at the Turkish State University in Istanbul. His other books include *Dante: Poet of the Secular World* (1929) and *Scenes from the Drama of European Literature* (1959).

JOAN BENNETT was a Lecturer in English at Cambridge University and Life Fellow of Girton College. In addition to *Virginia Woolf: Her Art as Novelist* (1945), she published *George Eliot: Her Mind and Her Art* (1948), *Sir Thomas Browne* (1962), and books on the metaphysical poets.

RACHEL BOWLBY is a reader in English at Sussex University. She is the author of *Just Looking* (1985) on femininity and shopping in turn-of-the-century novels; *Virginia Woolf: Feminist Destinations* (1988); and *Still Crazy After All These Years* (1992), to be followed by *Shopping with Freud* (1993). She has edited two volumes of Woolf's essays for Penguin: Woolf's *Orlando* in the World's Classics series and a collection of Woolf criticism in the Longman's Critical Readers series (all 1992).

MARGARET (COMSTOCK) CONNOLLY has taught English at NYU and at the University of Pennsylvania, and she served as Director of University Planning at St. Joseph's University in Philadelphia. She was a founding editor of the *Virginia Woolf Miscellany*. She lives with her family in Narberth, Pennsylvania.

MARGARET DRABBLE's novels include *The Millstone* (1965), *The Realms of Gold* (1975), *The Middle Ground* (1980), *The Radiant Way* (1987), and *A Natural Curiosity* (1989). She has also published studies of *Wordsworth* (1966) and of *Arnold Bennett* (1974), and she edited *The Oxford Companion to English Literature* (fifth edition, 1985).

RACHEL BLAU DUPLESSIS is Professor of English at Temple University. She is the author of *Writing Beyond the Ending* (1985), *H.D.: The Career of That Struggle* (1986), and of *The Pink Guitar: Writing as Feminist Practice* (1990), as well as of other essays on feminism and modernism. She co-edited *Signets: Readings of H.D.* (1990). She has also published several collections of poetry, including most recently *Tabula Rosa* (1987) and *Drafts 3–14* (1991).

CHRISTINE FROULA is Professor of English, Comparative Literature, and Literary Theory at Northwestern University. She is the author of *A Guide to Ezra Pound's Selected Poems* (1983), *To Write Paradise: Style and Error in Pound's Cantos* (1984), numerous essays on modernism, and *Joyce and Woolf: Gender Theory and the Literary Text* (1993).

GEOFFREY HARTMAN is Professor of English and Comparative Literature at Yale University. His books include *Wordsworth's Poetry 1787–1814* (1964), *Beyond Formalism* (1970), *Criticism in the Wilderness* (1980), *Easy Pieces* (1985), and most recently, *Minor Prophecies: The Literary Essay in the Culture Wars* (1991).

MARIANNE HIRSCH is Dartmouth Professor of French and Comparative Literature at Dartmouth College. Co-editor of *The Voyage In: Fictions of Female Development* (1983) and of *Conflicts in Feminism* (1990), she is also the author of *The Mother/ Daughter Plot: Narrative, Psychoanalysis, Feminism* (1989). Currently she is working on a book on family pictures.

MARGARET HOMANS is Professor of English at Yale University. She is the author of *Women Writers and Poetic Identity* (1980) and *Bearing the Word: Language and Female Experience in Nineteenth-Century Women's Writing* (1986), and has written essays on Victorian and contemporary women authors.

PATRICIA KLINDIENST JOPLIN is the author of "The Voice of the Shuttle Is Ours" (*Stanford Literature Review*, 1984) and of other essays on ancient and modernist literatures. When she wrote the essay included in this volume, she was Assistant Professor of English at Yale University. She is completing a book on Woolf.

JANE MARCUS is Distinguished Professor of English at the CUNY Graduate Center and The City College of New York, and Coordinator of Graduate Women's Studies at CUNY. She edited three volumes of essays on Virginia Woolf and is the author of *Virginia Woolf and The Languages of Patriarchy* (1987), *Art and Anger* (1988), and of essays on Woolf and on other British modernists. "Britannia Rules *The Waves*" is part of a book on Woolf and colonialism.

LUCIO P. RUOTOLO is Professor of English at Stanford University. A founding editor of *The Virginia Woolf Miscellany*, he also edited the two-volume Woolf manuscript special issue of *Twentieth Century Literature* (1975) and an edition of Woolf's play "Freshwater." In addition to *The Interrupted Moment*, his writings include *Six Existential Heroes* (1973) and numerous essays on Woolf. He is currently working on a book on the anarchist instinct in literature from romanticism to the present.

ALEX ZWERDLING is Professor of English at the University of California at Berkeley. He has published *Yeats and the Heroic Ideal* (1965), *Orwell and the Left* (1974), and *Virginia Woolf and the Real World* (1986).